LOOK 1

TEACHER'S BOOK

Katherine Bilsborough

Steve Bilsborough

COURSE CONSULTANTS

Elaine Boyd

Paul Dummett

NATIONAL GEOGRAPHIC
LEARNING

Australia • Brazil • Mexico • Singapore • United Kingdom • United States

National Geographic Learning,
a Cengage Company

Look 1 Teacher's Book

Authors: Katherine Bilsborough, Steve Bilsborough

Course Consultants: Elaine Boyd, Paul Dummett

Publisher: Sherrise Roehr

Executive Editor: Eugenia Corbo

Publishing Consultant: Karen Spiller

Senior Development Editor: Karen Haller Beer

Director of Global Marketing: Ian Martin

Heads of Regional Marketing:
  Charlotte Ellis (Europe, Middle East, and Africa)
  Kiel Hamm (Asia)
  Irina Pereyra (Latin America)

Product Marketing Manager: Dave Spain

Senior Content Project Manager: Nick Ventullo

Media Researcher: Leila Hishmeh

Art Director: Brenda Carmichael

Operations Coordinator: Hayley Chwazik-Gee

Manufacturing Planner: Mary Beth Hennebury

Composition: Composure Graphics, LLC

For permission to use material from this text or product,
submit all requests online at **cengage.com/permissions**
Further permissions questions can be emailed to
permissionrequest@cengage.com

ISBN: 978-1-337-79787-0

National Geographic Learning
20 Channel Center Street
Boston, MA 02210
USA

Locate your local office at **international.cengage.com/region**

Visit National Geographic Learning online at **ELTNGL.com**
Visit our corporate website at **www.cengage.com**

Printed in China
Print Number: 03 Print Year: 2020

Contents

Scope and Sequence

 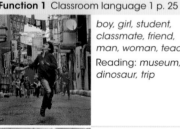

The World Is an Amazing Place

See something real

Children are naturally questioning and curious. They have an enormous appetite for learning about the world. *Look* taps into this curiosity by providing a window onto a fascinating world of real-life stories from diverse places and cultures: an underwater bedroom in Paris; a model town in the Netherlands; a boy dressing up for a festival in Mexico; a Thai girl wearing traditional costume. In each case, the topic is then related back to students' own lives and experiences in personalization activities: what is in *their* bedroom at home? what is *their* town or city like? what games and celebrations do *they* enjoy? what clothes do *they* like to wear? These real-life stories enhance the child's learning experience by:

- stimulating them with amazing facts about the world
- giving a meaningful context to the language learned
- making learning more memorable
- nurturing a spirit of open-mindedness and interest in others
- providing an opportunity for follow-up work on stories of particular interest

You don't need to worry about unfamiliar content. We have included background information in the teacher's notes on each real-world story and guides to the pronunciation of any names that are unfamiliar. Our hope is that you too will be inspired by these stories and then extend each topic. For example, getting students to design an amazing bedroom, making a map of a part of their town and labeling it, drawing pictures of festival costumes, and so on.

Get up close

As with every National Geographic Learning course, *Look* contains stunning photos. The photos are not just cosmetic. Each relates closely to the specific topic and is intended to warm students to it and to stimulate discussion. These opening photos are always accompanied by the question *What can you see?* You can ask this question or similar questions with any of the photos in the book, eliciting and revising items of vocabulary from previous lessons such as colors, clothes, objects, numbers, and actions as you go. Ask questions, such as: *Where are they? How many people can you see? Are they girls or boys? What color is his shirt?* You will find extra information about these photos in each lesson in the *About the Photo* box in the Teacher's Book. It is fine to tell your students more about the background to the photo in their first language. You can also return to these photos and use them as prompts for recalling words.

Make connections

We have included a range of video types in *Look*. All are in keeping with the theme of real-life stories and what an amazing place the world is. The *Lesson 7* video in every unit comprises recordings of children from around the world, describing their experiences. These interviews, interspersed with footage of the places and things they describe, feature the children answering questions about how the topics in the book relate to life in their countries: the food they eat, the games they play, the festivals they like, and so on. In this way, they give a fresh perspective on the topic. These videos reinforce the language learned throughout the unit and provide a speaking model for the students when they, in turn, talk about their own lives and experiences.

The second component is the *School Trip* videos. These center on visits to exciting places—a toy museum in Prague, an animal safari in the African savanna—and provide a springboard for the students to do their own mini-projects. When you have been through the activities on the page, you can try other techniques with these videos such as:

- turning the sound off and getting students to provide some commentary or narration
- pausing the video and asking students to remember what happened next
- asking students to watch and list different things they see (e.g. colors, toys)

Learn about the world and its stories

Each level of *Look* contains four extensive reading texts (*Reading Extra*). They are an opportunity for students to enjoy reading about the world rather than to practice language (although they do, of course, recycle language previously taught). Two of the reading texts are non-fiction (e.g. *Day and Night*) and two feature fables from around the world (e.g. *The Frog and the Butter*). In both cases, there is opportunity for motivating follow-up activities. For the former, the students can try at home to find out more about this subject and bring their ideas (or pictures) to the next class. For the latter, you can help students to dramatize the story (with actions, words, or both) or ask them to draw a scene from it. The fables also contain important moral lessons with universal significance, like the importance of never giving up in *The Frog and the Butter*. You may also choose to discuss the moral of these stories with your students in their own language.

Making Teaching and Learning a Joy

Songs and chants

Songs and chants are an important resource in any primary language-learning materials because their repetition and rhythm make them memorable. They're one of the best ways of providing language input for children. Children learn the words and structures along with the rhythms and patterns of the language. The chants and songs in *Look* are catchy and fun, and designed to help you present and recycle language in a motivating way. Songs and chants are also opportunities to develop learners' listening skills in general.

SONGS The best way to learn the songs is to listen to the recorded version and sing along to it. You shouldn't worry if your students don't pick up the song immediately. Each child will learn at his/her own pace. They can start by clapping to the rhythm and humming the tune, then focus on the chorus or the most memorable lines, building up to finally singing the whole song. This is how we learn songs in real life. When students are really confident with a song, they can sing along with the instrumental version. All the songs in *Look* come with step-by-step instructions for simultaneous actions. These help students grasp the meaning of the words, while providing opportunities for full-body movement and exercise—a necessity in any primary classroom.

CHANTS The chants in *Look* have two functions. The first is to present a language point in each unit. Each Lesson 2 chant contains a model of the target structure. Learning the chant enables students to internalize the grammar while following an excellent pronunciation model. Each Lesson 6 chant practices target sounds in the phonics section; these chants give the students a chance to focus on producing each sound and to link it to spelling.

The best way for students to learn a chant is by listening to it and then chanting along to the recorded version. But you can help students by building up the chant line by line, or chunk by chunk. For example:

Repeat after me: There's… / There's a beach ball … / There's a beach ball in the ocean.

Teachers are offered plenty of extra ideas for creative activities based on the chants and songs in *Look*. For example, you could ask your students to work in groups and write a new verse and record them performing it.

Games

There are four games lessons in *Look*. Children love playing games. A good game can make a lesson a fun, memorable event in the students' day. As well as consolidating learning, games can give lessons a boost in energy and enjoyment, and stimulate students to use English freely—but only if they are set up well. Here are the key ingredients to a successful game.

Preparation Make sure any materials, such as game pieces and slips of paper, are ready before the lesson. There is always a list of materials at the start of each lesson.

Clear instructions The Teacher's Book provides a clear procedure for how to set up each game by illustrating what to say, what to do on the board, demonstrating a dummy round, and doing examples with the class beforehand.

Monitoring Once students start playing, it's crucial that you check that students are following the rules and using English correctly.

Variety This level of *Look* features a variety of game types: *Spot the difference*, vocabulary revision games, *Snakes and ladders*, and a memory-based board game.

Clear language objectives Games should be fun, but in the English class, they must also help us meet our language goals. The games in *Look* encourage students to think about the language they have recently learned and practice it in an engaging and safe environment. You need to bear in mind these objectives from start to finish, provide students with the English they need, and correct errors where appropriate. *Look* games ensure students are using real English without detracting from the primary objective of winning!

Values

An important feature of *Look* is the attention it places on values. Besides being embedded throughout the materials, there is an explicit focus on one key age-appropriate value in every unit. Values education creates a healthy and often joyful learning environment, helping children develop social and relationship skills that last into adulthood. As students engage with positive values, they are equipped with attitudes and behaviors for success at school and beyond.

The values are reviewed and consolidated through fun and motivating activities in the corresponding unit of the Workbook.

A Multi-Strand Approach to Assessment

Exam practice

This level provides preparation and practice for the *Cambridge English Qualifications, Pre-A1 Starters* test. *Look* Student's Book and Workbook include tasks that represent all the different parts of the exam. Practice is focused on enabling students to master techniques which will allow them to perform at their best in formal assessment situations. These tasks give students the opportunity to familiarize themselves with each of the task types that appear in the exam and make connections to their own lives in order to build both their interest and confidence. A complete practice exam is included at the end of the Workbook.

Building young learners' confidence

To help students be less anxious and to relax in an exam situation, this Teacher's Book incorporates a range of strategies to build confidence, motivate, and make exams feel less scary. These strategies include activities to:

- **Personalize** These activities have students connect the context or situation of the task to their own lives. This allows them to see the relevance of what they are doing to real life.

- **Collaborate** These activities allow students to prepare tasks together, both to learn from each other and to give them the support they need before they have to "perform."

- **Help my friend** This encourages students to focus on what they can do well and allows them to use these skills and competences to help teach and support their classmates, so the class develops a pool of skills and knowledge.

- **Reflect** These activities give students time to check and consider their answers together so that they can reflect on the process they went through and look at how they can improve. This helps develop self-regulation and autonomous learning in young learners.

- **Second chance** These activities are suggested especially for productive tasks so that students have the opportunity to be successful in these performative parts of the exam. Once students have had some feedback and have considered their performance, they can repeat the task successfully to build confidence.

- **Own it!** These are tasks which have students start developing their own short tests in some way. This allows them to understand what tasks are testing and how they're testing it. It also shows that testing is not scary but can be fun with their classmates.

Formative assessment and feedback

Young learners need the support of constant feedback on their learning and progression in order to motivate them. To help teachers with this, we have included a framework for managing formative assessment and feedback on page 142. This framework outlines how each performance objective for the level can be assessed informally by you across the term or year. It suggests a range of feedback techniques and remedial activities which will support students' progression in each objective. The framework and photocopiable Student Log allow you to keep an objective, evidence-based record of each student's progress which you can use with the students themselves, their parents, or other stakeholders. You can also download the Student Log from the website.

Using formal criteria to assess productive skills

It may help you to use the assessment criteria applied in the *Cambridge English Qualifications* as these have been extensively trialed to match realistic performance expectations for young learners. These are available in the *Handbook for teachers* available on the Cambridge Assessment English website. The criteria can be overwhelming for students to process, so it is suggested that you apply individual criteria to each task as appropriate and work with one criterion at a time to allow young learners to focus on one feature of language they can improve.

- **Speaking** The three assessment criteria for the Speaking exam are Vocabulary, Pronunciation, and Interaction. In the different Speaking practice tasks, these are broken down so that one criterion is included with each task throughout the book. Advice is also given on how to apply each criterion as you are completing the specific task in class.

- **Writing** In the *Pre-A1 Starters* exam, the writing section (Part 5) is objectively marked as only one-word answers are required. The practice writing task includes guidance on this, but students need to be reminded that:
  - answers must represent what they can see in the support pictures (task completion)
  - answers must make sense with the words they are given on the page (grammatical accuracy)

Despite the fact that only short answers are required and so the writing is not extended, a very important long-term learning point is ensuring students understand they must address the task given and not invent their own ideas.

Unit Opener

Every unit starts with a full-page photo which stimulates students' interest in the topic and provides opportunities for photo-based questions and answers.

Students see people and places from all around the world and learn about how other children experience life.

A high-impact photo engages students' interest. The About the Photo section in the Teacher's Book allows you to satisfy your students' curiosity about the photo.

Even at low levels students can point and say, and thus interact with real-world photos.

Children in Japan

My Town

UNIT 7

Look at the photo. What can you see?

69

LESSON 1 **Words** and LESSON 2 **Grammar**

The vocabulary and grammar lessons are standalone lessons which are thematically linked. They move from word level (Words) to sentence level (Grammar).

Target vocabulary has been benchmarked against wordlists from international exams and the CEFR.

Students hear and see the target grammar in a catchy chant before focusing on the exponents in the grammar box in Activity 2.

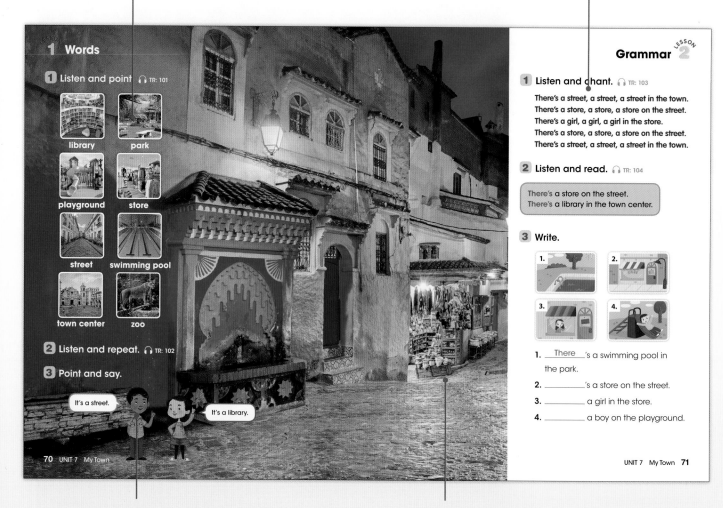

Activities are modeled by avatars of the video children from around the world.

A high-impact photo brings the real world into the classroom and provides further practice opportunities.

LESSON 3 Reading and LESSON 4 Grammar

The reading and grammar lessons are also standalone lessons. Students learn about the world as well as learning vocabulary and grammar, which they then use to talk about their own worlds.

New vocabulary is pre-taught in Activity 1, contextualized in the reading text, then practiced in Activity 3. All the target vocabulary is supported by flashcards and teaching notes.

Target grammar is presented in the grammar box, and then practiced using different skills: reading in Activity 1, writing in Activity 2, listening in Activity 3, and speaking in Activity 4.

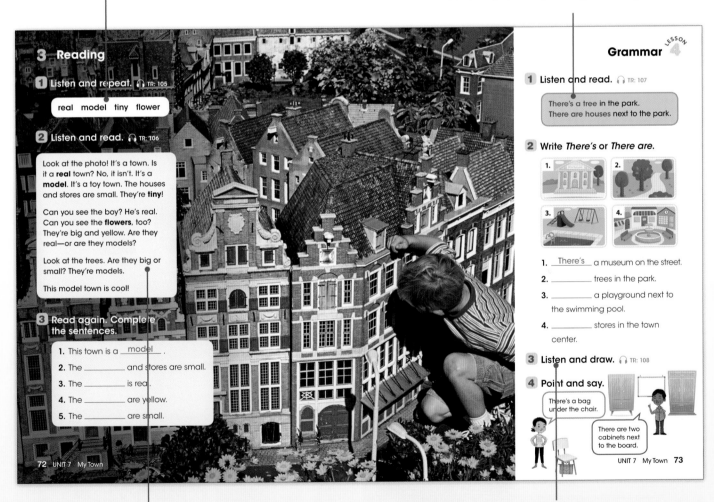

3 Reading

1 Listen and repeat. TR: 105

real   model   tiny   flower

2 Listen and read. TR: 106

Look at the photo! It's a town. Is it a **real** town? No, it isn't. It's a **model**. It's a toy town. The houses and stores are small. They're **tiny**!

Can you see the boy? He's real. Can you see the **flowers**, too? They're big and yellow. Are they real—or are they models?

Look at the trees. Are they big or small? They're models.

This model town is cool!

3 Read again. Complete the sentences.

1. This town is a __model__ .
2. The _____ and stores are small.
3. The _____ is real.
4. The _____ are yellow.
5. The _____ are small.

72   UNIT 7   My Town

Grammar LESSON 4

1 Listen and read. TR: 107

There's a tree in the park.
There are houses next to the park.

2 Write *There's* or *There are*.

1. __There's__ a museum on the street.
2. _____ trees in the park.
3. _____ a playground next to the swimming pool.
4. _____ stores in the town center.

3 Listen and draw. TR: 108

4 Point and say.

There's a bag under the chair.

There are two cabinets next to the board.

UNIT 7   My Town   **73**

The reading texts are about the real world. In this activity, students are asked to think critically by distinguishing between what is real and what is a model.

Exam task types are represented throughout the Student's Book. The accompanying teacher's notes offer guidance on assessment criteria and suggestions for boosting students' confidence.

LESSON 5 **Song** and LESSON 6 **Phonics**

The song pulls together all the language threads of the unit in a fun and active way. The phonics lesson uses the unit language to focus on target letters or letter combinations.

Two versions of the songs are provided (with and without vocals) so you can choose how much support your students need with singing.

The Level 1 phonics syllabus covers the sounds of the letters and introduces some common consonant–vowel–consonant (CVC) combinations.

The words containing the target letters are selected according to their level and frequency. Understanding meaning helps decoding, so the meaning of the words is supported with photos.

The songs have catchy, modern tunes.

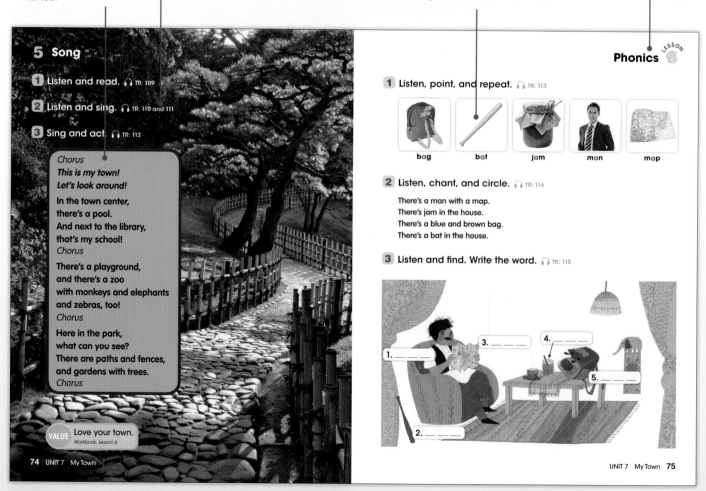

5 Song

1 Listen and read. TR: 109

2 Listen and sing. TR: 110 and 111

3 Sing and act. TR: 112

Chorus
This is my town!
Let's look around!
In the town center,
there's a pool.
And next to the library,
that's my school!
Chorus
There's a playground,
and there's a zoo
with monkeys and elephants
and zebras, too!
Chorus
Here in the park,
what can you see?
There are paths and fences,
and gardens with trees.
Chorus

VALUE Love your town.
Workbook, Lesson 6

74 UNIT 7 My Town

Phonics LESSON 6

1 Listen, point, and repeat. TR: 113

bag   bat   jam   man   map

2 Listen, chant, and circle. TR: 114

There's a man with a map.
There's jam in the house.
There's a blue and brown bag.
There's a bat in the house.

3 Listen and find. Write the word. TR: 115

1. _____
2. _____
3. _____
4. _____
5. _____

UNIT 7 My Town 75

LESSON
7 Video

Children representing sixteen different countries are interviewed about their lives and cultures. Students get a glimpse into how life is lived in different places around the world, and learn to embrace diversity and equality.

Three or four children are featured in each video. Their answers and descriptions are illustrated with photos and video footage.

After watching the video, students talk about their own lives and cultures. They are well prepared for this task because the language they need has been learned and practiced during the unit, and also modeled by the children on the video.

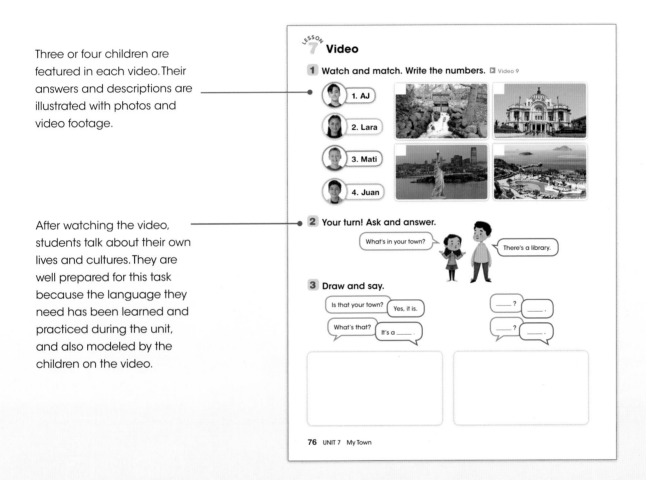

There are five types of modular lessons that sit outside the unit structure. The one-page lessons are: Game, Function, and Review. The two-page lessons are School Trip and Reading Extra; examples of these are shown on these two pages.

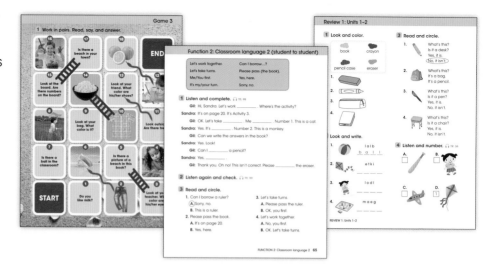

School Trip

The four video-based School Trip lessons take students to the four corners of Earth without leaving the classroom!

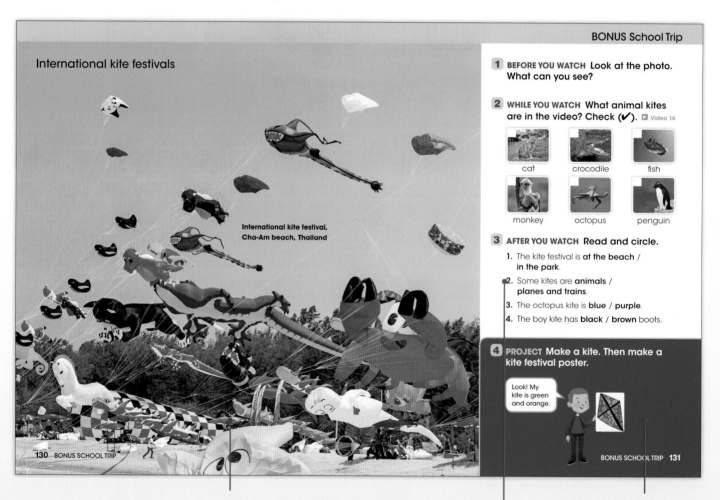

A stunning photo captures students' interest.

A carefully staged lesson activates students' prior knowledge (Activity 1) and works on comprehension (Activity 2) and memory (Activity 3).

The end-of-lesson project is often a craft activity that allows different students to shine in mixed-ability classes.

Reading Extra

The four extensive reading lessons comprise two real-world texts and two fables. The fables are traditional stories that teach a lesson, variations of which exist in many cultures. They often have important moral lessons with universal significance—in this case: the importance of never giving up.

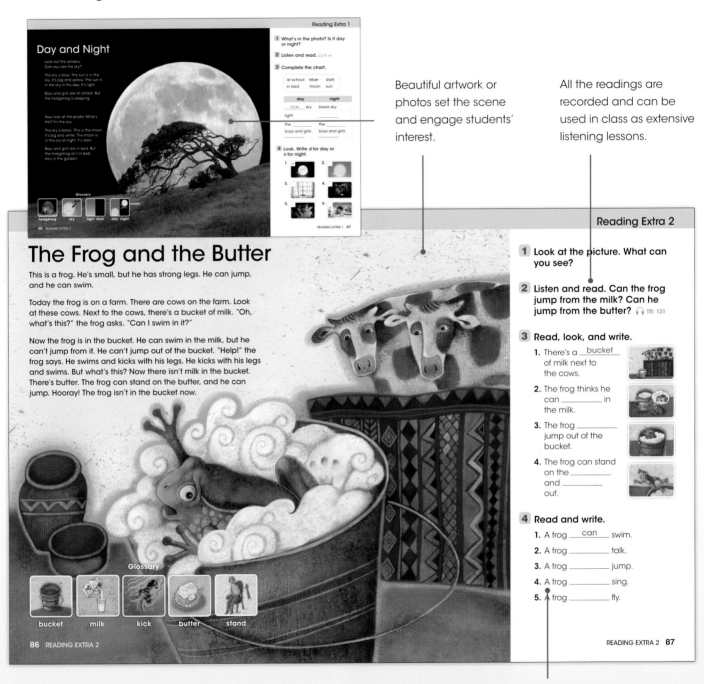

Beautiful artwork or photos set the scene and engage students' interest.

All the readings are recorded and can be used in class as extensive listening lessons.

The main focus of the activities is on comprehension and discussion. However, the language is carefully graded and also offers opportunities for language-based extension.

See the full list of Student and Teacher components for *Look* on the inside back cover.

1 **Listen and point.** 🎧 TR: 1

1 one	**2** two
3 three	**4** four
5 five	**6** six
7 seven	**8** eight
9 nine	**10** ten

2 **Listen and repeat.** 🎧 TR: 2

3 **Point and say.**

eight

three

4

Children in China

ABOUT THE PHOTO

This photo shows a group of children at the entrance of a school in China. In the Chinese education system, many children begin school at age three, and spend three years in an early childhood classroom that prepares them for school. Then, at the age of six or seven, they progress to elementary school, where they spend six years. They finish their compulsory education at secondary school, which they enter at the age of twelve. They spend between three and six years there. Since 1986, all children have the right to a minimum of nine years' education (six years in elementary and three in secondary). While in secondary school, students prepare for the *Gaokao*. This is a very difficult higher education entrance exam that takes nine hours to complete.

Look

In this unit, students will:

- recognize and use numbers, colors, and greetings.
- learn a chant about greetings.

Twenty-First Century Skills

Collaboration
Work in pairs to learn colors, Lesson 3

Communication
Greet each other, Lesson 1

Creativity
Make number shapes, Lesson 4

Critical Thinking
State a preference, Lesson 2

Look

In this lesson, students will:

- identify and say numbers 1–10.

Resources: Worksheets 1.0.1–1.0.3, Audio Tracks 1–2, Classroom Presentation Tool, Workbook p. 4, Online Practice

Warm Up

- Say *Hello* to students. Go around the class and say *Hello* to every student. Have students respond *Hello.* Then say *My name is....* Write your name on the board.
- Have two students stand up and greet each other. Have them say *Hello, [name]* and reply with *Hello, [name].* Then, have students move around the classroom so that they can greet all the other students.

- Hold up a copy of the Student's Book open to p. 4, and say *Open your book to page 4.* Say *Look at the numbers.* Point to the numbers and give students time to look at them.
- Read aloud the instructions. Point to your ear as you say *Listen* and then use your finger to model the word *point* as you say *Point.* Again, point to the numbers.
- Play **TR: 1** and point to the digits (1, 2, etc.) one at a time as you hear the words (*one, two,* etc).
- **Extra Challenge** Say the numbers in random order and have students point to them.
- **Extra Support** Pause after each number and draw a symbol on the board to represent that number. For instance, after *one,* draw and say *One star.*

2

- Direct students' attention to the instructions and read them aloud. Say *One, repeat. One. Two, repeat. Two.*
- Play **TR: 2**, pausing after the first word to model repeating for students. Continue with **TR: 2**, having students repeat the words as a class. Then play **TR: 2** again and call on individual students to repeat the words.
- **Extra Challenge** Collect different numbers of objects, such as two bags and three pencils. Put them all on your table. Point and ask *How many?* Have students say the number.

- **Extra Support** Say each number aloud and clap the corresponding number of times. Have students clap, too.

Optional Activity

- Show students how to write the numbers in order. Write each number slowly, line by line, on the board. Have students copy the number in their notebooks while you write it again.
- If students can already write numbers independently, do a dictation. Make sure you write the numbers you say on a piece of paper. When you finish, say each number again and write it on the board for students to check.

- Direct students' attention to the instructions. Say *Point and say.* Have students point with their finger. Then, to teach the meaning of *say,* say *Say* Hello. Have students say *hello.*
- Direct students' attention to the examples. Model pointing and saying the words.
- Point to one of the numbers again. Have a student say the word. Then have that student point to another number and call on a different student to say the word.
- **Extra Challenge** Have students add numbers to lists. For example, say *Three, five, seven* and have students say *nine.* Continue in this way with other patterns.
- **Extra Support** Have students point to and say the numbers in numerical order several times before they begin pointing to and saying them in random order.

Wrap Up

- Give instructions using classroom objects and numbers. For example, hold up an eraser and say *Three!* Call on a student to find three erasers, hold them up, and count them aloud. Repeat with other items and students until numbers one to ten have been reviewed.
- If you want to do the Optional Activity in Lesson 2, send home a request for permission to photograph students.

Additional Practice: Workbook p. 4, Worksheets 1.0.1–1.0.3, Online Practice

LESSON 2 Look

In this lesson, students will:
- chant about greetings.
- greet their classmates.

Resources: Audio Track 3; Classroom Presentation Tool; Flashcards 12, 14; Workbook p. 5; Workbook Audio Track 1; Online Practice

Materials: a camera, pins, markers, index cards, a photo of you, a timer, two dolls or two teddy bears

TEACHER TIP
Have students make name tags for themselves at the beginning of a new school year. Provide each student with a tag and have them write their name and decorate the tag. Collect the tags at the end of each class and hand them out again at the beginning of each new class. They will help you learn everyone's name.

Warm Up
- Review numbers. Say the name of a student and a number. For example, say *[Carla], two.* Have this student repeat *two* and clap twice. Have the student call on another student by saying his/her name and a number, for example, *[Pablo], four.* Now have the second student repeat *four* and clap four times, and then call on another student. Continue in this way for two or three minutes.
- **Use the Photo** Hold up a copy of the Student's Book and point to the photo on pp. 4–5. Say *Look! Children!* Point to children in the class to illustrate what you mean. Then point to the children in the photo and count aloud. Have students count with you. When you reach *ten,* stop and point to the whole group of children again and say *A lot of children!*

- Teach some of the language from the chant. If students have made name tags, have them wear them. Wear a name tag, too. Walk around the classroom having short conversations with students. Say *Hello!* and elicit *Hello!* in response. Then, to a student, ask *What's your name?* If necessary, model the answer. For example, say *My name's [your name],* pointing to your name tag. Repeat with a few more students. Then, ask *How old are you?* If students are unable to answer, ask *Five? Six?* Hold up the same number of fingers as you ask. Repeat the questions until students understand that you are asking their age. Have them respond with a nod (yes) or a shake (no) of the head. Finally, ask *How are you?* Model the answer and say *I'm fine, thanks.* Ask several students and have them answer.
- Hold up a copy of the Student's Book and point to p. 5. As you do, say *Look at page 5.*
- Read aloud the instructions. Point to your ear as you say *Listen.* Then play **TR: 3** from beginning to end.
- Play **TR: 3** again, pausing after each verse. Hold up a copy of the Student's Book at the same time and point to the words to indicate that students should follow in their books.

- Point to the chant and to the different-colored lines. Put students into two groups, green and orange. If you have a mixed class, the girls can be green and the boys can be orange. Say *I'm the teacher. I'm purple.* Explain that each group has to chant the words in their color. Point to your mouth and say *Now, listen and chant.*
- Play **TR: 3** again, pointing to each group when it's their turn to chant. Say the purple lines yourself as you listen and have students say the rest of the chant as they listen.
- **Extra Challenge** Have students close their books and try to remember the chant without reading the words, just listening and joining in with the recording.
- **Extra Support** Pause after each line for students to repeat the words.

Optional Activity
- If you've received permission from parents/caregivers, make a bulletin board with photos and names of each of the students. Take photos of the students. Then print them out and pin up each of the photos and have students make name labels to add under each photo. Alternatively, take a group photo and just have students label it around the outside. Write a title on the board such as *Our Class.* Add your own photo and name, too.

- Act out the verb *read.* Hold a copy of the Student's Book in front of you and pretend to read it. Say *Read.*
- Read aloud the instructions. Direct students' attention to the two characters. Then act out the conversation. Use the green and blue flashcards and raise each flashcard one at a time as you speak. Also, point to the characters.
- Ask *What's your name?* and have individual students answer. Then ask *How old are you?* Again, have individual students answer.
- Act out the conversation with a volunteer. Then have two volunteers act out the conversation.
- Have students do the activity in pairs. Monitor and make sure they understand that they have to give information that is true for them. Then have students move around the classroom so that they can give the same information to a lot of students in the class.
- **Extra Challenge** Set a timer for two minutes and challenge students to introduce themselves to at least five classmates in this time.
- **Extra Support** If necessary, remind students that English is read from left to right. Draw an arrow pointing to the right, and allow students to copy the arrow under or next to the models.

Wrap Up
- Use two dolls or two teddy bears to act out a role-play with the help of students. Start by using a funny voice and making the first doll speak. Have the doll say *Hello!* Have students respond *Hello!* for the other doll. Then continue, having a similar conversation to the conversation in Activity 2. Have students invent names and ages.

Additional Practice: Workbook p. 5, Online Practice

1 **Listen and chant.** 🎧 TR: 3

Hello! Hello!
What's your name?
My name's Xi.
My name's Wayne.

Hello! Hello!
How old are you?
Hello, I'm six.
I'm six, too!

Hello, Xi.
How are you?
I'm fine, thanks.
And I'm fine, too.

2 **Read and say.**

Hello!

Hello!

What's your name?

My name's Kaitlyn.
What's your name?

My name's Shiven.
How old are you?

I'm seven.
How old are you?

I'm ten.

Look

In this lesson, students will:
- identify and say colors.

Resources: Audio Tracks 4–5, Classroom Presentation Tool, Flashcards 11–19, Workbook p. 6, Workbook Audio Track 2, Online Practice

Materials: photos of colorful objects (balloons, jelly beans, etc.), crayons

ABOUT THE PHOTO

The photo shows a lantern store in Vietnam. Elaborate paper lanterns originated in China around 230 BCE, but soon became popular in Japan, Vietnam, and other Asian countries. The lanterns are made from paper or silk and are built around a light bamboo frame. They are lit from inside by a small candle. The earliest lamps were decorated with images from myths and legends. Modern lanterns can be decorated with just about anything, even pictures of teenage pop idols. The lanterns symbolize joy, good luck, celebration, and long life.

TEACHER TIP

Different students will have different levels of English at this stage, and some will know more words than others. Use the first lessons to gauge the amount of English that different students know. Tap into the students' knowledge and ask students who know more to help those who know less. But make sure that the skills of all students are recognized. For example, praise students for being neat, and for their drawing or coloring skills. Make sure students understand that everyone is good at something.

Warm Up

- **Use the Photo** Have students open their books to pp. 6–7. Hold up a copy of the Student's Book and point to one of the lanterns. Say *Look! Wow!* Smile and look in wonder. Encourage students to react in the same way to the beautiful lanterns. Then look at the photo as if you are trying to choose your favorite lantern. Make a thinking gesture. Then nod and point to one of the lanterns and say *Yes! I like this one!* Show students, and smile and nod. Make sure they understand that you have chosen your favorite lantern.
- Have students choose their favorite lantern. Say *Look and point! Which lantern do you like?* Use gestures. Point to your eyes and then do a pointing gesture. Point to the lanterns and then to the students when you say *you*. Have students hold up their books and point to their favorite lanterns.

- Say *Look at the colors.* Point to the nine colors and give students time to look at them.
- Make sure that students understand the instructions. Play **TR: 4**. Pause after the first word to check that students are pointing to the correct color. Then continue playing **TR: 4**, pausing if necessary to give students time to think, look, and point.
- **Extra Challenge** Have students close their books. Play **TR: 4** again, pausing after each color. This time have students point to something in the classroom that is that color. Make sure they have time to look and find an object. Display flashcards around the room for any colors that you don't already have in your classroom.
- **Extra Support** Hold up a copy of the Student's Book and point at the same time as the students.

- Read aloud the instructions and make sure students understand the word *repeat* (from Lesson 1).
- Play **TR: 5**, pausing after the first word to model repeating for students. Continue with **TR: 5**, having students repeat the words as a class.
- **Extra Challenge** Play **TR: 5** again, this time with students' books closed. As students say the word, have them point to something of that color in the classroom.
- **Extra Support** Hold up the color flashcards as students repeat each word.

Optional Activity

- Hold up objects that are different colors. Ask *What color?* Have students reply as a class by calling out the color each time. Alternatively, say each color one at a time and have students point to or touch an object of that color.

- Read aloud the instructions. Direct students' attention to the two characters and the examples. Model pointing and saying the words.
- Point to and say other colors. Make sure students are pointing to the correct colors in Activity 1. Have them repeat the colors.
- Hold up a copy of the Student's Book and point to one of the colors in Activity 1 again. Have a student say the word. Then have that student point to another color and call on a different student to say the word.
- Put students in pairs, A and B. Have Student A point to a color and have Student B say the word. Have students take turns pointing and saying. Walk around monitoring while students do the activity. Make sure they understand that one student has to point to a color and the other student has to say the word.

- **Extra Challenge** Have students do the activity as a game. Have them say *Red; Red, yellow; Red, yellow, orange,* etc. as their partner points to the colors. Have them go faster and faster with each word to see if they can keep their partner on track.

- **Extra Support** Hold up a copy of the Student's Book open to p. 7. Point to the green square and ask *Blue or green?* Have students choose from the two colors you say, by pointing and saying the correct color aloud.

- Read aloud the instructions. Hold up a copy of the Student's Book, and direct students' attention to the two characters and the examples. Say *Yellow,* point to a yellow lantern in the photo on pp. 6–7, and say *One.* Then point to a second yellow lantern in the photo and say *Two.* Continue to count up to ten and point to a different yellow lantern each time.

- Choose another color and count the lanterns in the same way. For example, say *Blue* and start counting. Have volunteers choose colors and start counting.

- Put students in pairs. Have one student say a color and the other start counting the lanterns. Then have students change roles.

- **Extra Challenge** Give students photos of other colorful objects (balloons, jelly beans, etc.), and have them point and count each color.

- **Extra Support** Before students do the activity with the lanterns in the photo, have them do the same activity with objects in the class. Have one student call out a color and one student point to an object of that color and say *one.* Then have another student point to an object of the same color and say *two.* Continue with other numbers and then with other colors. If there are more than ten objects of the same color in the classroom, stop at ten.

Wrap Up

- Play a colors game. Make sure each student has a variety of crayons: green, orange, purple, red, yellow, etc. Have them draw five circles and color each one in a different color. Let them choose any five colors. Then call out colors in a random order. Have students cross out their colors (or check them) as they hear them. When someone has crossed out (or checked) all five colors, have them call out *Colors!* That student wins the game.

- Have students play again in small groups, taking turns to be the caller. Alternatively, have them play the game using numbers instead of colors. When someone has crossed out (or checked) all five numbers, have them call out *Numbers!*

> **Additional Practice:** Workbook p. 6, Online Practice

A shop in Vietnam

1 **Listen and point.** 🎧 TR: 4

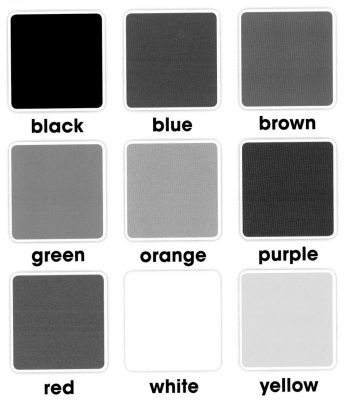

black   blue   brown

green   orange   purple

red   white   yellow

2 **Listen and repeat.** 🎧 TR: 5

3 **Point and say.**

white

orange

4 **Look, say, and point.**

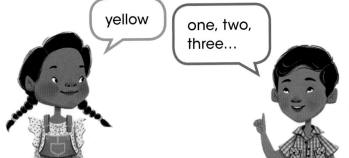

yellow

one, two, three...

7

Look

1 Say and point.

2 Play and say.

In this lesson, students will:

- review colors.
- review numbers.
- talk about size using *big* and *small*.

Resources: Classroom Presentation Tool, Workbook p. 7, Online Practice

Materials: a big ball and a small ball, a timer, colored clay or colored pipe cleaners (all nine colors per student), crayons

TEACHER TIP

Set up a system at the beginning of a new course to communicate regularly with parents and caregivers. This can easily be done by using a notebook which students take home at the end of each day and then bring in again for the next class. Make sure parents understand the system you set up and remember to inform them of homework tasks and examples of positive behavior, such as acts of kindness or a willingness to help and share.

Warm Up

- Say *Find something black* and model by pointing to something black in the classroom, such as a blackboard. Do the same with other colors. Then give instructions in a different order and have students point. Say *Find something green. Find something black.*
- Say *Find the number 3* and model by pointing to Activity 3 on Student's Book page 7, for example. Do the same with other numbers. Use the activity and page numbers within the Student's Book.

- Bring two balls into the classroom, one big and one small. Hold up each ball, one at a time, and say *Big* and *Small*. Walk around the classroom pointing to different objects. Say *Big* or say *Small* depending on their size, for example, a big bag, a small bag, a big pencil, and a small pencil. Then hold up each of the balls, one at a time, and ask *Big or small?* Have students reply as a class. Then point to the same objects again and have students call out *big* or *small*.
- Read aloud the instructions. Hold up a copy of the Student's Book, and direct students' attention to the two characters and the examples.
- Act out the activity in front of the class. Point to the character on the left and say *Orange.* Then point to the character on the right and to the orange letter *m* in the words and say *Small.* Then say *Yellow*, point to the corresponding letter *i*, and say *Big.*
- Choose another color and have a volunteer find the letter. Have the class say *big* or *small*.
- Put students in pairs. Have one student say a color and the other find the letter and say *big* or *small*. Then have students change roles.

- **Extra Challenge** Say three colors one after the other and have students say the three corresponding sizes. For example, you say *Black, red, green* and students say *big, big, small*.
- **Extra Support** Draw circles on the board and have students call out *big* or *small*.

- Direct students' attention to the box of colored numbers. Say *This is a game. We play a game.* Emphasize *play*. Then read aloud the instructions.
- Say *Point to number 9.* Have students point to the two numbers. Say *Big* and have students say the color. (brown) Then say *Small* and have students say the color. (orange)
- Hold up a copy of the Student's Book, and direct students' attention to the two characters and the examples.
- Act out the activity in front of the class. Point to the character on the left and say *Big, red.* Then point to the character on the right and to the big, red letter in the box, and say *Three.* Say *Small, green* and point to and say *Eight.* Then say *Big, green* and point to and say *One.* (There are two of every number except 1 and 10.)
- Choose another size and color and have a volunteer call out the number.
- Put students in pairs. Have one student say a size and color and the other say the number. Then have students change roles.
- **Extra Challenge** Set a timer for three minutes and see if students can cross off each number before the timer goes off.
- **Extra Support** Point out that the size comes before the color every time. Write *big, red* and *small, red* on the board. Point to each pair of words one at a time and nod your head.

Optional Activity

- Use colored clay or colored pipe cleaners to make number shapes. Divide the class into nine pairs or small groups. Have each pair make one of the figures (1–9). Then call out the numbers and have students say the corresponding colors.

Wrap Up

- Give each student a piece of paper and some crayons. Then give instructions of what to draw and color. Pause after each instruction. Say *Blue. A big three. Red. A small five.* Call on students to give instructions. Then put students into small groups to take turns giving instructions, drawing, and coloring.

Additional Practice: Workbook p. 7, Online Practice

UNIT 1 Things for School

In this unit, students will:

- talk about classroom objects.
- ask and answer questions about classroom objects using *What's this? It's a [pen].*
- read about a classroom.
- ask questions about classroom objects using *What's this? Is it a [pen]?*
- answer questions about classroom objects using *Yes, it is./No, it isn't.*
- listen to and sing a song about a school bus.
- identify and pronounce words with /æ/, /b/, /k/, and /d/ at the beginning.
- watch a video about classrooms in other countries.
- identify the value of taking care of your school things.

Language

Words
bag, book, crayon, eraser, pen, pencil, pencil case, ruler; board, chair, desk, poster

Grammar
- *What's this? It's a pen.*
- *Is it a classroom? Yes, it is.*
- *What's this? Is it a bag? No, it isn't.*

Phonics
/æ/ apple
/b/ bag
/k/ carrot
/d/ desk

Twenty-First Century Skills

Collaboration
Work with a partner to practice words, Lesson 1

Communication
Say a chant in two groups, Lesson 2

Creativity
Draw and speak about school things, Lesson 7

Critical Thinking
Identify the value of taking care of your school things, Lesson 5

In the Unit Opener, students will:

- respond to a photo of a girl painting a picture.
- talk about colors.

Resources: Home School Connection Letter, Classroom Presentation Tool

Materials: crayons

Introduce the Theme

- Hold up a red crayon and say *Look! Blue or red?* Have a volunteer answer and then say *Yes, it's red.* Repeat the word with the class. Say *Listen: red. Now repeat: red.*
- Hold up a pink crayon and say *Listen: pink. Now repeat: pink.*
- Go through all the colors, holding up a different crayon each time.
- Say *Look around.* Gesture around the room and say *Find something red.* Have students find things in the classroom that are red. Repeat this with other colors they've mentioned.

Use the Photo

- Have students open their books to p. 9. Say *Look at page 9.* Hold up a copy of the Student's Book open to p. 9 to show students the correct page. Make sure all students are on the correct page. Have students check that their classmates are on the same page.
- Read aloud the instructions at the bottom of the page and point to the photo. Ask *What colors can you see?* Have students point to things in the photo and say the colors. (black, blue, brown, green, orange, pink, white, yellow)
- Ask *Where is the girl? Is she at home?* (no) If necessary, draw an outline of a house to clarify the meaning of *home.* Then say *She's at school.* Gesture around the classroom. Repeat the word and say *School.*

TEACHER TIP
The best way to teach students how to do an unfamiliar activity is by demonstrating it a few times so that they can see exactly what is expected. Use different students each time you want to model an activity and repeat it as many times as necessary. That way, every student is clear about what needs to be done. As students get used to different activities and routines, there will be less need for demonstrations and modeling.

Things for School

ABOUT THE PHOTO

This photo shows a girl in elementary school in India. In India, children must begin elementary school at six years old. When children are eleven, they move into a middle school where they stay for four years. They take exams when they are fourteen. At that point, some children finish school while others continue on to secondary school.

A girl painting

Look at the photo. What can you see?

Words

1 Listen and point. 🎧 TR: 6

bag   book   crayon

eraser   pen   pencil

pencil case   ruler

2 Listen and repeat. 🎧 TR: 7

3 Point and say.

bag

eraser

Lesson 1 Words

In this lesson, students will:
- respond to the photo of a bag.
- compare their own bags.
- talk about classroom objects.

Resources: Audio Tracks 6–7, Classroom Presentation Tool, Flashcards 20–27, Workbook p. 8, Workbook Audio Track 3, Online Practice

Materials: two red crayons, a yellow crayon, sticky tack

Warm Up

- Draw a big circle on the board and in the middle write *Words in English*. Have students raise their hands if they know a word and say it when you say their name. Write the words that the students know on the board around the circle. Every student will know some words in English and some will know a lot, so you won't have time or space to write all the words they know on the board. This is an opportunity for students to realize how much they know.
- **Use the Photo** Help students open their books to pp.10–11. Point to the bag and say *Look! It's a bag. Show me your bag.* Have students take out or point to their schoolbags.
- Hold up two red crayons and say *Same.* Now hold up a red and a yellow crayon and say *Different.* Once you're certain students understand the meaning of *same* and *different*, gesture to the bags in the classroom and ask *Same?*
- Spend a few minutes comparing students' schoolbags with the bag in the photo. Find the bag in the classroom that's most similar to the one in the photo.

- Read aloud the instructions. Then direct students' attention to the photos. Point to each photo one at a time (except the bag) and ask *Is this in the bag? Yes or no?* Point to the bag in the main photo to make sure students understand that this is the bag you're referring to.
- Point to your ear and say *Let's listen.* Play **TR: 6** and point to the photos one at a time as you hear the words.
- Play **TR: 6** a second time. Hold up a copy of the Student's Book and model pointing to the photos as you hear the words. Have students point to the words as they listen.
- **Listening Strategy: Pointing** Have students point to the item as they listen to the word the first time. Students will be able to match the sound with the written word if they move their finger each time they hear a new word.

- Direct students' attention to the instructions and read them aloud. Play **TR: 7**, pausing after the first word to model repeating for students. Continue playing **TR: 7**, having students repeat the words as a class.
- Play **TR: 7** again and call on individual students around the class to repeat the words.

- **Extra Challenge** Write the eight words in a column on the board. Then collect a different number of each object (for example, two bags, three pencils, five books) and put them all on your table. Call on individual students to come to the table. Ask *How many [bags]?* Have students look, count, and write the number next to the word on the board. Have them use digits (for example, 2, 3) and not words.
- **Extra Support** Say each of the target words aloud and clap to each syllable. Say *Bag* (one clap), *Crayon* (two claps), and so on. Go through all the words, having students clap as you say them. Then, play **TR: 7** and have students clap at the same time.

- Read aloud the instructions. Direct students' attention to the examples. Model pointing and saying the words.
- Point to one of the photos in Activity 1 and ask a student to say the word. Then have that student point to another photo and call on a different student to say the word for that photo.
- Put the students in pairs, A and B. Have Student A point to a photo and have Student B say the word. Have students take turns to point and say until all the words have been practiced.

Optional Activity

- Hide eight classroom objects around the classroom, keeping a record of their colors. Write a list of the objects and their colors on the board, for example, *a red pen, a blue pencil case.*
- Have students search for the objects. Each time a student finds an object, have him/her bring the object to the front of the class and set it down for others to see. Then check the object off the list on the board.

Wrap Up

- Display the flashcards on the board and have students study them for a moment. Then have students close their eyes as you take one away. When they open their eyes, have students say the word for the missing flashcard. For an additional challenge, rearrange the position of the flashcards each time you remove one.

Additional Practice: Workbook p. 8, Online Practice

Grammar

In this lesson, students will:
- ask and answer questions about classroom objects using *What's this? It's a [pen].*
- say a chant about classroom things.

Resources: Audio Tracks 8–9, Classroom Presentation Tool, Flashcards 20–27, Workbook p. 9, Workbook Audio Track 4, Online Practice

Warm Up

- Challenge the students to remember the eight new words from Lesson 1: *bag, book, crayon, eraser, pen, pencil, pencil case,* and *ruler.* Write the first letter of each object on the board in a column and have students raise their hands to suggest a word. Write the words as students say them. Then say each word again and give students time to find and point to the object in the classroom.
- **Use the Photo** Have students open their books to pp. 10–11. Use the photo to review classroom objects. Point to a pencil in the photo and ask *Book or pencil?* (pencil) Be careful with plurals here. Refer to just one pencil, one book, and so on. Ask about other objects. Have students raise their hands when they want to answer. Choose a different student each time.

- Show students the *pen* and *book* flashcards. Say *Find these words on the page.* Have students scan the chant to find the words. Say *Point to the words.*
- Read aloud the instructions. Say *Listen to the chant.* Play **TR: 8.** Have students clap to the rhythm. Play **TR: 8** again. This time have students clap and chant *What's this?*
- Divide the class into two groups, A and B. Point to Group A and say *You say the purple.* Point to Group B and say *You say the green.* Play **TR: 8** again and have students chant their part. Then play **TR: 8** a final time, having groups switch roles.
- **Extra Challenge** Before students work in groups, chant the first three lines of the first verse. Then hold up another classroom object, such as a bag, and call on students to chant the fourth line with the word for the new object. Do the same with the second verse. Chant the first three lines of the second verse. Then hold up another classroom object, such as a crayon, and call on students to chant the fourth line with the word for this object.
- **Extra Support** Before students work in groups, chant the first three lines of the first verse. Then hold up a copy of the Student's Book and point to it. Call on students to chant the fourth line. Do the same with the second verse. Chant the first three lines of the second verse. Then hold up a pen and call on students to chant the fourth line.

- Read aloud the instructions. Direct students' attention to the grammar box. Say *Listen and read.* Play **TR: 9** one time as students read. Play **TR: 9** again and have students repeat the sentences as a class.
- Model the question in a real-life situation. Hold up a copy of the Student's Book and ask *What's this?* Then answer yourself, and say *It's a book.* Write the question and answer with contractions on the board. Write the full forms above:

What is this?	It is a book.
What's this?	It's a book.

- Circle the two contractions and repeat the question and answer, emphasizing the contracted forms. Have students repeat after you.
- Hold up other classroom objects and ask *What's this?* Have students raise their hands to suggest answers. They should use the contracted form.
- Erase the questions and answers on the board, then write *What's this?* Hold up a pencil. Ask the question and elicit the answer. Write *It's a pencil.* Then hold up an eraser and ask *What's this?* Write *an eraser* on the board. Then circle the *a* and the *an* in the two answers and draw lines to the first letter of *pencil* and *eraser.* Say *Some words start with* a, e, i, o, or u, *like* eraser. *For these words, we say* an.

- Read aloud the instructions. Direct students' attention to the example conversation. Holding an object, model the conversation with a volunteer. Then demonstrate the activity by practicing with another student. Hold up a copy of the Student's Book, point to an object in the photo on pp. 10–11, and ask *What's this?* Have the student answer.
- Have students do the activity in pairs while you monitor, helping when necessary.

Optional Activity

- Draw part of a pencil. Ask *What's this?* Have students raise their hands to guess.
- Have students work in pairs, A and B. Have Student A be the artist and draw part of an object. Then have Student A ask *What's this?* Have Student B guess. When Student B guesses correctly, have them change roles. Monitor students while they do the activity, helping when necessary.

Wrap Up

- Hold up one of the Lesson 1 flashcards facing you so that students can't see the picture. Ask *What's this?* Have students raise their hands to guess. They should say *It's a [pen].* If anyone guesses correctly, he/she wins the flashcard. If nobody guesses correctly, continue with another flashcard. Continue until all flashcards have been given out.

Additional Practice: Workbook p. 9, Online Practice

Grammar LESSON 2

1 **Listen and chant.** 🎧 TR: 8

What's this?
Take a look!
What's this?
It's a book.

What's this?
Look again.
What's this?
It's a pen.

What's this?
It's a room.
What's this?
Our classroom!

2 **Listen and read.** 🎧 TR: 9

> What's this? It's a pen.
> What's this? It's a bag.

3 **Point, ask, and answer.**

What's this?

It's a ruler.

Reading

1 Listen and repeat. 🎧 TR: 10

> poster   board   chair   desk

2 Listen and read. 🎧 TR: 11

Look at the photo. What's this?
It's a classroom.

What can you see in the classroom?
Can you see a **poster**? It's green.
Can you see a **board**? It's black.
Can you see a **chair**? It's red.
Can you see a **desk**?

3 Read again and circle.

1. I can see a **blue** / **green** poster.
2. I can see a **black** / **white** board.
3. I can see a **red** / **yellow** chair.

ABOUT THE PHOTO

The photo shows a teacher and some children in a math class. These days, teachers in a lot of elementary schools around the world are spending more time on STEM subjects (science, technology, engineering, and math) than in the past. There has also been a growth of after-school STEM clubs for students. Goals of STEM education include preparing students for the increasing number of careers that require knowledge of science and technology, as well as helping the general population become more knowledgable about these fields.

Reading

In this lesson, students will:

- read about a classroom.
- use new words to talk about a classroom.
- circle the correct word in sentences about the text.

Resources: Audio Tracks 10–11, Classroom Presentation Tool, Flashcards 28–31, Workbook p. 10, Workbook Audio Track 5, Online Practice

Materials: a box, a piece of cloth, sticky tack

Warm Up

- Put classroom objects into a box. When students aren't looking, take out an object, such as a book, from the box and cover it with a piece of cloth. Hold it up and ask *What's this?* Call on a student to say *It's a [book].* When a student guesses correctly, have that student come to the front of the class and choose another object from the box. Have him/her repeat the question and call on a classmate to respond. Have this continue until the box is empty.

- Have students open their books to p. 12. Read aloud the instructions. Play **TR: 10** and have students listen and repeat the words. Then use actions and descriptions to teach the new words. For example, find a poster in your classroom. Point and say *Look, what's this? It's a poster.* (Emphasize the word *poster.*) Have students point to other posters in the classroom and say the word.
- Explain the other words, one at a time, emphasizing each word as you teach it. Point to the board and say *Look, a board.* Have students point to the board as they say the word. Stand up, point to your own chair, and say *Look, a chair.* Have students stand up, point to their chairs, and say the word. Finally, point to a desk and say *Look, a desk.* Have students point to their own desk and say the word.
- Point to the text and say *Find the words here.* Have students scan the text to find the four new words. Make sure they understand that they don't have to read the whole text— they just have to find the words.
- Call on a volunteer to point to and read aloud the first of the words in the text. Make sure that all students are pointing to the correct word. As the volunteer says the word, hold up the corresponding flashcard. Repeat with the other Lesson 3 words and flashcards.

- Read aloud the instructions. Then point to the text and say *Read the first line.* Then say *Look at the photo.* Ask *What's this?* (a classroom) Say *Listen and read.* Play **TR: 11.** Have students listen to and read the whole text.
- Read aloud the questions starting with *Can you*, one at a time. Pause after each question and have students point to each object that is mentioned. At this stage, do not read aloud the answers.
- Play **TR: 11** again. Have students read the text again silently, taking their time to make sure they understand it.

- **Reading Strategy: Scanning for Specific Information** To find specific information in a text, such as the new words, it isn't necessary to read and understand the whole text. Students can look quickly through the text to spot the words. Point out that students should look for the first letter or the length of the words they're trying to find. By scanning to find the words, students can see where and how the new words are used before they begin to read.
- **Extra Challenge** Have students read the text again to memorize the order of the words. Have them test each other in pairs. Have one student read a question and the other point to an object in the photo or in their classroom.
- **Extra Support** Put students in pairs, A and B, to read aloud the text together. Have Student A read the first sentence. Then have Student B read the second sentence. Have them continue taking turns to read aloud to the end.

- Slowly draw a circle on the board and say *Circle* as you draw. Erase the circle. Then write the word *classroom* on the board, draw another circle around the word, and say *Circle.*
- Read aloud the instructions. Point to item 1 and read aloud the sentence with both colors. Hold up a copy of the Student's Book, point to the poster, and ask *Blue or green?* (green) Circle the answer with your finger so that students can see the example. Have students work in pairs to complete the activity.
- Discuss answers as a class and then write them on the board for students to check.

Optional Activity

- Read aloud the first question from the text *Can you see a poster?* Have students point to a poster in the classroom and call on a volunteer to say *It's [green, black and white].* Repeat with the other questions in the text and have students point.
- Ask questions with other classroom objects. For example, ask *Can you see a ruler?* Again, have students point to the objects and call on volunteers to say their colors.

Wrap Up

- Have students do an ordering activity. Say *Close your books.* Display the flashcards in a line on the board so that students can see them. Now ask students to put the flashcards in the order that the words appear in the text. (poster, board, chair, desk) Have volunteers come forward and move the flashcards into the correct position.
- When everybody has agreed on the order, say *Open your books and check.* Have students read the text again and check the order of the flashcards. If necessary, have them adjust the order of the flashcards.

Additional Practice: Workbook p. 10, Online Practice

Grammar

> **In this lesson, students will:**
> - ask questions about classroom objects using *Is it a [pen]?*
> - answer questions about classroom objects using *Yes, it is./No, it isn't.*
>
> **Resources:** Audio Track 12, Classroom Presentation Tool, Flashcards 20–31, Workbook p. 11, Workbook Audio Track 6, Online Practice
>
> **Materials:** sticky tack, crayons, an empty bag, an empty bag for each pair of students

Warm Up

- Use the Lesson 1 and 3 flashcards to review classroom objects. Display them around the classroom. Then have students stand up. Give instructions for students to follow. Say *Look at the pencil case.* Say *Look at* again and point to your eyes. Then say *Look at the pencil case* again and turn to face the *pencil case* flashcard. Have students turn to face the corresponding flashcard. Continue with different words. After you review all the words, call on volunteers to give the instructions.

- Have students open their books to p. 13. Read aloud the instructions. Point to the grammar box and say *Listen.* Play **TR: 12.** Have students listen and read. Play **TR: 12** again and have students repeat the questions and answers, first as a class and then individually.
- Use the Lesson 1 and 3 flashcards to make new questions and answers. Hold up the *ruler* flashcard. Ask *What's this? Is it a pencil?* (No, it isn't.) *What's this? Is it a ruler?* (Yes, it is.)
- Write on the board:

What's this? Is it a bag?	No, it isn't.
What's = What is	isn't = is not

- Point to and read aloud the questions and answer in the first line on the board, emphasizing the contractions. Then point to the apostrophes and to the information in the second line. Say *Look! What's means What is, and isn't means is not.* Emphasize the two separate contracted words and the contraction each time.

- Read aloud the instructions. Point to item 1. Read the questions and call on a student to answer. Hold up a copy of the Student's Book and circle the answer with your finger so that students can see the example.
- Have students complete the activity in pairs. Review answers as a class and write them on the board for students to check.

Optional Activity

- Hold a crayon behind your back so that students can't see it. Have students try to guess the color. Write on the board *Is it a [blue] crayon?* Call on students to ask the question. Answer each time and say *No, it isn't* until somebody guesses the color. Then answer and say *Yes, it is.*
- Put students in pairs, and give each pair several crayons. Have students do the activity in pairs, taking turns to hide a different-colored crayon each time.

- Put a few classroom objects into an empty bag, including a book. Read aloud the instructions. Holding the bag, direct students' attention to the example conversation. Point to the boy and say *Ask.* Then point to the girl and say *Answer.*
- Model the example conversation with a volunteer. Place your hand inside the bag and hold the book, but don't show it to the students. Start the conversation and ask *What's this?* Have the student respond and continue the conversation to the end. When you say the last line, pull the book out of the bag to show it to the class.
- Have students act out the conversation in pairs. Monitor and help when necessary.
- Have students do the activity in pairs. First, they put about six classroom objects into an empty bag and then take turns to put their hand into the bag and hold an object. Make sure that the other student can't see the object.
- Have students continue asking and answering about all the objects in their bags.
- **Extra Challenge** Have students do the activity again, this time in groups of four and with more objects in the bag. Have a different student hold the bag each time. Have the other students take turns to ask. When a student guesses correctly, he/she holds the bag.
- **Extra Support** Show students all the items that you're putting into the bag, naming them as you do so.

Wrap Up

- Take a bag and put a lot of classroom objects inside it. Let students see what you are putting in the bag. Include a book, a pencil case, a pen, a pencil, an eraser, a ruler, and a crayon. Have students come up one at a time, put on a blindfold, and feel around in the bag. Have them pull out an object and ask *What's this? Is it a [book]?* Have the rest of the students answer *Yes, it is* or *No, it isn't.* Have as many students as possible take a turn.

> **Additional Practice:** Workbook p. 11, Online Practice

Grammar

1 **Listen and read.**  TR: 12

> What's this? **Is it** a classroom?
> Yes, it is.
>
> What's this? **Is it** a bag?
> No, it isn't.

2 **Read and circle.**

1.  What's this? Is it a book?
   (Yes, it is.)
   No, it isn't.

2. What's this? Is it a chair?
   Yes, it is.
   (No, it isn't.)

3.  What's this? Is it a poster?
   Yes, it is.
   (No, it isn't.)

4. What's this? Is it a crayon?
   (Yes, it is.)
   No, it isn't.

3 **Point, ask, and answer.**

> What's this?   Is it a pencil?
>
> No, it isn't.   Is it a book?
>
> Yes, it is!

1 **Listen and read.** 🎧 TR: 13

2 **Listen and sing.** 🎧 TR: 14 and 15

3 **Sing and act.** 🎧 TR: 16

Chorus
This is the bus,
the bus to school.
It's a cat.
It's really cool!

What's this?
Is it the bus?
Yes, it is.
It's the bus to school!

What's this?
Is it a bag?
Yes, it is.
It's a bag for school!

What's this?
Is it a pencil?
No, it isn't.
It's a pen for school!
Chorus

VALUE **Take care of your school things.**
Workbook, Lesson 6

ABOUT THE PHOTO
The photo shows a school bus in Japan. It looks like a cat—and like the bus in one of the Totoro movies. While school buses look like normal buses in most parts of the world, Japan has all kinds of brightly colored and decorated school buses. Cat and dog buses are popular. Some buses even look like characters from popular animated movies and series such as Pikachu.

LESSON 5 Song

In this lesson, students will:

- listen to and sing a song about a school bus.
- act out a song.
- identify the value of taking care of your school things.

Resources: Audio Tracks 13–16, Classroom Presentation Tool, Flashcards 20–27, Workbook p. 13, Online Practice

Materials: a bag, sticky tack

Warm Up

- Use classroom objects and colors to review the structure from the previous lesson. Hold up a bag and ask *Is it blue?* Have students respond with *Yes, it is* or *No, it isn't.* Hold up more objects and ask more questions.
- Have students open their books to p. 14. Hold up a copy of the Student's Book and point to the photo. Point to the bus and ask *Is it big?* (yes) *Is it red and white?* (No, it's brown and white.)

- Display the Lesson 1 flashcards on the board. Ask *Which words are in the song?* Have students scan the song and find the words *bag, pencil,* and *pen.*
- Make sure students understand the word *cool.* Walk around the classroom, pick up objects or point, and say *Cool!* Smile to indicate that you think each object is nice.
- Read aloud the instructions. Play **TR: 13.** Have students listen to the song and follow in their books. Hold up a copy of the Student's Book and point to the chorus at the start of the song when you reach the end.

- Read aloud the instructions. Play **TR: 14.** Get a clapping or tapping rhythm going to accompany the song. Encourage students to sing along to the chorus.
- Divide the class into two groups, A and B. Point to Group A and say *You sing the green.* Point to Group B and say *You sing the purple.* Play **TR: 14** again and have students sing their part of the song.
- Play **TR: 15,** the instrumental version of the song, and have students sing their part of the song. Then play **TR: 15** a final time, having groups switch roles.
- **Extra Support** Hold up a bag as students sing the first verse. Do the same with a pen as they sing the second verse.

- Read aloud the instructions. Read aloud the line *This is the bus,* and at the same time act out holding your hands on the steering wheel of a bus. Have students act out the action, too. Establish an action for each line of the song, reading from the page each time.

This is the bus, (Hold your hands on the steering wheel of a bus.)
the bus to school. (Point to the classroom floor or make a roof shape for the school building with two hands.)
It's a cat. (Put your hands just above your ears to look like a cat's ears.)
It's really cool! (Smile and nod.)
What's this? (Hold your arms out to the side in a quizzical way.)
Is it the bus? (Hold your hands on the steering wheel.)
Yes, it is. (Nod.)
It's the bus to school! (As above)
What's this? (As above)
Is it a bag? (Touch your shoulder with your thumb to act out carrying a bag over your shoulder.)
Yes, it is. (Nod.)
It's a bag for school! (As above)
What's this? (As above)
Is it a pencil? (Use your hand to act out writing with a pencil.)
No, it isn't. (Shake your head.)
It's a pen for school! (As above)

- Play **TR: 16,** pausing after each line to make sure everybody remembers the actions. Change or simplify the actions as necessary for your students.
- Play **TR: 16** again. Have students sing the song and do the actions.
- **Extra Challenge** Have students create two more verses with different objects.
- **Value: Take care of your school things** At this point in the lesson, you can teach the value. Say *The value of this lesson is* Take care of your school things. Write *Things for school* on the board. Then hold up a bag and ask *Is this a thing for school?* (yes) Repeat with a pen. Then ask students to name other things for school. Ask *How can we take care of our school things?* Demonstrate careless behavior. Take some papers and books and shove them roughly into a bag. Then shake your head and say *No!* Then, show students how you carefully place your pen in a pencil case and put other things for school neatly on your table or desk. Smile at the class and say *Yes!* Have students act out taking care of their things for school neatly and with care. For additional practice, have students complete Lesson 6 of the Workbook in class or at home.

Optional Activity

- Have a singing competition. Divide the class into groups to perform the song. Have them sing along to **TR: 16** if they wish and turn their actions into a dance routine. Vote on the best version.

Wrap Up

- Play **TR: 13** and pause at the end of the first line. Have students sing the next line. Continue playing **TR: 13** and pause again at the end of the third line. Have students sing the next line. Continue until students have sung the entire song in this way.

Additional Practice: Workbook p. 13, Online Practice

LESSON 6 Phonics

In this lesson, students will:
- identify and write *a*, *b*, *c*, and *d*.
- identify and pronounce words with /æ/, /b/, /k/, and /d/ at the beginning.

Resources: Audio Tracks 17–19; Classroom Presentation Tool; Flashcards 20, 31–33; Workbook p. 12; Workbook Audio Track 7; Online Practice

Materials: a popular tune (on CD or Internet)

Warm Up

- Write the following letters on the board: *Aa*, *Bb*, *Cc*, and *Dd*. Point to and say each letter one at a time. Then point to each letter and have students say it. Finally, say *Today we're learning the sounds for these letters.*

- Have students open their books to p. 15. Hold up a copy of the Student's Book and point to the photos and words. Read aloud the instructions. Say *Listen.* Play **TR: 17**, pointing to each photo and word as students hear it.
- Play **TR: 17** again, pausing after the first word, *apple.* Hold up a copy of the Student's Book and point to the photo of the apple, saying the word aloud. Have students do the same. Then continue playing **TR: 17**. Have students point to and repeat each word. Monitor students carefully, making sure they pronounce the target sounds correctly.

- Read aloud the instructions. Point to the chant. Say *Listen. Can you hear /æ/, /b/, /k/, and /d/?* Say the sounds, not the letters.
- Play **TR: 18**. Pause after the first line of the chant. Ask *What sound do we hear? Is it /æ/, /b/, /k/, or /d/? Yes, we hear /æ/.* Hold up a copy of the Student's Book and point to the example in the first line. Continue playing **TR: 18**, pausing, asking, and eliciting the answer each time.
- Play **TR: 18** again. This time have students read and say the chant.

Optional Activity

- Choose a popular tune that students would be familiar with. Hum one or two lines of the tune. Then, say *Let's sing this song but with sounds, not words.*
- Put students into four groups, and assign each group one of the phonics flashcards. Have each group practice singing the tune with only their sound. Then, call on groups in alphabetical order to sing the tune with their sound.

- Read aloud the instructions. Give students a minute to look at the picture, read the words, and think about the sounds.
- Play **TR: 19** from beginning to end. Hold up a copy of the Student's Book and point to the example in item 1. Ask *What's the word?* (bag) Play **TR: 19** again, pausing after item 2. Ask *What's the word?* (desk) Have students write the letter in their books. Continue playing the audio, pausing each time to give students time to write the letter.
- Check answers by writing the four words on the board with the numbers 1–4. Then call out the numbers in order and have students say the words in chorus.

Script for TR: 19 *carrot, desk, apple, bag*

- **Extra Challenge** Say each letter in random order. Have students write the corresponding letter at the same time. Write a list as you say the letters so that you can check them with the class at the same time.
- **Extra Support** Do some writing practice if your students are able to write and know both lowercase and uppercase letters. Have students take out pencils and notebooks. Explain that they have to write the letters. Stand with your back to the students and say each letter, one at a time. Slowly trace the lowercase and uppercase letters with your finger in the air, and have students write the letters at the same time.

Wrap Up

- Use the phonics flashcards to review the target sounds. Hold up each flashcard, one at a time, and have students say the sound, the word, and the letter. Repeat the activity a few times, changing the order each time and speeding up so that students have to say the words more and more quickly.

Additional Practice: Workbook p. 12, Online Practice

Phonics

1 Listen, point, and repeat. 🎧 TR: 17

apple

bag

carrot

desk

2 Listen, chant, and circle. 🎧 TR: 18

What's this? It's an apple, an a, a, (a)pple.
What's this? It's a bag, a b, b, (b)ag.
What's this? It's a carrot, a c, c, (c)arrot.
What's this? It's a desk, a d, d, (d)esk.

3 Listen and find. Write the letter. 🎧 TR: 19

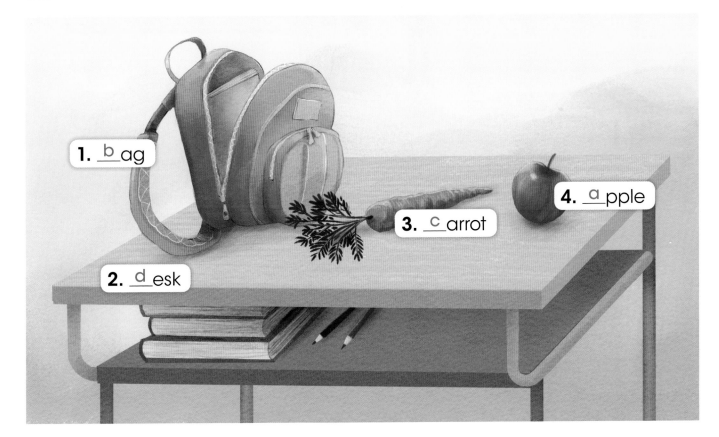

1. _b_ ag
2. _d_ esk
3. _c_ arrot
4. _a_ pple

Video

1 **Watch and match. Write the numbers.** ▶ Video 1

 1. AJ 2. Emilia 3. Jessica and Tracy

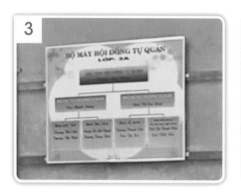

2 **Your turn! Ask and answer.**

ABOUT THE VIDEO

In this video, Jessica and Tracy talk about a classroom in Vietnam. Students start elementary school in Vietnam when they are six years old. In the first three years, they learn six subjects and in the final two years they learn nine subjects. Students often wear a school uniform. In many schools, girls wear white dresses, and boys wear blue or black pants and white shirts.

What's this? Is it a ruler?

No, it isn't. It's a pencil case.

3 **Draw and say.**

What's this? Is it a crayon?

No, it isn't. It's a _____ .

_____ ?
_____ ?

Yes, it is.

Video

In this lesson, students will:

- watch a video about classrooms in other countries.
- ask and answer questions about school things.
- draw and speak about school things.

Resources: Video 1, Classroom Presentation Tool, Online Practice

End-of-Unit Resources: Worksheet 1.1, Unit 1 Test, ExamView Assessment Suite

Warm Up

- Have students sit in a circle and think about their classroom. Point to the classroom and to the students and yourself, and say *Our classroom.* Point to something in the classroom and say *Look! A [desk].* Have each student point and say the name of an object one at a time. Smile and say *I like our classroom.* Say *Today's video is about classrooms.*

- Have students open their books to p. 16. Direct students' attention to the three photos at the top. Give students instructions. Say *AJ. Point to AJ! AJ is number one. Emilia. Point to Emilia! Emilia is number two.* Then do the same with the other children. Have students work in pairs and check they are pointing to the same photo.
- Point to the three photos at the bottom. Say *Look! Three things for school. One, two, three.*
- Point to the first photo. Say *Look! What's this?* (a poster) Repeat this for the second and third photos. (book, crayon)
- Read aloud the instructions and play **Video 1** from beginning to end. Have students match the three numbers and names at the top with the photos at the bottom and write the numbers in the boxes.
- If you like, play **Video 1** again for students to check their answers.
- Pause **Video 1** after segment 1 (AJ) and hold up the object (a book). Ask the narrator's questions from the segment and have students give full answers. Ask *Is it an eraser?* (No, it isn't.) *Is it a crayon?* (No, it isn't.) *Is it a book?* (Yes, it is.) Pause after segment 2, ask the narrator's questions, and have students give full answers. Do the same with segment 3, pointing to or showing a poster as necessary.
- **Extra Support** Play **Video 1** with the sound off the first time students watch it so that they can focus on the classroom objects. Play the video from beginning to end.

The script for **Video 1** *is available on the Teacher's Resource Website.*

- Read aloud the instructions. Hold up a pencil case and model the conversation with a volunteer. Then hold up a different object and ask the same student another question. For example, hold up a crayon and ask *Is it a bag?*
- Put students into pairs to ask and answer questions about their classroom objects.
- Monitor students while they speak and help when necessary.

Optional Activity

- Arrange students in two lines, A and B, facing each other. Have an equal number of students in each line. Have each student hold one classroom object. Have students make short conversations with the person facing them. Have them hold the same object and ask the same question each time.
- When students finish, clap your hands as a signal and move the students in one line along, so that they are facing a new partner. Have the student on the end of the line, without a new partner, walk around to the beginning of the line to face his/her new partner.
- Repeat the process until students have spoken to everybody in the opposite line. This kind of activity is an ideal opportunity for students to practice a language structure since they are forced to repeat the same information again and again.
- Have students choose a different object and repeat the activity. Have them ask the same question, or have them choose a different question.

- Read aloud the instructions. Use the board to demonstrate. Draw a picture of a poster. Point to the poster and model the conversation with a volunteer. Encourage the student to say *It's a poster.*
- Have students work individually to draw two objects, one in each box. When they finish, have students show their pictures to their classmates. Have them ask and answer questions. Encourage students to show their drawings to at least three other students.
- **Extra Challenge** Call on a volunteer to come to the front and hold up one of his/her pictures. Have students ask questions about the picture so that they elicit the answer *No, it isn't* each time. Repeat with other students holding up one of their pictures and answering questions.

Wrap Up

- Hold up a copy of the Student's Book and point to the middle photo in Activity 1. Take the role of the narrator and say *You're AJ. Answer the questions.* Ask the narrator's questions from the first segment and have students answer. If necessary, play **Video 1** again and pause after segment 1. Repeat with segment 2 and the photo on the right in Activity 1. Ask the narrator's questions which begin with *Is it...?* and have students answer. Then repeat with segment 3.

Additional Practice: Worksheet 1.1, Online Practice

UNIT 1   Things for School   **16a**

UNIT
2 Toys

In this unit, students will:

- talk about toys.
- use *This is my [ball]* to talk about possessions.
- read about the game of marbles.
- ask and answer questions about toys using *Is this your [game]? Yes, it is./No, it isn't.*
- listen to and sing a song about playing a game.
- identify and pronounce words with /ɛ/, /f/, /g/, and /h/ at the beginning.
- watch a video about toys in other countries.
- identify the value of sharing your toys.

Language

Words
ball, bat, doll, game, kite, plane, teddy bear, train; favorite, fun, marble

Grammar
- *This is my train.*
- *Is this your book? Yes, it is./No, it isn't.*

Phonics
/ɛ/ elephant
/f/ fish
/g/ goat
/h/ horse

Twenty-First Century Skills

Collaboration
Work with a partner to practice words, Lesson 1

Communication
Play a game with classroom objects, Lesson 4

Creativity
Draw and speak about your toys, Lesson 7

Critical Thinking
Identify the value of sharing your toys, Lesson 5

In the Unit Opener, students will:

- respond to a photo of a toy shop window.
- talk about toys.

Resources: Home School Connection Letter, Classroom Presentation Tool

Materials: some toys

Introduce the Theme

- Bring some toys into class. Arrange them on your desk for students to see. Say *Look! Toys!* Write the word on the board and call on students to come up and touch the toys. Hold up each toy and ask *Do you like this toy?* Look curious to show students what you mean. Smile and ask *Yes?* And then frown and ask *Or no?* Have students respond with *yes* or *no.*

- Have students draw their favorite toy. Give them no more than five minutes to do this. When they finish, have students compare their drawings. Encourage them to smile and show approval of each other's drawings.

- Collect together several toys and several objects that aren't toys, such as a pencil, a bag, a jacket, and an umbrella. Hold up each object, one at a time, and ask *Is it a toy?* Have students answer *yes* or *no* each time.

Use the Photo

- Hold up a copy of the Student's Book open to p. 17. and have students open their books to p. 17. Read aloud the instructions at the bottom of the page and point to the photo. Ask *What colors can you see?* Have students point to the objects in the photo and name the colors. Ask *What things can you see?* Then ask *Is this a school?* (no)

- Read aloud the caption *A toy shop.* Then point to the classroom window as you say *Window.* Then point to the photo again and say *This is a shop window. It's a toy shop window.*

TEACHER TIP

It's always a good idea to tell students how much time they have to complete a task and to tell them when half the time has passed. This will get them used to working within time limits and help to have all students finishing at more or less the same time. Giving students a time limit is especially useful for less structured tasks, such as drawing and coloring.

A toy shop

ABOUT THE PHOTO

This photo shows a window display in a toy shop in London, United Kingdom. The toys and games are old, but some are similar to toys that children play with today. Though video games have become more popular than board games, many people still play board games. The top three most popular board games around the world are *Chess*, *Stratego*, and *Monopoly*. *Monopoly* was invented in 1933. These days there are versions of *Monopoly* for most of the big cities around the world.

Look at the photo. What can you see?

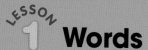
1 Listen and point. 🎧 TR: 20

ball

bat

doll

game

kite

plane

teddy bear

train

2 Listen and repeat. 🎧 TR: 21

3 Point, ask, and answer.

Is it a ball?

Yes, it is.

ABOUT THE PHOTO

The boy in this photo is playing with a simple model plane, probably made out of plastic, wood, or foam. Model airplanes have been around for more than a century. After the first successful airplane flight, in 1903, people began to take an interest in flying machines, and many aviators got their start by flying model planes. But these model planes were different than the one in the photo—they were actual airplanes, made in miniature. By the 1920s, model planes were being built to scale to resemble early airplanes, and they had small engines that allowed them to fly up to 80 kilometers per hour. Several organizations were established to promote and regulate the flying of model planes. These organizations held flying competitions around the globe. People still fly model airplanes today, though drones are a more popular and less expensive option for flying enthusiasts.

Words

In this lesson, students will:
- talk about toys.
- ask and answer questions about toys.

Resources: Audio Tracks 20–21, Classroom Presentation Tool, Flashcards 34–41, Workbook p. 14, Workbook Audio Track 8, Online Practice

Materials: a piece of colored paper

Warm Up

- On the board, draw a picture of one of the toys you showed students in the previous lesson. Draw slowly, building up the picture and pausing to ask students to guess what it is. Say *Look! Is it a toy?* (yes) Draw a pencil in the same way. Pause, and say *Look! Is it a toy?* (no) *What is it?* (It's a pencil.)
- Repeat the activity by drawing two or three toys and two or three other objects from Unit 1.
- **Use the Photo** Have students open their books to pp. 18–19. Hold up a copy of the Student's Book open to p. 18. Point to the boy and say *Look! A boy.* Point to the plane. Say *Look! It's a toy.* Ask *Is it red or white?* (white)

- Read aloud the instructions. Then direct students' attention to the photos. Point to each photo, one at a time. Then point to the boy and his toy plane, and then point to the photos under the instructions and say *Find the boy's toy here.* Have students look and point to the plane.
- Point to your ear and say *Let's listen.* Play **TR: 20** and point to the photos one at a time as you hear the words.
- Play **TR: 20** a second time. Hold up a copy of the Student's Book and model pointing to the photos as you hear the words. Have students point to the words as they listen.

- Direct students' attention to the instructions and read them aloud. Play **TR: 21**, pausing after the first word to model repeating for students. Continue with **TR: 21**, having students repeat the words as a class. Close your eyes as you say *Close your eyes* to students. Then say *Think of each word.*
- Play **TR: 21** again and call on individual students around the class to repeat the words.
- **Listening Strategy: Focusing** Have students close their eyes as they listen to the word. With their eyes closed, students will have fewer distractions in the classroom and they'll be better able to focus on hearing the new words.
- **Extra Challenge** Use the flashcards to practice the words. Hold up each flashcard, one at a time, and ask *What's this?* Elicit the answers from the class. Repeat, going faster each time.

- Read aloud the instructions. Direct students' attention to the example conversation. Model pointing and saying the conversation with a volunteer.
- Show students the *ball* flashcard and ask *Is it a plane?* (No, it isn't.) *Is it a ball?* (Yes, it is.) Put students in pairs to continue the activity. Walk around the room to monitor students as they work, offering help when necessary.

Optional Activity

- Show students a small section of a flashcard, covering the rest with a piece of colored paper. Ask *What is it?* Have students raise their hands to guess. If nobody guesses, show a little more of the flashcard or show a different section. Repeat with the other flashcards.
- **Extra Support** Before students begin, play **TR: 20** again to review the words.

Wrap Up

- Write the numbers 1–8 on the board. Point to 1, hold up one of the flashcards, and say *This is my favorite toy. This is 1.* Then point to 2, hold up another flashcard, and say *This is 2.* Do the same with the other flashcards.
- Have students classify the eight toys in order from the one they like best to the one they like least. Say *One* and call on students to name their favorite toy. Then continue with the other numbers. Have students name the toys.

Additional Practice: Workbook p. 14, Online Practice

LESSON 2 Grammar

In this lesson, students will:
- use *This is my [ball]* to talk about possessions.
- say a chant about toys.

Resources: Audio Tracks 22–23, Classroom Presentation Tool, Flashcards 34–41, Workbook p. 15, Workbook Audio Track 9, Online Practice

Materials: sticky tack, a brown paper bag for each group of students, different toys and classroom objects for each group of students

Warm Up

- Review the words from Lesson 1. On the board, write the first letter of a word and lines for the following letters. For example, write *b _ _ _* . Say *This is a toy. What's the word?* If students say *ball*, write the remaining letters. If they don't, write the next letter and ask again. Repeat for all eight words, leaving the words on the board each time.
- Hold up the corresponding Lesson 1 flashcard each time to confirm the meaning of the word.

- Have students open their books to p. 19. Read aloud the instructions and point to the activity. Say *Listen to the chant.* Play **TR: 22.** Have students clap to the rhythm.
- Divide students into two groups, A and B. Hold up a copy of the Student's Book and point to the purple lines. Turn to Group A and say *Look! You say the purple.* Turn to the other group. Point to the green lines. Say *Look! You say the green.*
- Play **TR: 22** again. Have Group A say the lines in purple and then have Group B say the lines in green.
- Display the eight toy flashcards from Lesson 1 on the board. Ask students to read the chant again and say which of the words is *not* in the chant. (game)
- **Extra Challenge** Have students say the chant and act out playing with each toy. Have them first do this as they read the chant. Then, have them close their books and do the actions as they listen to **TR: 22** and say the chant. Then have them close their books.
- **Extra Support** Hold up the *ball* flashcard and have students say the first line of the chant. Then hold up the other toy flashcards as the words appear in the chant, and have students say the rest of the chant.

- Read aloud the instructions. Direct students' attention to the grammar box. Say *Listen and read* and play **TR: 23.** Have students listen and read. Play **TR: 23** again and have students repeat the sentences as a class.
- Hold up classroom objects and say *This is my [pen].* Repeat with two or three other classroom objects. Then continue to make sentences and have students hold up the object you have mentioned. For example, say *This is my ruler* and have students hold up their ruler.

Optional Activity

- Prepare a bag with toys and classroom objects for each small group of students. Use a brown paper bag for each group and put one object in the bag for each student in the group. Make sure that the bags have a variety of objects and colors.
- Have students pass the bag around their group, each taking out an object and holding it up. Have students say *This is my [book].* Then have them say a simple description, such as *It's big and blue.*
- Have groups exchange bags and play several times.

- Read aloud the instructions. Direct students' attention to the picture of the pencil. Say *Look! What's this?* (It's a pencil.) Read the sentence below the picture aloud. Show students your pencil and say *This is my pencil.*
- Point to the sentence below the first empty box. Read it aloud and say *This is my bat.* Point to the empty box and indicate that students have to draw a picture there. Have students draw a baseball bat in the second box. Walk around the room to provide help when necessary.
- Have students complete the third item on their own. Then, call on three volunteers to draw the pictures on the board and say the sentences aloud.

Wrap Up

- Draw a bag on the board and a line below it. When you finish drawing, point to the line below the bag then write and say *This is my....* Pause before saying and writing *bag* and look at the students. Have them give the word *bag.*
- Have students draw something that belongs to them. Then have them take turns to hold up their drawing and tell the class what they have drawn, saying, for example, *This is my book.*

Additional Practice: Workbook p. 15, Online Practice

Grammar

1 **Listen and chant.** 🎧 TR: 22

This is my ball.
This is my plane.
This is my bat.
This is my train.

This is my doll.
This is my kite.
This is my teddy bear.
It's brown and white.

2 **Listen and read.** 🎧 TR: 23

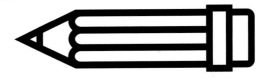

This is my **train**.
This is my **game**.

3 **Read and draw.**

This is my pencil.

This is my bat.

This is my eraser.

Reading

1 Listen and repeat. 🎧 TR: 24

> marble   favorite   fun

2 Listen and read. 🎧 TR: 25

Look at the photo. This is a game of **marbles**. Marbles is my **favorite** game. It's **fun**!

A marble is small. It's a small ball.

Find a blue marble. Find a red and white marble. Find a yellow marble. Yellow is my favorite color. Is this your favorite color, too?

3 Read again and match.

1. Marbles is a   ball.
2. A marble is   color.
3. A marble is a   game.
4. Blue is a   small.

ABOUT THE PHOTO

The photo shows a child playing with marbles. Marbles have been around for thousands of years. Nobody knows exactly when they first appeared, but there is evidence that a form of marbles was played in prehistoric times. The first marbles were made of clay, stone, or nuts.

LESSON 3 Reading

In this lesson, students will:

- read about the game of marbles.
- use new words to talk about marbles.
- match sentence parts in a comprehension activity.

Resources: Audio Tracks 24–25, Classroom Presentation Tool, Flashcards 34–43, Workbook p. 16, Workbook Audio Track 10, Online Practice

Materials: different-colored glass marbles, colored paper

Warm Up

- Bring some marbles into class and hold them up to show the students. Then call on students to pick the marbles up and hand them to you by color. Say *Give me the yellow marble.* Then say *Give me the red marble.* Repeat with the other colors.

- Have students open their books to p. 20. Read aloud the instructions. Play **TR: 24** and have students listen and repeat the words.
- Use actions and descriptions to teach the new words. For example, hold up a marble and say *Look, a marble.* Emphasize the word *marble.* Have students point and say the word. If you don't have a marble, hold up a copy of the Student's Book, open to p. 20, and point to a marble in the photo.
- Say *My favorite color is [blue].* Smile as you say the color and point to various things of that color. Then, to a few students, ask *What's your favorite color?* Each time, emphasize the word *favorite.* Listen to several students' responses.
- Hold up the *game* flashcard and say *Look, a game. Playing a game is fun!* Hold up the *train* flashcard and say *Look, a train. Playing with a train is fun, too!* Do the same with other toy flashcards from Lesson 1. Emphasize the word *fun* each time.
- Point to the text and say *Find the words here.* Have students scan the text to find the three new words. Make sure they understand that they don't have to read the whole text— they just have to find the words.
- Call on a volunteer to point to and read aloud the first of the words in the text. Make sure that all students are pointing to the correct word. As the volunteer says the word, hold up the corresponding flashcard. Repeat with the other Lesson 3 words and flashcards.

- Read aloud the instructions. Point to the text. Play **TR: 25.** Have students listen to and read the whole text.
- Ask questions about the text. Ask *Is a marble big or small?* (small) *What colors are the marbles? Do you have marbles?* Gesture to students to clarify the meaning of this last question.

- Say *Now, look again at the marbles.* Point to your head to indicate that you're thinking and say *Look at the blue marble. Is it big or small?* (big) Have students study the marbles, then close their eyes. Ask them questions about the sizes and colors of the marbles.
- Play **TR: 25** again. Have students read the text again and find the different colors referred to. Allow students to work in pairs, helping each other. Walk around the class to monitor students and make sure they are pointing to the correct marbles.
- **Reading Strategy: Visualizing** While students read, have them think about each sentence and try to visualize it, or make a picture of it in their mind. For example, students will read in this text *A marble is small. It's a small ball.* In these sentences, have them close their eyes and think about a small ball. If they do this after every couple of sentences, they can get a clear picture of what the reading is saying. Forming these mental pictures helps students to better retain the information from the text.
- **Extra Challenge** Have students read the text again using a piece of colored paper as a guide. Have them place the piece of paper under the line they are reading so that the remaining lines are hidden. Then have them read to the end of the line and guess or try to remember the next word at the beginning of the following line. Then, have them move the piece of paper down and continue.
- **Extra Support** Play **TR: 25** again and have students raise their hands when they hear the new words.

- Read aloud the instructions. Hold up a copy of the Student's Book and point to the first part of item 1 as you read it aloud. Then follow the line with your finger so that students can see the example.
- Have a volunteer read aloud the first part of item 2 and suggest the correct answer. Then have students complete the activity in pairs. When they finish, write the sentences on the board for them to check their work.

Optional Activity

- Bring enough marbles in for the class or request that students bring in any marbles they have at home. Demonstrate how to play the game of marbles with two students at the front of the class. Then put students into pairs or small groups to play. To play, you have to roll your marble so that it hits your partner's marble. If you hit the marble, you win it. If someone hits yours, you lose it.
- After playing, have students ask and answer questions about the marbles in their groups. Have them ask and answer questions about the size and color of the marbles, and then say whether the game is fun.

Wrap Up

- Play a memory game. Say *Close your books.* Have students call out words from the text and write them on the board.
- Have students open their books and read the text on p. 20 to check that the words on the board are in the text. See if students can list ten words.

Additional Practice: Workbook p. 16, Online Practice

Grammar

In this lesson, students will:

- use *This is my [ball]* to talk about possessions.
- ask and answer questions about toys using *Is this your [game]? Yes, it is./No, it isn't.*

Resources: Audio Track 26, Classroom Presentation Tool, Flashcards 20–27, Workbook p. 17, Workbook Audio Track 11, Online Practice

Materials: a box for each group of students

Warm Up

- Hold up a bag and say *This is my bag.* Then hold up a student's bag and ask *Is this my bag?* (No, it isn't.) Do this a few more times with different classroom objects and establish that each object belongs to a student. Hold up the student's bag again, look at the student it belongs to, and say *This is your bag,* emphasizing *your* but not offering an explanation yet. Repeat with the other objects, the other students, and *your.*

- Have students open their books to p. 21. Read aloud the instructions. Point to the grammar box and say *Listen.* Play **TR: 26.** Have students listen and read. Play **TR: 26** again and have students repeat the questions and answers, first as a class and then individually. Review the contraction *isn't* if necessary.
- Use the Lesson 1 flashcards from Unit 1 and students' things to further practice the structure. For example, show students the *bag* flashcard and ask *Is this your bag?* Model holding up your own bag and shaking your head. Say *No, it isn't. This is my bag. It's [blue].* Ask students questions about the flashcards or about their own classroom objects. Have students respond *Yes, it is/No, it isn't* and then show/describe their own object.
- **Extra Challenge** Pause the audio after *Yes* and have students complete the answer. Then do the same after *No.*
- **Extra Support** Pause the audio after each question and again after each answer for students to repeat.

- Read aloud the instructions. Point to the picture. Say *Look! This is Olga.* Say *Look at her toys. A doll, a marble,…* Elicit the words by pointing to each toy and looking at the students.
- Point to the doll in item 1 and to the doll in the main picture. Ask *Same or different?* Read the question in item 1 and ask *Is this your doll, Olga?* Hold up a copy of the Student's Book and circle the answer with your finger so that students can see the example.
- Point to the kite in item 2 and to the kite in the main picture. Have a volunteer answer the question.
- Have students complete the activity in pairs. Review answers as a class.

- Read aloud the instructions. Direct students' attention to the example conversation. Holding a pencil, model pointing and saying the conversation with a volunteer.
- Put students into groups of three or four and give each group a box with several classroom objects or toys in it. Have each student choose an object of his/her own and put it into the box without looking. Have students take turns taking something out of the box and asking a classmate *[Kim], is this your [pencil]?* Walk around to monitor the activity and make sure every student has the chance to ask and answer questions.

Optional Activity

- Have students draw three toys on separate pieces of paper. The drawings should be things that belong to them at home and that are in Unit 2, such as a ball, a bat, or a game. Say *Think of three toys. Your toys. Now, here are three pieces of paper. On each paper, draw one toy.* Make sure drawings are always singular and not plural.
- After they draw, have students play a game. Have them shuffle the drawings together to form a card game. Have them take turns to take a card from the pile, turn to a classmate, and ask *Is this your [ball]?* If it is the classmate's ball, have him/her say *Yes, it is.* Have the student who asks the question keep the picture. If not, have him/her put it at the bottom of the pile, and have the next student take a card. The winner is the student with the most cards when the pile is gone.

Wrap Up

- Have students close their books. Copy the questions and answers from Activity 1 on the board. Divide students into two groups, A and B. Explain that students in Group A are going to ask the questions and students in Group B are going to answer.
- Have the groups ask and answer the two questions. Erase the word *this* from the two questions and the word *it* from the two answers on the board. Have students repeat the questions and answers, saying the missing words from memory. Erase the word *your* from the two questions, and *is* and *isn't* from the two answers. Have students repeat the questions and answers again, saying the missing words from memory. Erase the remaining words and have students repeat the two questions and answers from memory.
- If time allows, have groups switch roles and repeat this activity, so that each student has a turn to ask questions and give answers.

Additional Practice: Workbook p. 17, Online Practice

Grammar

1 Listen and read. 🎧 TR: 26

> Is this your **book**? Yes, it is.
> Is this your **marble**? No, it isn't.

2 Read and circle.

Olga

1. Is this your doll, Olga?
   Olga: Yes, it is.
   Olga: No, it isn't.

2. Is this your kite?
   Olga: Yes, it is.
   Olga: No, it isn't.

3. Is this your marble?
   Olga: Yes, it is.
   Olga: No, it isn't.

4. Is this your teddy bear?
   Olga: Yes, it is.
   Olga: No, it isn't.

3 Point, ask, and answer.

Marcel, is this your pencil?

No, it isn't.

1 **Listen and read.** 🎧 TR: 27

2 **Listen and sing.** 🎧 TR: 28 and 29

3 **Sing and act.** 🎧 TR: 30

Chorus
Let's play bat and ball!

Is this your ball?
No, it isn't. My ball is red and blue.
Is this your ball?
Yes, it is! I can play with you.
Chorus

Is this your bat?
No, it isn't. My bat is white and blue.
Is this your bat?
Yes, it is. I can play with you!
Chorus

ABOUT THE PHOTO
The photo shows a child playing cricket in India. Early versions of the game of cricket were invented in the thirteenth century, and modern rules and equipment were developed in the sixteenth century. Since then it has spread around the world. Today, cricket is played throughout India. It is the country's most popular sport.

VALUE **Share your toys.**
Workbook, Lesson 6

Song

In this lesson, students will:

- listen to and sing a song about playing a game.
- act out a song.
- identify the value of sharing your toys.

Resources: Audio Tracks 27–30, Classroom Presentation Tool, Flashcards 34–41, Workbook p. 19, Online Practice

Materials: sticky tack; a bat, a ball, videos or photos of games using a bat and ball (optional)

Warm Up

- Have students open their books to p. 22. Point to the photo. Ask *What can you see?* (a boy) Point to his bat and ball, and ask *What's this?* Ask *What's the game?* Accept any reasonable answers. Some students will recognize the game of cricket. For some students, the game of *bat and ball* is a kind of no-rules game you play on the beach or at a park, where one person throws a ball and the other bats it away.

- Display the Lesson 1 flashcards on the board and ask *Which words are in the song?* Have students scan the song and find the words *bat* and *ball.* Then, point to the photo and ask *What's this song about?* (a game of bat and ball)
- Read aloud the instructions. Play **TR: 27**. Have students listen and follow in their books.

- Read aloud the instructions. Play **TR: 28**. Get a clapping or tapping rhythm going to accompany the song. Encourage students to sing along to the chorus.
- Hold up a copy of the Student's Book and point to the different-colored lines. Divide the class into two groups, A and B. Explain that students in Group A have to sing the green lines, students in Group B have to sing the purple lines, and all students have to sing the chorus (in black). Play **TR: 28** again for students to sing. Then play **TR: 29**, the instrumental version of the song. Have students sing again.
- **Extra Support** Play **TR: 29** again. Hold up a bat and a ball each time students sing the words.
- **Value: Share your toys** At this point in the lesson, you can introduce the value of sharing your toys. Say *The value of this lesson is* Share your toys. Write this on the board. Then ask a volunteer to help you demonstrate what this means through a role-playing activity. Use a ball to demonstrate. Take the ball, hold it up, and say *Look. This is my ball.* Hold the ball close to yourself, to show that it belongs to you. Then hold out the ball to the volunteer, smile, and say *You can share my ball.* Emphasize the word *share.* Change roles and have the student hold the ball first. Repeat the conversation. You may choose to have students act out sharing other toys, working in pairs, having mini-conversations while they hold a toy or a classroom object. For additional practice, have students complete Lesson 6 of the Workbook in class or at home.

- Read aloud the instructions. Establish an action to perform for each line. Here are some suggestions:
  Let's play bat and ball! (Make a batting-a-ball action.)
  Is this your ball? (Make a circle in the air with your finger.)
  No, it isn't. My ball... (Wave your forefinger in the air while shaking your head.)
  Is this your ball? (As above)
  Yes, it is... (Nod.)
  Is this your bat? (Make a batting action.)
  No, it isn't. My bat... (Wave your forefinger in the air while shaking your head.)
  Is this your bat? (As above)
  Yes, it is... (Nod.)
- Play **TR: 30**, pausing after each line to model the action and have students copy.
- Play **TR: 30** again. Have students sing their sections of the song and do the actions.
- **Extra Challenge** Have students close their books and sing the song from memory as they do the actions.

Optional Activity

- Show students a real bat and ball and, if you have access to an outdoor space, take students outside to play a game of bat and ball. If this isn't possible, find and show students some photos or videos of some games using bats and balls on the Internet (for example, cricket, baseball, table tennis, informal children's games). Always watch a video from the Internet before playing it in the classroom so that you can check the content is appropriate.

Wrap Up

- Have students choose a toy from Lesson 1. Then put students into pairs. Have them say the word they have chosen and make sure each pair has two different words.
- Have students sing the song again. Encourage them to use both size and color to describe the toy. You may want to play **TR: 29** again and call on pairs to sing their verses to the music.
- Have students bring in a toy (one of the toys from Lesson 1) for Lesson 7 Activity 2. You may also wish to contact parents to ask them to send in a toy with their child.

Additional Practice: Workbook p. 19, Online Practice

Phonics

In this lesson, students will:
- identify and write *e, f, g,* and *h.*
- identify and pronounce words with /ɛ/, /f/, /g/, and /h/ at the beginning.

Resources: Audio Tracks 31–33, Classroom Presentation Tool, Graphic Organizer: 4 x 4 Matrix, Flashcards 45–48, Workbook p. 18, Workbook Audio Track 12, Online Practice

Warm Up

- Review the letters and phonics from Unit 1. Draw four big circles on the board and write a letter (*a, b, c,* and *d*) in each one.
- Brainstorm words beginning with these letters and write them on the board in the corresponding circle. Let students look back at the Unit 1 Phonics lesson on p. 15 in their books.
- Erase the contents of the circles and replace the letters with *Ee, Ff, Gg,* and *Hh.* Point to and say each letter one at a time. Then point to each letter and have students say it. Finally, say *Today, we're learning more sounds. We're learning the sounds /ɛ/, /f/, /g/, and /h/.*

- Have students open their books to p. 23. Direct students' attention to the photos and words. Say *Listen.* Play **TR: 31,** pointing to each photo and word as students hear it.
- Play **TR: 31** again. Read the instructions aloud. Have students repeat each word. Walk around to monitor students carefully, making sure they pronounce the target sounds correctly.

- Read aloud the instructions. Point to the chant. Say *Listen. Can you hear /ɛ/, /f/, /g/, and /h/?*
- Play **TR: 32.** Pause after the first line of the chant. Ask *What sound do we hear—/ɛ/, /f/, /g/, or /h/?* When students answer /ɛ/, say *Yes, we hear /ɛ/.* Hold up a copy of the Student's Book and point to the example in the first line. Continue playing **TR: 32,** pausing at the end of each line and repeating the question. Have students answer the question each time.
- Play **TR: 32** again. This time have students read and chant.
- **Extra Challenge** Hold up a copy of the Student's Book, point to the elephant, and say *This is my elephant.* Have students continue the line of the chant and say *my e, e, elephant.* Point to the fish and say *This is my fish.* Have students continue the line of the chant and say *my f, f, fish.* Repeat with the other two animals and the other two lines. Then have volunteers point to a photo at random and say the first part of the corresponding line of the chant. Have the rest of the class continue the line.

- **Extra Support** Divide the class into four groups and give each group an animal from Activity 1. Have students draw the animal on a piece of paper. Have the four groups read and chant. Point to the students who have drawn an elephant and have them show their drawings and say the first line of the chant. Then point to the students who have drawn a fish and have them show their drawings and say the second line of the chant. Repeat with the other two groups. Then have students, each holding up their drawing, say the chant again.

- Read aloud the instructions. Give students a minute to look at the picture, read the words, and think about the sounds.
- Play **TR: 33** from beginning to end. Hold up a copy of the Student's Book and point to the example in item 1. Ask *What's the word?* (goat) Play **TR: 33** again, pausing after item 2. Ask *What's the word?* (elephant) Have students write the letter in their books. Continue playing the audio, pausing each time to give students time to write the letter.
- Check answers by writing the four words on the board with the numbers 1–4. Then call out the numbers in order and have students say the words in chorus.

  Script for TR: 33 *fish, horse, goat, elephant*

Optional Activity

- Give students a 4 x 4 matrix graphic organizer and have them fill it with upper and lowercase letters, *a–h,* writing one letter in each square, in random order, and using separate squares for uppercase and lowercase.
- Play a game. Say a letter and a word. For example, say *Gg, goat.* Have students find and cross off one of the *g*'s on their matrix. Continue, saying the following words in random order: *apple, at, bag, ball, carrot, cat, desk, doll, elephant, eraser, fish, fun, goat, game, hello,* and *horse.* The first student to get four letters in a row can yell "Four." Have the student say the letters and the words. This student is the winner if the words are correct.

Wrap Up

- Use the phonics flashcards to review the target sounds. Hold up each flashcard, one at a time, and have students say the sound, the word, and the letter. Repeat the activity a few times, changing the order each time, and speeding up so that students have to say the words more and more quickly.
- Have students bring in a toy (one of the toys from Lesson 1) for Activity 2 in the next lesson. You may also wish to contact parents to ask them to send in a toy with their child.

Additional Practice: Workbook p. 18, Online Practice

Phonics

1 **Listen, point, and repeat.** 🎧 TR: 31

elephant

fish

goat

horse

2 **Listen, chant, and circle.** 🎧 TR: 32

This is my elephant, my e, e, elephant.
This is my fish, my f, f, fish.
This is my goat, my g, g, goat.
This is my horse, my h, h, horse.

3 **Listen and find. Write the letter.** 🎧 TR: 33

3. _h_ orse

2. _e_ lephant

4. _f_ ish

1. _g_ oat

Video

1 Watch and match. Write the numbers. ▶ Video 2

 1. Aliyah

 2. Shiven

 3. Indiphile

ABOUT THE VIDEO

In this video, Indiphile talks about her favorite game, *Mancala*. *Mancala* is one of the oldest games in the world. It is played in Africa, Asia, and other parts of the world. It is played on a board with sections. Players use small pieces, such as stones or marbles. The goal of the game is to collect all your opponent's pieces. The word *mancala* comes from the Arabic word *naqala*, which means *to move*.

2 Your turn! Ask and answer.

Is that a plane?

No, it isn't. It's a kite.

3 Draw and say.

This is my _____ .

_____ .

Video

In this lesson, students will:

- watch a video about toys in other countries.
- ask and answer questions about toys.
- draw and speak about toys.

Resources: Video 2; Classroom Presentation Tool; Flashcards 20–27, 34–41; Online Practice

End-of-Unit Resources: Anthology Story 1, Anthology Teaching Notes p. 136, Worksheet 1.2, Unit 2 Test, ExamView Assessment Suite

Materials: photos of toys (from Internet or catalog), students' own toys (only toys from Lesson 1)

Warm Up

- Have students sit in a circle and think about toys. Bring in some photos of toys. Each time, ask *What is it?* Point to individual students and ask *Do you have a [train]?* Ask *Do you like this toy?* Have students respond with their personal ideas each time. Say *Today's video is about toys.*

- Have students open their books to p. 24. Direct students' attention to the three photos at the top. Give students instructions. Say *Aliyah. Point to Aliyah! Aliyah is number one. Shiven. Point to Shiven! Shiven is number two.* Then do the same with Indiphile. Have students work in pairs and check they are pointing to the same photo.
- Point to the three photos at the bottom. Say *Look! Three toys. One, two, three.* Point to the first photo. Say *Look! Is it a game?* (Yes, it is.) Point to the second photo. Say *Look! What is it?* (a train) Repeat with the third photo.
- Read aloud the instructions and play **Video 2** from beginning to end. Have students match the three numbers and names at the top with the photos at the bottom and write the numbers in the boxes. If you like, play **Video 2** again for students to check their answers.
- Pause **Video 2** after segment 1 (Aliyah) and say *You are Aliyah. Answer my questions.* Point to the photo of the teddy bear. Ask the narrator's questions from the segment and have students answer. Ask *Is this your teddy bear?* (Yes, it is.) *What's its name?* (Softie) *Is Softie your favorite toy?* (yes) Pause after segment 2 (Shiven) and say *You are Shiven. Answer my questions.* Point to the photo of the train, ask *Is this your favorite toy? What color is it?* and have students answer. Do the same with segment 3 and the photo of Indiphile's game. Ask *What's this? Is it your favorite game?*

*The script for **Video 2** is available on the Teacher's Resource Website.*

- Make sure every student has a toy for this activity. Have a few extra toys in the classroom just in case.
- Read aloud the instructions. Hold a toy, such as a game, and call on a volunteer to point to the toy and ask you a

question that requires a *no* answer, such as *Is it a bat?*

- Put students into pairs to ask and answer questions about their toys. The question they ask should require a *no* answer. Have them respond with *No, it isn't. It's a [train].* Have students change partners and repeat the activity.
- **Extra Challenge** Before students do the activity, use the Lesson 1 flashcards to review the words for toys. Show each flashcard very quickly to the students. Have students respond by calling out the word. Then call on students who have the toy to say *My [train] is [blue].*
- **Extra Support** Before students do the activity, use flashcards to review the words for toys. Write the word *Toys* on the board. Mix up the Lesson 1 flashcards from Units 1 and 2 so that students can't see them. Hold up the first flashcard in the pile, look at the picture, and say the word. Have students call out *yes* if the flashcard shows a toy and *no* if it shows a classroom object. When the flashcard shows a toy, hold up the flashcard so that students can see it. Say the word again and have students repeat.

Optional Activity

- Have a conversation similar to those in the video with a volunteer student. Say *Hello, [Olga]* and ask *How are you?* Then say *Show me a toy* and have the student show the toy from Activity 2. Ask some of the narrator's questions from the video. For example, ask *What's this? Is it your favorite toy?*
- Repeat the conversation with several students. Alternatively, students can suggest greetings and questions, and can speak to their classmates.

- Read aloud the instructions. Use the board to demonstrate. Draw a picture of a ball. Point and say *This is my ball.*
- Have students work individually to draw two toys. Make sure they draw one toy in each box.
- When they finish, have students walk around with their books and show their pictures to their classmates. Have them say what toys they have drawn.
- **Extra Support** When students finish drawing their toys, call on a volunteer to hold up his/her book and say what he/she has drawn. Have this student say *This is my [kite].* Call on other students who have drawn the same toy to hold up their book and repeat the sentence. Then call on a volunteer who has drawn a different toy to do the same.

Wrap Up

- Ask questions to find out how much students remember about the video. If necessary, play **Video 2** again.
- Suggested questions:
  Is Softie a teddy bear? (yes)
  How old is Softie? (nine)
  Is Shiven's plane small? (no)
  Is Shiven's train big or small? (small)
  Is Indiphile's toy a doll? (no)
  What is her favorite toy? (a game)

Additional Practice: Anthology Story 1, Worksheet 1.2, Online Practice

Function 1: Classroom language 1

In this lesson, students will:
- use functional language for communicating in the classroom.
- look at the language in a classroom conversation.

Resources: Audio Tracks 34–35, Classroom Presentation Tool, Workbook p. 20, Workbook Audio Track 13, Online Practice

Warm Up

- Draw a square on the board. Say *This is a classroom.* Write the heading *Classroom.* Draw the door and point. Ask *What's this?* Label the door. Draw a teacher (a stick person is fine) at the front of the class. Point and ask *Who's this?* If necessary, point and say *This is the teacher.* Label the teacher. Draw some desks and stick people to represent students. Point and say *Look! Students.* Label the students.
- Give students instructions, and have them listen and follow. Say *Point to the teacher.* Then say *Point to the door.* Repeat with *a boy, a girl, a book.* After students point to the pictures on the board, repeat the activity, having them point to people and objects in the classroom.
- Direct students' attention to the green functions box. Say *Today, we're going to learn words for speaking in the classroom.* Read aloud the expressions, pausing to have students repeat each one.

- Read aloud the instructions. Point to the conversation. Ask *Who's speaking?* (Sandra and her teacher) Say *Sandra is a girl.* Hold up a copy of the Student's Book, point to the example with your finger, and ask *What's the missing word?* (Come) Point to the expression in the green functions box as a reminder.
- Play **TR: 34** to the end. Have students listen to the conversation and follow in their books. Play **TR: 34** again. Have students write the missing words the second time they hear them. This activity can also be done orally.
- **Extra Support** Before students listen to **TR: 34**, write the missing words in alphabetical order on the board: *close, come, hand, open, please, sit, stand, thank.*

- Read aloud the instructions. Play **TR: 35** for students to check their answers.
- Play **TR: 35** again, pausing after each of Sandra's lines so that students can read them aloud.
- **Extra Challenge** Put students into pairs to read the conversation. Explain that they should read the lines but change the names to their own names. Encourage students to make their conversations as natural as possible. Have them say *Knock! Knock!* at the beginning. Monitor students as they read, helping when necessary and praising their efforts.

- Read aloud the instructions. Hold up a copy of the Student's Book and point to item 1 as you read this aloud. Then follow the line with your finger so that students can see the example.
- Have students complete the activity in pairs. Check answers. Read aloud each item one at a time and have students call out the letter.
- **Extra Support** Before students do the activity, practice the instructions. Hold up a copy of the Student's Book and point to the first picture. Say *Picture A* and then read aloud the first instruction. Say *Raise your hand.* Have students say *no.* Then read aloud the second instruction. Say *Come in.* Have students say *no.* Repeat with all the instructions for each picture.

Optional Activity

- Give an instruction. Say *Raise your hand.* Have students act out the instruction. Call on a volunteer to leave the room and knock on the door. Say *Come in.* Then give other instructions. Say *Close your books* and *Open your books.* Finally, say *Stand up* and *Sit down.* Have students act out the instructions.

Wrap Up

- Have students act out conversations using the expressions in Activity 3. Have a few pairs act out their conversations for the rest of the class, using classroom objects as props.

Additional Practice: Workbook p. 20, Online Practice

Function 1: Classroom language 1 (teacher to student)

> Open/Close your books.   Stand up.   Come in.   Thank you.
> Raise your hand.   Sit down.   Please.

1 **Listen and complete.** 🎧 TR: 34

Knock! Knock!

Teacher: ___Come___ in. Hello, Sandra. ___Sit___ down.
OK, boys and girls. ___Open___ your books. Let's read.

Sandra: Oh, no! This isn't my English book!

Teacher: Raise your ___hand___ , Sandra.

Sandra: Can I look at your book, ___please___ ?

Teacher: Yes, OK. Now be quiet, Sandra.

Teacher: ___Close___ your books now. Time to go home!
___Stand___ up, boys and girls. Goodbye!

Sandra: Here's your book.

Teacher: ___Thank___ you, Sandra.

2 **Listen again and check.** 🎧 TR: 35

3 **Read and match.**

1. Raise your hand.   2. Come in.   3. Open your books.   4. Sit down.

A.   B.   C.   D.

In this lesson, students will:

- watch a video about the Toy Museum in Prague, Czech Republic.
- use new words to talk about the Toy Museum.
- make a paper plane and then a paper plane mobile.
- present a project to the class.

Resources: Video 3, Classroom Presentation Tool, Project Guide, Workbook p. 21, Online Practice

Materials: a photo or brochure from a local museum, crayons or markers, thick colored paper (two colors per student), scissors, tape or sticky tack, colored thread, coat hangers

ABOUT THE VIDEO

The Toy Museum in Prague is located inside Prague Castle. It is said to be the second-largest toy museum in the world. The exhibits are displayed in seven rooms and include items from all over the world. The oldest toys are from ancient Greece and there are exhibits right up to the modern day. The museum also has an impressive display of Czech traditional toys including the cars, planes, and trains shown in the video.

Warm Up

- Write the words *toy museum* on the board. Say *Today, we're going on a school trip. We're going to a toy museum.* To teach the meaning of *toy museum*, first remind students of the meaning of *toy.* Ask *What toys can you name?* Have students share their ideas. Then name a local museum to teach students the meaning of the word *museum.* You may want to show a photo or a brochure from this museum. Ask if students know the museum.

- Say *Let's think about toy museums. What can we see in a toy museum?* Write the following words on the board: *ball, bat, doll, game, kite, plane, teddy bear,* and *train.* Point to each word, and ask *Can you see this in a toy museum? What do you think?* Listen to students' responses.

- Leave the list on the board. Say *Today, we're watching a video about a toy museum. Let's see what toys are in the museum.*

Introduce the Theme

- Have students open their books to pp. 26–27. Read aloud the title and say *There are a lot of old toys in this toy museum.* Make sure students understand *old.* If necessary, hold up a new pencil and an old pencil and use the two objects to teach both *new* and *old.* Hold up a copy of the Student's Book and point to the dolls. Ask *What can you see?* (dolls) Say *Yes. Old dolls.*

- Read aloud the instructions and point to the three sentences. Then read aloud the first sentence, saying both options. Say *Look at the photo. What word is it? Dolls or teddy bears?* (dolls) *That's right. We circle the word* dolls. Then have students work on their own to complete the activity. Check answers as a class.

- Say *Let's visit the Toy Museum.* Read aloud the instructions. Then hold up a copy of the Student's Book, point to each photo, and read aloud each word. Then play **Video 3** once.

- Play **Video 3** again and pause after the narrator says *Look! A sign* and ask *What color is the sign?* (white) Continue playing the video and pause after the narrator says *Look at the teddy bears.* Ask some questions. Ask *Can you see a big teddy bear? Can you see a small teddy bear? Can you see a white teddy bear? Do you like the teddy bears?* Guide students to check the photo of the teddy bear.

- Continue playing **Video 3** and pause again after the narrator says *There are a lot of toys.* Ask *What toys can you see now?* (planes, cars) Guide students to check the photo of the plane.

- Continue playing **Video 3** and pause again after the narrator says *There are girl dolls and boy dolls. Can you see?* Say *Point to a girl doll. Point to a boy doll.* Then guide students to check the photo of the doll.

- Continue playing **Video 3** and pause again after the narrator says *These trains are old.* Say *Point to a black train.* Then guide students to check the photo of the train.

- Continue playing **Video 3.** Then play the video again and have students check their answers. To review answers, read aloud each toy word one at a time and have students say *yes* or *no.* Ask *What toys are not in the video?* (ball, game)

- **Extra Support** Play the video with the sound off the first time students watch it so that they can focus on the toys. Play **Video 3** from beginning to end. Then play the video again and pause after the narrator says *There are girl dolls and boy dolls. Can you see?* Ask *Dolls or teddy bears?* Continue playing the video and pause after the narrator says *These trains are old.* Ask *Games or trains?*

Script for Video 3:

Let's go on a trip! Let's go to a museum.
Look! We're outside. What's this place? There are a lot of people. Look! A sign.
Look at the sign. Can you see it? It says TOY MUSEUM. Wow! A toy museum. Let's go inside and look at the toys. Come on!
Look at the teddy bears! There are a lot of toys. Planes and cars, dolls too. There are girl dolls and boy dolls. Can you see?
Look! More toys. What can you see? Trains! A lot of trains. These trains are old. There are toy houses, too. They're cool! The toy museum is fun!

3

- Ask *Is the Toy Museum cool? What do you think?* Listen to several students' responses before beginning the activity.
- Direct students' attention to the instructions. Read them aloud, pointing to the four sentences. Then read aloud the first sentence, saying both options. Repeat the sentence, emphasizing the word *outside*. Say *Look outside*, as you point out the window. Say *Remember the video. What word is it? People or toys?* (people) *That's right. We circle the word* people. Direct students' attention to item 4 and say the word *House*. Draw an outline of a house on the board as you say the word, to teach the meaning. Then have students complete the activity. Have students compare their answers with a partner. To review their work, read each sentence aloud with the correct word.
- **Extra Challenge** Have students work in pairs and take turns to say a toy they saw in the video.

Optional Activity

- Make sure students have a pencil, crayons or markers, and paper. Say *Draw your favorite toy from the toy museum.*
- Have students draw and color their favorite toy from the video. When students finish, have them hold up their drawings to show the class. Encourage them to say *My favorite toy at the museum is a [doll].* Display students' drawings in the classroom and have students look at their classmates' work.

4 Project

- Direct students' attention to the blue project box at the bottom of p. 27. Read aloud the instructions and make sure that students have the necessary materials to make a plane: thick colored paper, a pencil, scissors.
- Give each student a copy of the project guide or display the instructions. Say *Let's make a plane. Look!* Hold up a copy of the plane template, and point to each part as you say *It's a plane.* Then, give each student a copy of the plane template. Hold up a pair of scissors and say *Let's cut the shapes for our plane.* Have students cut out each of the three parts. Walk around to provide help as needed.
- After students finish cutting out the template, model putting the cut-out shape on the thick paper and tracing it with a pencil. To do this, use tape or sticky tack to put a piece of colored paper on the board. Hold up the template to the paper, and show students how to trace around it. Then say *Now you trace.* Make sure students have two colors of paper: one for the body and one for the wings. Walk around the room as they trace, offering help as needed.
- Once students finish tracing, hold up the scissors, and say *Cut the three shapes. Be careful!* As students are cutting walk around the room to complete Step 4—cutting the slit in the plane's body. Make sure the slit you cut in each student's plane is just slightly longer than the widest part of the wings.
- Say *Now, let's make our planes.* Hold up a set of wings

and a plane's body and model sliding both sets of wings through the body. Monitor students while they make their planes.

- When students finish, have them present their projects to the class, saying *This is my plane. It's [blue] and [green].* Have students hold their planes up and move them around to "fly" them as they say the colors.
- To assess the project, check that students followed directions and worked neatly and efficiently. You may wish to encourage to add designs to their planes, and offer points for creativity. Be certain to explain feedback orally so that students understand why they are receiving the grade they're getting.
- You may want to make class mobiles using the planes. Use pieces of colored thread to attach the planes to a coat hanger. Put no more than three or four planes on a single hanger. Make as many mobiles as necessary for your class. Then hang the mobiles in a high place so that students can admire their planes from below. (NOTE: Have students write their names on their planes with a marker so that when the mobile is dismantled they can take their plane home.)

Wrap Up

- Have students practice colors with the planes. Hold up a plane or point to one on a mobile and say *This plane is [green and yellow]* and have students who made a plane of this color call out *It's my plane.* Then call on individual students to talk about the colors of planes and other students to say *It's my plane.*

> **Additional Practice:** Workbook p. 21, Online Practice

1 BEFORE YOU WATCH Look at the photo. Circle.

1. They're **dolls** / teddy bears.

2. They're **brown** / pink.

3. They're new / **old**.

2 WHILE YOU WATCH What toys are in the video? Check (✔). ▶ Video 3

ball

doll

game

plane

teddy bear

train

3 AFTER YOU WATCH Read and circle.

1. You can see **people** / toys outside the museum.

2. You can see bags / **planes** and cars.

3. You can see blue and yellow / **boy and girl** dolls.

4. You can see toy classrooms / **houses**, too.

4 PROJECT Make a paper plane. Then make a plane mobile.

This is my plane. It's red and white.

1 Look and color.

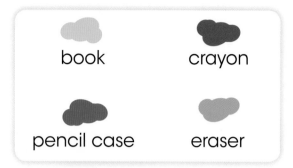

book   crayon

pencil case   eraser

1.

2. red

3. blue

4. yellow

2 Look and write.

1. l a l b
   b a l l

2. e t k i
   k i t e

3. l o d l
   d o l l

4. m a e g
   g a m e

3 Read and circle.

1. What's this?
   Is it a desk?
   Yes, it is.
   (No, it isn't.)

2. What's this?
   (It's a bag.)
   It's a pencil.

3. What's this?
   Is it a pen?
   (Yes, it is.)
   No, it isn't.

4. What's this?
   Is it a chair?
   Yes, it is.
   (No, it isn't.)

4 Listen and number. 🎧 TR: 36

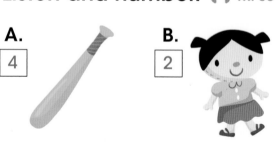

A.
4

B.
2

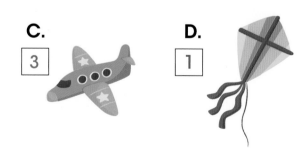

C.
3

D.
1

In this lesson, students will:

- review words and grammar from Units 1 and 2.

Resources: Audio Track 36, Classroom Presentation Tool, Flashcards 20–48, Workbook pp. 22–23, Online Practice

Warm Up

- Have students work in pairs to review the language from Units 1 and 2. Have each pair share a book and take turns to point and say something about each page. Hold up a copy of the Student's Book open to p. 20, point, and say *Look! A game.* Repeat for other pages. Then give students two minutes for this activity.

- Have students stand up at their desks. Give them instructions to review classroom objects. Hold up the *ruler* flashcard and ask *An eraser or a ruler?* (a ruler) Repeat with all the flashcards, asking an *or* question each time.
- Read aloud the instructions. Direct students' attention to the colors and words, and the four objects below. Point to item 1 and ask *What's this?* (an eraser) Then point to the box above and ask *What color?* (green) Point to the picture of the eraser and show how it's colored green as an example.
- Have students work individually to complete the activity. Walk around monitoring students as they do the activity and check they are using the correct colors.
- **Extra Support** Use the Lesson 1 flashcards to review Unit 1 words as a class before students begin.

Optional Activity

- Use all the flashcards from Units 1 and 2. Divide the class into two groups. Give half the flashcards to one group and half to the other. Have students find the photos in the units and remind themselves of the words their flashcards show.
- Have groups take turns to hold up a flashcard for the other group to identify. Have the other group say the word. If they can't immediately say the corresponding word for the flashcard, have them look through the units until they find it.

Task Guidance Notes

Starters Reading & Writing Part 3 Students have to write the word for each object in five pictures. The letters for each word are scrambled next to each picture. There are lines to show the number of letters in the word. Usually the words are from a single semantic set. This tests spelling and words.

Challenges Students need to know not only words but also spelling. They need word and picture recognition activities, but they also need practice in recognizing what kind of letters typically go together in English, such as, double consonants (for example, *p, t, s*) and silent letters (for example, final *e*).

Performance Descriptors

- Can write the letters of the English alphabet
- Can spell some very simple words correctly

- **Use What You Know** Have students close their books. Write two scrambled words (for example, *okob, maen*) and ask students to say the words. Check answers with the class.
- This activity practices a whole exam task. Read aloud the instructions for the activity. Go through the example with the class.
- Have students complete the activity individually. Monitor. Check answers with the class.
- **Own It!** Have students do three drawings of toys or classroom words they know and write the scrambled letters for the word under each drawing. Monitor and help. Have them exchange drawings with a classmate and write the correct words. Have students exchange drawings again and check each other's words.

- Hold up classroom objects and ask *What's this?* and *What's this? Is it [a pencil]?* Call on different students around the class to answer *It's [a pen]* or *Yes, it is./No it isn't.*
- Read aloud the instructions. Hold up a copy of the Student's Book and show students the object in item 1. Read aloud the questions and then the possible answers. Ask *Yes, it is or No, it isn't?* (No, it isn't.) Model circling the answer with your finger so that students can see the example.
- Have students work individually to complete the activity. Then read aloud each question and call on students to answer.

- Direct students' attention to the pictures. Point to the bat and ask *What's this?* Do the same with the other pictures.
- Read aloud the instructions. Play **TR: 36**, pausing after the first item on the audio. Hold up a copy of the Student's Book, point to the four pictures one at a time, and ask *A, B, C, or D?* (D) Point to the number 1 written in box D so that students can see the example.
- Continue playing **TR: 36** to the end. Point to your ear to indicate that students should listen and not write. Then play **TR: 36** again. Have students listen and write the numbers.
- Elicit the answers orally for students to check. Say each letter and have students call out the number.

Script for TR: 36 *1. This is my kite. 2. This is my plane. 4. This is my bat.*

- **Extra Challenge** Give students a moment to study the 16 pictures on the page. Then, have them close their books. Challenge students to remember at least ten of the items pictured.

Wrap Up

- Write the following on the board, and have students work in pairs to complete each item. When they finish, review students' answers as a class.
  1. *Name five things for school.*
  2. *Name five toys.*
  3. *Have a conversation starting with* What's this?
  4. *Have a conversation starting with* Is this your…?

Additional Practice: Workbook pp. 22–23, Online Practice

UNIT 3 People

In this unit, students will:

- talk about people.
- describe people using *he's* and *she's*.
- read about a school trip to a museum.
- use *Is he/she...?* and *Yes, he/she is; No, he/she isn't* to ask and answer questions about people.
- listen to and sing a song about friends.
- identify and pronounce words with /ɪ/, /dʒ/, /k/, and /l/ at the beginning.
- watch a video about portraits from other countries.
- identify the value of making friends at school.

Language

Words
boy, classmate, friend, girl, man, student, teacher, woman; dinosaur, museum, trip

Grammar
- *He's a boy. He's my classmate.*
- *She's a girl. She's my friend.*
- *Is he a teacher? Yes, he is.*
- *Is she your classmate? No, she isn't.*

Phonics
/ɪ/ insect
/dʒ/ jellyfish
/k/ kiwi
/l/ lamp

Twenty-First Century Skills

Collaboration
Work with a partner to practice words, Lesson 1

Communication
Ask and answer questions about people in the class, Lesson 4

Creativity
Draw and speak about people, Lesson 7

Critical Thinking
Identify the value of making friends at school, Lesson 5

In the Unit Opener, students will:
- respond to a photo of people.
- talk about people.

Resources: Home School Connection Letter, Classroom Presentation Tool

Materials: some photos of people (a mix of one person and groups of people), including boys and girls

Introduce the Theme

- Bring some photos of people into class, some with just one person and others with more than one person. Hold up a photo of one person and say *Look! A person. Can you see the person?* (yes) *How many?* (one) Hold up a photo of a few people and say *Look! People! Can you see people?* (yes) *How many?* Repeat with several photos, emphasizing *person* and *people* each time.
- Have a student come to the front of the class and stand to one side of you. Point and say *Look! A person. [Anna] is a person. One. One person.* Then have two students come to the front of the class and stand to the other side of you. Point and say *Look! People. [Jaime and Rachid] are people. One, two. Two people.*
- Repeat this activity with other single students and groups of students, each time changing the number and the gender mix in the group. Include yourself in the activity as well so that students understand *people*, not *boys, girls,* or *students.*

Use the Photo

- Hold up a copy of the Student's Book open to p. 29. Have students open their books to p. 29. Read aloud the instructions at the bottom of the page and point to the photo. Ask *What can you see?* (people) *What colors can you see?* (black, blue, green, orange, purple, red, white, yellow) Have students point to each color as they name it. Walk around, monitoring students to check they are pointing to the correct colors as they say them. Ask *How many people can you see?* (eleven) Point to two or three people in the photo and then point to your face and smile to show a happy face. Ask *Is he happy? Is she happy?* (yes)

TEACHER TIP
When students are doing a speaking activity, monitor carefully to make sure everyone is participating. Give plenty of encouragement and praise students for the effort they make and not only for the results. Shy students especially can benefit from plenty of praise and encouragement.

People

UNIT

3

ABOUT THE PHOTO

This photo shows a group of happy children running in a street in Istanbul, Turkey. A recent survey in Britain has shown that today children spend half the time their parents did playing outside. On average, children play outside for just over four hours a week, compared to 8.2 hours a week when the adults questioned were children. While more than four-fifths (83%) of parents questioned thought it was important their children learned to use technology, more than 90% of parents would prefer their children to spend their childhood outdoors because playing outdoors is important for their development.

Children running

Look at the photo. What can you see?

29

Words

1 Listen and point. 🎧 TR: 37

boy

girl

classmate
friend
student

man

woman

teacher

2 Listen and repeat. 🎧 TR: 38

3 Point and say.

Look! A girl!

Words

In this lesson, students will:

• talk about people.

• ask and answer questions about people.

Resources: Audio Tracks 37–38, Classroom Presentation Tool, Flashcards 49–52, Workbook p. 24, Workbook Audio Track 14, Online Practice

Materials: a photo of yourself and a friend

Warm Up

• **Use the Photo** Hold up a copy of the Student's Book open to pp. 30–31. Have students open their books to pp. 30–31. Point to the photo and ask *Where is it?* (a classroom) *Who can you see in the photo?* (people)

• Read aloud the instructions. Then direct students' attention to the photos under the instructions and the words in the boxes on the right.

• Point to your ear and say *Let's listen.* Play **TR: 37** and pause after the first word. Point to the photo so that students know what to do.

• Continue playing **TR: 37** and model pointing to the photos as you hear the words. Have students point to the words as they listen.

• Have a boy and girl stand up. Say *[Pierre] is a boy and [Natalie] is a girl.* Then go around the class saying students' names and having the class finish the sentence with *is a boy* or *is a girl.* Obviously this is only possible in classes with boys and girls. If you have a class with only boys or only girls, you could find photos of children in the Student's Book to refer to instead. Point to the photos, and say *Look, a boy. Look, a girl.*

• Point to a few students and say *Look! You're students. This is the English class. You're students.* Then say *This is the class. You're classmates.* Continue to point to include all the students. Choose two students who are friends and have them stand up. Point to them and say *Look! [Clara] and [George] are friends.* Then, show students a photo of yourself and a friend. Say *This is [Jon]. [Jon] is my friend.*

• Point to yourself and ask *Am I a boy?* (no) *Am I a girl?* (no) Say *I'm a man/woman.* Continue pointing to yourself and ask *Am I a student? Am I a classmate?* Shake your head as students say *no.* Then nod your head as you say *I'm a teacher.* Repeat the sentence a few times while you point to yourself.

• At this stage, try and have students understand that a classmate, a friend, and a student can be male or female. Hold up a copy of the Student's Book and point to the boy. Say *This boy is a student. He's a classmate and he's a friend.* Then point to the girl and say *This girl is a student. She's a classmate. She's a friend, too.*

• Read aloud the instructions. Play **TR: 38**. Pause after the first word. Repeat the word to model the activity for students. Continue playing **TR: 38** and have students repeat the words as a class.

• Play **TR: 38** again and call on individual students around the class to repeat the words.

• **Extra Support** Point to yourself and say *Teacher* and *[Woman/Man].* Tell individual students which words apply to them (for example, *boy/girl, student, classmate, friend*).

Optional Activity

• Write the letter *t* on the board and have students call out *teacher.* Erase *t* and write *g.* Have students call out *girl.* Repeat with the letters for other words from Activity 1.

• Use the flashcards to practice the words. Hold up the *boy* flashcard and ask *Boy or girl?* Repeat with all the flashcards, asking a question with *or* each time and having students say the answer together. Bear in mind that the *boy* and *girl* flashcard can also be used to mean *classmate, friend,* and *student,* and the *man* and *woman* flashcard can also be used to mean *teacher.*

• Read aloud the instructions. Direct students' attention to the example. If necessary, demonstrate what they have to do first. Point to someone in the class and say *Look! A [student].* Then point to someone else and say *Look! A [girl].*

• Divide students into pairs. Have one student say *Look! A [teacher]* and point, and the other student point to the same person and say *A [teacher].*

• **Extra Challenge** Have students close their books and work in pairs. Have one student point to other people in the class and the other student say the target words.

Wrap Up

• Have students sit in a circle, if possible. Join them in the circle and say *My name's [your name]. I'm a [man/woman]. I'm a teacher.* Point to the student sitting next to you and indicate that he/she should say *My name's [Paola]. I'm a student.* Continue around the circle until everyone has had a turn. For larger classes, model first with a small circle of students, while other students watch. Have students form several smaller circles to do the activity.

Additional Practice: Workbook p. 24, Online Practice

Grammar

In this lesson, students will:
- describe people using *he's* and *she's*.
- say a chant about people.

Resources: Audio Tracks 39–40, Classroom Presentation Tool, Flashcards 49–52, Workbook p. 25, Workbook Audio Track 15, Online Practice

Materials: sticky tack, sticky notes, photos of people

Warm Up

- Review the words from Lesson 1. Draw a boy on the board and write *b_ _* under it. Look at the class and shrug your shoulders. Ask *What's the word?* (boy) Write the missing letters to make the word *boy*. Do the same with *girl, man,* and *woman*. Point to two students in the class and say *Look! Class...what?* (classmates) Then point again to the two classmates and say *[Liv] and [Tania] are classmates and they are f... too.* Shrug your shoulders to indicate that you want students to say the missing word. (friends) Write *classmate* and *friend* on the board. Say *Yes! They're classmates and they're friends.* Draw a student on the board with a bag and some books. Write *s_ _ _ _ _ _* under it. Look at the class and shrug your shoulders. Ask *What's the word?* (student) Write *student* on the board. Point to yourself and ask *Student?* (no) *What?* (teacher) Write *teacher* on the board.
- **Use the Photo** Have students open their books to p. 31. Direct students' attention to the photo. Give students instructions. Say *Point to a boy. Point to a girl. Point to a teacher.* Check that students are pointing to the correct people.
- Then say *Look around the class. Point to a boy. Point to a girl. Point to a teacher. Point to your friend.* Have students listen and point.

- Display the Lesson 1 flashcards on the board. Ask students to find the words in the chant. Have them work in pairs to scan the chant and find the words. (boy, girl, student, classmate, friend) Ask *Which words are not in the chant?* (man, woman, teacher)
- Read aloud the instructions. Say *Listen to the chant.* Play **TR: 39**. Have students clap to the rhythm.
- Divide students into two groups, A and B. Hold up a copy of the Student's Book and point to the purple lines. Turn to Group A and say *Look! You say the purple lines.* Turn to the other group. Point to the green lines. Say *Look! You say the green lines.*
- Play **TR: 39** again. Have Group A say the lines in purple and then have Group B say the lines in green.
- Play **TR: 39** again. Have students change roles and say the chant again.

- Read aloud the instructions. Direct students' attention to the grammar box. Say *Listen and read.* Play **TR: 40** one time as students listen and read. Now say *Listen and repeat.* Play **TR: 40** again and pause after each sentence. Have students repeat the sentences as a class.
- Using the Lesson 1 flashcards, ask students to make new sentences. Hold up a flashcard. Have students say, for example, *He's a boy,* as a class. Then call on individual students to make sentences about each flashcard.
- **Listening Strategy: Understanding the Task** If students have to do a task which is based on the listening text, have them check that they have understood the task correctly before they listen. Understanding the task will motivate students to stay focused so that they can accomplish it.
- **Extra Challenge** Have students look through their Student's Book in pairs, pointing to people and saying *Look! He's a man, He's a boy, She's a woman* or *She's a girl.*
- **Extra Support** Write the words *he* and *she* on the board. Give each student a sticky note. Guide boys to write *he,* and girls to write *she.* Then, have students display the notes on themselves and keep them on throughout the class.

- Have a few students stand up. Point to each student one at a time and say *This is [Julio]. He's a boy. This is [Petra]. She's a girl.*
- Point to the photo in item 1 and ask *Is this a boy or a girl?* (a boy) Point to the photo in item 2 and ask *Is this a man or a woman?* (a woman)
- Read aloud the instructions. Point to the first photo again. Hold up a copy of the Student's Book and circle the correct option with your finger so that students can see the example.
- Have students circle the correct option in item 2. Review the answer together when everyone finishes.

- Read aloud the instructions. Model pointing and saying the example. To one of the students, say *Point to a friend in class.* Ask some more students to do this. Have them point and say *He's my friend* or *She's my friend.*
- Point to the teacher in the main photo. Say *She's a teacher.* Then point to a boy and say *He's a boy.*
- Have students do the activity in pairs, pointing to the people in the photo and to people in the class. Monitor as they speak, making sure they are using the correct form.

Optional Activity

- Bring some photos into class. Hold up the photos, point to the people, and have students say sentences about them, such as *He's a man.*

Wrap Up

- Hold up each Lesson 1 flashcard and say an incorrect sentence. For example, hold up the *boy* flashcard and say *She's a girl.* Have the class say *No! He's a boy!*

Additional Practice: Workbook p. 25, Online Practice

Grammar

1 **Listen and chant.** 🎧 TR: 39

Who's this?	Who's this?
This is Dan.	This is Kim.
He's a boy.	She's a girl.
He's a student.	She's a student.
He's my classmate.	She's my classmate.
He's my friend, too.	She's my friend, too.

2 **Listen and read.** 🎧 TR: 40

He's a boy. He's my classmate.
She's a girl. She's my friend.

3 **Read and circle.**

1. (He's) / She's a student.

2. He's / (She's) a teacher.

4 **Point and say.**

She's my friend.

3 Reading

1 Listen and repeat. 🎧 TR: 41

museum   dinosaur   trip

2 Listen and read. 🎧 TR: 42

Look at the photo. Is it a classroom?

Point to the girl. She's a student.

This isn't a classroom. It's a **museum**. Look! A **dinosaur**! It's big! The girl is on a school **trip**.

This museum is fun!

ABOUT THE PHOTO

The photo shows a young girl looking at a dinosaur exhibit in the Royal Tyrrell Museum of Palaeontology, in Alberta, Canada. The museum is very popular with visitors and is known for its fossil collection with more than 120,000 pieces. The museum is named after Joseph Burr Tyrrell, the geologist who found the dinosaur fossils in 1884. The museum opened in 1985.

3 Read again and match.

1. The photo is in   a student.
2. The girl is   a museum.
3. The dinosaur is — big.

Reading

In this lesson, students will:
- read about a school trip to a museum.
- use new words to talk about a school trip to a museum.
- match sentence parts in a comprehension activity.

Resources: Audio Tracks 41–42, Classroom Presentation Tool, Flashcards 53–55, Workbook p. 26, Workbook Audio Track 16, Online Practice

Materials: modeling clay (optional), photos of exhibits from a museum in your city

Warm Up

- **Use the Photo** Hold up a copy of the Student's Book open to pp. 32–33 and have students open their books. Direct students' attention to the photo. Point to the girl on p. 33 and ask *Is this a boy or a girl?* (a girl) *Is she in the classroom?* (no) Point to the big dinosaur on p. 32 and ask *Is this a toy?* (no) *Big or small?* (big) Point to the small dinosaur on p. 33 and ask *Is this a toy?* (yes) *Big or small?* (small)

- Read aloud the instructions. Play **TR: 41** and have students listen and repeat the words. Then use actions and descriptions to teach the new words. Draw a building on the board and write the name of a local museum above it (for example, *The National Museum*). Read aloud the word *museum* and point to the photo. Say *Look! A museum.* Ask *Do you know a museum?* If students can, have them name a museum in your area.

- Then hold up a copy of the Student's Book and point to the dinosaur. Say *Look! A dinosaur.* Write the word on the board.

- Finally, explain the word *trip.* If students have been on a trip recently, you can use this information in your explanation. Draw a picture of the school on the left side of the board. Draw a simple picture of a beach on the right side of the board. Draw a connecting road or pathway between the two locations and then draw a bus on the road. Point to three main elements of the picture one at a time (school, bus, beach) and follow the route that the bus takes from the school to the beach. Write *a trip* on the board. Point again and say *A trip.* Emphasize the new words each time.

- Point to the text and say *Find the words here.* Have students scan the text to find the three new words. Make sure they understand that they don't have to read the whole text—just find the words.

- Call on a volunteer to point to and read aloud the first of the words in the text. Make sure that all students are pointing to the correct word. As the volunteer says the word, hold up the corresponding flashcard. Repeat with the other Lesson 3 words and flashcards.

- Read aloud the instructions. Point to the text. Play **TR: 42**. Have students listen to and read the whole text.

- Ask questions about the reading text. Pause **TR: 42** after the first paragraph and ask *Is this a classroom?* (no) Continue playing **TR: 42** and pause after the second paragraph. Point to the girl and ask *Boy or girl?* (girl) *Is she a student?* (yes) Pause **TR: 42** after the third paragraph and ask *Is the girl at school?* (no)

- Have students read the text aloud as a class. Have them say the words in chorus. Read the text with them, but remain silent for some sentences, too.

- Hold up a copy of the Student's Book and point to the first part of the text. Say *One.* Then point to the other parts and say *Two. Three. Four.* Say the numbers one at a time and call on individual students to read aloud the corresponding part or paragraph of the text.

- **Reading Strategy: Working with Paragraphs** Have students notice the paragraphs in a text or story. Each paragraph is about a different topic. Identifying the text structure will help make it easier for students to understand each part.

- **Extra Challenge** Hold up a copy of the Student's Book and start counting the paragraphs. Have students call out the numbers, too. Then have them work in pairs and take turns to read. Have the first student read aloud the first paragraph while the second student follows. Then, have them change roles and continue with the next paragraph. Have them read the whole text, paragraph by paragraph, one at a time.

- **Extra Support** On the board, write *classroom, girl, museum, school.* Play **TR: 42** again and have students raise their hands each time they hear one of the words. They hear *classroom, girl,* and *museum* twice.

- Read aloud the instructions. Hold up a copy of the Student's Book and point to the first part of item 1 as you read it aloud. Then follow the line with your finger so that students can see the example.

- Have students complete the activity in pairs.

- Correct the activity by writing the full sentences on the board.

Optional Activity

- Have students draw dinosaurs. Have them copy dinosaur pictures or invent imaginary dinosaurs. Have them color their dinosaurs and give them names. Alternatively, have students make dinosaurs from modeling clay.

Wrap Up

- Show students some photos from a museum in your city or country. If necessary, use the Internet to show students photos of some exhibits. (Remember to check any website before accessing it in the classroom to make sure the content is appropriate for students.)

- Model showing wonder and awe and say *Look! Wow! Cool!* Encourage students to respond in the same way.

Additional Practice: Workbook p. 26, Online Practice

Grammar

In this lesson, students will:

- use *Is he/she…?* and *Yes, he/she is*; *No, he/she isn't* to ask and answer questions about people.

Resources: Audio Track 43; Classroom Presentation Tool; Flashcards 34–41, 49–55; Workbook p. 27; Workbook Audio Track 17; Online Practice

Warm Up

- Point to a boy in the class and say *He's a boy. He's a student.* Have a student point to the same boy and say *He's a boy. He's my classmate.* Choose another student to speak. Point to yourself and have students say *He's a man. He's my teacher* or *She's a woman. She's my teacher.* For single-gender classes, draw pictures on the board to represent the missing people.

- **Use the Photo** Have students open their books to pp. 32–33. Point to the girl and ask *Boy?* (no) *Teacher?* (no) *Woman?* (no) *Student?* (yes) *Girl?* (yes)

- Hold up the *girl* flashcard and ask *Boy?* (no) Hold up the *man* flashcard and ask *Man?* (yes) Continue with more flashcards, asking different questions and eliciting an answer from the class each time.

- Read aloud the instructions. Point to the grammar box and say *Listen.* Play **TR: 43.** Have students listen and read. Play **TR: 43** again and have students repeat the questions and answers, first as a class and then individually.

- Hold up a copy of the Student's Book and ask *Is it a book?* (Yes, it is.) Hold up a bag and ask *Is it a book?* (No, it isn't.) Emphasize *it* each time. Then point to a boy and ask *Is he a boy?* (Yes, he is.) Point to a girl and do the same. Say *Is it…oh, no, not it…Is she a girl?* (Yes, she is.) Emphasize the word *he* or *she* each time.

- **Extra Support** Use flashcards to check that students know when to use *it* and when to use *he* or *she.* Shuffle the Lesson 1 flashcards from Units 2 and 3. Hold up a flashcard and ask *It, he, or she?* Have students respond each time.

- Read aloud the instructions. Point to the photo in item 1. Then point to the question and the two answers on the right. Read aloud the question and point to the photo again. Then shrug your shoulders and point to the two possible answers again. Elicit *Yes, she is.* Circle the answer with your finger so students can see.

- Have students complete the activity in pairs. Go through the items as a class and elicit the answers orally. Read aloud each question and have students call out the answers in chorus.

- **Extra Challenge** Before students do the activity, have them work in pairs, A and B. Have Student A say the name of a person they both know. This can be someone in the classroom or school or a celebrity. Have Student B say *He's a man* or *She's a woman.* Then, have them change roles and have Student B say a name. Have them continue, taking turns to say names and say sentences.

- **Extra Support** Before students do the activity, say known words for people and have students say *he* or *she* for each one. For example, say *Girl* and have students say *she*, say *Man* and have students say *he.* Introduce words that can be both. For example, say *Friend* and have students say *he* or *she.* Say words from all three groups in random order and have students respond.

- Read aloud the instructions. Direct students' attention to the example conversation. Model pointing and saying the words. Model the conversation with a volunteer. Ask the questions yourself as you point. Then ask for two volunteers to act out the conversation. Explain that the first student should point to another person in the class and ask questions about this person. The first question should have a *no* answer. For example, if a student points to a boy, the question could be *Is he a teacher?* or *Is he a man?* The answer is *no.* The next question could be *Is he a boy? Is he a student? Is he a classmate?*, etc.

- Put students into pairs. Have students take turns to choose a person in the class and point to that person. Then have them ask and answer questions about the person.

Optional Activity

- Have students draw a picture of a person. Give them two or three minutes to draw. Call on a volunteer to hold up his/her picture. Point to the picture and ask students questions that elicit a negative answer first and then a positive answer. For example, ask *Is he a man?* (no) *Is he your friend?* (yes) Have students answer with full sentences. Then put students into small groups. Have them take turns to hold up their pictures and ask and answer questions.

Wrap Up

- Write the names of other people at your school on the board. For example, write the names of other teachers and students. Point to each name one at a time and ask a question. Begin with questions with a *no* answer. For example, as you point to a male name, ask *Is he a boy? Is he a teacher?* until students say *Yes, he is.*

- NOTE: You may also want to remind parents personally or in writing to send in a photo of the student's friend (for students to use in Lesson 7). Parents could also e-mail photos for display.

Additional Practice: Workbook p. 27, Online Practice

Grammar

1 **Listen and read.** 🎧 TR: 43

> Is he a teacher? Yes, he is.
> Is she **your classmate**? No, she isn't.

2 **Read and circle.**

1.
Is she a woman?
(Yes, she is.)
No, she isn't.

2.
Is he a boy?
Yes, he is.
(No, he isn't.)

3.
Is she a woman?
Yes, she is.
(No, she isn't.)

4.
Is he a boy?
(Yes, he is.)
No, he isn't.

3 **Point, ask, and answer.**

Is she a girl? — No, she isn't.

Is she a teacher? — Yes, she is.

5 Song

1 Listen and read. 🎧 TR: 44

2 Listen and sing. 🎧 TR: 45 and 46

3 Sing and act. 🎧 TR: 47

VALUE Make friends at school.
Workbook, Lesson 6

Chorus
Friends, friends, friends!

This is Jack. He's my friend.
He's my classmate, too.
Is he your brother?
No, he isn't.
He's my friend and classmate, too.
Chorus

This is Lily. She's my sister.
She's my best friend, too.
Is she your classmate?
No, she isn't.
She's my sister and best friend, too.
Chorus

ABOUT THE PHOTO
The photo shows two children, a boy and a girl, playing in a park in Beijing, China. Beijing is the capital of China. It has a population of more than 20 million. More than 5,500 people live in every square kilometer. These two children have escaped from the city's congestion to enjoy one of Beijing's many parks.

LESSON 5 Song

In this lesson, students will:
- listen to and sing a song about friends.
- act out a song.
- identify the value of making friends at school.

Resources: Audio Tracks 44–47, Classroom Presentation Tool, Flashcards 49–50, Workbook p. 29, Online Practice

Materials: a photo of a friend, sticky tack, photos of people

Warm Up

- Bring a photo of a friend of yours to class. Hold it up for students to see. Point to your friend and tell the class about this person. Say *This is my friend. [Her] name is [Anna].*
- **Use the Photo** Have students open their books to p. 34. Point to the photo. Ask *What can you see?* (a boy and a girl) *Are they at school?* (no) *Are they [friends]?* Listen to students' responses.
- Point to each child in the photo, one at a time, and ask *What's [his] name?* Have students scan the words of the song to find a boy's name and a girl's name. (Jack and Lily)

- Read aloud the chorus of the song. Ask *What is this song about?* (friends) Ask *Who are your friends?* Call on students to name several friends.
- Read aloud the instructions. Play **TR: 44**. Have students listen and follow in their books.

2

- Teach the words *brother* and *sister*. Draw a house shape on the board and draw a simple picture of a boy in front of it. Point and say *This is Raúl!* Then draw a girl next to him and say *This is Louisa!* Draw another boy on the other side of Raúl and say *This is Claudio.* Point to Raúl and then Louisa and say *Louisa is a sister.* Point to Raúl again and then to Claudio and say *Claudio is a brother.*
- Go around the class and ask *Brother?* Then ask *Sister?* If you know the name of a student's brother or sister, use this information to help students understand. Ask *Is [Nia] your classmate?* (no) *Is [Nia] your sister?* (yes)
- Read aloud the instructions. Play **TR: 45**. Encourage students to sing along to the chorus.
- Hold up a copy of the Student's Book and point to the different-colored lines. Divide students into two groups, A and B. Point to the green lines. Turn to Group A and say *Look! You sing the green lines.* Turn to the other group. Point to the purple lines. Say *Look! You sing the purple lines.* Point to everyone and say *You all sing the black lines.*
- Play **TR: 45** again for students to sing. Then play **TR: 46**, the instrumental version of the song. Have students sing again.
- **Extra Support** Play **TR: 46** again. Hold up the *boy* flashcard during the first verse. Hold up the *girl* flashcard during the second verse. Alternatively, if you have a mixed class, have boys stand up for the first verse and girls stand up for the second verse.

- Read aloud the instructions. Establish an action to perform for each line. Here are some suggestions:
  Friends, friends, friends! (Make a heart shape with both forefingers and thumbs.)
  This is Jack. He's my friend. (Stretch your arm out as if to introduce someone.)
  He's my classmate, too. (Point to people around the class.)
  Is he your brother? (Join your forefingers to show a family tie.)
  No, he isn't. (Shake your head.)
  He's my friend and classmate, too. (Make a heart shape with your hands and then point to people around the classroom.)
  This is Lily. She's my sister. (Stretch your arm out as if to introduce someone.)
  She's my best friend, too. (Place your hands on your heart.)
  Is she your classmate? (Point to people around the class.)
  No, she isn't. (As above)
  She's my sister and best friend, too. (Join your forefingers and then put your hands on your heart.)
- Play **TR: 47**, pausing after each line to make sure everyone remembers the actions. Then play **TR: 47** again. Have students sing their sections of the song and do the actions.
- **Extra Challenge** Have students invent a new verse for the song using the name of a friend and changing one or two other words, too.
- **Value: Make friends at school** At this point in the lesson, you can introduce the value. Say *The value of this lesson is Make friends at school.* Write this on the board. Then ask for a student to help you demonstrate what this means through a role-playing activity. Have a short conversation:
  You: Hello.
  Student: Hello.
  You: My name's [invented name]. What's your name?
  Student: My name's [name].
  (Shake hands.)
  You (to the class): [Student's name] is my friend.
  Student (to the class): [invented name] is my friend.
  Have students act out making friends, working in pairs, having mini-conversations with each other like the one above. For additional practice, have students complete Lesson 6 of the Workbook in class or at home.

Optional Activity

- Have students draw a picture of their best friend. Then display the pictures on a classroom wall. Have students point to their pictures and make sentences about their friend.

Wrap Up

- Bring some photos of a mix of people to class. Hold up a photo of a boy and make a thinking gesture. Then say *Look! This is Andy.* Have students ask you questions, such as *Is Andy a man? Is Andy your brother?* Do the same with other photos, inventing names and relationships. Then call on students to choose a photo to ask questions about. Have them start by saying *This is [name].*

Additional Practice: Workbook p. 29, Online Practice

Phonics

Warm Up

- Use the phonics flashcards from Units 1 and 2 to review these sounds: /æ/, /b/, /k/, /d/, /ɛ/, /f/, /g/, and /h/.
- Hold up each flashcard, one at a time, and elicit the word and the sound. Then, say *Let's play a sound game!*
- Choose four of the target sounds and elicit an action for each one. Say /æ/! *Clap your hands!* /æ/ Have students clap. Do the same with the three other sounds you've chosen. Suggested actions: *Jump! Turn around! Hands on head!*
- Have students stand up to play. Call out words with the four target sounds in random order. Repeat each word two or three times. Have students listen and do the action. If they do the wrong action, have them sit down. Continue playing until only a few students are left standing.

- Write the following letters on the board: *Ii, Jj, Kk,* and *Ll.* Point to and say each letter one at a time. Then point to each letter and have students say it. Finally, say *Today, we're learning more sounds. We're learning the sounds* /ɪ/, /dʒ/, /k/, *and* /l/.
- Have students open their books to p. 35. Direct students' attention to the photos and words. Say *Listen.* Play **TR: 48**, pointing to each photo and word as students hear it.
- Read the instructions. Play **TR: 48** again. Have students repeat each word. Monitor students carefully, making sure they pronounce the target sounds correctly.
- **Extra Challenge** Have students close their books. Say each sound one at a time and have students respond with the word. For example, you say /dʒ/ and have students respond *jellyfish.*
- **Extra Support** Say each word one at a time and have students respond with the sound. For example, you say *kiwi* and have students respond /k/.

- Read aloud the instructions. Point to the chant. Say *Listen. Can you hear* /ɪ/, /dʒ/, /k/, *and* /l/? Say the sounds, not the names of the letters.
- Play **TR: 49**. Hold up a copy of the Student's Book and point to the example in the first line. Have students work in pairs. Check answers together as a class by circling each letter with your finger so students can see and check.
- Play **TR: 49** again. This time have students read and chant.

- Read aloud the instructions. Give students a minute to look at the picture, read the words, and think about the sounds.
- Play **TR: 50** from beginning to end. Hold up a copy of the Student's Book and point to the example in item 1. Ask *What's the word?* (lamp) Play **TR: 50** again, pausing after item 2. Ask *What's the word?* (insect) Have students write the letter in their books. Continue playing the audio, pausing each time to give students time to write the letter.
- Check answers by writing the four words on the board with the numbers 1–4. Then call out the numbers in order and have students say the words in chorus.

  Script for TR: 50 *jellyfish, lamp, kiwi, insect*

Optional Activity

- Have students say the chant again. See if they can remember it without looking at the book. Say the chant in different voices to make it fun. For example, use a three-year-old's voice, a man's deep voice, a mouse's squeaky voice, etc.

Wrap Up

- Use the phonics flashcards from Units 1–3 to review the target sounds. Hold a flashcard so it is facing toward you and the students can't see it. Have one half of the class say a sound and have the other half respond with the corresponding word. For example, if the sound is /ɪ/, the word is *insect.* Only show the class the flashcard when the sound and word have been guessed correctly.
- Have students play the game several times. Use the phonics flashcards in a different order and have one half of the class say the sounds and the other half give the words.
- NOTE: Remind any students/parents who have not yet brought/sent in a photo of a friend to bring one in for the next class. Parents could also email photos for display.

Phonics

1 Listen, point, and repeat. 🎧 TR: 48

insect

jellyfish

kiwi

lamp

2 Listen, chant, and circle. 🎧 TR: 49

It's an insect, an i, i, insect.
It's a jellyfish, a j, j, jellyfish.
It's a kiwi, a k, k, kiwi.
It's a lamp, a l, l, lamp.

3 Listen and find. Write the letter. 🎧 TR: 50

1. __l__amp

2. __i__nsect

3. __j__ellyfish

4. __k__iwi

Video

1 Watch and match. Write the numbers. ▶ Video 4

 1. Emilia   2. Kaitlyn   3. Marcel

ABOUT THE VIDEO

In this video, Emilia talks about the *Mona Lisa*. This is a portrait painted by the Italian Renaissance artist Leonardo da Vinci between 1503 and 1519. There has been much speculation about the identity of the woman in the portrait, but no one can say with certainty who she was. The painting has been in The Louvre in Paris, France, since 1804.

2 Your turn! Ask and answer.

Who's that?

My friend.

3 Draw and say.

Who's that?

My _____ .

_____ ?

_____ .

Video

In this lesson, students will:
- watch a video about portraits from other countries.
- ask and answer questions about people.
- draw and speak about people.

Resources: Video 4, Classroom Presentation Tool, Online Practice

End-of-Unit Resources: Worksheet 1.3, Unit 3 Test, ExamView Assessment Suite

Materials: photos of paintings showing people, students' photos of friends (provided ahead of time by parents)

Warm Up
- Hold up photos of famous paintings with people in them one at a time. Each time, have students point and say *Look! A [man].* Have students say whether or not they like each painting. Say *Today's video is about paintings of people.*

- Have students open their books to p. 36. Direct students' attention to the three photos at the top. Give students instructions. Say *Emilia. Point to Emilia! Emilia is number one. Kaitlyn. Point to Kaitlyn! Kaitlyn is number two.* Then do the same with Marcel. Have students work in pairs and check they are pointing to the same photo.
- Point to the first painting. Say *Look! Is it a painting?* (yes) Point to the other drawing and painting, one at a time, and ask the same question.
- Read aloud the instructions and play **Video 4** from beginning to end. Have students match the three numbers and names at the top with the paintings and drawing at the bottom and write the numbers in the boxes.
- If you like, play **Video 4** again for students to check their answers.
- Pause **Video 4** after Emilia's segment, and point to her picture in the book. Ask questions about the picture and have students answer. Ask *Is she a girl?* (no) *Is she a woman?* (yes) Pause after segment 2 (Kaitlyn) and say *Point to the man in the picture. Point to the horse.* (NOTE: There are three women in the video segment, but only two women in the picture.) Do the same with segment 3, asking students to point to people in the picture.
- **Extra Challenge** Before playing the video, have students point to each painting or drawing one at a time and say the people they can see there. For example, you can see *a man, a woman,* and *four boys* in the painting on the left.
- **Extra Support** Before playing the video, say the people you can see in each painting or drawing one at a time. For example, say *A woman.* Have students point to the woman in the painting on the left. Then say *a baby* and have students point to the baby. Repeat this with *a man* and *four boys.* Then say who you can see in the drawing in the middle.

*The script for **Video 4** is available on the Teacher's Resource Website.*

- Read aloud the instructions. Call on two students to act out the conversation in front of the class.
- Have students bring in photos of their friends. Put students into pairs to ask and answer questions about the people in the photos. Have them point and ask *Who's that?* Have them answer *It's [my brother].* Then, have students change partners and repeat the activity a few more times. Monitor students while they speak and help when necessary.

- Read aloud the instructions. Use the board to demonstrate. Draw a picture of a woman. Point to the woman and model the conversation with a volunteer. Have the student point to the drawing on the board as he/she asks the question and say *My sister.*
- Have students work individually to draw two people, one in each box. When they finish, have them walk around with their books and show their pictures to their classmates. Have them ask and answer questions.

Optional Activity
- Review words for animals. Say *h* and have students guess the animal. If they can't guess it, write *h _ _ _ _* on the board. Elicit that the word is *horse.* Repeat with *cat, elephant, fish, goat, insect,* and *jellyfish* in random order.

Wrap Up
- Hold up a copy of the Student's Book and point to the paintings and drawing in Activity 1. Say *1 Emilia* and have students point to the painting on the right. Point to the woman and ask *Who's that?* (a woman) Then say *2 Kaitlyn* and have students point to the drawing in the middle. Ask *Who's that?* as you point to the man on the left. Then ask *What's that?* as you point to the horse. Continue, asking about the other people in this drawing. Then, have students ask and answer questions about the people in the painting on the left.

Additional Practice: Worksheet 1.3, Online Practice

In this unit, students will:

- talk about families.
- talk about a family using *I have* and *I don't have.*
- read about a birthday party.
- use *His/Her name is* to identify people.
- listen to and sing a song about a family of monkeys.
- identify and pronounce words with /m/, /n/, /a/, and /p/ at the beginning.
- watch a video about cartoon families from other countries.
- identify the value of giving things to your friends.

Language

Words

aunt, baby, cousin, dad, grandma, grandpa, me, mom, uncle; birthday cake, birthday party, middle

Grammar

- *I have a grandpa.*
  I don't have a sister.
- *His name is Victor.*
  Her name is Arneta.

Phonics

/m/ mom
/n/ nose
/a/ orange
/p/ pencil

Twenty-First Century Skills

Collaboration

Talk about family photos in pairs, Lesson 4

Communication

Tell the class about your family, Lesson 2

Creativity

Draw and speak about family members, Lesson 7

Critical Thinking

Identify the value of giving things to your friends, Lesson 3

In the Unit Opener, students will:

- respond to a photo of a family.
- talk about people.

Resources: Home School Connection Letter, Classroom Presentation Tool

Materials: photos of families

Introduce the Theme

- Bring some photos of family groups into class. Hold up each photo one at a time for students to see. Say *Look! Families!* Write the word *family* on the board.
- Point to the adults and ask *Is this a man? Is this a woman?* Then point to the children and ask *Is this a man?* (no) *Is this a woman?* (no) *Is this a boy? Is this a girl?* Have students answer each question.
- Hold up each photo. Ask *How many people?* Call on individual students to say the number. Then ask about students' own families. For example, ask *How many people in your family, [Pablo]? How many [men] in your family, [Anna]? Is your family [big], Laurent?* Have students give one-word answers.

Use the Photo

- Hold up a copy of the Student's Book open to p. 37. Have students open their books to p. 37. Make sure all students are on the correct page. Have students check that their classmates have the same page.

- Point to the photo and to the question at the bottom of the page. Ask *What can you see?* (a family) Then point to the man and ask *Is this a man?* (yes) Point to one of the children and ask *Is this a boy?* (no) *Is this a girl?* (yes) Point to the whole family and ask *Are they at school?* (no) *Are they happy?* (yes) Smile and point to your mouth to help with understanding. Then ask *How many people?* (four) *How many girls?* (three)

- NOTE: You may want to remind parents personally or in writing to send in a photo of someone in the student's family (for students to use in Lesson 4). Parents could also e-mail photos.

TEACHER TIP

Show students what to do, don't tell them. Giving instructions about how to carry out an activity, what to do in pairwork, or how to play a game can be difficult without reverting to students' first language. To keep the class moving in English, it's often better to demonstrate how to do things rather than explain. So, for example, if you want to set up a pairwork activity where Student A asks Student B about something, take the part of Student A yourself and ask a volunteer to take the part of Student B to model the conversation. Then have two students model the conversation. In this way, everyone can see what it is they have to do.

ABOUT THE PHOTO

This photo shows a Korean family having fun on a sled at the Hwacheon Sancheoneo Ice Festival. This festival takes place every year in January. More than 200,000 people come to the frozen river to celebrate winter and have fun in the snow and ice. The main attraction is fishing through small holes in the ice. When people catch fish, they cook them over a grill and enjoy eating them with their families and friends.

A family in Korea

가족썰매
134

Look at the photo. What can you see?

37

Words

1 Listen and point. 🎧 TR: 51

grandpa grandma

dad   mom

uncle   aunt

baby

me

cousin

2 Listen and repeat. 🎧 TR: 52

3 Point and say.

grandpa

LESSON 1

Words

In this lesson, students will:
- talk about families.

Resources: Audio Tracks 51–52; Classroom Presentation Tool; Flashcards 49–52, 60–68; Workbook p. 30; Workbook Audio Track 19; Online Practice

Warm Up

- Use the Lesson 1 flashcards from Unit 3 to review words for people. Hold up the *boy* flashcard and say *Look! She's a girl. Yes or no?* Have students respond by saying *No! He's a boy.* Continue with all the flashcards, making an untrue comment each time and having students correct you.
- **Use the Photo** Hold up a copy of the Student's Book open to pp. 38–39. Have students open their books to pp. 38–39. Say *Look at the big photo* and point to the main photo of the family in the mountain village. Say *Look! A family.* Give instructions, and have students listen and point. For example, say *Point to the woman. Point to the man. Point to the boy. Point to the girl.* Ask *Are the children in school?* (no) *Are they happy?* (yes)

- Read aloud the instructions. Then direct students' attention to the photos under the instructions. Point to the photo of the boy in the middle and say *Look, a boy! This is a photo of a boy. The boy is me.* Point to the other photos around the boy and say *Look, this is the boy's family.*
- Point to your ear and say *Let's listen and point.* Play **TR: 51** and pause after the first pair of words. Point to the photo. As you point, say what you are thinking. Say (thinking aloud) *Where's the grandpa? Oh yes, this is the grandpa. Look! Point to the photo of the grandpa. There are two people in this photo, a grandpa and a grandma. Point to the grandpa. Now point to the grandma.* Continue playing **TR: 51** and repeat this with the other photos.
- Play **TR: 51** again and model pointing to the photos as you hear the words. Have students point to the words as they listen.

- Read aloud the instructions. Play **TR: 52**. Pause after the first word. Repeat the word to model the activity for students. Continue playing **TR: 52**, having students repeat the words as a class.
- Play **TR: 52** again and call on individual students around the class to repeat the words.
- **Extra Challenge** Have students close their books. Then call on students to name all the family members. Alternatively, set a time limit of 30 seconds and call on students to name as many family members as they can in that time. Write a list on the board as students say the words.

- **Extra Support** Play **TR: 52** again. If you're female, only repeat the words for girls and women. If you're male, only repeat the words for boys and men. Make sure students understand that either gender can say *baby, me,* and *cousin.* Play **TR: 52** again. Have the girls say the words for girls and women, the boys say the words for boys and men, and everyone say *baby, me,* and *cousin.*

- Use the flashcards to practice the words. Hold up each flashcard one at a time and ask *Who's this?* Elicit the answers from the class.
- Show students the *baby* flashcard and ask *Is this a mom?* (no) *Is this a baby?* (yes)
- Read aloud the instructions. Direct students' attention to the example. Model pointing and saying the word. Ask students to point to the correct photo. Point to another photo and say the word. Have students point to the same photo. Then call on individual students to point to photos and say the words.

Optional Activity

- Have students draw pictures of animal families. First, demonstrate on the board. Choose an animal like a mouse. Draw a mouse and label it *me.* Then say *This is me. I'm a mouse.* Draw other mice around the first mouse. Point each time and say *This is my dad. This is my mom.* Make the drawings funny. Allow students time to draw their pictures. Then have them hold up their pictures and tell each other who the animal family members are. Have them do this as a class or, if the class is too large, in smaller groups.

Wrap Up

- Practice the words using the flashcards. Show students a flashcard very quickly, for just a second or two. Ask *Who is it?* Have students call out the family word. If nobody knows, say the word aloud and then put the flashcard at the bottom of the pile to be reviewed again. Continue until students say the correct family word. Do the same for all the flashcards.

Additional Practice: Workbook p. 30, Online Practice

Grammar

LESSON 2

In this lesson, students will:
- talk about a family using *I have* and *I don't have*.
- say a chant about families.

Resources: Audio Tracks 53–54, Classroom Presentation Tool, Flashcards 49–52, Workbook p. 31, Workbook Audio Track 20, Online Practice

Materials: eight large index cards, sticky tack, photos of families (from the Internet or a magazine)

Warm Up

- Review the words from Lesson 1. Write each of the eight words on an index card. (Don't include *me*.) Then display the Lesson 1 flashcards in a row across the board, leaving space below each flashcard for students to display a word card. Hold up each word card, one at a time, and elicit the word from the class. Then have volunteers come to the board each time to display the word card in the correct place under its corresponding flashcard.
- When all the word cards are on the board, remove the flashcards. Hold up each flashcard, one at a time, and elicit the word. Then repeat the activity, this time having students display the flashcards back on the board in their corresponding place above the word cards.

- Display the Lesson 1 flashcards. Ask students to read the chant quickly and say which of the words are in the chant. (cousin, grandma, grandpa, uncle) Remind students of the words *brother* and *sister* (from Unit 3). If possible, use examples from the class. For example, say *This is Paula. Paula has a sister. Her name's Clara.*
- Read aloud the instructions. Say *Listen to the chant.* Play **TR: 53**. Have students listen to the chant and clap to the rhythm.
- Play **TR: 53** again. Have students say the chant.
- Play **TR: 53** a third time. This time, encourage students to raise their hands when a sentence about family members is true for them. For example, have any students who have two brothers and one sister raise their hands at the end of the first line, and have any students who don't have a cousin raise their hands at the end of the second line.

Extra Challenge Have students invent and say a new verse for the chant. Write this model on the board for them to complete:

I have a ＿＿ and a ＿＿ , too.
I don't have a ＿＿ . What about you?

- **Extra Support** Say *I have two brothers* and encourage students who have two brothers to raise their hands. Say *I have a sister* and encourage students who have a sister to raise their hands. Say *I don't have a cousin* and encourage students who don't have a cousin to raise their hands. Repeat with three more sentences about a grandma, a grandpa, and an uncle.

- Read aloud the instructions. Direct students' attention to the grammar box. Say *Listen and read* and play **TR: 54**. Play **TR: 54** again and have students repeat the sentences as a class.
- Hold up a pencil. Point to yourself and say *I have a pencil.* Nod your head and say *I have a pencil* again. Repeat with a few other classroom objects. Then point to something on a student's desk that you don't have and shake your head. For example, point to a pencil case and say *I don't have a pencil case.* Emphasize the word *don't*. Repeat with a few more objects you don't have.
- Write *don't* on the board. Draw a long vertical line in a different color between the *o* and the *n* so that they are separated. Then erase the apostrophe and write an *o* in its place. Now write *do not = don't* on the board. Say *Don't means* do not.

Optional Activity

- Have students work in pairs to say what they have on their desks or in their bags. If necessary, start with a review of classroom objects. Hold up a pen, nod your head, and say *I have a pen.* Shake your head and say *I don't have a pencil.* Then put students in pairs to take turns to say what they have and don't have.

- Read aloud the instructions. Direct students' attention to item 1 as you read aloud the two sentences. Point to the three pictures and ask some questions, thinking aloud. Say *I have an uncle. An uncle is a man. Which pictures have a man?* (a, c) *I don't have an aunt. An aunt is a woman. I don't have an aunt. So, there's no woman. Let's circle picture c.* Hold up a copy of the Student's Book and follow the line with your finger so that students can see the example.
- Point to items 2 and 3 and indicate that students should work with a partner to match the sentences with the other pictures. Monitor and then check answers.

- Read aloud the instructions. Direct students' attention to the example and read it aloud.
- Have students work in pairs and tell each other true information about their own families using *I have* and *I don't have*.

Wrap Up

- Practice *I have* and *I don't have* using photos of families from magazines or a website. Show students a photo of a family and point to one member. Say *This is me!* Then point to members of the family and say *I have [a mom].* Then shake your head and say *I don't have [an uncle].* Continue until you describe all the people in the photo.
- Give each student or pair of students a photo and have them describe their imaginary family, using *I have* and *I don't have*.

Additional Practice: Workbook p. 31, Online Practice

Grammar LESSON 2

1 **Listen and chant.**  TR: 53

> I have two brothers and a sister, too.
> I don't have a cousin. What about you?
>
> I have two grandmas and a grandpa, too.
> I don't have an uncle. What about you?

2 **Listen and read.** TR: 54

> I have a grandpa.
> I don't have a sister.

3 **Read and match.**

1. I have an uncle.
   I don't have an aunt.

2. I have an uncle,
   and I have an aunt.

3. I have an aunt.
   I don't have an uncle.

a

b

c

4 **Say.**

> I have a brother.
> I don't have a sister.

3 Reading

1 Listen and repeat.
🎧 TR: 55

> middle
> birthday party
> birthday cake

ABOUT THE PHOTO

In this photo, three sisters—triplets—are celebrating their birthday. They may have just sung the birthday song. "Happy Birthday" is the most recognized song in the English language. It was originally written with the lyrics "Good morning to you!" by Kentucky schoolteacher Patty Smith Hill and her sister Mildred. The "Happy Birthday" version appeared in a piano song book in 1912 and later in a Broadway musical called *The Band Wagon*. On hearing the song, Patty and Mildred's family took legal action and eventually the two sisters were credited as the authors. Until recently if filmmakers wanted to include "Happy Birthday" in a movie, they had to pay a fee to the owners.

2 Listen and read.
🎧 TR: 56

Look at the photo. It's a family. Can you see Mom?

Count the girls. One, two, three. Look at the girl in the **middle**. Her name's Atdhetare. She's five today! Her sister Arneta is five today, too. And her sister Agnesa...she's five, too!

This is a **birthday party**. Look! A **birthday cake**. Happy birthday, Atdhetare, Arneta, and Agnesa!

3 Read again. Write *T* for True or *F* for False.

1. This is a class photo. | F |

2. Mom is in the photo. | T |

3. Arneta is in the middle. | F |

4. Atdhetare is her sister. | T |

5. Agnesa is five today. | T |

LESSON 3 Reading

In this lesson, students will:
- read about a birthday party.
- use new words to talk about a birthday party.
- decide whether sentences about a text are true or false.
- identify the value of giving things to your friends.

Resources: Audio Tracks 55–56; Classroom Presentation Tool; Flashcards 49–52, 60–71; Workbook pp. 32, 35; Workbook Audio Track 21; Online Practice

Materials: a video of a birthday party

Warm Up
- Have students act out a birthday scene. Say *[Monika] is [seven] today. Happy birthday, [Monika]!* Have students say *Happy birthday!* to the student and if they know the birthday song, have them sing the song.
- **Use the Photo** Have students open their books to pp. 40–41. Direct students' attention to the photo. Point and ask *How many girls can you see?* (three) Say *Look! It's a birthday!*

- Read aloud the instructions. Play **TR: 55** and have students listen and repeat the words. Hold up the flashcards one at a time. Then use actions and descriptions to teach the new words.
- Point to the text and say *Find the words here.* Have students scan the text to find the new words. Make sure they understand that they don't have to read the whole text— they just have to find the words.

- Read aloud the instructions. Point to the text. Play **TR: 56** from beginning to end. Have students listen to and read the whole text. Then ask *How old are the sisters today?* (five)
- Have students read the text again in groups of three or four. Have them take turns to read one or two sentences at a time, following along in their books carefully.
- **Reading Strategy: Making Word Associations** Students can sometimes recognize words that are similar to words in their own language. They can also recognize words related to other words, such as *my* and *me* or *birthday cake* and *birthday party.* When students don't know a word, have them check to see if it reminds them of another word.
- **Extra Challenge** Have students work in pairs. Have them take turns to read aloud the text as quickly as they can. Have them use a timer to see how quickly they can do it.
- **Extra Support** Play **TR: 56** and have students raise their hands when they hear the new words.

- Teach students the meaning of *true* and *false.* Hold up a book and say *I have an apple. This is* false. *I don't have an apple. I have a book.* Hold up a pencil. Say *I have a pencil. This is* true. *This is a pencil! It's true. It isn't false.* Repeat with other classroom objects and say true and false sentences. Have students call out *True* or *False* each time.

- **Predict** Ask students to cover the text and look at the photo and think of all the words they know in the photo. This encourages them to think before they answer and to feel confident that they know enough words. Then read the instructions and make sure students understand what to do. Go through the example. This practices identifying things.
- Have students work individually to complete the exercise. Monitor.
- **Help My Friend** Have students check answers in pairs and help each other with any incorrect answers. Check answers with the class.
- **Value: Give things to your friends** At this point in the lesson, you can introduce the value. Say *The value of this lesson is* Give things to your friends. Write this on the board. Then have three students help you demonstrate what this means through a role-playing activity. Hold out a classroom object to one of the volunteers, smile, and say *Here, you can have my [pencil].* Repeat with two other objects and the other two volunteers. Have students act out giving each other things. Then put students into pairs and have them act out mini-conversations with classroom objects. For additional practice, have students complete Lesson 6 of the Workbook in class or at home.

Optional Activity
- Find a video of a birthday party on the Internet and play it. If the scene includes singing the birthday song, encourage students to join in if they know the words. Pause the video from time to time and ask questions about it. For example, ask *How many people can you see? What color is the birthday cake?* Call on different students to respond each time.

Wrap Up
- Have students imagine they are at the birthday party in the photo. Say *Look at the photo. This is a birthday party. Now you draw a present for one of the girls.* Have students draw a picture of their birthday present. Then have them show the class their present and speak about it.
- NOTE: Remind any students/parents who have not yet brought/sent in a photo of someone in the student's family to bring one in for the next class. Parents could also e-mail photos.

Additional Practice: Workbook pp. 32, 35; Online Practice

Grammar

In this lesson, students will:

- use *His/Her name is* to identify people.
- match and say possessive adjectives (his/her) according to gender.

Resources: Audio Tracks 57–58, Classroom Presentation Tool, Workbook p. 33, Workbook Audio Track 22, Online Practice

Materials: dolls or puppets; photos of people, including people in your own family; modeling clay; students' photos of someone in their family (provided ahead of time by parents)

Warm Up

- Review *What's your name?* and *My name's [Peter]*. Use puppets or dolls to act out a role-play. Have students invent their names. Then have them work in pairs to ask and answer questions.

- Teach *his* and *her*. Point to boys in the class (or use photos in the Student's Book) and say *His name is [Arturo]*. Repeat with girls and say *Her name is [Luisa]*.

- Hold up a copy of the Student's Book open to pp. 40–41. Use the photo to remind students of the names of the three girls. Say *Her name is...* each time. (NOTE: You might like to listen to **TR: 57** before the lesson and note the pronunciation of the girls' names.)

- Hold up photos of men or boys. You can also use dolls or puppets. Point to each person one at a time and give that person a make-believe name. Say *His name is* each time.

- Hold up a photo of a woman or use a female doll and say *Her name is [Betty]*. Have students repeat. Then hold up another photo of a woman or a doll. Ask *His name is [Meg]. Is this correct?* Have students respond. (no)

- Have students open their books to p. 41. Read aloud the instructions. Point to the grammar box and say *Listen*. Play **TR: 57**. Have students listen and read.

- Play **TR: 57** again and have students repeat the sentences, first as a class and then individually.

- **Extra Support** Point to the grammar box and read aloud the first sentence. Ask *Is Victor a boy or a girl?* (a boy) *Is Arneta a boy or a girl?* (a girl)

- Read aloud the instructions. Point to and read aloud item 1. Ask *Is a grandpa a man or a woman?* (a man) Point to the second sentence and read aloud both options. Then ask *Is it His or Her?* (His) Have students circle *His* with a pencil.

- Have students complete the activity in pairs. Check answers as a class. Read aloud both *I have* sentences and have students say the correct option in the second sentences.

Optional Activity

- Have students make a family of four from modeling clay and give each person a name. Have students then introduce their families to the rest of the class.

- Read aloud the instructions and point to the two columns. Say *Brother* and ask *Boy or girl?* (boy) Say *Sister* and ask *Boy or girl?* (sister) Repeat with the other two family members. Then say *Ann* and ask *Boy or girl?* (girl) Repeat with the other names.

- Point to all the words on the page. Count the words and then say *Nine words. You are going to hear these nine words. They're the important words.*

- Play **TR: 58**, pausing after the first sentence. Hold up your book and point to item 1. Then follow the line with your finger so that students can see the example.

- Play the rest of **TR: 58**, pause after each description and have students complete the activity. Then check answers as a class.

- **Listening Strategy: Focusing on Key Words** It isn't necessary for students to understand every single word. Make sure they realize that they can ignore words that they think are less important and focus instead on the words that are important.

Script for TR: 58

1. I have a brother. His name is Mark.
2. I have a sister. Her name is Lucy.
3. I have a cousin. Her name is Ann.
4. I have a baby brother. His name is Hugo.

- Read aloud the instructions. Direct students' attention to the examples. Point to the girl and say *Look! A photo. A photo of a man.* Call on a volunteer to model the conversation with you. Have this student ask you the question. Then say *Dad is a man. The question is: What's his name?*

- Hold up a photo of a woman in your family. To a volunteer, say *Now ask a question about a woman.* Have this student point to your photo and ask *What's her name?* Respond with the name of a female and say her relationship to you. For example, say *[Manuela.] She's my mom.*

- Have students bring in photos of family members. Divide the class into pairs. Have students ask and answer questions about the person in their photos. Remind students to include *his* or *her* in questions and *He* or *She* in answers.

- **Extra Challenge** Say *His name's [Carlo]. He's my [brother].* Call on volunteers to talk about people in their family.

Wrap Up

- Use the Lesson 1 flashcards from Units 3 and 4 to practice the language. On the board write *I have a grandma. Her name is [Carmen]*. Hold up the *grandma* flashcard. Look at the flashcard and indicate that you are using your imagination. Then say *Her name is [Carmen]*. Hold up the rest of the flashcards, one at a time, and call on students to say *His/Her name is...* depending on whether the person is female or male. Have them invent a name each time.

Additional Practice: Workbook p. 33, Online Practice

VALUE Give things to your friends.
Workbook, Lesson 6

Grammar

1 **Listen and read.** 🎧 TR: 57

His name is Victor.
Her name is Arneta.

2 **Read and circle.**

1. I have a grandpa.
   (His)/ Her name is Dan.

2. I have an aunt.
   His /(Her) name is May.

3. I have a sister.
   His /(Her) name is Jill.

3 **Listen and match.** 🎧 TR: 58

1. brother   Ann
2. sister   Hugo
3. cousin   Mark
4. baby brother   Lucy

4 **Point, ask, and answer.**

What's his name?

Franco.
He's my dad.

5 Song

1 **Listen and read.** 🎧 TR: 59

2 **Listen and sing.** 🎧 TR: 60 and 61

3 **Sing and act.** 🎧 TR: 62

Chorus
I'm a monkey in a tree.
This is my family, my family and me.
I'm a monkey in a tree.
This is my family, my family and me.

I have a mom and a dad.
I have a grandma, too.
I have a baby sister.
What about you?
Chorus

I have a big brother,
an aunt, and an uncle, too.
I have a lot of cousins.
What about you?
Chorus

ABOUT THE PHOTO

The photo shows a family of squirrel monkeys: a father, a mother, and a baby monkey. Squirrel monkeys live in families within large troops. There are usually around 40 animals in a troop, but troops of up to 500 monkeys have been counted. The monkeys sleep together at night and then break up into smaller groups to feed during the day. Squirrel monkeys live in Central and South America. They mostly eat fruits and insects. Sometimes they eat leaves, flowers and eggs. The name refers to the fact that the monkey resembles a squirrel.

LESSON 5 Song

In this lesson, students will:
- listen to and sing a song about a family of monkeys.
- act out a song.

Resources: Audio Tracks 59–62, Classroom Presentation Tool, Flashcards 60–68, Online Practice

Materials: photos of animal families (from the Internet or a magazine)

Warm Up

- Use the Lesson 1 flashcards to review the family words. Hold up the *dad* flashcard and ask *Is this mom?* (No, it's dad!) Say *That's right! It's dad.* Emphasize *Her* and say *Her name is Jon. Is that right?* (no) *What's wrong?* (*His* name is Jon.) Repeat with all the flashcards, asking some questions which elicit a *no* answer and having students give the correct information each time.
- **Use the Photo** Have students open their books to p. 42. Point to the photo. Ask *What can you see?* (monkeys) *Where are they?* (in a tree) Point to the baby monkey. Ask *Is this the mom?* (no) *Is this the dad?* (no) *Is this the baby?* (yes) *Do you like monkeys?* Have students raise their hands to respond.

- Have students read the first line of the chorus. Ask *What is this song about?* (a family of monkeys)
- Explain *a lot of.* Hold up a single pencil and say *A pencil.* Repeat with two pencils and say *Two pencils.* Then hold up a handful or a jar of pencils and say *I have a lot of pencils.*
- Read aloud the instructions. Play **TR: 59**. Have students listen and follow along in their books.

- Read aloud the instructions. Play **TR: 60**. Get a clapping or tapping rhythm going to accompany the song. Encourage students to sing along to the chorus. Then play **TR: 60** again and have students sing the chorus and the verses.
- Play **TR: 61**, the instrumental version of the song, for students to sing.
- **Extra Support** Before playing **TR: 61**, play **TR: 60** again and have students clap their hands each time they hear a family word (mom, dad, grandma, sister, brother, aunt, uncle, cousins).

- Read aloud the instructions. Establish actions to perform during the chorus.
  I'm a monkey in a tree. (Make monkey movements, with your arms curved under and your hands pointing upward.)
  This is my family, my family and me. (Make outstretched hands as if indicating your family members, then point to yourself on *me*)
- Establish an action for each line of the verses.
  I have a mom and a dad, (Place fingers in the air counting one, then two.)
  I have a grandma, too. (Continue with three fingers.)
  I have a baby sister. (Nurse a baby to and fro.)
  What about you? (Point to other people.)
  I have a big brother, (Use a hand to indicate someone tall.)
  an aunt, and an uncle, too. (Hold up first one, then two fingers.)
  I have a lot of cousins. (Point around the room to indicate a lot of people.)
  What about you? (As above)
- Play **TR: 62**, pausing after each line to make sure everyone remembers the actions. Change or simplify the actions if necessary.
- Play **TR: 62** again. Have students sing the song again and do the actions.
- **Extra Challenge** Have students work in small groups or pairs to write a new verse for the song. Write this model on the board to help:

> I have a ＿＿ and a ＿＿ ,
> I have a ＿＿ , too.
> I have a ＿＿ .
> What about you?

Optional Activity

- Play a memory game. Say *You're the baby monkey. Tell me about your family.* Have individual students make a sentence each about the baby monkey's family. For example, have them say *I have a [a dad].*

Wrap Up

- Show students some more photos of animal families. Start by pointing to individual animals as you say *Look! This is a dad! Look, here's a baby,* etc. Then have students come to the front of the class and do the same with other photos. Encourage them to point to individual animals and say *Look! This is a dad,* etc.

Additional Practice: Online Practice

Phonics

In this lesson, students will:
- identify and write *m, n, o,* and *p.*
- identify and pronounce words with /m/, /n/, /a/, and /p/ at the beginning.

Resources: Audio Tracks 63–65; Classroom Presentation Tool; Flashcards 20, 25, 31–33, 45–48, 56–59, 63, 72–73; Workbook p. 34; Workbook Audio Track 23; Online Practice

Warm Up

- Use the phonics flashcards to review the sounds and letters from Units 1–3. Put all the flashcards together and mix them up. Hold up one of the flashcards and call on a student to say the word. Then ask *What's the first sound? What's the first letter?* For example, hold up the *apple* flashcard and ask *What's the word?* (apple) *What's the first sound?* /æ/ *What's the first letter?* (a) Repeat with the other flashcards.

- Write the following letters on the board: *Mm, Nn, Oo,* and *Pp.* Say the letters of the alphabet. Then say *Today we're learning the sounds for these letters.*
- Have students open their books to p. 43. Direct students' attention to the photos and words. Say *Listen.* Play **TR: 63,** pointing to each photo and word as students hear it.
- Play **TR: 63** again. Read aloud the instructions. Have students repeat each word. Monitor students carefully, making sure they pronounce the target sounds correctly.
- **Extra Support** Say each word again and then the sound. Have students read the word and then repeat the sound.

- Read aloud the instructions. Point to the chant. Say *Listen. Can you hear* /m/, /n/, /a/, *and* /p/? Say the sounds, not the letters. Play **TR: 64.** Hold up a copy of the Student's Book and point to the example in the first line. Have students work in pairs and circle the letters in the other lines. Check answers as a class by holding up a copy of the Student's Book and circling each letter with your finger so students can see and check.
- Play **TR: 64** again. This time have students read and chant.
- **Extra Challenge** Have students read the text from p. 40 again and identify more /m/, /n/, /a/, and /p/ sounds at the beginning of words. Have them say the words aloud. If your students are able to write, have them write the words in a list in their notebooks (*mom, middle, name, party*).

- Read aloud the instructions. Play **TR: 65,** pausing after the first word. Then point to the picture and say *Pencil! Where's the pencil? Ah! Here it is. It's number one.* Use your finger to trace the letter *p* and say *It says* pencil! Continue playing **TR: 65,** pausing after each word on the audio to give students time to find the item in the picture and write the letter.
- Check answers as a class.

  Script for TR: 65 *orange, nose, pencil, mom*

Optional Activity

- Say each word from this lesson and have students call out the sound. Begin with the words in alphabetical order and then say them in random order. Then say each sound and have students call out the word. Again, begin with the sounds in order and then say them in random order. Have individual students say the words one at a time and their classmates respond with the sound. Then have individual students say the sounds and their classmates respond with the word.

Wrap Up

- Use the phonics flashcards from Units 1–4 to review the target sounds. Hide the flashcards around the room, and say *I'm looking for* /p/. Say the sounds, not the letters. Call on a volunteer to find and give you the flashcard each time. For an additional challenge, give instructions to find another person or thing with the sound /p/. Have students give you a pen, a pencil, a paper, something *purple.* Repeat with the other sounds.

Additional Practice: Workbook p. 34, Online Practice

Phonics

1 Listen, point, and repeat. 🎧 TR: 63

mom

nose

orange

pencil

2 Listen, chant, and circle. 🎧 TR: 64

I have a mom, a m, m, (m)om.
I have a nose, a n, n, (n)ose.
I have an orange, an o, o, (o)range.
I have a pencil, a p, p, (p)encil.

3 Listen and find. Write the letter. 🎧 TR: 65

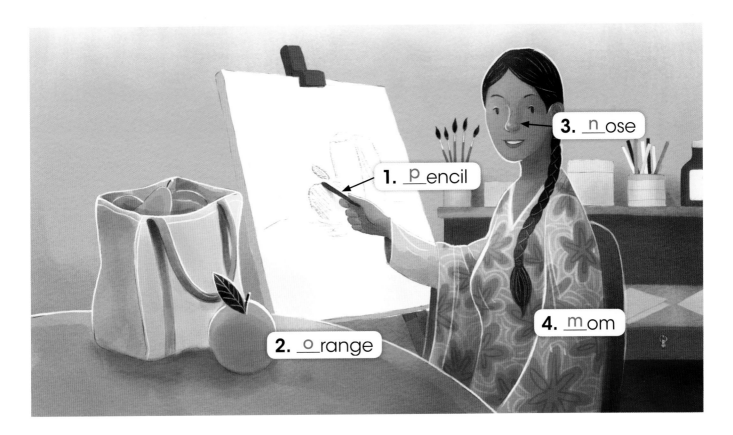

3. _n_ose

1. _p_encil

4. _m_om

2. _o_range

Video

1 **Watch and match. Write the numbers.** ▶ Video 5

1. Emilia

2. AJ

3. Yurara

4. Aliyah

3

4

1

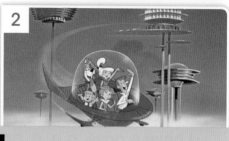

2

ABOUT THE VIDEO

In this video, Yurara talks about the cartoon film *My Neighbor Totoro*. Totoro is an animal-like character with rabbit ears and a big, round body. He makes friends with two sisters, Mei and Satsuki, and together they have a lot of adventures. Totoro is known and loved in Japan and around the world.

2 **Your turn! Ask and answer.**

Who's in your family?

I have a mom, a dad, and a sister.

3 **Draw and say.**

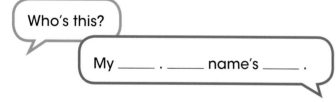

Who's this?

My _____ . _____ name's _____ .

_____ ?

_____ . _____ name's _____ .

In this lesson, students will:

- watch a video about cartoon families from other countries.
- ask and answer questions about family members.
- draw and speak about family members.

Resources: Video 5, Classroom Presentation Tool, Online Practice

End-of-Unit Resources: Anthology Story 2, Anthology Teaching Notes p. 137, Worksheet 1.4, Unit 4 Test, ExamView Assessment Suite

Materials: a picture of a family, or some family members, from a TV series or story that students are familiar with (from Internet or magazine)

Warm Up

- Hold up the picture of a family or some family members from a TV series or a story that students are familiar with, point to the characters, and ask *Do you know this family?* Then point to the male characters one at a time and ask *Who's this? What's his name? Is he a boy or man?* Repeat with the female characters: *Who's this? What's her name? Is she a girl or woman?* Say *Today's video is about families.*

- Have students open their books to p. 44. Direct students' attention to the four photos on the left. Give students instructions. Say *Where's Yurara? Point to her! Yurara is number three.* Then do the same with the other children. Have students work in pairs and check they are pointing to the same photo.
- Point to the four pictures on the right. Say *Look! Four families. One, two, three, four.*
- Read aloud the instructions and play **Video 5** from beginning to end. Have students match the pictures with the four numbers and names on the left and write the numbers in the boxes.
- If you like, play **Video 5** again for students to check their answers.
- Pause **Video 5** after segment 1 (Emilia) and say *I'm Emilia. I have a mom,….* Have students finish the sentence if they can. (I have a mom, a dad, and a sister.) Then pause again after segment 2 (AJ) and say *I'm AJ. I have a mom,….* Again, have students finish the sentence. (I have a mom, a dad, and a sister.) Pause again after segment 3 (Yurara) and then after segment 4 (Aliyah). Have students say *I have a mom, a dad, and a brother* and *I have a mom.*
- **Extra Challenge** Before students watch **Video 5** the first time, have students work in pairs to tell each other three things about each of the four pictures on the right.

- **Extra Support** Before students watch **Video 5** the first time, have them look more closely at the four pictures on the right. Write these questions on the board: *How many people? Who? Where?* Give students time to think about the questions.

*The script for **Video 5** is available on the Teacher's Resource Website.*

- Read aloud the instructions. Call on two students to act out the conversation in front of the class.
- Put students into pairs to ask and answer questions about their families. Monitor students while they speak and help when necessary.

Optional Activity

- Arrange students in two lines, A and B, facing each other. Have an equal number of students in each line. Have students make short conversations with the person facing them. Have them think about their extended family (including grandparents, aunts, uncles, cousins, etc.) and make notes. Then, have them each ask and answer the question in Activity 2.
- When students finish, clap your hands as a signal and move the students in one line along so that they are facing a new partner. Have the student on the end of the line walk around to the beginning of the line to face his/her new partner.
- Repeat the process until students have spoken to everybody in the opposite line. This kind of activity is an ideal opportunity for students to practice a language structure since they are forced to repeat the same information again and again.

- Read aloud the instructions. Use the board to demonstrate. Draw a picture of a man. Point to the man and model the question and answer with a volunteer. Have the student point to the drawing on the board as he/she asks *Who's this?* Say *My brother. His name's [David].*
- Have students work individually to draw two people, one in each box. When they finish, have them walk around with their books and show their pictures to their classmates. Have them ask and answer questions.

Wrap Up

- Ask questions to find out how much students remember about the video. If necessary, play **Video 5** again.
- Suggested questions:
  Is Pinocchio a boy or a girl? (a boy)
  Does Pinocchio have a mom? (no)
  Is Elroy a boy or a girl? (a boy)
  What animal is Astro? (a dog)
  Is Totoro big or small? (big)
  Is Mei big or small? (small)
  Is Michael a baby? (yes)
  Does Wendy have three brothers? (no)

Additional Practice: Anthology Story 2, Worksheet 1.4, Online Practice

Game 1

In this lesson, students will:
- review words from previous units.
- compare and contrast two pictures.
- play a game.

Resources: Classroom Presentation Tool; Flashcards 20–31, 34–43, 49–55, 60–71; Workbook p. 36

Warm Up

- Use the Lesson 1 and 3 flashcards to review words from Units 1–4. Shuffle all the flashcards and place them facedown on the table. Put students into two or four teams, depending on the size of the class.
- Turn over and hold up one flashcard at a time. For example, hold up the *book* flashcard. Say *This is a book. It isn't a ruler. The book is small.* Have teams take turns to talk about the flashcard. Have students say three sentences about each flashcard. One sentence should be negative.
- Make sure each team is given the same number of opportunities. Award one point for each correct sentence. Add up the points at the end to find the winning team with the most points.

- Put students into pairs, A and B. Have each pair share a book. Have students open their books to p. 45. Read aloud the instructions and direct students' attention to the two pictures. Have the A students point to picture A and the B students point to picture B.
- Say *Look! There are two pictures. A lot of things are the same.* Point to the top picture and ask *Where's this?* (a classroom) Point to the teacher and ask *Who's this?* (a teacher) Point to things in the top picture that appear in both pictures (for example, a cabinet, a table, a chair, a board, crayons, a picture, a pencil case, an elephant) and ask *What's this?* Then point to the same things in the bottom picture and have students say the words.
- Say *Look at the pictures. Five things are different.* Give students simple instructions to play the game. Point to the two pictures again and say *Take turns, A and B. Find five different things. Point and say.* Give an example. Point to the two teachers and say *Look! Two teachers—one, two. Are they the same or different?* (different) Emphasize *same* and *different.* Say *Good! That's one different thing. In picture A, the teacher is a woman. In picture B, the teacher is a man.*
- Have students continue playing in pairs. Walk around the classroom, monitoring while they play the game and helping when necessary.
- When they finish playing, call on students to tell you a difference between the two pictures. Choose a different student each time and make sure he/she is using complete sentences.

- **Extra Challenge** Before students play the game, have them work in pairs to describe one picture each in turn. Model a few sentences first. For example, say *A teacher is in the classroom. She is a woman. The board is green.*
- **Extra Support** As students start to play the game, write a few questions on the board to help them find the differences. For example, write *Is the teacher a man or a woman? Is the child a boy or a girl? What color is the ball? What color is the birthday cake? Is the book big or small?*

Optional Activity

- Have students work in pairs to make two spot-the-difference pictures. Give each pair of students a piece of paper. Have them divide it into two halves by folding it. Model doing this and provide help if necessary. Then have them draw the same picture in both halves but with four differences. Have them draw different objects and people, and use different colors. Give students ideas for differences before they start. For example, say *Big or small, blue or green, boy or girl, dog or cat, two flowers or three flowers.*
- Have students exchange their paper with another pair and find the four differences. Have them take turns to find and say a difference.

Wrap Up

- Have students close their books and say from memory the differences between the two pictures on p. 45. Write these words on the board as prompts: *teacher, student, book, ball,* and *birthday cake.*
- Call on students around the class to say one difference each. Write notes on the board, then have students open their books to p. 45 again and check.

Additional Practice: Workbook p. 36

1 Work in pairs. Find the differences. Point and say.

Day and Night

Look out the window.
Can you see the sky?

The sky is blue. The sun is in the sky. It's big and yellow. The sun is in the sky in the day. It's light.

Boys and girls are at school. But the hedgehog is sleeping.

Now look at the photo! What's this? It's the sky.

The sky is black. This is the moon. It's big and white. The moon is in the sky at night. It's dark.

Boys and girls are in bed. But the hedgehog isn't in bed. He's in the garden!

Glossary

hedgehog

sun

sky

light dark

moon

day night

In this lesson, students will:

- respond to a photo of a night scene.
- read about day and night.
- compare and contrast day and night.

Resources: Audio Track 66, Classroom Presentation Tool, Workbook p. 37, Workbook Audio Track 24, Online Practice

Materials: pieces of drawing paper (one per student), sticky tack, index cards (six per pair of students)

ABOUT THE PHOTO

The photo shows an oak tree blowing in the wind with the moon in the background. The photo has been taken at night when there is a rising full moon. The moon is Earth's only natural satellite. It takes 27.3 days to orbit Earth. Because Earth is moving around the sun at the same time, the moon takes 29.5 days to complete its cycle of phases. When the moon appears to be growing in size, it is *waxing*. When it appears to be decreasing in size, it is *waning*. When the moon is facing the sun, it is a *full moon*, like the one in the photo.

Warm Up

- Introduce the concepts of *day* and *night*. Draw a line down the center of the board and draw the same simple outdoor picture on both sides. Start with a tree on both sides of the board. Then write the headings *Day* and *Night* above each tree.
- Build up the picture of the day scene. Add some children, the sun in the sky, some flowers, etc. Then build up the picture of the night scene. Add a moon and stars in the sky so that it looks dark.
- Point to the first picture and say *Day!* Point to the second picture and say *Night!*
- Have students draw day and night pictures. Give each student a piece of paper and have them draw a line down the center. Have students start by drawing the same outdoor picture on both sides of the paper. Then have them make one picture a day scene and the other picture a night scene.
- Display the pictures on a classroom wall.
- **Use the Photo** Hold up a copy of the Student's Book open to pp. 46–47. Point to the photo. Ask *Is it day or night?* (night) Point to the moon and ask *Is it big or small?* (big) Point to the tree and say *Look! This is a tree.* Then point out the classroom window and ask *Is it day or night?* (day)
- Have students open their books to pp. 46–47. Direct students' attention to the title of the text. Point and ask *What is this about?* (day and night) Read aloud the first two sentences. Point to the sky through the classroom window. Ask *Can you see the sky?* Point again if necessary. If the sky is blue, ask *What color is it?* and teach the meaning of *sky* through its color. For example, say *I can see the sky. It's blue today.*

- Point to other things outside the classroom and ask *What other things can you see?* Accept any appropriate responses, for example, trees, boys, girls, birds, cars.

- Read aloud the question. Direct students' attention to the photo again. Have students raise their hands to respond. Ask *Is it day or night?* (night)
- Draw students' attention to the glossary on p. 46. Point to the first photo and say *Look! This is a hedgehog. A hedgehog is a small animal. It comes out at night.* Point to the second photo and say *Look! This is the sky.* Ask *What color is the sky?* (blue) *Yes, the sky is blue.* Then point to the sun and say *And this is the sun. What color is the sun?* (yellow) *Yes, the sun is yellow. The sun is in the sky.* Point to both sides of the third photo and say *Look! This photo is outside.* Then point to the left side and say *Sometimes it's light, like this. When it's light, we can see the sky.* Point to the right side and say *But sometimes it's dark, like this. When it's dark, we can't see the sky. We can't see anything.* Shake your head for emphasis. Point to the left side of the last photo. Say *Look! This photo shows the sky. This is the sky in the day. Can you see the sun? Yes, that's right. The sun is in the sky in the day.* Then point to the right side and say *Look! This is the sky at night. Is it blue or black?* (black) *That's right. The sky is black at night.* Point to the moon and say *This isn't the sun. It's the moon. The moon is in the sky at night.*

- **Listen and Read** Read aloud the instructions. Point to the text. Play **TR: 66** from beginning to end.
- Play **TR: 66** again, pausing after *It's light.* Have students listen to and read the first two paragraphs of the text. Ask some questions to check students understand. Ask *What color is the sky?* (blue) *Where is the sun?* (in the sky) *Is the sun small?* (No, it's big.) *Is the sun blue?* (No, it's yellow.) *Is it dark in the day?* (No, it's light.)
- Continue playing **TR: 66**, pausing after *sleeping.* Have students listen to and read the third paragraph of the text. Ask some questions to check students understand. Ask *Where are boys and girls?* (at school) *Is the hedgehog sleeping?* (yes)
- Continue playing **TR: 66**, pausing after *It's dark.* Have students listen to and read the fourth and fifth paragraphs of the text. Ask some questions to check they understand. Ask *What color is the sky?* (black) *Is the moon in the sky in the day?* (no) *Is the moon in the sky at night?* (yes) *Is it dark or light?* (dark)
- Play the last part of **TR: 66**. Have students listen to and read the final paragraph of the text. Ask some questions to check understanding. Ask *Where are boys and girls?* (in bed) *Is the hedgehog in bed, too?* (no) *Where's the hedgehog?* (in the garden)
- Have students read the text again and find the eight new words from the glossary in the text. Allow students to work in pairs, helping each other.
- Review the reading strategy *scanning for specific information*. Say *Look quickly at the text. How many colors are in the text?* (four: blue, yellow, black, and white)

Reading Extra 1

- **Listen Only** If you choose to do this as a listening-only activity, have students close their books. Follow the instructions above, pausing after each section of the text and asking the comprehension questions.
- Review the listening strategy *focusing.* Have students close their eyes when they listen to the audio. This will help them to actively pay attention to what they are listening to.
- **Extra Support** Write the eight words from the glossary on the board. Play **TR: 66** again and have students listen. Have them raise their hands each time they hear one of the words.

- Read aloud the instructions. Hold up a copy of the Student's Book and point to the word box. Say *Here are the words.* Point to the chart and say *Here is the chart.* Point to the two headings and read them aloud (*day* and *night*).
- Point to the word *blue* that has been crossed out in the box. Say *Blue!* Then point to the place in the chart where *blue* has been written as an example. Say *Look! Blue sky.* Say *The sky is blue in the day* while you point again to the heading *day.*
- Have students work in pairs to complete the activity. Monitor while they work, checking that they understand what they have to do and helping when necessary. This activity can also be done orally (see Extra Support).
- Elicit the answers. As you do this, draw a completed chart on the board for students to check their answers.
- **Listen Only** Play **TR: 66** again before students complete the activity.
- **Extra Support** Write the words in the box on index cards and have students, in pairs, divide them into two columns (day/night) on their desks instead of writing answers in the book.

- Read aloud the instructions. Hold up a copy of the Student's Book and point to the photos. Point to the first photo and ask *Day or night?* (night) Point to the example *n* written in the corner of the first photo.
- Have students work individually to complete the activity. Monitor while they work, helping when necessary.
- When everyone finishes, check answers. Call out the number of a photo and have students respond as a class with *day* or *night*, or *d* or *n.*
- **Extra Challenge** Before students do the activity, have them work in pairs. Have one student describe a night scene and one describe a day scene using very simple sentences. For example, they can say *It is night. It is dark. The moon is in the sky. The moon is big.*

Optional Activity

- Draw a picture on the board of you in the garden. Say *This is me. I'm in the garden. It's day.* Then have each student draw two pictures, one showing him/her in the day and one showing him/her at night. Have students hold up one of their pictures and describe it to the class.

Wrap Up

- Have students draw a sun on one side of a piece of paper and a moon on the other side. Read aloud sentences from the text or make new sentences. Have students listen and hold up the corresponding picture. Suggested sentences: *We are at school. It's dark. It's light.,* etc.

> **Additional Practice:** Workbook p. 37, Online Practice

1 What's in the photo? Is it day or night? *night*

2 Listen and read. 🎧 TR: 66

3 Complete the chart.

> at school   ~~blue~~   dark
>
> in bed   moon   sun

day	night
blue sky	black sky
light	_dark_
the _sun_	the _moon_
boys and girls _at school_	boys and girls _in bed_

4 Look. Write *d* for day or *n* for night.

1.  n
2.  d

3.  d
4.  n

5.  n
6.  d

1 **Look and read. Write a (✔) or an (✗).**

1. This is a baby. ✔

2.  This is a girl. ✗

3.  This is a woman. ✗

4.  This is a man. ✔

2 **Match.**

1. brother
2. dad
3. grandpa
4. man
5. uncle

aunt
grandma
mom
sister
woman

3 **Read and match.**

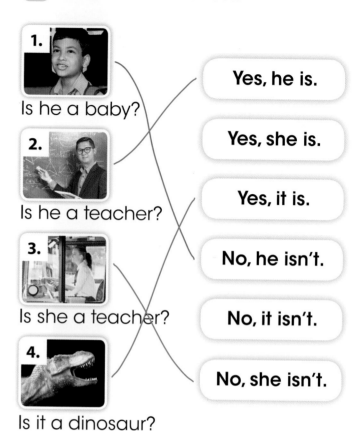

1. Is he a baby?

2. Is he a teacher?

3. Is she a teacher?

4. Is it a dinosaur?

Yes, he is.

Yes, she is.

Yes, it is.

No, he isn't.

No, it isn't.

No, she isn't.

4 **Read and circle.**

1. (His) / Her name is Hugo.

2. His / (Her) name is Eva.

3. (His) / Her name is Matt.

4. His / (Her) name is Judy.

5. (His) / Her name is Nico.

In this lesson, students will:

- review words and grammar from Units 3 and 4.

Resources: Classroom Presentation Tool; Flashcards 49–52, 60–68; Workbook pp. 38–39; Online Practice

Materials: index cards

Warm Up

- Have students work in pairs to review the language they learned in Units 3 and 4. Have each pair share a book and open it to p. 29. Have students take turns to point to and say something about each page until they reach p. 48, or as time allows. Hold up a copy of the Student's Book and give a few examples. For example, on p. 30, point and say *Look! A woman.* Then on p. 33, point to the boy character in Activity 3 and say *Look! Is he a boy?* Have students answer *Yes, he is.*

Task Guidance Notes

Starters Reading & Writing Part 1 Students have to read five short sentences, each with a picture. Have them put a check if the sentence matches the picture or an **✗** if it doesn't. This tests recognition of some words, singular and plural forms, and understanding short sentences.

Challenges Students tend to rush at this because the pictures look easy. The words are often in the same semantic or sound set, which students are likely to confuse, such as *socks* and *shoes; mouse* and *house.* Encourage students to take a ten-second pause before answering each one. They should not panic if they don't know one of the words because they have five sentences.

Performance Descriptor

- Can read and understand some simple sentences

- **Memorize** With their books closed, have students draw a baby. Ask *Is a baby big? Is a baby small?* Then have them draw a boy or a girl (they choose). Have individual students hold their drawing up. Ask *Is it a boy? Is it a girl?* Have students draw a man or a woman. Have individual students hold their drawing up. Ask *Is it a man? Is it a woman?*

- Have students look at the photo in item 1 in Activity 1. Ask *Is this a man? Is this a woman? Is this a baby?* Make sure students understand the instructions, then ask them to complete the activity individually. Check answers with the class.

- **Own It!** Have students exchange their drawings with a partner. Have students say a *This is a…* sentence for each of their three drawings. Tell them one must be incorrect. Have the partner listen to each sentence and correct the one incorrect sentence. For example, *This isn't a boy. This is a girl.*

Optional Activity

- Use the Lesson 1 and 3 flashcards from Units 3 and 4 to play a game. Write the corresponding words on index cards, one word for each flashcard. Then share the cards around the class, giving half the class the pictures and the other half the words. Students can't show anyone their cards. Have students try to find their partner by asking and answering simple questions. For example, they can ask *Do you have a picture of [a baby]?* and answer *No, I don't. I have a picture of [a man].* Print off more flashcards for larger classes and play in smaller groups.

- Read aloud the instructions. Hold up a copy of the Student's Book and draw students' attention to the example line joining the pair of words in the two columns.

- Have students work individually to complete the matching activity. When everyone finishes, check answers. Read aloud each word on the left (1–5) and have students call out the matching words.

- Read aloud the instructions. Hold up a copy of the Student's Book and show students the two columns. Point to item 1 and have students look at the photo. Read aloud the question. Then follow the blue line with your finger to its matching answer. Read aloud the question and answer. Say *Is he a baby? No, he isn't.*

- Have students work individually to complete the matching activity. When everyone finishes, check answers. Read aloud each question and call on students to say the corresponding answer. Have students raise their hands if they want to suggest an answer.

- Read aloud the instructions. Hold up a copy of the Student's Book and show students the picture. Point to the child numbered 1 in the picture. Then point to item 1 and read aloud the sentence, saying both *His* and *Her.* Show students the blue circle around *His.*

- Point to each of the children in the picture and ask *Boy* or *girl?* Have students answer as a class. Then have them work individually to complete the circling activity.

- When everyone finishes, check answers. Say each number and call on students to read the correct sentence.

Wrap Up

- Give each of the following instructions one at a time and allow students thinking time before answering. Elicit the answers from the class, choosing a different student each time.
  1. *Name people in a family (for example, mom, uncle).*
  2. *Name people not in a family (for example, man, friend).*
  3. *Point to people in the classroom and say* His name is… *or* Her name is….

Additional Practice: Workbook pp. 38–39, Online Practice

In this unit, students will:

- use words for parts of the body.
- talk about parts of the body using *This is* and *These are.*
- read about a painted face.
- describe people using *He/She has* and *He/She doesn't have.*
- listen to and sing a song about parts of the body.
- watch a video about masks from other countries.
- identify and pronounce words with /kw/, /r/, /s/, /t/, and /ʌ/ at the beginning.
- identify the value of being active.

Language

Words

arm, ear, eye, foot, hand, head, leg, mouth; body, face, hair, skeleton

Grammar

- *This is my head. These are my hands.*
- *He has black hair.*
  She doesn't have blue eyes.

Phonics

/kw/ queen
/r/ rabbit
/s/ sofa
/t/ table
/ʌ/ umbrella

Twenty-First Century Skills

Collaboration

Point to and talk about body parts, Lesson 1

Communication

Play a guessing game in pairs, Lesson 4

Creativity

Draw and speak about friends and family members, Lesson 7

Critical Thinking

Identify the value of being active, Lesson 5

In the Unit Opener, students will:

- respond to a photo of colorful hands.
- talk about boys and girls.

Resources: Home School Connection Letter, Classroom Presentation Tool

Materials: photos of boys and girls (Internet or magazine)

Introduce the Theme

- Stand at the front of the class and do a series of actions using different parts of your body. Have students stand up and face you, and copy each action. The idea is to have students think about how their body works and all the amazing things it can do. Give instructions. For example, say *Stand up. Watch and copy me. Bend down and touch your toes. That's right. Very good. Now stand up again. Put your hands up in the air like me and clap your hands.*
- Suggested actions:
  Bend down and touch your toes.
  Stand up.
  Put your hands in the air.
  Clap your hands.
  Jump up and down.
  Pretend to kick a ball.
  Nod your head.
  Raise your arms over your head.
  Stretch out your arms.
  Tap your knees.
  Turn around.
  Wave your hands.

- Put students into three groups, A, B, and C. First, Group A does a series of actions like those above. Groups B and C copy the movements. Then, Group B does the actions first and finally Group C. Say *Our bodies can do a lot of things.* Emphasize the word *body* and gesture to your own body. Then say *In this unit, we learn to talk about our body.*

Use the Photo

- Practice colors. Point to objects in the classroom and have students call out the colors. Remind students that they were introduced to the word *pink* in Unit 1. Point to something pink in the classroom and say *Pink. That's pink.*
- Have students open their books to p. 49. Make sure all students are on the correct page. Have students check that their classmates have the same page.
- Hold up a copy of the Student's Book open to p. 49 and point to the photo. Say *Look! Hands.* Ask *How many hands can you see?* (nine) *What color are the hands?* (blue, pink, purple, orange, red, yellow) Then hold up your hands and say *Look at your hands.* Ask *Are your hands blue?* (no) Then repeat with one or two other colors.

TEACHER TIP

Wait time is an important aspect of classroom management. Different students need different amounts of time to complete tasks, so it's useful to pay attention to the amount of time students are taking so that you can determine the average amount of time that a task should take. It's a good idea to tell students how much time they've got to work before doing a task. For example, say *Look at the photo for one minute.* Also, if students haven't replied to your question in five to seven seconds, offer them more support. When reviewing an activity, avoid always calling on the first student with a hand up. Wait until at least five hands go up before calling for an answer.

ABOUT THE PHOTO

This photo shows a group of children celebrating the Holi festival in India. The Holi festival is an ancient festival. It is celebrated in spring and is sometimes called *The Festival of Love*. These days, people celebrate the festival in many countries around the world. It lasts for one night and one day and includes Rangwali Holi, a tradition of covering each other from head to foot with multicolored powders. These powders are called *gulal*. They were originally made from spices (like bright yellow turmeric), plants, and flowers. They were even known to have beneficial properties for the skin. These days most *gulal* come from synthetic sources, though there is a desire by some to return to using natural colors.

Colorful hands

Look at the photo. What can you see?

1 Listen and point. 🎧 TR: 67

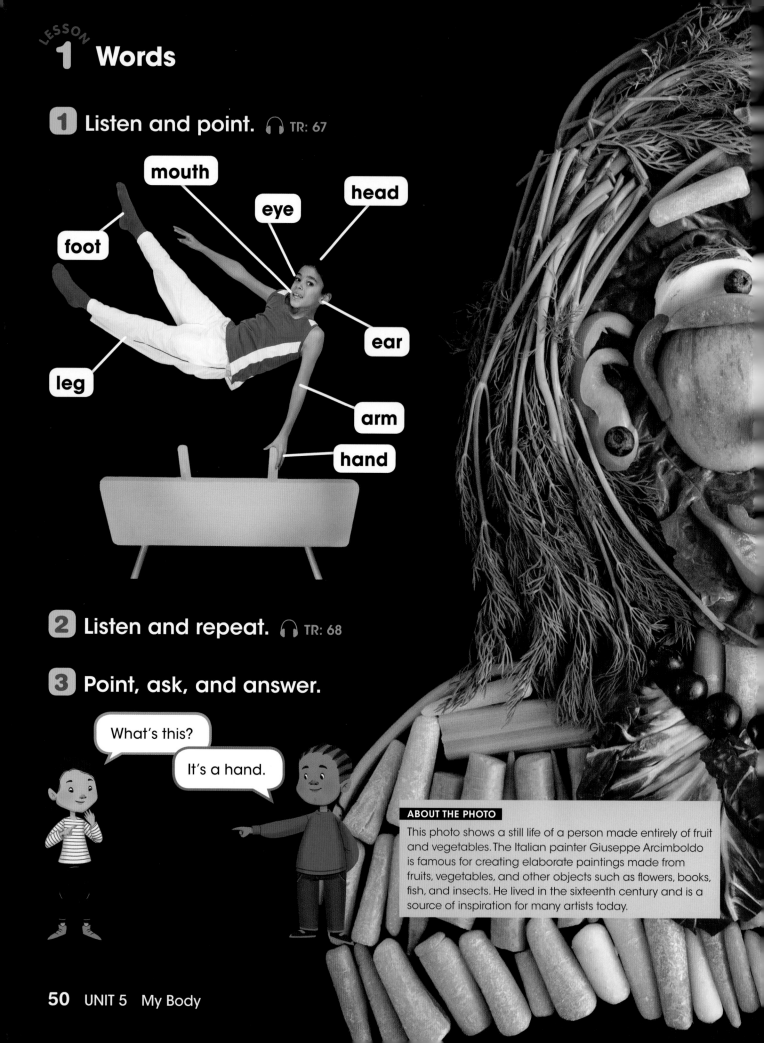

mouth

eye

head

foot

ear

leg

arm

hand

2 Listen and repeat. 🎧 TR: 68

3 Point, ask, and answer.

What's this?

It's a hand.

ABOUT THE PHOTO

This photo shows a still life of a person made entirely of fruit and vegetables. The Italian painter Giuseppe Arcimboldo is famous for creating elaborate paintings made from fruits, vegetables, and other objects such as flowers, books, fish, and insects. He lived in the sixteenth century and is a source of inspiration for many artists today.

Words

In this lesson, students will:
- use words for parts of the body.
- draw faces made of fruit and vegetables.

Resources: Audio Tracks 67–68, Classroom Presentation Tool, Flashcards 74–81, Workbook p. 40, Workbook Audio Track 25, Online Practice

Materials: photos of some of these fruits and vegetables: an apple, a pepper, orange and white carrots, black and green grapes, spinach, peas, fennel or other leafy greens, red cabbage, etc.; sticky tack; beans, pasta, pulses, and grain; cardboard, glue, buttons, ribbons, scrap paper and paper clips; dance music

Warm Up

- **Use the Photo** Have students open their books to pp. 50–51. Point to different parts of the photo and hold up a pencil and paper. Ask *Is it a drawing?* (no) *Is it a photo?* (yes) Point to the apples and ask *Apples?* (yes) Point to the carrots and ask *Carrots?* (yes) Point to the whole photo and say *Fruits and vegetables.*

- Give a few other instructions to review words students were introduced to in the phonics lessons from Units 1 and 4. Say *Point to the apple. Count the carrots.*

- Bring in some photos of fruit and vegetables from the Internet or from magazines and show students a photo of another vegetable that has been used to make the face in the Student's Book. Hold up a photo of a pepper and say *Point to this in the photo.* Have students point to the same vegetable in the photo in the Student's Book. Repeat with other photos of vegetables, having students look at the photo, then find and point in the Student's Book each time. Then repeat with *grape.*

- To finish, ask *Is it a person?* (yes) Point and say *This is the head. Now let's talk about the body.* As you speak, use your hands to indicate your head and then your body.

- Read aloud the instructions. Then direct students' attention to the photo of the boy under the instructions and the words.

- Point to your ear and say *Let's listen.* Play **TR: 67** and pause after the first word. Point to the correct place in the photo (leg) so that students know what to do.

- Play **TR: 67** again and model pointing to the parts of the photo as you hear the words. Have students point to the words as they listen. Have a student come to the front of the class. Point to the student's head and say *Head.* Repeat and say *Head.* Then point to the student's mouth, foot, leg, eye, ear, arm, and hand. Each time you point, say the body part. Have students repeat the body words.

- If possible, have students stand up at their desks. Give instructions. Say *Point to your [eye].* Have students listen and point. Repeat with all the body parts.

  Script for TR: 67 *leg, foot, mouth, eye, head, ear, arm, hand*

- Read aloud the instructions. Play **TR: 68**. Pause after the first word. Repeat the word to model the activity for students. Continue with **TR: 68** as students repeat the words as a class.

- Play **TR: 68** again and call on individual students to repeat the words.

- **Extra Support** Point to your own body parts as you play **TR: 68** and have students repeat the words. Then play the audio again, and have students point to their body parts as they listen and repeat.

- Use the flashcards to practice the words. Hold up the *eye* flashcard and say *This is an arm.* Have students shout *False!* Then say *This is an eye.* (True!) Repeat with all the flashcards, saying a sentence each time and having students call out *True* or *False.*

- Display the flashcards in a column on the board, leaving a space to the left of each flashcard to write the article. Point to the *hand* flashcard and say *Hand.* Then say *A hand* and write *a* to the left of the *hand* flashcard. Say *It's a hand,* emphasizing *a.* Point to the *arm* flashcard and say *Arm.* Then say *An arm* and write *an* in front of the *arm* flashcard. Say *It's an arm,* emphasizing *an.* Continue with the other words, establishing that we use *an* before words beginning with a vowel.

- Read aloud the instructions. Point to your hand as in the example and ask *What's this?* Then say *It's a hand.* Do the same with one or two more body parts.

- Put students into pairs. Have them take turns to point to parts of their own body, and to ask and answer.

- **Extra Challenge** Put students into pairs. Have them take turns to point to a part of their own body and say a sentence. For example, have one student point to his/her arm and say *This is a leg.* Have the other respond with *False! It's an arm.*

Optional Activity

- Bring a collection of beans, pasta, pulses, and grain into class and have students use them to make faces on cardboard. Give each student a piece of cardboard and some glue. Have students draw a simple face on the cardboard. Then have them use different dried food to map out the contours of the face. Have them add glue to one section at a time and then carefully add the beans, etc. When they finish, have students hold up their picture and describe the face, for example, *This is my face. The hair is brown and the eyes are black. The nose is white. The mouth is red.* Have students also use other objects, such as buttons, ribbons, scrap paper, and paper clips, to make their faces.

Wrap Up

- Play some dance music. Say *Move your [arms]* and model doing this. Repeat with more actions as students dance.

Additional Practice: Workbook p. 40, Online Practice

Grammar

In this lesson, students will:
- talk about parts of the body using *This is* and *These are*.
- say a chant about parts of the body.

Resources: Audio Tracks 69–71, Classroom Presentation Tool, Flashcards 74–81, Workbook p. 41, Workbook Audio Track 26, Online Practice

Materials: sticky tack, a soft ball or similar (one per class or several for a larger class)

Warm Up

- Review the words from Lesson 1. Have students stand up and face you. Say *Ear* and indicate that students should touch their ear. Then continue, saying body parts one at a time, slowly at first, pausing after each word. Have students listen and touch the body part you say each time. Start saying the words faster and faster so that students have to react more and more quickly.

- Display the Lesson 1 flashcards on the board. Ask students to find the words in the chant. Have them work in pairs so they can help each other. Have students scan the chant to find the words. (mouth, ear[s], head, eye[s], hand[s])
- Read aloud the instructions. Play **TR: 69**. Have students listen to the chant and clap to the rhythm.
- Play **TR: 69** again. Have students touch their body parts as they say the chant.

- Read aloud the instructions. Direct students' attention to the grammar box. Say *Listen and read* and play **TR: 70**. Have students listen and read. Play **TR: 70** again and get students to repeat the sentences as a class.
- Hold up a hand and say *This is my hand.* Emphasize *this.* Then hold up two hands and say *These are my hands.* Emphasize *these.* Point to one of your legs and say *This is my leg.* Emphasize *this.* Then point to both legs and say *These are my legs.* Emphasize *these.* Repeat with one foot and both feet. Write *one foot* and *two feet* on the board.
- Have students stand up. Give instructions and have students point to one or two parts of their body. For example, say *This is my arm. These are my eyes.* Have students listen and point.
- **Extra Challenge** Say a body part and have students point to their own body part and make a sentence. For example, say *Nose.* Have students point to their nose and say *This is my nose.* Remind them to use both hands if they are pointing to plural body parts.
- **Extra Support** Say a body part and point to your own body part as you say it. Have students respond by pointing to their own body parts and saying *This* or *These.* Reinforce the idea of *This* and *These* with more familiar vocabulary, such as classroom objects.

- Point to the first picture and ask *Is this an arm?* (No, it's a head.) Point to the second picture and ask *Are these hands?* (No, they're legs.) Point to the third picture and ask *Are these ears?* (No, they're arms.) Point to the fourth picture and ask *Is this a nose?* (No, it's a mouth.)
- Read aloud the instructions. Look at the example with the class. Elicit that this is the first body part students will hear in the audio. Play **TR: 71** from beginning to end. Have students listen to the sentences and follow in their books. Play **TR: 71** again. Have students listen and write the numbers.
- Check answers with the class. Play **TR: 71** again, pausing at the end of each sentence. Have students call out the number and the body part and then point to the corresponding picture.
- **Listening Strategy: Using Visual Clues** Have students use any visual clues on the page to help them understand what they hear. Have them look at the photos or pictures and remind themselves of the words they are most likely going to hear. This way they will hear words they are expecting and will find the activity easier.

Script for TR: 71
1. This is my mouth.
2. These are my legs.
3. This is my head.
4. These are my hands.

- Read aloud the instructions. Direct students' attention to the examples. Point and read the sentences to model.
- Have students do the activity in pairs, taking turns to point and say. Monitor as they speak, making sure they are using the correct form (*This is* or *These are*).

Optional Activity

- Point to body parts as in Activity 4 and say a false sentence. For example, point to your feet and say *These are my hands.* Have two students correct you. Have one student point to his/her own feet and say *No, these are my feet* and another student hold up his/her own hands and say *No, these are my hands.* Repeat with another body part.
- Divide the class into groups of three. Have one student point to a body part and make an incorrect sentence. Have the other two students point and say correct sentences.

Wrap Up

- Have students sit in a circle. Throw a soft ball or other small object to a student. Then point to a part of the student's face or body. Point to either a singular part, such as a nose, or plural parts, such as two eyes or two hands. Have the student say *This is my [nose]* or *These are my [eyes].* Then have the student throw the ball to another student and point to a part of that student's body. The game continues with students throwing the ball to a new student each time. For larger classes, group students into several smaller circles.

Additional Practice: Workbook p. 41, Online Practice

Grammar

^{LESSON} **2**

1 **Listen and chant.** 🎧 TR: 69

This is my mouth.
My mouth is red.
These are my ears.
This is my head!

These are my eyes.
My eyes are blue.
These are my hands.
One and two!

2 **Listen and read.** 🎧 TR: 70

This is my head.
These are my hands.

3 **Listen and number.** 🎧 TR: 71

4 **Point and say.**

These are my eyes.

This is my head.

3 Reading

1 Listen and repeat. 🎧 TR: 72

> skeleton   hair   body   face

2 Listen and read. 🎧 TR: 73

Look at the photo. Is it a **skeleton**? No! Look again. This is a boy.

He has black **hair** and brown eyes. He isn't a skeleton! He doesn't have a skeleton **body**.

Look at his **face**. He has white paint on his face, and black paint on his eyes and mouth.

Face paint is fun!

3 Read again and match.

1. black — eyes
2. brown — face
3. white — hair

Reading

LESSON 3

In this lesson, students will:

- read about a painted face.
- use new words to talk about a painted face.
- match words from a text in a comprehension activity.

Resources: Audio Tracks 72–73, Classroom Presentation Tool, Flashcards 82–85, Workbook p. 42, Workbook Audio Track 27, Online Practice

Materials: a toy skeleton or a photo of a skeleton, glue, cotton swabs, black foam, white foam, scissors

Warm Up

- **Use the Photo** Have students open their books to pp. 52–53. Direct students' attention to the photo. Ask *Is this a boy or a girl?* (a boy) Give instructions. Say *Point to his eyes.* Repeat with other body parts. Say *Point to his nose, Point to his mouth, Point to his ears, Point to his hand.* Point to the boy's face as you say *Look! Paint.* Ask *What color is the paint?* (black and white)

- Read aloud the instructions. Play **TR: 72** and have students listen and repeat the words. Then use actions and descriptions to teach the new words.
- Use both your hands to show the outline of your body. Say *This is my body.* Emphasize the word *body* and write it on the board.
- Use a toy skeleton or a photo of a skeleton to teach the word *skeleton.* Hold it up for the class to see. Say *Look! This is a skeleton. We have a skeleton inside our body.* Gesture to help students understand what you mean.
- Use a doll to teach the words *hair* and *face.* Point to the doll's hair and say *Look! This is her hair. Her hair is on her head.* Point and say *Look! This is her face.* Point and say *Her eyes, her nose, and her mouth are on her face.*
- Point to the text and say *Find the words here.* Have students scan the text to find the four new words. Make sure they understand that they don't have to read the whole text—just find the words.
- Call on a volunteer to point to and read aloud the first of the words in the text. Make sure that all students are pointing to the correct word. As the volunteer says the word, hold up the corresponding flashcard. Repeat with the other Lesson 3 words and flashcards.

- Read aloud the instructions. Point to the text. Play **TR: 73** from beginning to end. Have students listen to and read the whole text.

- Play **TR: 73** again, pausing after the first paragraph. Have students listen and read. Point to the photo and ask *Is this a skeleton or a boy?* (a boy) Continue playing **TR: 73**, pausing after the second paragraph. Have students listen and read. Ask *What color is his hair?* (black) Point to the boy's body and ask *Is this a skeleton?* (no) Play the last part of **TR: 73**. Have students listen and read. Ask *What color paint is on his face?* (white) *What color paint is on his eyes?* (black)
- Play **TR: 73** again, and have students read the text without stopping. Then, have students read aloud the text in pairs, reading aloud one sentence at a time.
- **Reading Strategy: Using Visual Clues** Before reading, have students look at any visuals for clues about the text. Have them try to guess what the text is going to be about and also which words they might see in the text.
- **Extra Support** On the board, write *skeleton, hair, body,* and *face.* Play **TR: 73** again and have students raise their hands each time they hear one of the words. They hear *skeleton* and *face* three times.

- Read aloud the instructions. Hold up a copy of the Student's Book and point to the first word. (black) Point to the three body words and read them aloud. Ask *What's black? His eyes? His face? His hair?* (hair) Use your finger to trace a line from *black* to *hair.* Have students draw the line in their books.
- Have students complete the matching activity on their own.
- Correct the activity by calling out the colors and having students respond with the body words as a class.
- **Extra Challenge** Have students give whole sentences as they do the matching activity. For example, *He has black hair* or *His hair is black.*

Optional Activity

- Have students glue cotton swabs onto black foam to make a skeleton. Have them glue one swab vertically and four horizontally across the vertical to make the body. Then have them use two more swabs for each arm (attached to the top horizontal swab) and leg (attached to the bottom horizontal swab). Use about one-third of the length of a swab for each foot and finger. Then cut out the skull from white foam and use more black foam to make eyes, a nose, and teeth for the mouth. When they finish, have students hold up their skeletons and say *This is my skeleton. This is [his] hand,* etc.

Wrap Up

- Practice the words for colors and parts of the body. Say a color, such as *red,* and write it on the board. Then say a body part, such as *arm,* and write it on the board. Say other colors and body parts at random one at a time. Have students say the word on the board under which you should write this word. For example, if you say *yellow* after *arm,* then you should write *yellow* under *red.* They are both colors!

Additional Practice: Workbook p. 42, Online Practice

Grammar

In this lesson, students will:

- describe people using *He/She has* and *He/She doesn't have.*

Resources: Audio Tracks 74–75, Classroom Presentation Tool, Workbook p. 43, Workbook Audio Track 28, Online Practice

Materials: construction paper or cardboard, colored paper, ribbons

Warm Up

- Point to your hair and say *Look at me. I have [black] hair.* Point to your eyes and say *I have [brown] eyes.* Then have students describe their own hair and eyes.

- Read aloud the instructions. Point to the grammar box and say *Listen.* Play **TR: 74.** Have students listen and read. Play **TR: 74** again and have students repeat the sentences.
- Point to your own eyes and say *I have [brown] eyes.* Point to a boy student and say *He has [green] eyes.* Repeat with a girl student. Write the three sentences on the board. Then point and say *I don't have [white] hair.* Repeat with *doesn't have* and sentences about boy and girl students.
- Write *don't* and *doesn't* on the board. Explain that they mean *do not* and *does not* and that *n't* means *not.*

- Read aloud the instructions. Have students complete the activity in pairs. Check answers as a class.
- **Extra Challenge** Have students work in pairs to extend the acitvity by talking about their classmates, saying, for example, *He has brown hair. She doesn't have blue eyes.*

Task Guidance Notes

Starters Listening Part 1 Students have to look at a big picture of people doing different things. They listen to a conversation and match the names around the picture to people by drawing lines. There is an extra name and an extra character they do not need. The conversation has pauses to allow students to draw a line. This tests understanding names and descriptions.

Challenges Students can get confused by similar characters. Give them time to look at the picture before they start. Encourage them to think about words they know so that they can predict what they are listening for.

Performance Descriptor

- Can understand some simple spoken descriptions of people such as name, age, gender, or appearance

- **Predict** This activity practices matching a name to a description. Have students look at each photo and think of all the words they know. This encourages them to think before they listen and to feel confident that they know the words. Then ask them to say as many words as they can for each photo. Make a list on the board.
- Look at the names with the class. Read aloud each name and have students repeat.
- Make sure students understand the instructions and look at the example with the class. Play the first part of **TR: 75** and follow the blue line with your finger.
- Play **TR: 75** to the end. Have students complete the activity individually. Play the recording again for students to check their answers. Check answers with the class.
- **Personalize** Ask students to each draw two children they know, such as a sister or classmate. Have them color their hair and eyes. Then have them exchange with a classmate and take turns to say one description while their classmate listens and checks. Monitor and help.

Script for TR: 75

This is Sue. She has brown hair. She has blue eyes.
This is Peter. He has brown hair, and he has big blue eyes.
This is Jack. He has brown hair and brown eyes.
This is Marion. She doesn't have blue eyes. She has brown hair.

- Read aloud the instructions. Point to the example conversation and explain that this is a guessing game about someone in the classroom. Model the conversation with a volunteer. Then choose a boy in the class (without telling the students) and describe him. Have students guess who you are describing.
- Put students into pairs. Have them take turns to think of a person in the class. Then have them describe the person and ask questions until they guess who the person is.
- **Extra Support** Before students do the activity, point to a boy student and say *He has.* Have other students complete the sentence, for example, *He has blue eyes, He has brown hair.* Repeat with *doesn't have.* Again, have other students complete the sentence. Repeat with *She has* and *She doesn't have.* Then have individual students point and say *He/She has* and *He/She doesn't have.*

Optional Activity

- Have students make their own masks from construction paper or cardboard. Have them draw scary or funny faces and color them in bright colors. If you have time, have students decorate the masks with pieces of colored paper, ribbons, etc. When they finish, have students hold up their masks and say *It has a green head, it has purple eyes,* etc.

Wrap Up

- Practice *has* and *doesn't have.* Say *This person has [black] hair.* Have students point to someone who this sentence describes. Then say *This person doesn't have [green] eyes.* Have students point to someone who this sentence describes. Repeat with other sentences.

Additional Practice: Workbook p. 43, Online Practice

Grammar

1 **Listen and read.** 🎧 TR: 74

> He has black hair.
> She doesn't have blue eyes.

2 **Read and circle.**

1. (He has)/ He doesn't have black hair.

2. He has /(He doesn't have) green eyes.

3. She has /(She doesn't have) brown hair.

4. (She has)/ She doesn't have blue eyes.

3 **Listen and draw lines.** 🎧 TR: 75

Jack   Marion   Peter   Sue

4 **Say, ask, and answer.**

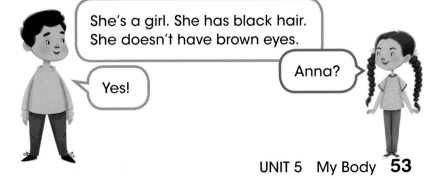

She's a girl. She has black hair.
She doesn't have brown eyes.

Anna?

Yes!

Song

1 **Listen and read.** 🎧 TR: 76

2 **Listen and sing.** 🎧 TR: 77 and 78

3 **Sing and act.** 🎧 TR: 79

Chorus
This is my finger.
I point to my nose.
These are my feet.
These are my toes.

Wave your arms
around and around.
Nod your head
up and down.
Chorus

Stamp your feet.
Jump in the air.
With your finger,
point to your hair.
Chorus

Open your mouth.
Close it and then
close your eyes
and count to ten!
One, two, three…!

VALUE Be active.
Workbook, Lesson 6

Lesson 5 — Song

In this lesson, students will:

- listen to and sing a song about parts of the body.
- act out a song.
- identify the value of being active.

Resources: Audio Tracks 76–79, Classroom Presentation Tool, Workbook p. 45, Online Practice

Warm Up

- Have a drawing dictation to practice body parts. Have students listen to your instructions and draw. Give instructions one at a time, pausing after each instruction to give students time to draw.
- Say *Let's draw a doll. Draw a big head. Now draw a big body. Draw two arms. Draw two hands. Now draw two legs and two feet. Now let's draw the face. First, draw two small eyes. Now, draw a big nose and a big mouth. Draw two big ears. Draw the doll's hair.*
- Give students a few minutes to show their classmates' their drawings.
- **Use the Photo** Have students open their books to p. 54. Point to the photo. Ask *What can you see?* (a girl) *Is she at school?* (no) *Is she happy?* (yes)
- Draw two hands and two feet on the board. Point to the fingers and the toes. Say *Look! Fingers.* Ask *How many fingers do we have?* (ten) Do the same with *toes*.
- Say *Look at the girl again. Listen to me and point. Point to her legs. Now point to her arms.* Repeat with other body parts. Have students listen and point.

- Point to your eyes. Ask *How many eyes?* (two) Hold up your hands. Ask *How many hands?* (two) Repeat with *ears, legs, arms, feet*. Now wiggle your fingers and ask *How many fingers?* (ten)
- Read aloud the instructions. Play **TR: 76**. Have students listen and follow in their books.
- **Extra Support** Play **TR: 76** again and have students clap their hands when they hear any body words (finger, nose, feet, toes, arms, head, feet, finger, hair, mouth, eyes).

- Read aloud the instructions. Play **TR: 77**. Get a clapping or tapping rhythm going to accompany the song. Encourage students to sing along to the chorus.
- Teach each verb in the song. First, say the verb aloud. Then, read the phrase or the whole sentence with the verb. For example, say *I point to my nose* and do the action. Have students do the action, too.
- Play **TR: 77** again for students to sing. Then play the audio a third time for students to change roles and sing again.
- Play **TR: 78**, the instrumental version of the song, and have students sing the song.

- **Extra Challenge** Put students into small groups. Have individual students give instructions for others to act out. First, have them read the instructions from the song itself. Then, have them close their books and give instructions from memory.

- Read aloud each line of the song and have students invent an action. For example, read aloud and say *This is my finger* and have students hold up one finger. Then read aloud and say *I point to my nose* and have students point to their nose with their finger. Repeat for each line and practice each action with the class.
- Play **TR: 79**, pausing after each line to make sure everyone remembers the actions.
- Play **TR: 79** again. Have students sing the song and do the actions.
- **Value: Be active** At this point in the lesson, you can introduce the value. Say *The value of this lesson is* Be active. Write *Be active* on the board. Then ask for a student to help you demonstrate what this means through a role-playing activity. Have the student follow your instructions. If necessary, demonstrate the actions yourself. Give simple instructions for warm-up activities. For example, say:
  Move one leg up and down.
  Move the other leg up and down.
  Jump three times.
  Touch your toes.
  Put your arms up.
  Wave your arms.
  Jump again.
  Stop!
  Point to the active student and say *Very good! Being active is good.* If you have space in the classroom, have the class stand up and follow the instructions. For additional practice, have students complete Lesson 6 of the Workbook in class or at home.

Optional Activity

- Have a performance with students singing and acting in groups. Put students into groups and give them time to practice. Have them sing and do a dance routine. Have each group take a turn to give their performance.

Wrap Up

- Give students instructions using *Please*. For example, say *Please point to your feet. Please pick up a bag. Please jump in the air. Please nod your head three times.* Then play a game. Give instructions. If you say *Please*, students have to follow the instruction. If you don't say *Please*, they shouldn't follow the instruction. If anyone makes a mistake, he/she sits down. End the game when just a few students are left standing.

Additional Practice: Workbook p. 45, Online Practice

Phonics

> **In this lesson, students will:**
> - identify and write *q, r, s, t,* and *u.*
> - identify and pronounce words with /kw/, /r/, /s/, /t/, and /ʌ/ at the beginning.
>
> **Resources:** Audio Tracks 80–82; Classroom Presentation Tool; Flashcards 25, 56–59, 63, 72–73, 86–90; Workbook p. 44; Workbook Audio Track 29; Online Practice
>
> **Materials:** sticky tack

Warm Up

- Use the Lesson 6 flashcards to review the sounds from Units 3 and 4. Display the eight flashcards on the board. Point to each flashcard one at a time and have students say the word and then the sound. Then have students say the letter for each flashcard.

 1

- Write the following letters on the board: *Qq, Rr, Ss, Tt,* and *Uu.* Say the letters of the alphabet. Then say *Today we're learning the sounds for these letters.*
- Have students open their books to p. 55. Direct students' attention to the photos and words. Read aloud the instructions. Play **TR: 80**, pointing to each photo and word as students hear it.
- Play **TR: 80** again. Have students repeat each word. Monitor students carefully, making sure they pronounce the target sounds correctly.
- **Extra Support** Say each word again and then the sound. Have students read the word and then repeat the sound.

 2

- Read aloud the instructions. Point to the chant and look at the example with the class. Say *Listen. Can you hear /kw/, /r/, /s/, /t/, and /ʌ/?* Say the sounds, not the letters. Play **TR: 81**. Have students circle the letters as in the example. Have students work in pairs. Check answers together as a class by holding up a copy of the Student's Book and circling each letter with your finger so that students can see and check.
- Play **TR: 81** again. This time have students read and chant.
- **Extra Challenge** Have students say the chant before they listen to the audio.

 3

- Have students look at the picture. Give them instructions. Say *Point to the queen.* Have students listen, look, and point. Then repeat with *rabbit, sofa, table,* and *umbrella.*
- Read aloud the instructions. Give students a minute to look at the picture again and read the words. Look at the example with the class. Use your finger to trace the letter *u.*
- Play **TR: 82** from beginning to end. Have students do the activity individually.
- Check answers by playing **TR: 82**, pausing after each word and eliciting students' answers.

  Script for TR: 82 *rabbit, table, queen, sofa, umbrella*

Optional Activity

- Say each word from this lesson and have students call out the sound. Begin with the words in alphabetical order and then say them in random order. Then say each sound and have students call out the word. Again, begin with the sounds in order and then say them in random order. Continue with words and sounds from Units 1–4. If you like, have students do this activity in pairs.

Wrap Up

- Use the phonics flashcards from Units 1–5 to review the target sounds. Divide the class into two teams, A and B. Display all the phonics flashcards on the board. Have one member from Team A come to the board, point to a flashcard, and say a sound. If the sound matches the picture, have the student take the flashcard for Team A. If the sound doesn't match the picture, the flashcard remains on the board and another student (from either team) can try and say the sound correctly for the picture. When there are no more flashcards on the board, the team with the most flashcards is the winner.

> **Additional Practice:** Workbook p. 44, Online Practice

1 Listen, point, and repeat. 🎧 TR: 80

queen   rabbit   sofa   table   umbrella

2 Listen, chant, and circle. 🎧 TR: 81

This is a queen, a q, q, (q)ueen.
This is a rabbit, a r, r, (r)abbit.
This is a sofa, a s, s, (s)ofa.
This is a table, a t, t, (t)able.
This is an umbrella, an u, u, (u)mbrella.

3 Listen and find. Write the letter. 🎧 TR: 82

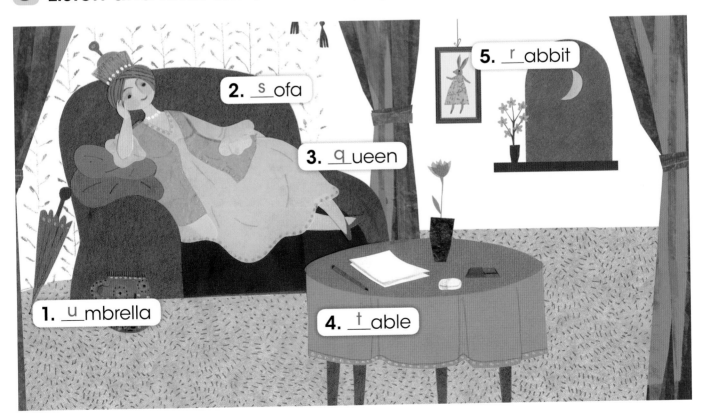

5. _r_ abbit

2. _s_ ofa

3. _q_ ueen

1. _u_ mbrella

4. _t_ able

Video

1 Watch and match. Write the numbers. ▶ Video 6

 1. Shiven

 2. Marcel

 3. Kaitlyn

 4. Juan

 2

 4

 1

 3

ABOUT THE VIDEO

In this video, Kaitlyn talks about a Chinese dragon. Dragons are very important in Chinese culture. Dragons symbolize prosperity, wisdom, and good fortune. You can see them in paintings, and on decorated plates and clothes. At some festivals, you can watch a traditional Chinese dragon dance. This is a special performance where a group of dancers hides under an enormous dragon head and body.

2 Your turn! Ask and answe

What color are your eyes?

They're brown.

3 Draw and say.

This is my friend, _____ .
_____ has _____ _____ .

_____ , _____ .
_____ has _____ _____ .

In this lesson, students will:
- watch a video about masks from other countries.
- ask and answer about eyes and hair color.
- draw and speak about friends and family members.

Resources: Video 6, Classroom Presentation Tool, Online Practice

End-of-Unit Resources: Worksheet 1.5, Unit 5 Test, ExamView Assessment Suite

Materials: photos of people wearing masks (from Internet or magazine), a video clip from the Internet of a Chinese dragon dance

Warm Up
- Bring in some photos of people wearing masks, particularly cultural rather than scary masks. Hold up one of the photos and say a few sentences to describe the mask. Say *Look! It's a [man]. He has [black] eyes. He doesn't have [black] hair. He has [green] hair.*
- Hold up more photos and have students say sentences to describe the people in the photos. Prompt students when necessary by saying parts of the face. Say *Today's video is about masks.*

- Have students open their books to p. 56. Direct students' attention to the four photos on the left. Give students instructions. Say *Where's Juan? Point to him! Juan is number four. Where's Kaitlyn? Point to her. Kaitlyn is number three.* Then do the same with the other children. Have students work in pairs and check they are pointing to the same photo.
- Point to the four photos on the right. Say *Look! One, two, three, four photos.*
- Read aloud the instructions and play Video 6 from beginning to end. Have students match the photos with the four numbers and names on the left and write the numbers in the boxes.
- Play Video 6 again. Pause the video after Shiven says *This is a photo of four men* and ask *How many men can you see?* (four) Continue and pause again after Shiven says *I can see their legs and feet* and ask *Can Shiven see legs and feet?* (yes) Pause again after Marcel says *This is a woman* and ask *Is this a man or a woman?* (a woman) Pause again after Kaitlyn says *This is a woman* and ask *Is this a man or a woman?* (a woman) Pause again after Kaitlyn says *Its eyes are green* and ask *What color are the dragon's eyes?* (green) Pause again after Kaitlyn says *It has a ball in its mouth* and ask *What's in its mouth?* (a ball) Then pause again after Juan says *I can see his head, his hair, and his ears under the mask* and ask *Can Juan see the man's ears?* (yes)

- **Extra Challenge** Before students watch Video 6 the first time, have them look more closely at the four photos on the right. Have students work in pairs. Have them choose one photo each, point to it, and describe it. For example, they can say *Big eyes, yellow face, red and black mouth, pink hair.* Monitor students as they speak.
- **Extra Support** Before students watch Video 6 the first time, have them look more closely at the four photos on the right. Have them point to and say the colors in the photos.

The script for Video 6 is available on the Teacher's Resource Website.

Optional Activity
- Find a video on the Internet of the Chinese dragon dance. Play the clip for students to watch and ask them to describe the dragon's face and say what color its head, eyes, and mouth are.

- Read aloud the instructions. Act out the conversation with a volunteer. Then ask *What color's your hair?* and have volunteers respond. If necessary, teach the word *fair*.
- Call on two students to act out the conversations in front of the class.
- Put students into pairs to ask and answer about their eyes and hair. Monitor and help when necessary.

- Read aloud the instructions. Use the board to demonstrate. Draw a picture of a boy or girl. Say *This is my friend, [Claudio]. He has [blue] eyes.*
- Have students work individually to draw two people, one in each box. When they finish, have them walk around with their books and show their pictures to their classmates. Have them describe the people. For example, they can say *This is my sister, Marta. She has green eyes.*

Wrap Up
- Play a game to see how much students remember about the video. Have students close their books. If necessary, play Video 6 again. Then put students into teams. Ask each team a question one at a time. Have students raise their hands to answer. Award a point for each correct answer. The winner is the team with the most points.
- Suggested questions:
  Where is Shiven's festival? (India)
  How many men have masks? (four)
  What color are the flowers on their heads? (yellow)
  Who sees a photo of a carnival? (Marcel)
  What color is the woman's hair? (red)
  How many hands can Marcel see? (one)
  Where is the dragon? (China)
  Is the dragon's head big or small? (big)
  Is it blue and yellow? (no)
  What color is the mask in Juan's photo? (yellow)
  Is the head big or small? (big)
  What does Juan think is cool? (the hair)

Additional Practice: Worksheet 1.5, Online Practice

UNIT
6 Homes

In this unit, students will:

- talk about homes.
- talk about where things are using *Where's...?* and *It's in the....*
- read about a bedroom under the water.
- use *next to*, *on*, and *under* to talk about where things are.
- listen to and sing a song about a game of hide-and-seek.
- identify and pronounce words with /v/, /w/, /j/, and /z/ at the beginning.
- identify and pronounce words that include /ks/.
- watch a video about homes in other countries.
- identify the value of playing with your friends.

Language

Words

bathroom, bed, bedroom, cabinet, kitchen, living room, shower, TV; clock, house, water

Grammar

- *Where's the sofa?*
  It's in the living room.
- *The table is next to the bed.*
- *The game is on the bed.*
- *The bedroom is under the water.*

Phonics

/v/ violin
/w/ wall
/ks/ box
/j/ yogurt
/z/ zebra

Twenty-First Century Skills

Collaboration
Complete sentences in pairs, Lesson 2

Communication
Play a memory game, Lesson 2

Creativity
Draw and speak about rooms in your home, Lesson 7

Critical Thinking
Identify the value of playing with your friends, Lesson 5

In the Unit Opener, students will:

- respond to a photo of a tree house.
- talk about houses.

Resources: Home School Connection Letter, Classroom Presentation Tool

Materials: five photos of homes in different parts of the world, sticky tack

Introduce the Theme

- Bring five photos of homes in different parts of the world into class. Try to get a range of house styles and settings that might be unfamiliar to students, including at least one apartment. Display the photos on the board for students to see. Say *These are homes!* and call on students to come up and look at the photos.
- Show students that you are looking at the five photos and thinking. Use gestures and expressions for this. Then choose a house, point to it, and then put both hands on your heart and smile to show you like it best. Write a heading on the board: *My favorite homes.* Point and say *This is my favorite home. Then this one. Then this one.* Continue until you've put all the homes in order of preference.
- Have students come to the board, look at the five photos, and then point and say their favorites in order.
- Find out the class favorite by pointing to each home one at a time and having students raise their hands if it is their favorite.

Use the Photo

- Hold up a copy of the Student's Book open to p. 57 and point to the photo. Ask *Is this in [name of your town]?* (no) Point to the tree house and ask *What color is this?* (brown) Point to the tree house and the trees around it and say *These are trees. Is this house in the trees?* (yes) Look at the caption and say *A tree house.* Ask *Do you like this tree house?*
- Have students open their books to p. 57. Read aloud the question at the bottom of the page and have students share their ideas. Accept single words, colors, and so on. Say *This is a tree house.*

TEACHER TIP

Try to find out about your students and be sensitive to their personal situations. Students are sometimes expected to talk about aspects of their personal lives, such as their homes. If you think this will show inequality (for example, when some students have luxurious homes and others have very simple homes), change the focus and have students instead talk about an imaginary situation.

ABOUT THE PHOTO
This photo shows a tree house on the Edisto River in South Carolina, in the United States. The tree house is part of a large wildlife refuge popular with tourists. When visitors arrive, they have to get to their tree house by paddling up the river in a canoe.

A tree house

Look at the photo. What can you see?

LESSON 1 Words

1 Listen and point. 🎧 TR: 83

bathroom

bedroom

kitchen

living room

bed

cabinet

shower

TV

2 Listen and repeat. 🎧 TR: 84

3 Say.

shower

bathroom

ABOUT THE PICTURE

This picture is based on a typical house in Spain. Notice the roof. In Spain, homes often have clay tile roofs. Clay is fire-resistant and inexpensive, as well as being durable and easy to maintain. The tiles in this picture are made from a kind of clay called *terracotta*, an Italian word that means "baked earth." The type of tile in this picture is also popular in parts of North, Central, and South America—a legacy of Spanish colonization.

Words

LESSON 1

In this lesson, students will:
- talk about homes.

Resources: Audio Tracks 83–84, Classroom Presentation Tool, Flashcards 91–98, Workbook p. 46, Workbook Audio Track 30, Online Practice

Materials: sticky tack

Warm Up

- **Use the Picture** Have students open their books to pp. 58–59. Say *Look! A house.* Have students listen, look, find, and point. Give instructions to find and point to different things in the picture. Say *Point to something green* and *Point to something white.* Then say *Point to a chair.* Repeat this with *a lamp, a picture, a sofa, a table.*

- Read aloud the instructions. Then direct students' attention to the pictures under the instructions. Point to the top four pictures and say *Look, four rooms: one, two, three, four.* Point to the lower four pictures and say *Look, four things in a house.*
- Point to your ear and say *Let's listen.* Play **TR: 83** and point to the pictures one at a time as you hear the words.
- Play **TR: 83** again, and model pointing to the pictures as you hear the words so that students know what to do.

- Read aloud the instructions. Play **TR: 84**. Pause after the first word. Repeat the word to model the activity for students. Continue with **TR: 84** as students repeat the words as a class.
- Play **TR: 84** again and call on individual students to repeat the words.
- **Extra Challenge** Write the new words on the board in one long word snake with no spaces. Have students come to the board one at a time to find and circle the eight items.

- Use the flashcards to practice the words. Hold up each of the four room flashcards one at a time and ask *What's this?* Elicit the answers from the class. Display the four room flashcards in a row on the board, leaving space under each one to display another flashcard.
- Hold up the *bed* flashcard and ask *What's this?* Hold the *bed* flashcard under the *kitchen* flashcard on the board and ask *Here?* (no) Repeat the action, holding the flashcard under different rooms until you hold it below the bedroom. When students say *yes*, say *That's right! A bed in the bedroom.* Repeat with the remaining three furniture flashcards. Make sure students match flashcards as in the main picture, even if the item of furniture could be found in more than one room.

- Read aloud the instructions. Direct students' attention to the models. Say the words with a volunteer. Say an item of furniture and have the student say the room it's in in the main picture.
- Put students in pairs to do the activity. Monitor students while they do the activity, making sure they are taking turns to say an item of furniture.
- **Extra Support** Leave the paired flashcards on the board for students to refer to while they do the activity.

Optional Activity

- Have students draw and talk about their own houses. Have them start with a basic picture of a rectangular house shape, split into four rooms. Then have them add at least one object in each room.
- Have students share their pictures with a partner. Have them compare their pictures and say a few things about their houses. For example, *This is the living room in my house. The big television is in the living room.*

Wrap Up

- Practice the words using the flashcards. Display the flashcards facedown in random order on the board so that students are unable to see the pictures. Write a number next to each flashcard (1–8). Call on students to say two numbers. Turn over the corresponding flashcards. Have the student say the words. If they match, the student wins the pair of flashcards. If they don't match, the flashcards remain facedown on the board and another member (from either team) can try and match them correctly. Matching flashcards: bathroom and shower, bedroom and bed, kitchen and cabinet, living room and TV.

Additional Practice: Workbook p. 46, Online Practice

Grammar

Warm Up

- Review the words from Lesson 1. Write each of the eight new words on an index card. Then display the eight Lesson 1 flashcards in a row across the board, leaving space below each card for students to display a word card.

- Hold up each word card one at a time and elicit the word from the class. Then have volunteers display the word card under its corresponding flashcard.

- When all the word cards are on the board, remove the flashcards. Hold up each flashcard, one at a time, and elicit the word. Then repeat the activity, this time having students display the flashcards back on the board in their corresponding place above the word cards.

- Read aloud the instructions. Say *Listen to the chant.* Play **TR: 85**. Have students listen and clap to the rhythm.

- Play **TR: 85** again. Divide students into two groups, A and B. Point to the purple lines of the chant and say *Group A, say the purple lines.* Point to the green lines of the chant and say *Group B, say the green lines.*

- Play **TR: 85** again. Have students stand up to say the chant. Have them jump and sit at the end of the verses.

- Read aloud the instructions. Direct students' attention to the grammar box. Say *Listen and read* and play **TR: 86**. Play **TR: 86** again and have students repeat the questions and answers as a class. Have them point to the items of furniture in the main picture as they speak.

- Copy the first question and answer from the grammar box onto the board. Underline the two contractions: *Where's* and *It's.* Read aloud the question, emphasizing the contraction. Then do the same with the answer.

- Write on the board *Where's = Where is.* Make sure students understand that the meaning is the same, but when we speak we use *Where's.* Remind students that *It's* means *It is.*

- Arrange the following objects on your table: *a pencil case, a bag, a book, a ruler, an eraser, a pencil, a pen,* and *a crayon.* Make sure students can see all the objects. Then put the crayon, the eraser, and the pencil inside the pencil case. Put the ruler, the book, and the pen inside the bag. Place the bag and the pencil case side by side. Ask *Where's the [crayon]?* and elicit full answers.

- **Extra Challenge** Divide students into groups of three. Have them choose an empty pencil case and an empty bag and place them side by side on a desk. Then have them choose four classroom objects to put in the pencil case and four classroom objects to put in the bag. Have them choose more than one of the same object and ask questions like *Where's the [red] pencil?* Have students take turns to ask and answer. Monitor as they do the activity, helping when necessary.

- Read aloud the instructions. Direct students' attention to the first question and point to the *'s* that has been added as an example. Read aloud the sentence. Point to the answer and indicate that students should work with a partner to complete the sentence.

- Monitor students as they work and then elicit the answers orally from the class. Call on volunteers to read aloud each question and answer.

Optional Activity

- Take a dollhouse and doll furniture into the classroom and use them to practice the language. Alternatively, use some boxes of different sizes to form different rooms in a house and smaller objects as pretend furniture. Place the furniture in different rooms to practice the preposition *in.* Use the opportunity to have a little fun and make things silly. For example, put the sofa in the bathroom and ask *Where's the sofa?* (It's in the bathroom.) *Is that right?* (no!)

- Read aloud the instructions. Give students a minute to study the picture before having them close their books. Demonstrate with a volunteer. Ask questions about the main picture for the volunteer to answer from memory. For example, ask *Where's the TV? Where's the lamp?*

- Have students work in pairs. Have them take turns to ask and answer questions.

- **Extra Support** Have students work in groups of three as two of them ask and answer questions. Have the third check, by looking at the main picture, that the answers are correct.

Wrap Up

- Practice using *Where's the...?* and *It's in the....* Divide the board into four equal parts. Draw a large bag shape in each section. Use a different color for each bag, for example, blue, green, red, yellow.

- Have students copy the four bags on a piece of paper or in their notebooks.

- Give students drawing instructions. Have students listen and draw, but also have them engage in a conversation:
  Teacher: Draw a pencil.
  Students: Where's the pencil?
  Teacher: It's in the red bag.

- When you finish the activity, ask students to give you instructions so that you can draw the same items in the same places on the board.

Grammar

1 **Listen, point, and chant.**

 TR: 85

Where's the bed?
Where is it?
The bed's in the bedroom.
Jump on it!

Where's the sofa?
Where is it?
The sofa's in the living room.
Sit on it!

2 **Listen and read.** 🎧 TR: 86

> Where's the sofa?
> It's in the living room.
>
> Where's the table?
> It's in the kitchen.

3 **Write.**

1. Where __'s__ the shower?
   It's __in__ the bathroom.

2. __Where's__ the lamp?
   It's __in__ the bedroom.

4 **Close your book. Ask and answer.**

3 Reading

1 Listen and repeat. 🎧 TR: 87

> house   clock   water

2 Listen and read. 🎧 TR: 88

Look at the photo. This is a bedroom. It isn't in a **house**. It's in an aquarium. Can you see the table? The table is next to the bed. It's white. The **clock** is on the table. It's small. The game is on the bed. It's yellow, red, and blue. The toy fish are on the bed, too.

Look at the fish in the **water**. This bedroom is under the water!

3 Read again and circle.

1. This is a **bedroom** / kitchen.
2. The table is **white** / yellow.
3. The clock is **big** / **small**.

ABOUT THE PHOTO

The photo shows a bedroom built inside a shark tank in the Paris Aquarium. It was built as a prize for a competition organized by Airbnb, a rental company where people can find unusual vacation homes around the world. Three lucky winners were able to spend a night in the underwater bedroom, watch sharks from every angle, and visit the rest of the aquarium the following day.

Reading

In this lesson, students will:
- read about a bedroom under the water.
- use new words to talk about a bedroom.
- choose the correct words in sentences about a text.

Resources: Audio Tracks 87–88, Classroom Presentation Tool, Flashcards 99–101, Workbook p. 48, Workbook Audio Track 32, Online Practice

Materials: a photo of an aquarium, photos of unusual rooms (from Internet or magazine), sticky tack

Warm Up
- Draw a picture of a bedroom on the board. Draw part of each item of furniture, pausing to ask *What's this?* for each item. Have students watch and raise their hands to make suggestions each time you ask a question. Have different students answer each time. Add these items to the bedroom: a bed, a chair, a desk, a TV, a toy plane hanging from the ceiling, a train on a track, etc.
- **Use the Photo** Have students open their books to pp. 60–61. Direct students' attention to the photo. Point and ask *What colors can you see? Is this a kitchen?* (no) *Is this a living room?* (no) *Is this a classroom?* (no) *Is this a bedroom?* (yes)
- Give students instructions. Say *Point to the bed.* Then repeat with *book, clock, game, table, water.* Have students listen, look, and point each time.
- Bring in a photo of a traditional aquarium. Point to the photo in the book and say *An aquarium is a home for fish. Look! This is an aquarium.*

- Read aloud the instructions. Play **TR: 87** and have students listen and repeat the words. Then use actions and descriptions to teach the new words.
- Hold up the *house* flashcard and say *Look! A house.* Ask *What color is the house?*
- Hold up the *clock* flashcard and say *Look! A clock!*
- Hold up the *water* flashcard and say *Look! Water.* Then, on the board, draw various forms of water (a glass of water, a river, the sea, a lake, raindrops, etc.). Point to all the pictures and say *Water* each time.
- Point to the text and say *Find the words here.* Have students scan the text to find the three new words. Make sure they understand that they don't have to read the whole text—just find the words.
- Call on a volunteer to point to and read aloud the first of the words in the text. Make sure that all students are pointing to the correct word. As the volunteer says the word, hold up the corresponding flashcard. Repeat with the other Lesson 3 words and flashcards.

- Read aloud the instructions. Point to the text. Play **TR: 88** from beginning to end. Have students listen to and read the whole text.
- Ask *Do you like this bedroom?* Elicit answers from different students.
- Have students read the text again. Have them read aloud in groups, one sentence at a time. Encourage them to help each other with the meaning of any unknown words.
- **Reading Strategy: Using Context for Understanding** If a student doesn't understand a word in a text, it's a good idea to read on before asking. Often other words later in a sentence will help them understand an earlier word. For short texts, it's a good idea to read the whole text to the end, and then go back and read it again.
- **Extra Challenge** Have students work in pairs, A and B. Have Student A with the book open and Student B with the book closed. Have Student A read the first half of the text (to *on the table*) a line at a time, pausing before the final word in each sentence. Have Student B say the missing word each time. Have students change roles and have Student B continue reading from *It's small* to the end while Student A says the final word in each sentence.
- **Extra Support** Play **TR: 88** again and have students raise their hands when they hear the new words.

- Read aloud the instructions. Point to item 1 and read aloud the first sentence, saying and emphasizing both options. Ask *Bedroom or kitchen?* (bedroom) Have students complete the activity in pairs.
- Correct the activity by reading aloud each sentence, pausing before the options, and having students call out the correct word to complete the sentence.

Optional Activity
- Have students design their ideal bedrooms. Have them spend a minute thinking, then have them draw the bedroom. When they finish, display their drawings. Then have students come to the front and say three things about their bedroom. Have students vote on the coolest idea.

Wrap Up
- Find some photos of unusual rooms. Show each photo one at a time and have students respond with *Wow!* if they like it or *No!* If they don't.

Additional Practice: Workbook p. 48, Online Practice

Grammar

In this lesson, students will:
- use *next to*, *on*, and *under* to talk about where things are.
- identify the correct prepositions in sentences.

Resources: Audio Tracks 89–90, Classroom Presentation Tool, Workbook p. 49, Workbook Audio Track 33, Online Practice

Warm Up

- Review *in*. Ask *What's in your pencil case?* and have students take out the contents of their pencil cases and put them on their desks. Have students take turns to pick up an object, put it back in their pencil case, and say *My [ruler]'s in my pencil case*.

- Have students open their books to p. 61. Read aloud the instructions. Point to the grammar box and say *Listen and read*. Play **TR: 89**. Have students listen and read. Play **TR: 89** again and have students repeat the sentences, first as a class and then individually.
- Direct students' attention to the main photo of the bedroom under the water. Point to the table and the bed, and say *Look! The table is* next to *the bed*. Emphasize the words *next to*. Point to the game on the bed and say *Look! The game is* on *the bed*. Emphasize the word *on*. Then point to the whole bedroom and the water outside the window and say *Look! The bedroom is* under *the water*. Emphasize the word *under*.
- **Extra Support** Draw three simple tables in a row on the board. Draw a ball on the first table and say *On*, a ball under the second table and say *Under*. Then draw a ball next to the third table and say *Next to*. Point to the first table and ask *Where's the ball?* (It's on the table.) Point to the other pictures, ask the questions, and elicit the answers.

- Read aloud the instructions. Point to the picture and read item 1 with both options. Then say *Look at the picture*. Ask *Next to* or *on?* (on) Have students circle *on* with a pencil.
- Have students complete the activity in pairs. Check answers as a class. Call on students to read aloud each correct sentence.
- **Extra Challenge** Have students draw a similar picture to the one in the activity. Underneath, have them write three more *Read and circle* sentences with a correct preposition and an incorrect preposition. Have them exchange notebooks with a partner to do the activity their partner created.

- Make sure students are prepared for the activity with a piece of drawing paper or a notebook and a pencil.
- Read aloud the instructions. Then play **TR: 90** from beginning to end. Say *Table* and then encourage students to say other words that they recognize and remember from the audio.

- Play **TR: 90** again, pausing after the first element to check that students are drawing. Play the rest of **TR: 90**, pausing to give students time to draw each element. Play **TR: 90** again if necessary. Have students compare their drawings in small groups when they finish.
- **Listening Strategy: Listening Twice** When students are doing a listening task that involves doing something while they listen, it's a good idea to play the audio twice. The first time have students just listen. The second time have them complete the task. This extra listening stage helps them to familiarize themselves with the context and the language so that when they do the activity they can focus on the actual task.

Script for TR: 90

Draw a table. Now draw a book. The book is on the table. Now draw a pen. The pen is on the table, too. It's next to the book.
Now draw an umbrella. The umbrella is under the table. Now draw a cabinet. Draw a small cabinet. The cabinet is next to the table.

- Read aloud the instructions. Direct students' attention to the example conversation. Put your bag under your table and model saying the conversation with a volunteer. Say the text on the left and have the volunteer say the text on the right. Then put students into pairs to read the conversation.
- Have students continue the activity in pairs, A and B. Have Student A arrange classroom objects on, next to, and under his/her own desk while Student B closes his/her eyes. Then have them play the guessing game, with Student B asking questions at random because he/she can't see the objects. Have them take turns to choose an object, and to ask and answer. Monitor students as they speak and help when necessary.

Optional Activity

- Practice the prepositions. Put your bag on the table and say *My bag's on the table*. Then put your bag under, in, or next to something else in the classroom and say where it is.
- Have students tell the class about other objects in the classroom, for example, *It's next to the board*. If necessary, have students place the object first. Have students listen and guess the object.

Wrap Up

- Have students arrange the following objects on their desks: a pen, a pencil, a ruler, an eraser, a crayon, a book, and a pencil case. Give students instructions about how to arrange the items. Have students listen and put each item in its place. Say *Put the pencil in the pencil case. Now put the eraser next to the pencil case. Put the book under the pencil case, etc.* Call on students around the class to give instructions using *next to*, *on*, *under*, and *in*.

Additional Practice: Workbook p. 49, Online Practice

Grammar

1 **Listen and read.** 🎧 TR: 89

> The table is **next to** the bed.
> The game is **on** the bed.
> The bedroom is **under** the water.

2 **Read and circle.**

1. The clock is **next to** / **on** the cabinet.

2. The bed is **on** / **under** the lamp.

3. The cabinet is **next to** / **under** the bed.

3 **Listen and draw.** 🎧 TR: 90

4 **Say, ask, and answer.**

It's under the table. What is it?

Is it a book?

No, it isn't.

Is it a bag?

Yes, it is.

1 **Listen and read.** 🎧 TR: 91

2 **Listen and sing.**
🎧 TR: 92 and 93

3 **Sing and act.** 🎧 TR: 94

ABOUT THE PHOTO

The photo shows children playing hide-and-seek in Istanbul, Turkey. The game has been around for hundreds of years, and there are many variations in countries around the world. The game is mentioned in records from second-century Greece. It was called *apodidraskinda* in those days, but today it's called *kryfto*. In Spain, it's called *el escondite*. In France, it's called *jeu de cache-cache*. In South Korea, it's called *sumbaggoggil*, and in Bolivia, it's called *tuja*. These days there is even a hide-and-seek world championship. It is held in Italy every summer.

Chorus
Close your eyes.
Turn to the wall.
Count to ten.
Then call out, "Coming!
Ready or not!"

Where's Hana?
Where's Paul?
She's in the kitchen.
He's in the hall.

Where's Fiza?
Where is she?
She's in the yard
next to the tree.

Where's Claude?
Where is he?
Under the table.
Can you see?
Chorus

VALUE **Play with your friends.**
Workbook, Lesson 6

LESSON 5 Song

In this lesson, students will:

- listen to and sing a song about a game of hide-and-seek.
- act out a song.
- identify the value of playing with your friends.

Resources: Audio Tracks 91–94, Classroom Presentation Tool, Workbook p. 51, Online Practice

Materials: a board game per group of students (optional); puppets, stuffed toys or dolls

Warm Up

- Teach and review some words from the song using places in the classroom and the wider school area. Point to the classroom wall and say *Look! A wall.* Ask *How many walls in the classroom?* (four) If you have a hall in the school, take students there. Say *Let's go to the hall.* When you are there, ask *What's in the hall?* Accept any reasonable ideas. Repeat with the schoolyard, if time and weather permit.
- **Use the Photo** Have students open their books to p. 62. Point to the photo and ask *Are the children in a house?* (no) *Is this a game?* (yes) *How many girls can you see?* (three) *How many boys?* (one) *Do you know this game?*

 1

- Have students read through the song. Ask *What's the song about?* (a game)
- Read aloud the instructions. Play **TR: 91**. Have students listen and follow in their books.
- **Extra Support** Allow students time to read the song before they listen and read. Have them read aloud in pairs, taking turns with each line and pausing to check they both understand. If a pair of students doesn't understand, have this pair raise their hands and say *We don't understand [wall].* Call on another student to explain.

 2

- Read aloud the instructions. Play **TR: 92**. Get a clapping or tapping rhythm going to accompany the song.
- Divide students into two groups, A and B. Explain that students in Group A have to sing the green lines, students in Group B have to sing the purple lines, and all students have to sing the chorus (in black). Play **TR: 92** again for students to sing.
- Play **TR: 93**, the instrumental version of the song, and have students sing their part of the song. Then play **TR: 93** again having groups switch roles.

 3

- Read aloud the instructions. Establish actions to perform during the chorus.
  Close your eyes. (Close your eyes.)
  Turn to the wall. (Turn to face a wall.)
  Count to ten. (Count silently on fingers.)
  Then call out, "Coming! Ready or not!" (Have two hands open by your mouth in a calling gesture.)

- Establish an action for each line of the verses.
  Where's Hana? (Look left and right with your hand across your eyes to indicate searching.)
  Where's Paul? (As with Hana)
  She's in the kitchen. (Point to a place on the left.)
  He's in the hall. (Point to a place on the right.)
  Where's Fiza? (As with Hana)
  Where is she? (As with Hana)
  She's in the yard (Point to a place on the left.)
  next to the tree. (Make a tree shape—stand tall, with your arms outstretched like branches.)
  Where's Claude? (As with Hana)
  Where is he? (As with Hana)
  Under the table. (Point under a table.)
  Can you see? (Point to your eyes.)

- Play **TR: 94**, pausing after each line to make sure everyone remembers the actions. Simplify the actions if necessary.
- Play **TR: 94** again. Have students sing the song and do the actions.
- **Extra Challenge** Have students invent a new version of the song using the names of friends and changing the objects and places, too.
- **Value: Play with your friends** At this point in the lesson, you can introduce the value. Say *The value of this lesson is* Play with your friends. Write *Play with your friends* on the board. Then put students into small groups to play games. Give each group a board game or have them play games with paper and pencils. After playing for five minutes, say *This is fun. Playing with your friends is fun!* Give students a brief evaluation on how they feel after playing with friends. Draw a grid on the board for students to copy. Draw a smiling face with a number 5, then a frowning face with a number 1. Point to the number 5, smile, and say *I'm very happy playing with my friends.* Point to the number 1, frown, and say *I'm not happy playing with my friends.* Have students rate the experience. Find out how many chose 5 and then say *Look! [number] say 5! Playing with friends is good.* For additional practice, have students complete Lesson 6 of the Workbook in class or at home.

Optional Activity

- Play a game of hide-and-seek. If appropriate, go outside to the schoolyard. Choose one student to turn to the wall and count to ten while the other students hide. Teach the student the phrase *Ready or not, here I come!* When the student has counted to ten, have him/her call out the phrase then run around looking for the other students. If this isn't appropriate, play a different hiding game. Have students put their heads on their desks and close their eyes. Hide a teddy bear or another object somewhere in the classroom. Count to ten and then tell students to get up and look for the teddy bear.

Wrap Up

- Use puppets, stuffed toys, or dolls in the song. Give them names and then sing the song again. Use the song as a model, but change the names and use the puppets, toys, or dolls to act out the lines of the song.

Additional Practice: Workbook p. 51, Online Practice

Phonics

LESSON 6

In this lesson, students will:
- identify and write *v, w, x, y, z.*
- identify and pronounce words with /v/, /w/, /j/, and /z/ at the beginning of words.
- identify and pronounce words that inlcude /ks/.

Resources: Audio Tracks 95–97; Classroom Presentation Tool; Flashcards 20, 25, 31–33, 45–48, 56–59, 63, 72–73, 86–90, 102–106; Workbook p. 50; Workbook Audio Track 34, Online Practice

Warm Up

- Use the Lesson 6 flashcards to review the phonics from Units 1–5. Put all the flashcards together and jumble them up. Hold up each flashcard one at a time and have students say the word as a class. Listen to the pronunciation of the initial sound and say the word aloud yourself if you think students need to hear it again.

- Write the following letters on the board: *Vv, Ww, Xx, Yy,* and *Zz.* Say the letters of the alphabet. Then say *Today we're learning the sounds for these letters.*
- Have students open their books to p. 63. Direct students' attention to the photos and words. Read aloud the instructions. Then say *Listen.* Play **TR: 95**, pointing to each photo and word as students hear it. Point to the word *box* and say *Look! Box doesn't begin with an x. It ends with an x.* Shake your head and say *There aren't many words starting with an x.*
- Play **TR: 95** again. Have students listen, point, and repeat each word. Monitor students carefully, making sure they pronounce the target sounds correctly.
- **Extra Support** Say the sounds in random order. Say each sound more than once. For example, say /z/, /z/, /z/. Have students listen and point to the photos.

- Read aloud the instructions. Point to the chant. Say *Listen. Clap when you hear* /v/, /w/, /ks/, /j/, *and* /z/. Say the sounds, not the letters. Play **TR: 96**. Have students circle the letters. Have students work in pairs. Check answers together as a class by circling each letter with your finger so they can see and check.
- Play **TR: 96** again. This time have students read and chant.
- **Extra Challenge** Hold up the phonics flashcards in random order. For example, hold up the *yogurt* flashcard and say *Where's the yogurt, the y, y, yogurt?* Repeat with the other flashcards and encourage students to join in as you say lines from the chant. At first, have students do this with their books open. Then have them close their books, look at the flashcards as you hold them up, and say the lines of the chant.

- Point to the wall, the yogurt, the box, the zebra and the violin, one at a time. Each time, ask *What's this?* Call on different students to answer.
- Read the instructions aloud. Give students a minute to look at the picture, read the words, and think about the sounds.
- Play **TR: 97**, pausing after each word to give students time to find the item in the picture and write the letter.
- Check answers by saying the number of each word and having students say the letter.

  Script for TR: 97 *wall, zebra, box, yogurt, violin*

Optional Activity

- Have one student say a sound and other students say words beginning with that sound. Continue around the class. For example, say /b/ and have students call out *bag, ball, bat, bed, bathroom, boy.*

Wrap Up

- Use the phonics flashcards to review the target sounds. Hold up each flashcard one at a time and have students say the word. Repeat the activity a few times, changing the order each time and speeding up so that students have to say the words more and more quickly.

Additional Practice: Workbook p. 50, Online Practice

---

1 Listen, point, and repeat. 🎧 TR: 95

violin   wall   box   yogurt   zebra

2 Listen, chant, and circle. 🎧 TR: 96

Where's the violin, the v, v, (v)iolin?
Where's the wall, the w, w, (w)all?
Where's the box, the x, x, bo(x)?
Where's the yogurt, the y, y, (y)ogurt?
Where's the zebra, the z, z, (z)ebra?

3 Listen and find. Write the letter. 🎧 TR: 97

1. _w_ all

5. _v_ iolin

4. _z_ ebra

2. _y_ ogurt

3. bo _x_

Video

1 **Watch and match. Write the numbers.** ▶ Video 7

 1. Rhiane   **2. Pablo**   **3. Rafi**

ABOUT THE VIDEO

In this video, Rafi talks about a house in Saudi Arabia. The house is painted white. Temperatures in Saudi Arabia reach 50°C in the summer. In very hot countries like this, most houses are painted white. This is because white paint reflects the sun's rays and helps keep the houses cooler inside. Dark paint absorbs the heat from the sun and makes the houses even hotter.

2 **Your turn! Ask and answer.**

What's in your living room?

A sofa, two chairs, and a TV.

3 **Draw and say.**

This is my bedroom.
The _____ .

Video

Warm Up

- Hold up a photo of a room and describe it. For example, say *Look! A big, yellow sofa. Look! No TV in this living room.*
- Hold up other photos and have students describe them. Then say *Today's video is about homes.*

- Have students open their books to p. 64. Direct students' attention to the three photos at the top. Point to the three people one at a time and say their names. Then point to the three photos at the bottom. Say *Look! Three houses. One, two, three.*
- Read aloud the instructions and play **Video 7** from beginning to end. Have students match the photos with the three numbers and names at the top and write the numbers in the boxes.
- Pause **Video 7** after Rhiane says *Books are on the table* and ask *Where are the books?* (on the table) Continue and pause again at the end of segment 1 and ask *Is there a TV in this room?* (no) Pause after Pablo says *A table and five chairs* and ask *How many chairs?* (five) Then pause again after he says *The living room has a big, brown sofa* and ask *What color's the sofa?* (brown) Play and then pause again after Rafi says *But not this big* and ask *Is this house small?* (No, it's big.) Play and pause again after he says *It has three chairs* and ask *How many sofas are in this living room?* (two)
- **Extra Challenge** Before students watch **Video 7**, have them think of all the words the speakers might use to describe the houses in the photos. Write the word *colors* on the board and have students suggest colors. Then write *rooms* and have students name the rooms of a house. Then ask *What's in the rooms?* and have students name items of furniture and other objects, such as *a clock.*
- **Extra Support** Before students watch **Video 7**, have them guess whose house is shown in each photo. Point to the photo on the left and say *Rhiane is from Argentina. Is this a house in her country?* Encourage students to raise their hands and say *Yes, it is* if they think it is a house in Argentina. Repeat with Pablo and Spain, and with Rafi and Saudi Arabia. Do not tell students the answers at this point.

*The script for **Video 7** is available on the Teacher's Resource Website.*

- Read aloud the instructions. Call on two students to act out the example conversation in front of the class.
- Put students into pairs to ask and answer questions about their living rooms. Monitor students while they speak and help when necessary.
- Complete the activity by asking students about their partner's living room. For example, point to a student and then to his/her partner and ask *What's in [his] living room?* Have students tell the class about their partner's living room.

Optional Activity

- Divide students into pairs or small groups. Have them look at the photos in Activity 1 again one at a time and say what's in the living room. For example, point to the photo in the middle and ask *What's in the living room?* Play **Video 7** again if necessary so that students can remind themselves.
- Check answers as a class. Again, point to each photo one at a time and ask *What's in the living room?* Play **Video 7** again so that students can check their answers.

- Read aloud the instructions. Use the board to demonstrate. Draw a picture of a bedroom. Draw the bed next to the window. Point to the bedroom and say *This is my bedroom. The bed is next to the window.*
- Have students work individually to draw their bedroom. When they finish, have them walk around with their books and show their picture to their classmates. Have them describe their bedroom.

Wrap Up

- Put students into three groups and give each group a name (Rhiane, Pablo, Rafi). Have each group work together to say everything they remember about their person's video segment and the home mentioned.
- Call on one person from each group to tell the rest of the class what they remember. If necessary, write the first words of some sentences on the board as support. For example, write *[Rhiane]'s house is in… The house is… We can see a… In the [living room], there's a… It's [color].,* etc.
- NOTE: Have students bring in a doll or teddy bear for the Optional Activity in Review: Units 5–6. You may also wish to contact parents to ask them to send in a doll or teddy bear with their child.

Function 2: Classroom language 2

Warm Up

- Review the words for classroom objects. Give students instructions and have them listen and follow. For example, say *Hold up a pencil.* Repeat with *red crayon* and *eraser.* Then say *Point to a bag.* Repeat with *pencil case* and *desk.* Then say *Touch a book.* Repeat with *pen* and *ruler.*
- Direct students' attention to the green functions box. Say *Today we're going to learn words for speaking with other students in the classroom.* Read aloud the expressions, pausing to have students repeat each one.

- Read aloud the instructions. Point to the conversation. Ask *Who is speaking?* (Gil and Sandra) Say *Gil and Sandra are classmates.* Hold up a copy of the Student's Book, point to the first space with your finger, and ask *What's the missing word?* (together) Point to the expression in the green box as a reminder.
- Play **TR: 98** to the end. Have students listen to the conversation and follow in their books. Play **TR: 98** twice if necessary. Have students write the missing words the second time they hear them.
- **Extra Challenge** Have students try to complete the spaces before they listen. Have them do this in pairs orally, without writing anything. Then have them listen and do the activity as outlined above.
- **Extra Support** Provide students with two or three options for each space. Write them on the board before starting the activity. For example, for the first space, *together/turns/first;* for the second space, *first/turns/turn.*

- Read aloud the instructions. Play **TR: 99** for students to check their answers. Then divide students into two groups (Gil and Sandra). Play **TR: 99** again, pausing after each line so that students can read them aloud.

Optional Activity

- Have a student come to the front to model the conversation again with you. Sit down next to the student and make sure you have a book, a pencil, and an eraser on the desk. Read aloud the conversation with the student, sounding as natural as possible and using the classroom objects to help you act out the conversation.
- Put students into pairs to read the conversation. Explain that they should read the lines but change the names to their own names. Encourage students to make their conversations as natural as possible and to use a real book, eraser, and pencil. Monitor students as they read, helping when necessary and praising students' efforts.

- Read aloud the instructions. Point to item 1 and read aloud the question. Circle the correct option with your finger so that students can see the example. Have two students repeat the question and the response.
- Have students complete the activity in pairs. Check answers. Read aloud the first sentence each time and have students give the correct response as a class.

Wrap Up

- Have students act out conversations using the expressions in Activity 3. Have a few pairs act out their conversations for the rest of the class, using classroom objects as props.
- Have students work out short conversations for the unused options in Activity 3. Give an example for item 1. Say *This is a ruler.* Then say *Can you see This is... in the conversation in Activity 1? Yes. This is a cat.* Elicit and write a conversation and the names of two students on the board *[Matteo]: Let's take turns. You first.* and below *[Gianni]: Number 1. This is a ruler.* Have these two students read aloud the conversation. Then have students work out and practice conversations for the other three unused options.
- NOTE: Have students bring in a doll or teddy bear for the Optional Activity in Review: Units 5–6. You may also wish to contact parents to ask them to send in a doll or teddy bear with their child.

Function 2: Classroom language 2 (student to student)

> Let's work together.
>
> Let's take turns.
>
> Me/You first.
>
> It's my/your turn.
>
> Can I borrow…?
>
> Please pass (the book).
>
> Yes, here.
>
> Sorry, no.

1 **Listen and complete.** 🎧 TR: 98

Gil: Hi, Sandra. Let's work __together__ . Where's the activity?

Sandra: It's on page 20. It's Activity 3.

Gil: OK. Let's take __turns__ . Me __first__ . Number 1. This is a cat.

Sandra: Yes. It's __my turn__ . Number 2. This is a monkey.

Gil: Can we write the answers in the book?

Sandra: Yes. Look!

Gil: Can I __borrow__ a pencil?

Sandra: Yes, __here__ .

Gil: Thank you. Oh no! This isn't correct. Please __pass__ the eraser.

2 **Listen again and check.** 🎧 TR: 99

3 **Read and circle.**

1. Can I borrow a ruler?

   (A.) Sorry, no.

   B. This is a ruler.

2. Please pass the book.

   A. It's on page 20.

   (B.) Yes, here.

3. Let's take turns.

   A. Please pass the ruler.

   (B.) OK, you first.

4. Let's work together.

   A. No, you first.

   (B.) OK. Let's take turns.

Animals in the Savanna, Africa

In this lesson, students will:

- watch a video about animals in the savanna in Africa.
- use new words to talk about animals.
- make a cutout monkey and then a class monkey mobile.
- present a project to the class.

Resources: Video 8, Classroom Presentation Tool, Project Guide, Workbook p. 53, Online Practice

Materials: a world map; photos of an elephant, a monkey, a lion (both male and female), a zebra, and a meerkat; modeling clay; tape or sticky tack; thick white paper (one sheet per student); scissors; crayons or markers; a coat hanger

ABOUT THE VIDEO

The savanna is a biome, a large community of flora and fauna that occupies a specific habitat. It has two seasons, one very dry and the other very wet. A savanna lies between a forest and a grassland. The biggest area of savanna is in Africa. There are others in Australia, India, and South America. The savanna has few trees and a lot of grass. This makes it an ideal place for grazing animals like elephants and zebras. These animals are herbivores. Because of their presence, other animals, like lions, which are carnivores, are attracted to the savanna as a place to find food. The savanna in Africa is an important tourist attraction because people enjoy coming to see the animals.

Warm Up

- Write the words *Animals in the African savanna* on the board. Say *Today, we're going on a school trip. We're going to the savanna in Africa.* To teach the meaning of *Africa,* show Africa on a world map. Say *The savanna is a big place where animals live.*

- Say *Let's think about the savanna in Africa. What animals can we see?* Have students make suggestions and write each animal word on the board. Accept any reasonable ideas.

- Leave the list on the board. Say *Today we're watching a video of animals in the savanna in Africa. Let's see the animals in the video.*

Introduce the Theme

- Have students open their books to pp. 66–67. Read aloud the title. Hold up a copy of the Student's Book and point to the lion. Ask *Look at this animal. What is it?* Teach the word *lion* if necessary. Say *Lions live in the African savanna. Other animals live in the savanna, too.*

- Read aloud the instructions and point to the three questions. Then read aloud the first question. Ask *What's the answer? Big or small?* (big) *That's right. It's big.* Then read aloud the second question. Draw a tail on the board and point to the tail. Say *Look. It's a tail. Do you have a tail?* Look behind yourself, laugh, shake your head, and say *I don't have a tail.* Then point to the lion and ask *Does a lion have a tail?* (yes)

- Read aloud the third question. Point to your hair and then the lion's hair. Say *Look at this lion's hair. Yes, this lion is a dad.* You might like to show students a photo of a female lion to show the difference.

- **Extra Support** Give students an extra question clue for each question. Before question 1, ask *Is an eraser big or small?* (small) Before question 2, ask *Do you have a tail?* (no) Before question 3, say *Look at the photo. Which lions have hair like this, boys or girls?* (boys)

- Say *Let's visit the savanna in Africa.* Read aloud the instructions. Then hold up a copy of the Student's Book and point to the box of animal words. Read aloud the words and hold up a photo of each animal as you say it. Then play **Video 8** once.

- Play **Video 8** again and pause after the narrator says *Look! What can you see in the tree?* and ask *What can you see?* (a monkey) Continue playing the video and pause after the narrator says *This is Mom. Can you see the baby?* Ask some questions. For example, ask *How many monkeys can you see?* (two) *Can you see Mom? Can you see the baby? Do you like the monkeys?* Guide students back to the word box on the page and have them circle the word *monkeys.*

- Continue playing **Video 8** and pause again after the narrator says *This is a family of lions.* Ask *How many lions can you see?* (three) Guide students back to the word box on the page and have them circle the word *lions.*

- Continue playing **Video 8** and pause again after the narrator says *Can you see the tails?* Say *Point to the lion's tail.* Ask *How many tails can you see?* (two) Continue playing **Video 8** and pause again after the narrator says *This is a family of meerkats.* Ask *How many meerkats can you see?* (five) Guide students back to the word box on the page and have them circle the word *meerkats.*

- Continue playing **Video 8**. Then play the video again and have students check their answers. To review answers, read aloud each animal word one at a time and have students say *yes* or *no.*

Script for Video 8

Let's go on a trip to Africa.
This is the savanna. Can you see the trees? Let's look at the animals!
Look! What can you see in the tree? Monkeys! This is Mom. Can you see the baby? Mom has a long tail! The baby has a long tail, too. Goodbye, monkeys!
Let's look at another animal family. Look! This is a family of lions. The big lion is the dad. He has a big mouth. There are two baby lions. One, two. A baby lion is called a cub. A lion has a long tail. Can you see the tails? Goodbye, lions!
Let's look at another animal family. Look! This is a family of meerkats. Meerkats are funny. A meerkat can stand on two legs. Look! It has big eyes. How many meerkats can you see? Let's count. One, two, three, four, five. Five meerkats! A meerkat has a long tail, too. Goodbye, meerkats!
A monkey has a long tail. A lion has a long tail. And a meerkat has a long tail, too!

- Ask *Is the savanna in Africa cool? What do you think?* Listen to several students' responses before beginning the activity.
- Read aloud the instructions. Then read aloud the first sentence, saying both options. Say *Remember the video. What word is it,* dad *or* mom*?* (mom) *That's right. We circle the word* mom. Review prepositions if necessary. Then allow time for students to complete the activity on their own.
- Have students compare their answers with a partner. To review their work, read each sentence aloud with the correct word.
- **Extra Challenge** Have students work in pairs to make their own sentences. Have them take turns to say something they saw in the video.

Optional Activity

- Have students make clay animals and then talk about them. Before handing out the modeling clay, have students think about the animal they are going to make. Show them the animal photos and ask *Which animal are you going to make?*
- Give students clay for their animals and tell them how much time they have. Then, when everyone finishes, have each student hold up their animal one at a time. Have them say what animal it is and then say two or three sentences to describe it.

4 Project

- Direct students' attention to the blue project box at the bottom of p. 67. Read aloud the instructions and make sure that students have the necessary materials to make a monkey: thick white paper, a pencil, scissors, and crayons or markers.
- Give each student a copy of the project guide or display the instructions. Say *Let's make monkeys. Look!* Hold up a copy of the monkey template and say *It's a monkey.* Then,

give each student a copy of the monkey template. Hold up a pair of scissors and say *Let's cut.* Have students cut out the monkey template. Walk around to provide help as needed. (NOTE: If you think this will be too difficult for your students to cut out independently, cut out five or six monkeys before class begins for students to trace.)

- After students finish cutting out the template, model putting the cut-out shape on the thick paper and tracing it with a pencil. To do this, use tape or sticky tack to put a piece of thick white paper on the board. Hold up the template to the paper, and show students how to trace around it. Then say *Now you trace.*
- When students finish tracing, say *Now let's cut out our monkeys.* Walk around the room as students trace and cut, offering help as needed.
- Read aloud Step 4 and point to the picture on the project guide. Say *Draw the monkey's face. Two small eyes, a nose, and a big mouth.* Do a drawing action so that students understand. Then have students color the monkey.
- Read aloud Step 5. Ask *What's your monkey's name?* Have each student say their monkey's name before writing it on the monkey.
- When students' monkeys are finished, have individual students present their projects to the class, saying *This is my monkey. Its name is [Joey].*
- Point to the picture of the monkey mobile at the bottom of the project guide. Say *Look! This is a monkey mobile. Let's make a monkey mobile.* Hang a monkey from a coat hanger and hang the coat hanger from a high spot in the classroom. Then add the monkeys, one at a time, hooking each bent hand over a bent foot. You may need to create three or four mobiles for your class. Leave the monkey mobiles on display and use them to review numbers and counting, colors, and body parts.
- To assess the project, check that students followed directions and worked neatly and efficiently. You may also want to offer points for creativity. Be certain to explain feedback orally so that students understand why they are receiving the grade they're getting.

Wrap Up

- Write these words from this video on the board: *lion, monkey, meerkat, savanna,* and *tail.* Point to the first word, *lion,* and call on a student to use that word in a sentence about the video, such as *A lion is an animal.* Then call on a different student to give another sentence using the same word, such as *The dad lion is in the video.*
- Continue until students make at least two sentences using each word. Repeat this with each of the words. Challenge the class to go beyond two sentences if possible.
- NOTE: Have students bring in a doll or teddy bear for the Optional Activity in the next lesson. You may also wish to contact parents to ask them to send in a doll or teddy bear with their child.

Additional Practice: Workbook p. 53, Online Practice

1 **BEFORE YOU WATCH** Look at the photo.
Answer.

1. This is a lion. Is it big or small?
   big
2. Does a lion have a tail?
   yes
3. Is this lion a mom or a dad?
   a dad

2 **WHILE YOU WATCH** Watch and circle.

▶ Video 8

elephants (monkeys) (lions)
zebras (meerkats)

3 **AFTER YOU WATCH** Read and circle.

1. The monkeys are a **dad** / (**mom**) and
   a baby.

2. They are (**in a tree**) / **next to a house**.

3. The baby lions are with a (**dad**) / **mom**.

4. **Four** / (**Five**) meerkats are in the video.

4 **PROJECT** Draw and color a monkey.
Then make a class monkey mobile.

This monkey's
name is Joe!

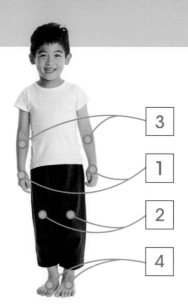

1 Read and number.

1. These are my hands.

2. These are my legs.

3. These are my arms.

4. These are my feet.

3

1

2

4

2 Complete the chart. Use the words in the box.

bed   cabinet   shower   TV

bedroom	bathroom	living room	kitchen
bed	shower	TV	cabinet

3 Write *has* or *doesn't have*.

1. She _____has_____ brown hair.

2. She __doesn't have__ brown eyes.

3. He _____has_____ brown hair.

4. He _____has_____ brown eyes.

4 Listen and circle. 🎧 TR: 100

1. Where's the boy?

    A.    B.

2. Where's the girl?

    A.    B.

3. Where's the cabinet?

    A.    B.

4. Where's the clock?

    A.    B.

In this lesson, students will:

• review words and grammar from Units 5 and 6.

Resources: Audio Track 100, Script for TR: 100, Classroom Presentation Tool, Workbook pp. 54–55, Workbook Audio Track 36, Online Practice

Materials: students' own dolls or teddy bears

Warm Up

• Have students work in pairs to review the language from Units 5 and 6. Have each pair share a book and take turns to point and say something about each page.

• Hold up a copy of the Student's Book open to p. 68. Read aloud the instructions. Direct students' attention to the example.

• Have students work individually to complete the activity. Check answers. Read aloud each sentence and have students respond with a number.

Optional Activity

• Have students bring a favorite doll or teddy bear into class. Have them take turns to hold up their doll and describe its features using *has* and *doesn't have*.

• Read aloud the instructions. Hold up a copy of the Student's Book and show students the word box and the chart. Point to the word *bed* in the box and say *Look! Bed.* Then point again to the chart and read aloud the four headings. Ask *Where can we see a bed?* (in a bedroom) Direct students' attention to the example in the first column.

• Have students work individually to complete the chart. Then check answers. Say each room and have students call out the item of furniture that belongs in that room.

• Read aloud the instructions. Have students work individually to complete the activity. Then check answers.

Task Guidance Notes

Starters Listening Part 3 Students have to listen to five short, separate conversations and choose the correct answer from three pictures for each question. The pictures might be very similar, so they need to listen for detail. This tests understanding of specific information.

Challenges Students worry about listening for differences when the pictures are similar. They tend to choose their answer at the first mention of something they hear. Each question tells them what to focus on.

Performance Descriptors

• Can understand very simple spoken descriptions
• Can understand very short conversations

• **Collaborate** Have students in pairs look at all the photos, think about which room each photo shows, and what they can see in each photo. (NOTE: There are only four different photos.) See which pair can get the most words. Share ideas with the class and write words on the board.

• This activity practices listening for differences. Make sure students understand the instructions. Play the first segment of **TR: 100** and make sure that students understand why B is correct.

• Play **TR: 100** to the end. Have students complete the activity individually. Play **TR: 100** again for students to check their answers. Check answers with the class.

• **Reflect** Have students in pairs look at the script and find/ underline the words that give the answer to each question. Check ideas with the class.

Script for TR: 100

1. **A:** *Where's the boy?*
   B: *I don't know. He isn't in the kitchen.*
   A: *Is he in the bedroom?*
   B: *Yes, he is.*
2. **A:** *Where's the girl?*
   B: *I don't know. Is she in the kitchen?*
   A: *No, she isn't.*
   B: *What about the bathroom? Is she in the bathroom?*
   A: *Yes, she is!*
3. **A:** *Where's the cabinet?*
   B: *I don't know. Is it in the living room?*
   A: *The living room? No, it isn't. It's in the bathroom.*
4. **A:** *Where's the clock?*
   B: *I don't know. Is it in the living room?*
   A: *No, it isn't.*
   B: *Where is it?*
   A: *It's in the bedroom.*
   B: *Oh, yes!*

Wrap Up

• Give each of the following instructions one at a time and allow students thinking time before answering. Elicit the answers from the class, choosing a different student each time.
1. *Name five parts of your head and face, and five parts of your body.*
2. *Name four rooms in a house and name one thing in each room.*
3. *Describe a classmate using* He/She has *and* He/She doesn't have.
4. *Say where three objects in the classroom are using* in, on, next to, *and* under.

Additional Practice: Workbook pp. 54–55, Online Practice

UNIT
7 My Town

In this unit, students will:

- talk about places in a town.
- say what is in a town using *There's a*.
- read about a model town.
- describe where things are in a town using *There's a* and *There are*.
- listen to and sing a song about a town.
- identify and pronounce CVC words with /æ/ in the middle.
- watch a video about cities in other countries.
- identify the value of loving your town.

Language

Words

library, park, playground, store, street, swimming pool, town center, zoo; flower, model, real, tiny

Grammar

- *There's a store on the street.
  There's a library in the town center.*
- *There's a tree in the park.*
- *There are houses next to the park.*

Phonics

/æ/ *bag, bat, jam, man, map*

Twenty-First Century Skills

Collaboration
Take turns to talk about the classroom, Lesson 4

Communication
Describe a photo of a town, Lesson 3

Creativity
Draw and speak about places in your town, Lesson 7

Critical Thinking
Identify the value of loving your town, Lesson 5

In the Unit Opener, students will:

- respond to a photo of children in Japan.
- locate places in a town on a map.

Resources: Home School Connection Letter, Classroom Presentation Tool

Materials: a simple map of your town, sticky tack, drawing paper, crayons

Introduce the Theme

- Display a simple map of your town in the classroom, where all students can see it. Show students and say *This is [name of your town]. This is our town.* Point out the location of your school. Say *Look! Our school.*
- Point out other familiar places in town without saying the target words in Lesson 1. Point and say *Look!* each time. Have students find street names and features on the map and start thinking about their town.
- Give students drawing paper and crayons. Say *Draw our town.* Allow students several minutes to draw a picture of their town. You may choose to draw your own picture to show them as an example. Then, call on students to hold up their drawings, one at a time. Say encouraging things about them, such as *Wow! I like your town. Look! Our school. This is great!*
- Say *Think about our town. Is it big or small? Do you like our town?* Listen to several students' responses.

Use the Photo

- Have students open their books to p. 69. Read aloud the instructions at the bottom of the page and point to one of the children in the photo. Ask *Is it a man?* (no) *Is it a woman?* (no) *Is it a child?* (yes) Ask *How many children can you see?* (three) *Are they friends?* (yes) *Are they happy?* (yes)

- Point to different things in the photo, such as a bag, a face, a nose, a mouth. For each item, ask *What's this?* Repeat with plural items (eyes, ears, etc.) and ask *What are these?* Call on different students to respond.

TEACHER TIP

It's important to have clear rules in the classroom. Rules protect a student's right to learn and to enjoy the experience. They also protect a teacher's right to teach. Rules should be positive, telling students what to do, with the goals of eliciting good, on-task behavior. For example, rules should be *Listen to the teacher, Stay in your seat, Be kind to your classmates,* and so on. Avoid telling children what *not* to do. Make sure you define each rule during the first few lessons. Model good behavior and be consistent.

My Town

Children in Japan

Look at the photo. What can you see?

1 Words

1 Listen and point. 🎧 TR: 101

library

park

playground

store

street

swimming pool

town center

zoo

2 Listen and repeat. 🎧 TR: 102

3 Point and say.

It's a street.

It's a library.

Words

In this lesson, students will:
- talk about places in a town.
- make a poster of a town.

Resources: Audio Tracks 101–102, Classroom Presentation Tool, Flashcards 107–114, Workbook p. 56, Workbook Audio Track 37, Online Practice

Materials: colored paper, photos of places in towns from the Internet or from magazines, large pieces of paper (one per group of four students), glue

Warm Up

- Write the name of the town where your school is located on the board. Point and say *This school is in [town].* Write more names of towns that students know on the board. Point and say *[Town name] is a town.* Ask *Do you know a town?* Elicit the names of different towns students know.
- **Use the Photo** Have students open their books to pp. 70–71. Point to the photo and ask *Is this a town?* (yes) *That's right! It's a colorful town! This town has colorful buildings.* Point to different parts of the photo and ask *What color is this?* Finish and ask *Do you like this town?* Have students answer *yes* or *no.*

- Read aloud the instructions. Then direct students' attention to the eight small photos.
- Point to your ear and say *Let's listen.* Play **TR: 101** and point to the photos, one at a time, as you hear the words.
- Use the flashcards to present the new words. Hold up the *library* flashcard and say *Look! A library. You can read books in a library.* Then, ask *Is there a library in our town?* Gesture to the whole class with your arm to clarify the meaning of *our.* Hold up the *park* flashcard and say *Look! A park. You can play in a park.* Again, ask if this place is in your town. Hold up the *playground* flashcard and say *Look! A playground. You can play in a playground.* Ask *Is there a playground at our school?* Hold up the *store* flashcard and say *Look! A store. You can buy things in a store.* Ask *Is there a store next to our school?* Hold up the *street* flashcard and say *Look! A street. This school is on [name] street.* Hold up the *swimming pool* flashcard and say *Look! A swimming pool.* Do a swimming action and ask *Is there a swimming pool in our town?* Hold up the *town center* flashcard and say *Look! The town center.* Walk to the center of the classroom and say *This is the center of the classroom. Center* means middle. Hold up the *zoo* flashcard and say *Look! A zoo. You can see animals in a zoo.* Ask *Is there a zoo in our town?*
- Play **TR: 101** a second time. Walk around the classroom to make sure students are pointing to the correct photos.

- Read aloud the instructions. Play **TR: 102.** Pause after the first word to model repeating for students. Continue playing **TR: 102,** having students repeat the words as a class.
- Play **TR: 102** again and call on individual students around the class to repeat the words.
- **Extra Support** Hold up the corresponding flashcard as you hear each item on **TR: 102.**

- Review the words. Say a prompt for each place and have students call out the word. For example, say *Read a book* (library), *Play soccer* (park), *Climb with your friends* (playground), *Buy a toy* (store), *Walk* (street), *Play in water* (swimming pool), *Look around* (town center), *See animals* (zoo).
- Read aloud the instructions. Direct students' attention to the models. Point and say the sentences.
- Put students into pairs, A and B. Have Student A point to a photo and have Student B say a sentence. Have students take turns to point and say until all the photos have been used.
- **Extra Challenge** Put students into pairs, A and B. Have the B students cover the words under the first pair of photos (*library, park*) with a piece of colored paper. Then have Student A point to one of these photos and have Student B say *This is a [library].* Have students take turns to cover the words under the pairs of photos, and point and say until all the photos have been used.

Optional Activity

- Have students work in groups of four to make a poster of a town. Have them draw and cut out different places and/or use photos from the Internet or from magazines. Have them display the places on a large piece of paper with the town center in the middle. Draw a sign on the board for them to copy: *Welcome to [name of town].*

Wrap Up

- Hold up each flashcard one at a time and have students say the word aloud. Clap the same number of syllables. If necessary say *Listen! Store* (one clap), *playground* (two claps). Then, have students work in pairs, saying each word aloud, counting the syllables and clapping the appropriate number of times.

Additional Practice: Workbook p. 56, Online Practice

Grammar

In this lesson, students will:

• say what's in a town using *There's a.*

• say a chant.

Resources: Audio Tracks 103–104, Classroom Presentation Tool, Flashcards 107–114, Workbook p. 57, Workbook Audio Track 38, Online Practice

Materials: sticky tack, colored paper, building blocks

Warm Up

• Review the words from Lesson 1. Draw a fictitious town on the board. Build it up item by item. Start by drawing a street, a park, a playground, and buildings. On the buildings, draw symbols to show what they are (a book for the library, a loaf of bread for the store, a monkey for the zoo, water for the swimming pool, and so on). As you draw each place, pause and ask *What's this?* Call on a student to think of a name for the town and write it as a heading.

• Display the Lesson 1 flashcards on the board. Have students open their books to p. 71. Direct students' attention to the chant. Ask students to find two of the words in the chant. Have students scan the text to find the words in the chant. Then, have an individual come to the board and point to the *street* flashcard and the *store* flashcard.

• Read aloud the instructions. At the same time, point to the chant. Say *Listen to the chant.* Play **TR: 103.** Have students listen to the chant and clap to the rhythm.

• Play **TR: 103** again. This time, encourage students to do actions when they hear the words *street* (walk their fingers on their desk) and *store* (hand over money and buy something).

• **Extra Support** Point to the chant and count aloud the lines. Have students notice which lines in the chant are the same. Say *1 There's a street, a street, a street in the town.* Then ask *Is line 2 the same?* (no) *Is line 3 the same?* (no) Repeat with lines 4 and 5. Then read aloud line 2, etc. Have students use highlighters to color the lines of the chant that are the same (1 and 5; 2 and 4).

• Read aloud the instructions. Direct students' attention to the grammar box. Play **TR: 104.** Have students listen and read. Play **TR: 104** again and have students repeat the sentences as a class.

• Display the *zoo* flashcard on the board. Point to the animal in the zoo. Say *Look! There's an animal in the zoo.* Point to the animal again. Under the flashcard, write *There's an animal in the zoo.* Read the sentence aloud, emphasizing the contraction in *There's.* If students ask, point to the animal and say *Lion. This is a lion. There's a lion in the zoo.* Read the sentence on the board aloud, emphasizing the contraction in *There's.* Point to the apostrophe. On the board, write *There's = There is.*

• Point to a few things in the classroom and say *Look! There's a [board] in the classroom.* Repeat with *poster* and *girl.* Emphasize the contracted form each time. Call on students to point to things and say *There's a [desk] in the classroom.*

• Point to the first picture and ask *Is it a library?* (No, it isn't. It's a swimming pool.) Point to the second picture and ask *Is it a park?* (No, it isn't. It's a store.) Point to the third picture and ask *Is it a boy?* (No, it isn't. It's a girl.) Point to the fourth picture and ask *Is it a street?* (No, it isn't. It's a playground.)

• Point to the sentences below the pictures. Direct students' attention to the example in the first sentence and read it aloud.

• Have students complete the other sentences, while you monitor, encouraging and helping when necessary.

• Have students cover the sentences with a piece of paper. Read aloud each sentence again in random order, and have students point to the corresponding picture. (Or have students do this in pairs.)

• **Extra Challenge** Have students work in pairs. Have them cover the sentences below the pictures with a piece of colored paper and try to remember them. Have them say aloud each sentence from memory, and then look and check.

• **Extra Support** Before students start writing, make sure they realize that sentences 3 and 4 don't include *'s* and that they have to write it.

Optional Activity

• Give students some building blocks and have them build a street in groups. Then call on students to say what's on their street. Have them point to each block one at a time and say *There's a [library]. It's [green and red].*

Wrap Up

• Divide the class into pairs. Have students write another line for the chant, such as *There's a monkey, a monkey, a monkey in the zoo, There's a bus, a bus, a bus in the town center.* Have pairs chant their lines, one at a time.

Additional Practice: Workbook p. 57, Online Practice

Grammar

1 **Listen and chant.** 🎧 TR: 103

There's a street, a street, a street in the town.
There's a store, a store, a store on the street.
There's a girl, a girl, a girl in the store.
There's a store, a store, a store on the street.
There's a street, a street, a street in the town.

2 **Listen and read.** 🎧 TR: 104

> There's a store on the street.
> There's a library in the town center.

3 **Write.**

1. ___There___'s a swimming pool in the park.

2. ___There___'s a store on the street.

3. ___There's___ a girl in the store.

4. ___There's___ a boy on the playground.

3 Reading

1 Listen and repeat. 🎧 TR: 105

> real   model   tiny   flower

2 Listen and read. 🎧 TR: 106

Look at the photo! It's a town. Is it a **real** town? No, it isn't. It's a **model**. It's a toy town. The houses and stores are small. They're **tiny**!

Can you see the boy? He's real. Can you see the **flowers**, too? They're big and yellow. Are they real—or are they models?

Look at the trees. Are they big or small? They're models.

This model town is cool!

3 Read again. Complete the sentences.

1. This town is a __model__ .

2. The __houses__ and stores are small.

3. The __boy__ is real.

4. The __flowers__ are yellow.

5. The __trees__ are small.

ABOUT THE PHOTO

The photo shows the model town, Madurodam, in The Hague, the Netherlands. It is a popular tourist attraction with replicas of famous Dutch buildings and monuments, including museums, ports, and windmills. The park opened in 1952. Since then, tens of millions of people have visited Madurodam.

Reading

LESSON 3

In this lesson, students will:
- read about a model town.
- use new words to talk about a town.
- complete sentences about the text.

Resources: Audio Tracks 105–106, Classroom Presentation Tool, Workbook p. 58, Workbook Audio Track 39, Online Practice

Materials: a bag, modeling clay

Warm Up

- **Use the Photo** Have students open their books to pp. 72–73. Direct students' attention to the photo. Say *What's this? It's a town.* Give instructions. Say *Point to the boy. Point to a tree.* Then say *Point to something white.* Repeat with other colors.

- Read aloud the instructions. Play **TR: 105** and have students listen and repeat the words. Then use actions and descriptions to teach the new words.

- Hold up a real pencil and say *Look! A pencil. This is a real pencil.* Emphasize *real.* Draw a picture of a pencil on the board and say *Look! A pencil.* Point to the drawing and say *This isn't a real pencil. This is* not *a real pencil.*

- Point to the photo of the model town and ask *Is this a real town?* (no) Ask *Is this a drawing of a town?* (no) Point again and say *This is a* model *of a town.* Emphasize *model.*

- Draw two flowers on the board, one big and one small. Point to the big flower and say *Look! It's a flower.* Emphasize *flower.* Ask *Is it big or small?* (big) Then ask *How many flowers?* (two) Point to the small flower and ask *Is this flower big or small?* (small) Now draw a tiny flower. Point to the three flowers one at a time and say *Look! A big flower, a small flower, and a* tiny *flower.* Emphasize *tiny.*

- Point to the text and say *Find the words here.* Have students scan the text to find the four new words.

- Read aloud the instructions. Point to the text and play **TR: 106.** Have students listen to and read the whole text.

- Play **TR: 106** again, pausing after the first paragraph. Point to the photo and ask *Is this a photo?* (yes) *Is this a town?* (yes) *Is this a real town?* (no) *Is it a model?* (yes) *Are the houses big?* (no) *Are they tiny?* (yes) Continue playing **TR: 106,** pausing after the second paragraph. Ask questions about the paragraph.

- Have students read the text again silently, taking their time to make sure they understand it.

- **Reading Strategy: Focusing on Key Words** While reading a text for the first time, have students focus on key words such as nouns, verbs, and adjectives and not worry about smaller words. This will help them locate the main points of a text.

- **Extra Challenge** Have students read aloud the text in pairs. Have one student read and pause after each question. Have the other student answer the question.

- **Extra Support** Read the text again. Point to parts of the photo as you mention the things, nod and shake your head when there are questions and answers, and demonstrate the meaning of the adjectives (*small, tiny,* etc.).

Task Guidance Notes
Starters Reading & Writing Part 5 Students have to look at three pictures which tell a story and read questions. They then have to write one-word answers. Each picture has one or two questions. The questions usually relate to <u>where</u> people or objects are or <u>what</u> they are doing and includes some numbers. This tests students' knowledge of question forms, words, prepositions, and activity verbs.

Challenges Students can feel overwhelmed by the amount they have to read and write. Help them to understand that they can look at each picture in isolation and that there are only one or two questions per picture. Help them break the questions/sentences down into key words, for example, <u>What</u> are the <u>children</u> <u>playing</u> with?

Performance Descriptors
- Can read and understand questions
- Can spell some simple words correctly
- Can write the letters of the English alphabet

- **Collaborate** Ask students to cover the text and look at the photo. Ask *What can you see?* Do an example. Write *town* on the board. Ask *Is it big?* (no) *Are houses in the town?* (yes) Then write *small* and *houses* next to *town.* Ask students in pairs to do the same with all the words they know to describe towns. Check words and extra information with the class and make a list on the board.

- Make sure students understand the instructions and direct their attention to the example. Ask students to underline important words in the sentences (*1. town 2. The, stores, small 3. The, real 4. The, yellow 5. The, small*). Then have them read the text again individually, and complete the activity.

- Have students check with another pair. Then check answers with the class.

- **Own It!** Have students write one or more sentences of their own about the photo. Have them check with a classmate. Have them read the sentence(s) aloud to the class.

Optional Activity

- Write nouns from Units 1–7 on strips of paper so that there is a different word for each student. Put the strips of paper in a bag and have each student take a word. Give students some modeling clay and have them use the clay to make a model of the item on their paper. When they finish, have them hold up their clay model for the class to guess what it is.

Wrap Up

- Put students into groups of four. Give each group a word (real, model, tiny, flower). Give groups two minutes to make sentences using their word. Ask each group to appoint a leader to say their sentences to the rest of the class.

Additional Practice: Workbook p. 58, Online Practice

Grammar

Warm Up

• Stand at the front of the class. Look around the classroom and gesture to show you are thinking. For example, if you use a whiteboard, say *There's a [white] thing in the classroom. It isn't small. It's big. What is it?* Have students raise their hands to guess what it is. Repeat with *table* and *poster* starting with *There's a…* each time and having students guess.

• Have students open their books to p. 73. Read aloud the instructions. Point to the grammar box and say *Listen.* Play **TR: 107**. Have students listen and read. Play **TR: 107** again and have students repeat the sentences, first as a class and then individually.

• Remove everything from your table so that the surface is clear. Then put a pencil on the table and say *There's a pencil on the table,* emphasizing *There's.* Have students repeat the sentence. On the board write *There's = There is.* Point and say *Look! There's means There is.* Ask *How many pencils?* (one)

• Put another pencil on the table so that there are two. Say *There are pencils on the table,* emphasizing *are* and the plural *s.* Have students repeat the sentence. Ask *How many pencils?* (two) Do the same with other objects (books, crayons, erasers).

• Point to the first picture and ask *What's this?* (a museum) Point to the second picture and ask *What are these?* (trees) Repeat for the last two pictures.

• Read aloud the instructions. Look at the first sentence with the class and direct students' attention to the example.

• Have students complete the activity on their own or in pairs. Then have individual students give the answers orally, reading aloud each completed sentence for the rest of the class to check.

• **Extra Support** Point to each picture and say what it is before students begin, being sure to point out singular and plural.

• Make sure students have a piece of paper or a notebook and a pencil. Read aloud the instructions. Then play **TR: 108** from beginning to end. Play **TR: 108** again, pausing after each instruction for students to draw.

• Have students compare their drawings in pairs. Then play **TR: 108** again, and draw the scene on the board for students to check their work.

• **Listening Strategy: Taking Notes** When students are listening for key information, it can be useful to take notes as they listen. Train students how to write notes, just one or two key words from a whole sentence. In this activity, have them actively listen carefully for the items they have to draw and any numbers. As they hear these words, have them write them on a piece of paper.

• **Extra Challenge** Have students work in pairs to describe their drawings. This means that they restate the audioscript in their own words.

Script for TR: 108
There are three trees. This is a park. Draw three trees in a park.
There are flowers in the park, too.
There's a boy in the park. There's a woman, too. She's with the boy. She's his mom.

• Read aloud the instructions. Direct students' attention to the models. Put your bag under a chair and model pointing and saying the first sentence. Then model the second sentence. If necessary, change this sentence so that it is about your classroom. For example, say *There's a cabinet under the window. There are two chairs next to the board.*

• Put students into pairs. Have students take turns to point and say something about the classroom using *There's* or *There are.*

Optional Activity

• Bring in some photos of outdoor scenes in cities or parks from the Internet or from magazines. Display one photo on the board and have students point and say *There's a…* and *There are…* to talk about what's in the photo.

• Set the timer for two minutes. Give each pair or small group of students a photo and have them talk about it. When the time is up, have students exchange photos and repeat the activity a few times.

Wrap Up

• Hold up your book open to p. 9. Say *There's a girl in the photo. There are orange hands.* Write these two sentences on the board. Then have students, in pairs, look back at the Unit Opener photos from Units 1–7. Have them write two sentences using *There's a* and *There are* for each photo. Then have them read aloud their sentences for the rest of the class to find the photo.

Grammar

1 **Listen and read.** 🎧 TR: 107

> There's a tree in the park.
> There are houses next to the park.

2 **Write *There's* or *There are*.**

1. ___There's___ a museum on the street.

2. ___There are___ trees in the park.

3. ___There's___ a playground next to the swimming pool.

4. ___There are___ stores in the town center.

3 **Listen and draw.** 🎧 TR: 108

4 **Point and say.**

There's a bag under the chair.

There are two cabinets next to the board.

UNIT 7   My Town   **73**

5 Song

1 Listen and read. 🎧 TR: 109

2 Listen and sing. 🎧 TR: 110 and 111

3 Sing and act. 🎧 TR: 112

ABOUT THE PHOTO

The photo shows a path in Ritsurin Garden, one of the most famous historical gardens in Japan. The garden is in the city of Takamatsu, in the southern part of the country. *Ritsurin* means "chestnut grove." The garden was created in the early seventeenth century and contains bridges, tea houses, lakes, a pavilion, and footpaths like the one in the photo. There are also small hills in the garden where people can stand and enjoy views across the garden and the surrounding scenery.

Chorus
This is my town!
Let's look around!

In the town center,
there's a pool.
And next to the library,
that's my school!
Chorus

There's a playground,
and there's a zoo
with monkeys and elephants
and zebras, too!
Chorus

Here in the park,
what can you see?
There are paths and fences,
and gardens with trees.
Chorus

VALUE Love your town.
Workbook, Lesson 6

LESSON 5 Song

In this lesson, students will:
- listen to and sing a song about a town.
- act out a song.
- identify the value of loving your town.

Resources: Audio Tracks 109–112; Classroom Presentation Tool; Flashcards 107–109, 112–114; Workbook p. 61; Online Practice

Materials: photos of students' town or town's website with photos of important places and buildings

Warm Up

- Play a memory game about a town. Say *In my town, there's a school.* Have a student repeat the sentence. Then indicate that this student should extend the sentence. Say *In my town, there's a school and….* Have the student complete the sentence, for example, *…a park.* Point to another student, and have this student repeat the sentence and add a third item, for example, *In my town, there's a school, a park, and a library.* Point to a few more students and have them repeat the sentence, adding one more item each time and remembering all the previous items. See if students can get at least eight words.

- **Use the Photo** Have students open their books to p. 74. Point to the photo. Make statements about the photo and have students say *True* or *False.* Say *This is a town center.* (false) *This is a park.* (true) *There are trees.* (true) *There are people.* (false)

1

- Have students say the new words they've learned so far in this unit. Write the words on the board as students say them. Point to the song and have students scan it to find any words that are on the board. (town center, [swimming] pool, library, playground, zoo) Have them say the words and check each one on the board as they say it.

- Read aloud the instructions. Play **TR: 109.** Have students listen and follow in their books.

- **Extra Support** Play **TR: 109** again and hold up the *town center* flashcard, the *swimming pool* flashcard, the *library* flashcard, the *zoo* flashcard and the *park* flashcard as each word is sung.

2

- Hold up a copy of the Student's Book open to p. 74 and point to the path in the photo. Say *Path,* write *path* on the board and have students repeat. Then, point to the fence and repeat. Then play **TR: 110.** Get a clapping or tapping rhythm going to accompany the song. Encourage students to sing along with the chorus.

- Play **TR: 111,** the instrumental version of the song, for students to sing.

3

- Read aloud each line of the song and demonstrate an action. Have students make the action, too.
  This is my town! (Hold out your hand with your arm extended to indicate the space around.)
  Let's look around! (Use an open hand above your eyes as you turn your head from side to side.)
  In the town center, (Point to a spot in the distance.)
  there's a pool. (Make a swimming action.)
  And next to the library, (Make a reading action)
  that's my school! (Gesture around the classroom.)
  There's a playground, (Make a climbing action.)
  and there's a zoo (Extend your arms to indicate a place.)
  with monkeys and elephants (Make a monkey action and move your arms like a trunk for elephants.)
  and zebras, too! (Make a galloping motion.)
  Here in the park, (Point your finger down to your feet to indicate *here.*)
  what can you see? (Shrug and then point to your eyes.)
  There are paths and fences, (Stretch your arms out, and move them in bends to indicate a path.)
  and gardens with trees. (Place your hands together, move them up and then separate them for *tree.*)

- Play **TR: 112,** pausing after each line to make sure everyone remembers the actions. You can change or simplify the actions if necessary.

- Play **TR: 112** again. Have students sing the song again and do the actions.

- **Extra Challenge** Put students into pairs, A and B. Have Student A do an action from the song and have Student B say the line of the song. Have them take turns acting and identifying.

- **Value: Love your town** At this point in the lesson, you can teach the value. Say *The value of this lesson is* Love your town. If possible, organize a walk around the town, and have students point out places they like. During the walk, model picking up litter, and ask *Is this good?* (yes) Then say *I love my town.* Then, pretend to do something harmful, such as dropping litter or similar, and ask *Is this bad?* (yes) *This is* not *how I love my town.* If it isn't possible to take a walk, show photos of places in your town that children will take an interest in. Also, look for appropriate photos of litter in a town, and point out that this is NOT a good way to love your town. For additional practice, have students complete Lesson 6 of the Workbook in class or at home.

Optional Activity

- Have students work in groups to draw an imaginary park. First, have them draw in groups. Then, have them hold up their drawings and describe them using *In the park, there's a…*

Wrap Up

- Sing the first line and part of the second line of the song, stopping before the last word, and calling on students to sing the missing word. Continue in this way until you've sung the entire song.

Additional Practice: Workbook p. 61, Online Practice

Phonics

In this lesson, students will:
- identify and pronounce CVC words with /æ/ in the middle.
- form three-letter words with the letter *a*.

Resources: Audio Tracks 113–115; Classroom Presentation Tool; Flashcards 20, 35, 51, 119–120; Workbook p. 60; Workbook Audio Track 41; Online Practice

Warm Up
- Play a drawing game with students. Begin drawing a bag on the board. Pause and ask *What is it?* Then continue drawing the bag, pause, and repeat the question. Continue until a student is able to guess what you're drawing. Do the same with drawings of a bat and a man. Then point and say Bag, bat, man. *Today we're learning words with the /æ/ sound in the middle.*

- Have students open their books to p. 75. Direct students' attention to the photos and words. Read aloud the instructions. Play **TR: 113**, pointing to each photo and word as students hear it.
- Play **TR: 113** again. Have students repeat each word. Monitor students carefully, making sure they pronounce the target sound (/æ/) correctly. Ask *What sound are we learning today?* (/æ/) Remind students that they are practicing this sound in the middle of words.
- Say *We're learning vowel sounds. Vowels are a, e, i, o, u. All other letters are consonants. B, c, d, k, and p are consonants.* Call on students to give additional examples of consonants. (NOTE: Students are practicing CVC words—words made up of a consonant, a vowel, and another consonant.)
- Have students say the alphabet and write it on the board, one letter at a time. Say *Vowel* and call on a student to say the first vowel. Underline the letter *a* in the alphabet on the board. Repeat with the other four vowels. Point to the letter *a* again and say *This is the vowel we're practicing today.*
- **Extra Challenge** Write the five target words on the board, but scrambled: *gba, tba, maj, nma, pam.* Have students unscramble the letters and write the words. Then point to each word and have students say it aloud.
- **Extra Support** Write _ _ g, _ _ t, _ _ m, _ _ n, _ _ p on the board. Have students copy and write the missing letters.

Optional Activity
- Have students think of and say their own sentences with the five target words. For example:
  This is my bag.
  My bat is small.
  The jam is on the table.
- Call on students to read aloud a sentence, one a time. Have the rest of the class listen and call out the target CVC word.

- Read aloud the instructions. Point to the chant. Say *Listen. Can you hear /æ/ in the middle of a word?* Play **TR: 114**. Have students circle the letter *a* each time. Have students work in pairs. Check answers together as a class by saying each word, one at a time, and writing the word on the board. Make sure students only circle the letters in the target words and not the other *a* letters (in *a* and *and*).
- Play **TR: 114** again. This time have students read and chant.

- Have students look at the picture. Give them instructions. Say *Point to the man.* Repeat with *map, jam,* and *bat.* Have students listen, look, and point. Point to the bag and ask *What's this?* Then point to the photo of the bag in Activity 1. Do the same with the other four items so that students understand that in this activity they can copy the words from Activity 1.
- Read aloud the instructions. Give students a minute to look at the picture again, and think about the words and the sounds.
- Play **TR: 115**. Have students do the activity individually.
- Walk around the classroom, monitoring students as they do the activity and checking to see that they have written the words correctly.

Script for TR: 115 *bat, jam, map, bag, man*

Wrap Up
- Use the phonics flashcards to review the target sounds. Hold up the *bag* flashcard and say *This is a bag. A bag, bag, bag.* Have students repeat after you. Then hold up the other flashcards and elicit the same chant each time with the different target words.

Additional Practice: Workbook p. 60, Online Practice

1 **Listen, point, and repeat.** 🎧 TR: 113

bag   **bat**   **jam**   **man**   **map**

2 **Listen, chant, and circle.** 🎧 TR: 114

There's a m**a**n with a m**a**p.
There's j**a**m in the house.
There's a blue and brown b**a**g.
There's a b**a**t in the house.

3 **Listen and find. Write the word.** 🎧 TR: 115

1. m a n
2. b a t
3. m a p
4. j a m
5. b a g

1 **Watch and match. Write the numbers.** ▶ Video 9

1. AJ

2. Lara

3. Mati

4. Juan

3

4

1

2

ABOUT THE VIDEO

In this video, AJ talks about the Statue of Liberty. This gift from the French was designed by Frédéric Auguste Bartholdi and built by the engineer Gustave Eiffel in 1886. The statue represents *Libertas*, the Roman goddess of liberty.

2 **Your turn! Ask and answer.**

What's in your town?

There's a library.

3 **Draw and say.**

Is that your town?

Yes, it is.

What's that?

It's a _____ .

_____ ?

_____ .

_____ ?

_____ .

Video

In this lesson, students will:

- watch a video about cities in other countries.
- ask and answer about places in their town.
- draw and speak about places in their town.

Resources: Video 9, Script for Video 9, Classroom Presentation Tool, Online Practice

End-of-Unit Resources: Worksheet 1.7, Unit 7 Test, ExamView Assessment Suite

Materials: a map of the world, photos of places in your town (one per group of students)

Warm Up

- Ask students if they know the names of any cities around the world. Have students raise their hands to make suggestions. Write the cities they know on the board. If some of the cities are in the same country, group them together on the board.
- If students don't mention New York or Mexico City, name them, too, and write them on the board.

- Have students open their books to p. 76. Direct students' attention to the four photos on the left. Say the name of one of the children. For example, say *Juan*, and have students say the corresponding number. Do the same with the other names.
- Point to the four photos of cities. Say *Look! Four cities.*
- Read aloud the instructions and play **Video 9** from beginning to end. Have students match the four numbers and names on the left with the photos on the right and write the numbers in the boxes.
- Write the names of the four cities on the board: 1. *New York*, 2. *Bodrum*, 3. *Gdansk*, 4. *Mexico City*. Show the class where these places are on a map of the world.
- Write the eight places from Lesson 1 on the board. Play **Video 9** again and pause after each segment. Write 1 next to *library* and next to *store*. Ask *Number 1?* and point to the list again. Have students call out other places in the segment about New York (street). Repeat for the other segments. (Answers: 1. (New York) store, library, museum; 2. (Bodrum) store, playground, swimming pool; 3. (Gdansk) zoo, park, store, street; 4. (Mexico City) park, zoo, library, museum)

*The script for **Video 9** is available on the Teacher's Resource Website.*

Optional Activity

- Put students in groups and give each group a photo of a place in your town. Make sure each group has a different place. Have groups write two or three sentences about this place.

- Have groups choose a leader. Ask the leader of one of the groups to come to the front and hold up his/her group's photo. Play the role of the narrator and ask some questions, as in the video and corresponding to the photo that is being held up. Guide the student to answer. If you have permission, you may choose to record this and replay the video interview. Repeat with the other photos.

- Read aloud the instructions and model the conversation with a volunteer. Ask the question again and have another student answer. Encourage students to say other places. Continue asking the question until a student answers *There are stores.* If you're all from the same town, you can use the name of the town in the question.
- Put students into pairs to ask and answer the question. Encourage them to use the places in Lesson 1 and to use a variety of places in their answer. Monitor students while they speak and help when necessary.
- **Extra Challenge** Have students in pairs identify other features of a town. Ask them to say the words for places and write a list on the board, for example, *statue, museum, hotel,* and *café.* Have students use actions to demonstrate the meaning of these words. Then have them use the words in their answers.
- **Extra Support** Write the model answer on the board and erase the word *library.* Then call on another volunteer to make a sentence using another word, for example, *There's a zoo.* Repeat with other students and other words.

- Read aloud the instructions. Use the board to demonstrate. Draw a picture of a store in a town or town center. Point to the store and say *What's that? It's a store.*
- Have students work individually to draw two places, one in each box. When they finish, have them walk around with their books and show their pictures to their classmates. Have them ask and answer questions about their drawings.

Wrap Up

- Play a game to see how much students remember about the video. If necessary, show **Video 9** again. Then put students into small groups. Write these sentences on the board and ask the groups to copy them and write the name of the person who said the sentence.
- Suggested sentences:
  My favorite place is my town. (Mati)
  Yes, that's true. (AJ)
  They come for vacation. (Lara)
  There are lots of stores in the town center. (Juan)
  There's a beautiful park, too. (Mati)
  There are libraries and museums, too. (AJ)
  It is next to the Aegean Sea. (Lara)
  There's a great zoo. (Mati)
  There are many hotels. (Lara)
  You can see art and listen to music. (Juan)

Additional Practice: Worksheet 1.7, Online Practice

UNIT
8 On the Farm

In this unit, students will:

- talk about farm animals.
- talk about things animals are able to do using *can* and *can't*.
- read about a farm.
- use *can* to ask about abilities.
- listen to and sing a song about animals.
- identify and pronounce words with /ɛ/ in the middle.
- watch a video about farm animals in other countries.
- identify the value of being kind to animals.

Language
Words
bee, bird, chicken, cow, dog, donkey, duck, sheep; farmer, food, pen
Grammar
- *A dog can run. A cat can't swim.*
- *Can you see the lamb? Yes, I can.*
- *Can a duck talk? No, it can't.*
Phonics
/e/ bed, leg, pen, pet, yes

Twenty-First Century Skills
Collaboration
Take turns to identify animal sounds, Lesson 1
Communication
Find animals in a picture, Lesson 5
Creativity
Draw and speak about your favorite animal, Lesson 7
Critical Thinking
Identify the value of being kind to animals, Lesson 3

In the Unit Opener, students will:
- respond to a photo of a sheep.
- talk about animals.

Resources: Home School Connection Letter, Classroom Presentation Tool

Materials: photos of animals (farm, wild/zoo, and pets), sticky tack

Introduce the Theme

- Bring to class photos of animals. Make sure you have a mix of farm animals, wild animals, and pets. Hold up a few photos and say *Animals.* Write the word *animal* on the board. Say it aloud and have students repeat after you. Point out that *animal* begins with /æ/.
- Draw a barn and farmland on the board. Say *This is a farm.* Then hold up the photos one at a time and ask *Is this animal on a farm?* Ask a few other questions about each animal, too. Ask *Is it big or small? What color is this animal?*
- Say *On the farm.* Hold up the photos one at a time again. Have individual students point to photos of animals which can be on a farm.
- Don't worry about the names of the animals, but if any students know the name of an animal, have them say it for the rest of the class.
- Display the animal photos on the wall of the classroom. Ask *What's your favorite animal?* Have students think and choose their favorite animal from the selection. Say *Point to your favorite animal.*
- You might like to play a guessing game. Choose an animal from the photos and describe it in a few sentences. Have students point to the correct photo. For example, say *This is a big animal. It's white. It lives on a farm.* (sheep) Students do not need to say the name of the animal at this point.

Use the Photo

- Have students open their books to p. 77. Read aloud the instructions at the bottom of the page and point to the photo.
- Ask *Is this an animal?* (yes) *What color is it?* (white)
- Give instructions to students. Say *Point to the head.* Repeat with *body, nose, mouth.* Then say *Point to the ears.* Repeat with *eyes, legs.* Ask *What color are the eyes?* (yellow) *How many legs does it have?* (four)
- Read aloud the caption. Say *A sheep.* Point and say *This animal is a sheep. It's on a farm.*

TEACHER TIP
Have students work in pairs as much as possible. Working in pairs will make them feel more confident, and encourage them to share their ideas and knowledge. Make sure students change partners frequently, too. With students this age, it is best to organize pairs and not have students choose their own partners. This will help keep students from getting too talkative with their partners. It will also help students to get to know classmates other than their close friends. Pairing can also be fun. For example, have students find somebody who has the same favorite color, who is the next person alphabetically in a list of first names, and so on. This variety will ensure that students get the chance to work with many different classmates.

On the Farm

A sheep

ABOUT THE PHOTO

This photo shows a sheep in a field in Cornwall, UK. Sheep were first domesticated more than 10,000 years ago in Central Asia. However, we have been making wool from sheep since long before then, probably since around 3500 BCE. A female sheep is called a *ewe* /juː/, and a male sheep is called a *ram*. Sheep live together in groups called *flocks*.

Look at the photo. What can you see?

Words

1 Listen and point. 🎧 TR: 116

bee

bird

chicken

cow

dog

donkey

2 Listen and repeat. 🎧 TR: 117

ABOUT THE PHOTO

This photo shows a herd of cows on a farm in Northern Ireland. Cows have surprisingly sharp senses. They can smell something up to nine kilometers away. They can also hear high- and low-frequency sounds better than people. They have almost 360° vision, too—they can see almost all the area around them, without turning their heads. All cows are color-blind and they can't distinguish between red and green.

3 Listen, ask, and answer. 🎧 TR: 118

What's the animal?

It's a donkey.

Words

In this lesson, students will:
- talk about farm animals.

Resources: Audio Tracks 116–118, Classroom Presentation Tool, Flashcards 121–128, Workbook p. 62, Workbook Audio Track 42, Online Practice

Materials: photos of animals from Unit Opener, sticky tack, modeling clay

Warm Up

- **Use the Photo** Have students open their books to pp. 78–79. Point to the cows and say *Look! Animals.* Ask *Are they big or small?* (big) *How many can you see?* (five)

- Have students listen, look, find, and point to things in the main photo. Give instructions to find and point to different things. Say *Point to something green.* Then repeat with *brown.* Say *Point to a head.* Then repeat with *body, ear,* and *eye.* Divide the class into pairs and have students check that their partner is pointing to the correct thing.

- Write the words *Big* and *Small* on the board as headings. Write *Big* on the left side of the board and *Small* on the right side.

- Bring the animal photos into class and display them where students can see them. Point to each photo one at a time and ask *Is this a big animal?* or *Is this a small animal?* Have students respond, then move the photo to the correct side of the board.

- Point to the group of big animals. Point to each photo one at a time and ask *Big or very big?* Hold your hands hip-width apart to indicate *big* and then extend them further apart to indicate *very big.*

- Indicate that you want the biggest animal. When you have the biggest animal from the photos, display it on the far left side of the board. Then repeat the procedure to find the smallest animal.

- Have students order the animals from the biggest to the smallest, displaying them on the board each time. It might be necessary to display two or more photos in the same position, one above the other.

- Read aloud the instructions. Then direct students' attention to the photos under the instructions. Point and say *Look. Animals. Eight animals.*

- Point to your ear and say *Let's listen.* Play **TR: 116** and point to the photos one at a time as you hear the words.

- Play **TR: 116** a second time. Walk around the classroom to make sure students are pointing to the correct photos.

- Read aloud the instructions. Play **TR: 117.** Pause after the first word to model repeating for students. Continue with **TR: 117,** having students repeat the words as a class.

- Play **TR: 117** again and call on individual students around the class to repeat the words.

- **Extra Challenge** Have students cover the words under the photos. Play **TR: 117** again and have students listen, repeat, and point.

- Have students close their books. Use the flashcards to review the words. Hold up the *bee* flashcard and ask *Is it a bee or a bird?* (a bee) Repeat with the other flashcards, using *or* and the name of two animals each time.

- Hold up the *bee* flashcard and say *This is a bee. A bee says* bzzzzzz. Ask *What sound does a bee make?* Have students respond with bee sounds. Repeat with the other flashcards, eliciting animal sounds each time.

- Have students open their books again to p. 78. Read aloud the instructions. Play **TR: 118,** pausing after the first animal sound. Direct students' attention to the models. Model pointing and saying the sentences with a volunteer.

- Put students into pairs. Play **TR: 118,** pausing after each animal sound for students to ask and answer. Monitor students while they do the activity, making sure they are taking turns and saying the correct animal.

- Check answers with the class. Play **TR: 118** again, pausing after each animal sound. Have pairs of students ask and answer in front of the class.

- **Listening Strategy: Listening for Sounds** Listening for sounds can help provide context. For example, if students hear car horns and foot traffic, they'll understand that the passage is set on a city street. If they hear a refrigerator door opening, and some pots and pans, they'll understand that it is in a kitchen. The sounds can give clues that help students better understand the context of a given listening passage.

- **Extra Support** Play **TR: 118** from beginning to end before students do the pairwork. Have students write the animal they think they hear.

Script for TR: 118

1. sound of donkey braying
2. sound of cow mooing
3. sound of sheep bleating
4. sound of bird song
5. sound of dog barking
6. sound of bee buzzing
7. sound of duck quacking
8. sound of chicken clucking

Optional Activity

- Have students work individually and make one farm animal each from modeling clay. Have them each make an animal, hold it up, and say three sentences about it, for example, *This is a cow. It's black and white. It says* Mooo! Go around the class as students start work, making sure that they are making all eight animals from Activity 1.

Wrap Up

- Have students play a guessing game in groups. Have them take turns pretending to be an animal. Have the other students guess which animal it is by asking *Are you a [donkey]?* The student can respond *Yes, I am* or *No, I'm not.*

Additional Practice: Workbook p. 62, Online Practice

Grammar

In this lesson, students will:

- talk about things animals are able to do using *can* and *can't*.
- say a chant.

Resources: Audio Tracks 119–120, Classroom Presentation Tool, Flashcards 121–128, Workbook p. 63, Workbook Audio Track 43, Online Practice

Materials: a photo of a cat

Warm Up

- Review the words from Lesson 1. Hold up each animal flashcard, one at a time, and have students say the animal word and make the corresponding sound. For example, *A bee! Bzzzzzz.*
- Have a volunteer make an animal sound and choose a classmate to name the animal. Repeat with other volunteers and sounds until all of the Lesson 1 words have been reviewed.

- Have students open their books to p. 79. Point to the chant. Say *Listen to the chant.* Play **TR: 119.** Have students listen to the chant and clap to the rhythm. As each action is mentioned in the chant, act it out so that students understand the meaning (run, talk, swim, walk, sing, fly).
- Hold up a photo of a cat. Say *Look! This is a cat.* Ask students to repeat the word and write it on the board. If appropriate, ask if anyone has a cat at home and what their cat's name is.
- Read aloud the second line of the chant, and repeat the word *cat.* Have students turn back to p. 14. Point to the bus and ask *What's this?*
- Have students turn back to the chant on p. 79. Play **TR: 119** again. This time have students chant, too.
- Write the actions from the chant on the board: *run, talk, swim, walk, sing,* and *fly.* Have students stand up. Say each action, one at a time, and have students do the action. If you like, have students copy the words for the actions into their notebooks.

- Read aloud the instructions. Direct students' attention to the grammar box. Say *Listen and read* and play **TR: 120.** Have students listen and read. Play **TR: 120** again and get students to repeat the sentences as a class.
- Hold up the *bird* flashcard. Say *Look! A bird. A bird* can *fly!* Emphasize the word *can.* Do a flying action, pretending your arms are wings, flapping up and down.
- Hold up the *sheep* flashcard. Say *Look! A sheep. A sheep* can't *fly!* Emphasize the word *can't.* On the board write *can't = cannot.* Explain that *can't* means *cannot,* but make sure students understand that *can't* is more commonly used.

- Demonstrate *can* and *can't* with personalized expressions. Say *I can speak English.* Pick up a book and pretend to read and say *I can read.* Say *I can't fly.* Continue, practicing *can* and *can't* with several more examples.

- Hold up the *bird* flashcard. On the board write *A bird can…* and *A bird can't….* Point to and read aloud each sentence. Call on students to give a verb for each, such as *fly* or *read.* Complete the sentences on the board. Underline *can* and *can't,* and say each sentence for students to repeat.
- Read aloud the instructions and point to the four pictures. Each time, ask *What is it?* (a chicken, a bird, a sheep, a boy)
- Point to the sentences below the pictures. Direct students' attention to the example in item 1 and read aloud the sentence. Say *Jump* and remind students of its meaning. Demonstrate jumping and say the word again.
- Have students complete the other sentences, while you monitor, encouraging and helping when necessary. Make sure students have written *can* in the space in the second sentence. If necessary, direct students' attention to items 5 and 6 which are personal responses.
- Have students work in pairs to look at the pictures, read the sentences, and write *can* or *can't.*
- Elicit the answers orally from the class. Have students read aloud each complete sentence.
- **Extra Challenge** Have students write other sentences beginning with *I.* For example, *I can run, I can't swim, I can walk.*
- **Extra Support** Before students complete the sentences, have them do the action in each sentence to establish whether or not the animals can or can't do the action. Start with item 1. Point to the word *jump* and say *Jump!* Have students listen and act out the action.

Optional Activity

- Hold up the *cow* flashcard and say *A cow can walk, A cow can swim, A cow can't fly, A cow can't talk.* Then ask *Read?* Have students make a sentence. (*A cow can't read.*) Repeat the activity with the other Lesson 1 flashcards and different verbs (*fly, speak, read, sing, jump, walk,* etc.).
- Have students work in pairs and choose an animal. Have them draw a picture of the animal and then write as many *can* and *can't* sentences as they can about the animal.

Wrap Up

- Practice using *can* and *can't* in a memory game. Say *A cat can run.* Have a student repeat the sentence and add a second sentence with *can't* (*A cat can run, A chicken can't sing.*). Repeat the two sentences and add a third with *can.* Say *A cat can run, A chicken can't sing, A girl can read.* Continue with a few more students repeating the sentences each time and adding a new sentence with *can* or *can't.*
- Have students play in groups of four or five. Monitor, making sure students are using *can* and *can't* correctly.

Additional Practice: Workbook p. 63, Online Practice

duck   sheep

Grammar

1 **Listen and chant.** 🎧 TR: 119

A dog can run, but a dog can't talk.
A cat can't swim, but a cat can walk.
A bird can sing, and a bird can fly.
A bird can fly very, very high.

2 **Listen and read.** 🎧 TR: 120

> A dog **can** run.
> A cat **can't** swim.

3 **Write** *can* **or** *can't*.

1. A chicken ____can____ jump.

2. A bird ____can____ fly.

3. A sheep ____can't____ swim.

4. A boy ____can____ sing.

5. I ____can____ talk.

6. I ____can't____ fly.

3 Reading

1 Listen and repeat. 🎧 TR: 121

pen   farmer   food

2 Listen and read. 🎧 TR: 122

Can you play with animals at school? No! You can play with your friends at school. Can you play with animals on a farm? Yes! Look at this farm.

This is a **pen**. But it isn't a pen for writing. It's a sheep pen. A pen is a sheep's "house." Look! Can you see the **farmer**? She has **food** for the sheep.

Look at the boy! He has food for the sheep, too. Do you like this farm?

3 Read again. Complete the sentences.

animals̶   food   friends   pen   sheep

1. You can't play with __animals__ at school.

2. You can play with your __friends__ at school.

3. A __pen__ is a house for sheep.

4. The farmer has food for the __sheep__ .

5. The boy has __food__ , too.

LESSON 3 Reading

In this lesson, students will:
- read about a farm.
- use new words to talk about a farm.
- choose the correct words to complete sentences about a text.
- identify the value of being kind to animals.

Resources: Audio Tracks 121–122; Classroom Presentation Tool; Flashcards 121–131; Workbook pp. 64, 67; Workbook Audio Track 44; Online Practice

Warm Up

- Play a guessing game about animals. Point to your head to show you are thinking. Choose one of the Lesson 1 flashcards, but do not show it to the class. Say *Can you guess the animal?* Give clues such as *It's very small* or *It can fly*, one at a time, and have students raise their hands if they want to guess. Give clues using *big* and *small*, colors, and *can* and *can't*.
- **Use the Photo** Have students open their books to pp. 80–81. Direct students' attention to the photo. Point and ask *What animals can you see?* (sheep) Ask *How many sheep can you see?* (two) *How many people can you see?* (two)

- Read aloud the instructions. Play **TR: 121** and have students listen and repeat the words. Then use drawings, actions, and descriptions to teach the new words.
- Hold up the *pen* flashcard (129) and say *Look! A pen!* Say *A pen is a house for sheep.* Hold up the *farmer* flashcard and say *Look! A farmer!* Ask *Is a farmer a person?* (yes) Say *Yes, a farmer works on a farm. I'm a teacher. A teacher works in a school.* Draw a picture of a sheep on the board. Point and ask *What's this?* (a sheep) Draw a stick figure next to the sheep and say *Look! A farmer.* Draw a bucket of food in the farmer's hand. Point and say *Look! Food.* Ask *Is the food for the farmer?* (no) *Is the food for the sheep?* (yes) Hold up the *food* flashcard.
- NOTE: If necessary, direct student's attention to the irregular plural *sheep*. Say *One animal* and *Three animals*, write the words next to each other on the board and underline the *s*. Then, say *One sheep* and *Three sheep*, point to the sheep in the photo and write the words below the others on the board.
- **Extra Support** Help students understand the text by holding up flashcards of the new words as they appear.

- Read aloud the instructions and point to the text. Have students write one question about the photo and/or the text before they read. Then, play **TR: 122**. Have students listen to and read the whole text. Have them find the answer to their question if it is in the text.
- Play **TR: 122** again, pausing after the first paragraph. Ask *Who can you play with at school?* (friends) *Is this a farm?* (yes) *What can you play with here?* (animals)

- Continue playing **TR: 122**, pausing after the second paragraph to ask more questions. Ask *Is this a pen for writing?* (no) *Is it a pen for sheep?* (yes) *Do these sheep have food?* (yes)
- Continue playing **TR: 122** to the end. Have students listen and read. Point to the child and ask *Is this a girl?* (No, it's a boy.) *Do you like this farm?* Say *The people in this photo are kind to animals. They are kind to these sheep.*
- **Reading Strategy: Asking and Answering Questions** One way to engage students' interest in a text is to have them write the questions that they would like to see answered. Even if the questions they created are not answered in the text, the process of writing the questions helps prepare students before reading and then focuses their attention when they read.
- **Value: Be kind to animals** At this point in the lesson, you can teach the value. Say *The value of this lesson is* Be kind to animals. Write this on the board. Explain the meaning of *kind*. Ask a student to help you move some books from your table to a shelf, for example. When he/she finishes, smile and say *Thank you. You are very kind.* Draw and ask questions about being kind to animals, accepting any reasonable responses. For example, draw a cat on the board and ask *How can we be kind to a cat?* Listen for students' responses. Then draw a bowl of milk next to it and say *Cats like milk. We can give them milk and food.* Say *Now you choose another animal. Draw a picture of you and that animal. Draw a picture of you being kind to that animal.* For additional practice, have students complete Lesson 6 of the Workbook in class or at home.

- Read aloud the instructions. Direct students' attention to the word box and the example in the first sentence and read aloud the sentence. Point to the word box again and show how the word *animals* has been crossed out. Have students complete the activity in pairs.
- Correct the activity by calling on students to read aloud each complete sentence.
- **Extra Challenge** Have students try to complete the sentences without looking at the word box.

Optional Activity

- Have students work in pairs and take turns to describe a farm, saying what animals there are and what food they have. Have the partner draw what he/she hears. Have them take turns speaking and drawing until each has a complete picture.

Wrap Up

- Have students close their books. Write the three new words on the board: *pen*, *farmer*, and *food*. Have students write a sentence about a farm, including each word.

Additional Practice: Workbook pp. 64, 67; Online Practice

LESSON 4 Grammar

> **In this lesson, students will:**
> • use *can* to ask about abilities.
>
> **Resources:** Audio Track 123, Classroom Presentation Tool, Flashcards 121–128, Workbook p. 65, Workbook Audio Track 45, Online Practice

Warm Up

• Turn the Lesson 1 flashcards facedown on the table. Call on a student to pick up the top flashcard and show it to the class without you seeing it. Try to guess the animal by saying what it *can/can't* do. For example, say *This animal can fly.* Have students call out *true or false* for each of your sentences. Continue until you think you know the animal. Then ask *Is this animal a [cow]?* Have students call out *Yes, it is* or *No, it isn't.* Have the student with the flashcard show it to you. Play again with a few more flashcards.

• Have students open their books to pp. 80–81. Point to a sheep and say *Look! This is a sheep.* Then say *A lamb is a baby sheep.*

• Read aloud the instructions. Point to the grammar box and say *Listen.* Play **TR: 123.** Have students listen and read. Play **TR: 123** again and have students repeat the sentences, first as a class and then individually.

• Hold up the *bird* flashcard and ask *Can you see the bird?* Have students answer *Yes, I can.* Hold the flashcard behind your back so the students can't see it. Ask *Can you see the bird?* Emphasize the word *you.* Have students answer *No, I can't.* Say the answer with the students, emphasizing the word *I.* Repeat with a few more flashcards.

• Hold up the *cow* flashcard and ask *Can a cow walk?* Have students answer *Yes, it can.* Say the answer with students, emphasizing the word *it.* Ask *Can a cow swim?* Have students answer *No, it can't.* Say the answer with students, emphasizing the word *it.* Repeat with a few more flashcards.

• **Extra Support** Copy the questions and answers from the grammar box onto the board. Draw a stick figure next to the first question and a duck next to the second. Then circle *you* and *I* in the first question and answer, and circle *a duck* and *it* in the second. Read aloud each question and answer, pointing first to the small picture and then to the words you have circled.

Optional Activity

• Draw this chart on the board:

Can	you	swim	?
	a bird	read	
	a cow	sing	
	a cat	dance	
	a dog	jump	
	a sheep	fly	
	a duck	run	

• Ask questions using the chart. Point to the words in the three columns as you make each question. Ask *Can a dog dance?* Elicit a full answer from the class. (No, it can't.)

• Have students work in pairs. Have them take turns to ask questions and answer with complete sentences. Remind students to ask questions in a random order. Make sure students understand that they can ask silly questions, too. You might like to provide a few examples. For example, ask *Can a cow jump on a sofa?* Listen to some of the students' questions and responses.

• Read aloud the instructions. Point to the questions. Direct students' attention to the example answer for the first question, and read aloud both the question and answer.

• Have students continue the activity in pairs. Have them work with different partners.

• Check answers as a class. Read aloud each question one at a time and call on a different student to provide the answer each time.

• **Extra Challenge** Have students do the activity again orally in pairs, replacing the animal in each sentence.

• Read aloud the instructions. Direct students' attention to the model. Hold up the *bird* flashcard and model saying the conversation with a volunteer. Begin the conversation and say *Can you guess the animal?*

• Choose another flashcard, but don't show it to the class. Say *Can you guess the animal?* Call on volunteers to ask questions and have the class guess the animal. Show the flashcard when they have guessed the animal correctly.

• Put students into pairs to read the conversation. Have them take turns to read each part.

• Have students do the activity in pairs. Have them take turns choosing an animal and asking questions about an animal. Monitor students as they work and help them when necessary.

Wrap Up

• Have students think about what they *can* and *can't* do. On the board, draw some pictures to represent activities or actions. Draw a stick figure swimming, riding a bike, dancing, reading, jumping, playing a guitar, playing a drum, playing soccer, climbing a mountain, riding a horse, etc. Point to a picture and to a student, ask *[Julia], can you do this?* Elicit *Yes, I can* or *No, I can't.* Go around the class pointing and asking different students each time.

> **Additional Practice:** Workbook p. 65, Online Practice

Grammar

1 **Listen and read.** 🎧 TR: 123

> Can you see the lamb?
> Yes, I can.
>
> Can a duck talk?
> No, it can't.

2 **Read and answer.**

1. Can a bird fly?   Yes, it can.

2. Can a cat run?
   Yes, it can.
3. Can a chicken swim?
   No, it can't.
4. Can a dog jump?
   Yes, it can.
5. Can a cow read a book?
   No, it can't.

3 **Ask and answer.**

Can you guess the animal?

Can it swim?

No, it can't.

Can it fly?

Yes, it can.

It's a bird.

VALUE **Be kind to animals.**
Workbook, Lesson 6

UNIT 8   On the Farm   **81**

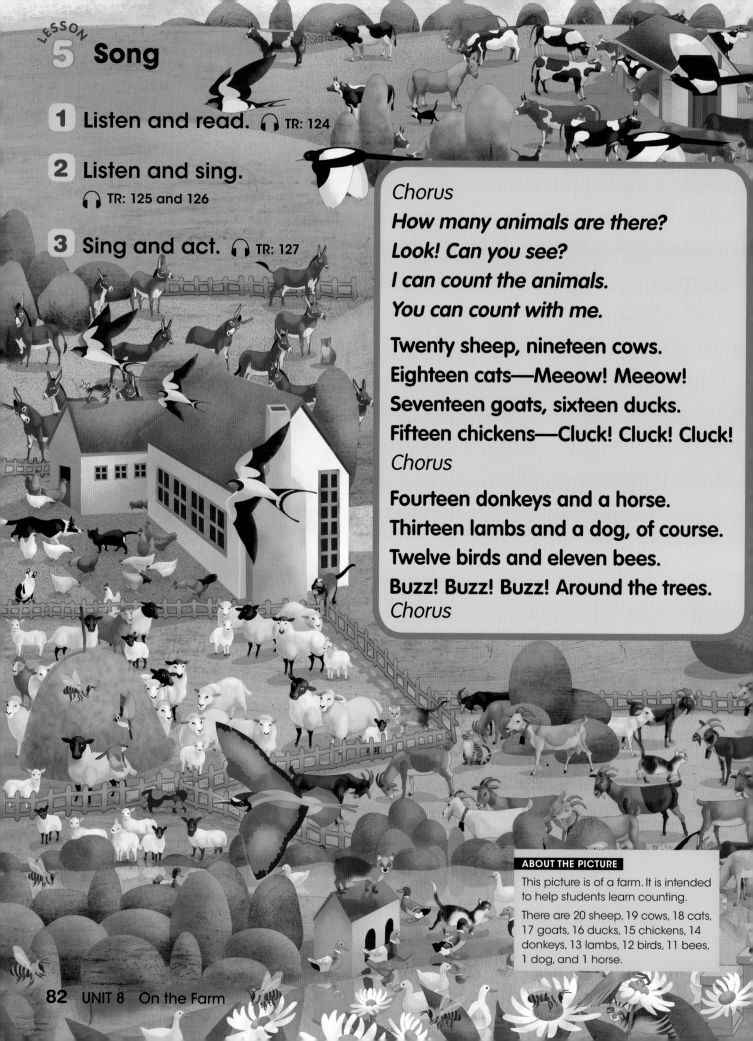

1 **Listen and read.** 🎧 TR: 124

2 **Listen and sing.**
🎧 TR: 125 and 126

3 **Sing and act.** 🎧 TR: 127

Chorus

How many animals are there?
Look! Can you see?
I can count the animals.
You can count with me.

Twenty sheep, nineteen cows.
Eighteen cats—Meeow! Meeow!
Seventeen goats, sixteen ducks.
Fifteen chickens—Cluck! Cluck! Cluck!
Chorus

Fourteen donkeys and a horse.
Thirteen lambs and a dog, of course.
Twelve birds and eleven bees.
Buzz! Buzz! Buzz! Around the trees.
Chorus

ABOUT THE PICTURE

This picture is of a farm. It is intended to help students learn counting.

There are 20 sheep, 19 cows, 18 cats, 17 goats, 16 ducks, 15 chickens, 14 donkeys, 13 lambs, 12 birds, 11 bees, 1 dog, and 1 horse.

LESSON 5 Song

In this lesson, students will:
- listen to and sing a song about animals.
- act out a song.

Resources: Audio Tracks 124–127; Classroom Presentation Tool; Flashcards 47–48, 121–141; Online Practice

Materials: index cards or small pieces of paper (six per student)

Warm Up
- Review the numbers 1–10 and the animal words in the song. Say *Four sheep* and have students clap four times and make a sheep sound. Continue with different numbers and different animals. Have students listen, clap the correct number of times, and make the animal sound. Start slowly and gradually build up speed so that students end up clapping as quickly as they can.
- **Use the Picture** Have students open their books to p. 82. Point to the picture. Ask *What can you see?* (a farm and animals) Give instructions to the class. Say *Point to the farm.* Repeat with *a flower, a tree, a dog, a fence,* etc.
- Remind students of the difference between *sheep* and *lamb*. Point to a sheep and say *Look! This is a sheep. It's a mom or dad.* Then point to a lamb and say *Look! This is a lamb. It's a baby sheep.*
- NOTE: The following animals are in the picture: *bee, bird, cat, chicken, cow, dog, donkey, goat, lamb,* and *sheep.*

- Review the numbers 1–10 and then teach the numbers 11–20. Use the board and drawings. Draw a stick boy on the board and say *How many boys?* Have students answer as a class with *One boy.* Write the number 1 under the boy. Then add another boy and repeat the question. Elicit *Two boys* and write the number 2. Continue in this way until you have ten boys. Then continue adding boys and numbers. Each time, say *Look! Another boy. Now there are [11] boys.* Write the numbers eleven to twenty under the digits 11 to 20 on the board. Point to each number, one at a time, say it, and have the class repeat it after you.
- Practice numbers with students in the class if there are more than 20 students in the class. Call out each number and have that number stand up. For example, say *Ten* and have ten students stand up. Then say *Eleven* and have one more stand up. Point to the word and the number on the board. Then say *Twelve* and have one more stand up, etc. Leave the numbers 11 to 20 on the board.
- Dictate numbers to the class in random order. For example, say *Thirteen* and have students write *13* and *thirteen* in their notebooks. Also, have them draw 13 stars. Repeat with the other numbers. Make sure you write a list so that you can check answers. Call on an individual to say the first number you dictated. Write the digit, the word and the correct number of stars on the board, one at a time. Repeat with other students and the other numbers.

- Have students read through the song quickly and find all the animal words. Ask *What's the song about?* (animals)
- Read aloud the instructions. Play **TR: 124**. Have students listen and follow in their books.
- **Extra Support** Play **TR: 124** again for students to sing. Hold up number flashcards and animal flashcards as the animals are mentioned. (NOTE: There's no *cat* flashcard and no *lamb* flashcard, so have two students draw these.)

- Read aloud the instructions. Play **TR: 125**. Get a clapping or tapping rhythm going to accompany the song. Encourage students to sing along to the chorus.
- Play **TR: 126**, the instrumental version of the song, for students to sing.

- Read aloud each line of the chorus and demonstrate an action. Have students make the action, too.
  How many animals are there? (Count silently on your fingers and shrug.)
  Look! Can you see? (Point to the distance.)
  I can count the animals. (Point to yourself, then silently count on your fingers.)
  You can count with me. (Point to someone and then point to yourself.)
- Read aloud each phrase of the song and have students point to the correct animal in the picture. Have a volunteer stand next to the board and point to each number (11–20) as it is mentioned.
- Play **TR: 127** more than once. Have students sing the song.
- **Extra Challenge** Have students sing along to the instrumental version of the song, holding up number flashcards and animal flashcards. Have each student hold up a number flashcard and/or an animal flashcard and sing the corresponding word as it features in the song.

Optional Activity
- Give each student six index cards or small pieces of paper. Have them make three number cards from 11 to 20 and three animal cards with either the picture of the animal or the word. (Discourage them from choosing a series of numbers, such as 20, 19, 18 or 17, 16, 15.)
- Play **TR: 125** again and have students sing the song, holding up the correct number card and animal card as they hear them mentioned. Keep track of animals or numbers that weren't used, and review them at the end.

Wrap Up
- Have students find numbers and animals in the song, for example, *twenty sheep,* and then look carefully for the animals in the picture.

> **Additional Practice:** Online Practice

Phonics

In this lesson, students will:
- identify and pronounce CVC words with /ɛ/ in the middle.
- form three-letter words with the letter *e*.

Resources: Audio Tracks 128–130; Classroom Presentation Tool; Flashcards 20, 24, 35, 51, 80, 95, 142–143; Workbook p. 66, Workbook Audio Track 46, Online Practice

Warm Up
- Use the five phonics flashcards to review the sound from Unit 7 (/æ/). Put all the flashcards together and jumble them up. Hold up one flashcard at a time and have students say the word as a class. Listen to the pronunciation of the key sound and say the word aloud yourself if you think students need to hear it again.

- Have students open their books to p. 83. Direct students' attention to the photos and words. Read aloud the instructions. Play **TR: 128**, pointing to each photo and word as students hear it.
- Play **TR: 128** again. Have students repeat each word. Monitor students carefully, making sure they pronounce the target sound (/ɛ/) correctly. Ask *What sound are we learning today?* (/ɛ/) Remind students that they are practicing this sound in the middle of words. Remind them that *e* is a vowel, and each of these words follows a consonant, vowel, consonant pattern with *e* in the middle.
- **Extra Support** Write _ _ d, _ _ g, _ _ n, _ _ t and _ _ s on the board. Have students copy and write the missing letters.

Optional Activity
- Practice the new sound. Have students stand up. Then say a series of words, one after the other. Have students jump when they hear a word with the sound /ɛ/. Say *Yes, bat, pen, bag, leg, jam, pet, map, bed, man.*
- Repeat each word with the sound /ɛ/ and show the flashcard each time.

- Read aloud the instructions. Point to the chant. Say *Listen. Can you hear /ɛ/ in the middle of a word?* Play **TR: 129**. Have students work in pairs to circle the letter *e* each time. Check answers together as a class by saying each word, one at a time, and writing the word on the board. Make sure students only circle the letters in the target words (for example, in *Yes*) and not the other *e* letters (for example, in *see*).
- Play **TR: 129** again. This time have students read and chant.
- **Extra Challenge** Hold up the *bed* flashcard and have students say the corresponding line of the chant without looking at their book. Repeat with the other three flashcards and three lines of the chant.

- **Extra Support** Have students say the alphabet and write it on the board, one letter at a time. Say *Vowel* and call on a student to say the first vowel. Underline *a* in the alphabet on the board. Repeat with the other four vowels. Point to the letter *e* again and say *This is the vowel we're practicing today.*

- Have students look at the picture. Give them instructions. Say *Point to the bed.* Repeat with *leg, pen, pet,* and *yes.* Have students listen, look, and point. Then point to the photo of the bed in Activity 1. Do the same with the other four items so that students understand they can copy the words from Activity 1.
- Read aloud the instructions. Give students a minute to look at the picture again, read the words, and think about the sounds.
- Play **TR: 130**. Have students do the activity individually.
- Walk around the classroom, monitoring students as they do the activity and checking to see that they have written the words correctly.

    Script for TR: 130 *pet, yes, leg, bed, pen*

Wrap Up
- Repeat the chant from Activity 2. Use the four phonics flashcards from the questions in the chant to review the target sounds. Hold up the *bed* flashcard and say *Can you see a bed?* Have students say *Yes, I can.* Then hold up the other flashcards one at a time, ask a *Can you…?* question, and have students respond.
- Hand out the four flashcards to volunteers. Have them ask the questions and have the rest of the class respond.

Additional Practice: Workbook p. 66, Online Practice

Phonics

1 Listen, point, and repeat. 🎧 TR: 128

bed   leg   pen   pet   yes

2 Listen, chant, and circle. 🎧 TR: 129

Can you see a bed? Yes, I can!
Can you see a leg? Yes, I can!
Can you see a pen? Yes, I can!
Can you see a pet? Yes, I can!

3 Listen and find. Write the word. 🎧 TR: 130

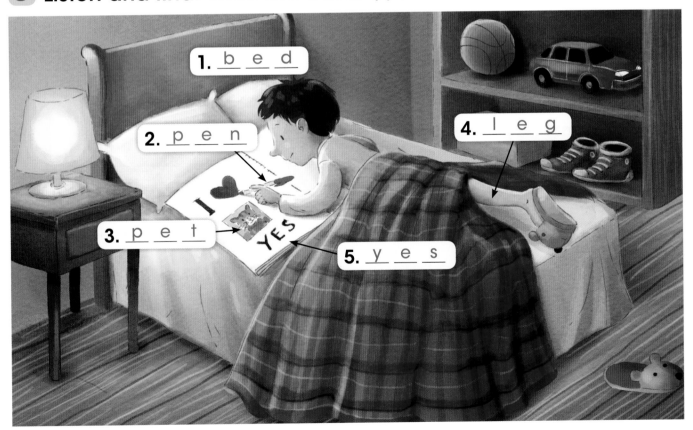

1. b e d
2. p e n
3. p e t
4. l e g
5. y e s

Video

1 Watch and match. Write the numbers. ▶ Video 10

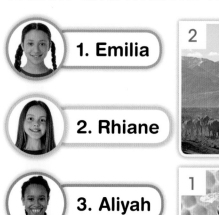

1. Emilia

2. Rhiane

3. Aliyah

4. Safia

2

4

1

3

ABOUT THE VIDEO

In this video, Emilia talks about bees. Bees are important. They help other plants grow because they are pollinators, carrying pollen, or other plants and seeds, from one plant to another. Honeybees live in hives with one queen bee, male drone bees, and lots of female worker bees. Honeybees are very important for the environment and need to be protected because bee numbers are in decline. For example, across Europe, nearly 10% of bee species face extinction.

2 Your turn! Ask and answer.

What's your favorite farm animal?

A horse.

3 Draw and say.

This is my favorite animal.

It's a/an _____ .

_____ .

_____ .

Video

In this lesson, students will:

- watch a video about farm animals in other countries.
- ask and answer about favorite farm animals.
- draw and speak about favorite animals.

Resources: Video 10, Classroom Presentation Tool, Flashcards 121–128, Online Practice

End-of-Unit Resources: Anthology Story 4, Anthology Teaching Notes p. 139, Worksheet 1.8, Unit 8 Test, ExamView Assessment Suite

Warm Up

- Show the class the Lesson 1 flashcards. Show the *bee* flashcard and say *Look! This is a bee. A bee is yellow and black. A bee can fly.* Show the remaining flashcards, and have students point and say.
- For each flashcard, elicit four or five sentences. Continue until each student has had a chance to speak.

- Have students open their books to p. 84. Direct students' attention to the four photos on the left. Say the name of one of the children. For example, say *Emilia*, and have students say the corresponding number. Do the same with the other names.
- Point to the four photos of animals. Say *Look! Animals.* Ask *What animals can you see?* (cows, goats, bees, sheep)
- Read aloud the instructions and play **Video 10** from beginning to end. Have students match the four numbers and names on the left with the photos on the right and write the numbers in the boxes.
- Pause **Video 10** after the narrator says *This person is called a beekeeper* and ask *What is this man called?* (a beekeeper) Continue and pause again after Emilia's segment and ask *How many bees are there?* (15) Pause again after Rhiane's segment and ask *Which two animals are on the farms in Argentina?* (horses and cows) Play and pause again after Aliyah's segment and ask *What color are the sheeps' faces?* (black) Play and pause again after Safia's segment and ask *Where are the goats?* (in a tree)
- **Extra Support** Play **Video 10** again and pause during each segment when the animals for counting first appear on-screen. (These are the photos in Activity 1.) Play the video as the children start counting the animals. Have students count aloud as the children in the video count.

*The script for **Video 10** is available on the Teacher's Resource Website.*

- Read aloud the instructions and model the conversation with a volunteer.
- Put students into pairs to ask and answer questions about their favorite animals. Have students work with more than one partner.
- Monitor students while they speak and help when necessary.

- **Extra Challenge** Before starting the activity, play a memory game. Divide the class into pairs and give students two minutes to write a list of farm animals. Then call on volunteers to write one animal each on the board. Have students cross out words that are on their lists.

Optional Activity

- Write the following headings on the board: *Six legs, Four legs, Two legs,* and *No legs.* Say an animal and have students decide how many legs it has. For example, say *Elephant* and have students call out *four legs.* Write *elephant* under *Four legs* on the board. Then say *Fish* and have students call out *no legs.* Write *fish* under *No legs* on the board. Continue with the names of a few other animals.
- Divide the class into small groups. Have students choose animals and say how many legs they have. Have one student from the group write a list of animals.
- Check answers. Have one student call out an animal, another say the number of legs, and another write the animal under the correct heading on the board.

- Read aloud the instructions. Use the board to demonstrate. Draw a picture of a bird. Point to the picture of the bird and say *This is my favorite animal. It's a bird.*
- Point to the box on the right. Ask *What's your favorite color?* and have students answer. Then ask *What's your favorite toy?* and have students answer. Point to the box on the left and say *Animal.* Point to the box on the right and say *You choose.*
- Have students work individually to complete the activity. When they finish, have them walk around with their books and show their pictures to their classmates. Have them talk about their drawings.

Wrap Up

- Have students close their books. Play a game to see how much students remember about the video. Put students into pairs. Ask *What are the animals in the video? What are the numbers?*
- If necessary, play **Video 10** again. Have students work in pairs and choose the number and name of the animals. Ask *What's the number and what are the animals in Emilia's segment?* and have individual students answer. Repeat with the other animals.

Additional Practice: Anthology Story 4, Worksheet 1.8, Online Practice

Game 2

In this lesson, students will:
- review words from previous units.
- ask and answer questions about photos.
- play a game.

Resources: Classroom Presentation Tool; Flashcards 74–85, 91–101, 107–118, 121–128; Workbook p. 68

Materials: sticky tack, sticky notes

Warm Up

- Use Lesson 1 and 3 flashcards to review words from Units 5–8. Shuffle all the flashcards and place them facedown on the table. Put students into two or four teams, depending on the size of the class.
- Turn over and hold up one flashcard at a time. Have teams take turns to respond to three *True* or *False* sentences about the photo. For example, hold up the *shower* flashcard. Say *It's a shower.* (true) *A shower is in a bedroom.* (false) *This shower is red.* (false)
- Make sure each team is given the same number of turns. Award one point for each correct response. Add up the points at the end to find the team with the most points.
- Display all the flashcards on a wall or on the board. Have students work in pairs, A and B. Have Student A choose a flashcard and make a sentence about it. For example, *This is in the bathroom.* Have Student B guess which flashcard is being described and say the word. (shower) Then have A and B change roles. Have students continue playing for a few minutes.

- Have students open their books to p. 85 and use the photos in the game to review language. First, have students name the item in each photo. If necessary, have them look back through Units 5–8 to find the correct names. Then, point to each photo and ask a series of questions. For example, ask *What's this? What color is the [cabinet]? How many [people] are in the photo? Where is the [sofa]?*
- Hold up a copy of the Student's Book open to p. 85. Point to START and say *Start.* Then start counting 1–16 across the page, then down, then across, etc. until you come to END. Say *End.* Then say *There are sixteen photos in this game.*
- Continue to hold up the Student's Book and say *I'm Student A and you're Student B.* Point to the photo on the right in the first pair and ask *What's this?* If a volunteer answers *It's a sheep*, then have another volunteer ask you about the other photo in the pair. If no one can answer your question, have students look back through Units 5–8 until they find the answer. Then ask *What's this?* again and have a volunteer answer: *It's a sheep.*
- Divide students into pairs, A and B, and have them share a Student's Book. Have Student A point to the photo on the right each time and ask *What's this?* Have students take turns to ask and answer questions from memory. Students score one point for each correct answer. The student with the most points at the end is the winner.

- Have students play in pairs. Walk around the classroom, monitoring students while they play the game and helping when necessary.
- When students finish, have them play the game again with a different partner.
- **Extra Challenge** Have students ask each other more questions about each photo. Write these examples on the board for students to ask (and answer):
  Animal photos: What is it? Can a [sheep] [swim]? How many [legs] does it have?
  Home photos: What is it? What color is the [shower]? Is there a [shower] in the [school]?
  Places: Where's this? Is there a [swimming pool] in our town? What can we do in this place?
  Parts of the body: What's this? or What are these? How many [noses] do we have?
- **Extra Support** Have students go through the game board twice. Have them ask questions starting with *Is it a…?* The second time, have them change roles and photos.

Optional Activity

- Have students create another board game of their own, drawing different things for each space, making drawings on small sticky notes, and placing them on top of the current photos or writing new words instead of drawings. Then have students play the game for additional practice. Alternatively, have them exchange games to play.

Wrap Up

- Use the photos to review the words in a personalized way. Point to a photo and then point to yourself. Say a sentence that is true for you. For example, say *I have a big shower in my home. My nose is small. There are ducks in the park in this town.*
- Have students work in groups of three or four, working their way through the pairs of photos, choosing one each time and saying something true about themselves. When students finish, call on groups to share their sentences with the class.

Additional Practice: Workbook p. 68

1 Work in pairs. Point, ask, and answer.

START

END

The Frog and the Butter

This is a frog. He's small, but he has strong legs. He can jump, and he can swim.

Today the frog is on a farm. There are cows on the farm. Look at these cows. Next to the cows, there's a bucket of milk. "Oh, what's this?" the frog asks. "Can I swim in it?"

Now the frog is in the bucket. He can swim in the milk, but he can't jump from it. He can't jump out of the bucket. "Help!" the frog says. He swims and kicks with his legs. He kicks with his legs and swims. But what's this? Now there isn't milk in the bucket. There's butter. The frog can stand on the butter, and he can jump. Hooray! The frog isn't in the bucket now.

Glossary

bucket   milk   kick   butter   stand

In this lesson, students will:
- respond to a picture of a farmyard scene.
- read a story about a frog.
- find out how butter is made.

Resources: Audio Track 131; Classroom Presentation Tool; Flashcards 49–52, 60–68; Workbook p. 69; Workbook Audio Track 47; Online Practice

Materials: empty containers which used to hold milk, cheese, cream, yogurt and butter; a video from the Internet of butter being churned; a large piece of paper

ABOUT THE STORY

The story originates in Africa and reminds readers that even if they stumble, they should keep on going because eventually things will work out. For example, here, the milk turns into butter after a while, allowing the frog to get out of the pail. The moral is about perseverance.

Warm Up

- Take empty containers which used to hold milk, cheese, cream, yogurt, and butter, into class and display them on the table at the front of the room. Hold up the empty milk container and say *Look! Milk.* Ask *Do you like milk?* Then ask *What animal gives us milk?* (a cow) (NOTE: In some countries, goat's milk or sheep's milk is more common, so accept those answers, too.) Then point to the other empty containers and say *All these come from milk.* Point to the milk container again. Then hold up the cheese container and say *Look! This is cheese. We make it with milk.* Ask *Do you like cheese?* Repeat with the other containers

- **Use the Picture** Have students open their books to pp. 86–87. Point to the picture. Say *Point to the cows.* Ask *How many cows can you see?* (two) Point to the frog and say *Do you know the name of this animal?* If necessary, say *It's a frog.* Point to the liquid in the bucket and ask *What's this? Can you guess?* Accept any reasonable ideas.

- Direct students' attention to the title of the story. Say *This story is about a frog and butter.*

- Direct students' attention to the glossary on p. 86. Point to the picture of the bucket and say *This is a bucket.* Ask *What can we put in a bucket?* Accept any reasonable ideas. Point to the picture of milk and say *Look! Milk.* Point to the picture for *kick* and say *Look! He's kicking.* Do a kicking action and say *We can kick a ball.* Point to the picture of butter and say *Look! Butter.* Then point to the picture of *stand* and say *Look! Stand.* Then, to the class, say *Stand!* and indicate the movement with your hand. Have students stand up and then say *Sit!* Indicate the movement with your hand and have them sit down.

- Read aloud the instructions. Say *Look at the picture. What can you see?* Direct students' attention to the picture again. Ask students to raise their hands to share their ideas.

- **Listen and Read** Read aloud the instructions. Point to the text. Play **TR: 131** from beginning to end.

- Play **TR: 131** again, pausing after *he can swim.* Have students listen to and read the first paragraph of the text. Ask some questions to check that students understand. Point to the frog and ask *What animal is this?* (a frog) *Is it big or small?* (small) *Can a frog jump?* (yes) *Can a frog swim?* (yes)

- Continue playing **TR: 131**, pausing after *Can I swim in it?* Have students listen to and read the second paragraph of the text. Ask some questions to check they understand. Ask *Where's the frog?* (on a farm) *What animals are on the farm?* (cows) *What's in the bucket?* (milk)

- Continue playing **TR: 131**, pausing after *But what's this?* Have students listen to and read the first part of the last paragraph. Ask some questions to check understanding. Ask *Where's the frog now?* (in the bucket) *Can the frog swim in the milk?* (yes) *Can the frog jump out of the bucket?* (no) Say *The frog swims and … what else?* (kicks)

- Play the last part of **TR: 131**. Have students listen to and read to the end of the text. Ask some questions to check understanding. Ask *Is there milk in the bucket now?* (no) *What's in the bucket now?* (butter) *Can the frog jump out of the bucket now?* (yes) *Is the frog happy now?* (yes)

- Ask the two questions again. Ask *Can the frog jump from the milk?* (no) *Can the frog jump from the butter?* (yes)

- Have students read the text again and find the five new words from the glossary in the text. Allow students to work in pairs, helping each other.

- Review the reading strategy *using visual clues.* Say *Look at the picture. Point and say.* Have students point to different parts of the picture and say what they can see from the story. Encourage them to say *This is the [frog] from the story.*, etc.

- Bring out the empty milk and butter containers, and display them on the table. Point and say *This is milk and this is butter.* Ask *How can we make butter?* Indicate that students should use actions to show how to make butter from milk (mixing fast). If you have Internet access in the classroom, show students a video of butter being churned. Remember to always watch a video before showing it in class to check that the contents are appropriate.

Reading Extra 2

- **Listen Only** If you choose to do this as a listening-only activity, have students close their books. Follow the instructions above, pausing after each section of the text and asking the comprehension questions.
- Play **TR: 131** again, and have students raise their hands when they hear each of the five new words from the glossary.
- Divide students into pairs and have them write the most important words from the story. Ask individual students for a word each and write a list on the board of the important words in order. For example, write *milk/bucket/frog/swim/ can't jump/kick/butter/stand/can jump.*

Optional Activity

- Have students work in groups of three or four to make a storyboard for the story. First have them decide how many pictures they need to draw. Model the first frame of the storyboard on the board. Draw a square. Have students suggest what the first picture should be. Draw the picture.
- Give each group a large piece of paper to make their storyboards. Give them ten minutes to draw and color their pictures. Walk around and help as necessary. When they finish, make a display and have students read each other's storyboards.

- Read aloud the instructions. Hold up a copy of the Student's Book and point to the four sentences and the four pictures. Direct students' attention to the example in the first sentence and read aloud the sentence.
- Have students work in pairs to complete the activity. Monitor while they work, checking that they understand what they have to do and helping when necessary.
- Have three different students read aloud the other sentences for the rest of the class to check.
- **Listen Only** Play **TR: 131** again if you think students need to hear the story again before completing the activity.

- Read aloud the instructions. Hold up a copy of the Student's Book and point to the sentences. Direct students' attention to the example in the first sentence and read aloud the sentence.
- Have students work individually to complete the activity. Monitor while they work, helping when necessary.
- When everyone finishes, check answers. Call out a number (1–5) and have students respond as a class by reading the complete sentence.

Wrap Up

- Put students into pairs and have them take turns reading and acting out each scene from the story. Have one student reread the story as the other does the actions. Walk around the classroom watching students as they read and do the actions. Encourage them to say things like *Help! I can't get out!*

> **Additional Practice:** Workbook p. 69, Online Practice

1 **Look at the picture. What can you see?**

2 **Listen and read. Can the frog jump from the milk? Can he jump from the butter?** 🎧 TR: 131

No, he can't. Yes, he can.

3 **Read, look, and write.**

1. There's a ___bucket___ of milk next to the cows.

2. The frog thinks he can ___swim___ in the milk.

3. The frog ___can't___ jump out of the bucket.

4. The frog can stand on the ___butter___ and ___jump___ out.

4 **Read and write.**

1. A frog ___can___ swim.

2. A frog ___can't___ talk.

3. A frog ___can___ jump.

4. A frog ___can't___ sing.

5. A frog ___can't___ fly.

1 Look and read. Write (✔) or (✗).

1.

2.

3.

4.

This is a street. ✗

This is a library. ✔

This is a store. ✗

This is a park. ✔

2 Listen and write the numbers. 🎧 TR: 132

1. There are __nine__ on the farm.

3. There are __eight__ .

2. There are __three__ .

4. There are __four__ .

3 Write *There's* or *There are*.

1. __There are__ animals in the zoo. __There's__ a store, too.

2. __There's__ a library in my town. __There are__ stores, too.

4 Write.

1. a bird / walk   Can __a bird walk__ ? Yes, it __can__

2. a donkey / sing Can __a donkey sing__ ? No, it __can't__ .

3. a cow / talk   __Can a cow talk?__ ? __No, it can't__

4. a dog / run   __Can a dog run?__ ? __Yes, it can.__

In this lesson, students will:

• review words and grammar from Units 7 and 8.

Resources: Audio Track 132, Classroom Presentation Tool, Workbook pp. 70–71, Workbook Audio Track 48, Online Practice

Warm Up

• Have students work in pairs to review the language from Units 7–8. Have each pair share a book and take turns to point and say something about each page in the units.

• Read aloud the instructions. Point to the first photo and read aloud the sentence. Direct students' attention to the example for item 1. Say *This isn't a street.* Have students correct the sentence. (*It's a zoo.*)

• Have students work individually to complete the activity. Then check answers as a class.

Task Guidance Notes

Starters Listening Part 2 Students have to listen to a conversation and write a name or a number for five questions. There is a picture to support the conversation, but it may not illustrate all the answers. After each part of the conversation, there is a pause for students to write an answer. This tests numbers and spelling.

Challenges Students may panic because they have to listen very carefully for numbers and especially spelling. Make sure they know how to predict what type of word they are listening for by reading the questions. Practice writing letters from the alphabet quickly and neatly.

Performance Descriptors

• Can understand letters of the English alphabet when heard

• Can understand some very short conversations that use familiar questions and answers

• **Predict** Ask students to look at the photos. Ask *Where are we?* Ask students to identify all the animals in the photos. Ask a question about each photo. For example, say and ask *Look at the photos. 1. Are they horses?* (no) *2. Are they ducks?* (no) *3. Are they sheep?* (yes) *4. Are they cows?* (no)

• **Build Confidence** Say numbers and have students write them quickly. Start slowly, then get faster so that they don't have too much writing time. This will give students confidence that they can listen and write quickly as well as fast spelling practice.

• This activity practices listening to and writing numbers. Make sure students understand the instructions and direct their attention to the example. Play the first part of **TR: 132**, pause after *horses*, and write the number *nine* on the board.

• Play the rest of **TR: 132**. Have students complete the activity individually. Play **TR: 132** again for students to check their answers. Check answers with the class.

• **Own It!** Ask *How many posters are in the classroom?* Then ask students in pairs to take turns to ask and answer questions about things they can see. Monitor and help. When they finish, ask them to make a list, for example, *three posters,* etc.

Script for TR: 132
A: *Tell me about the animals on the farm. Let's start with cows.*
B: *Well, there are nine cows. And there are two horses.*
A: *What about donkeys?*
B: *There are three donkeys, Bill, Ben, and Bingo.*
A: *Bill, Ben, and Bingo! They're nice names. And sheep?*
B: *Sheep? There are eight sheep.*
A: *Eight sheep. And ducks?*
B: *There are four ducks.*
A: *Four!*

• Read aloud the instructions. Hold up a copy of the Student's Book and show students the four sentences. Direct their attention to the example and read it aloud.

• Have students work individually to complete the activity, writing *There's* or *There are* in each space.

• When everyone finishes, check answers. Call on students to read the sentences for the rest of the class to check.

• Read aloud the instructions.

• Have students work in pairs, using the prompts to write the questions and answers.

• When everyone finishes, check answers. Call on two students, one to read the questions and the other to read the answers for the rest of the class to check.

Optional Activity

• Divide the class into two halves and then divide each half into pairs. Have students in the first half make a new Activity 3 and the second half make a new Activity 4. Have students make a rough draft. Check their work, then have them transfer the activity onto a clean piece of paper and record the answers in a separate place.

• Have pairs exchange their papers with a pair from the other half of the class and do their activity. When they finish, have the two pairs work together to check their answers.

Wrap Up

• Give each of the following instructions one at a time and allow students thinking time before answering. Elicit the answers from the class, choosing a different student each time.
  1. Name five places in a town.
  2. Name five animals on a farm.
  3. Point and say a true sentence using *There is*….
  4. Point and say a true sentence using *There are*….
  5. Ask and answer a question using *Can you*…?

• You may want to ask parents or guardians to send in a traditional costume for the next lesson, if possible.

Additional Practice: Workbook pp. 70–71, Online Practice

In this unit, students will:

- talk about clothes.
- ask and answer questions about clothes using *Are these your [shoes]? Yes, they are/No, they aren't.*
- read about a scarecrow.
- talk about the color of things using *It's [black], They're [green].*
- listen to and sing a song about clothes on a clothesline.
- identify and pronounce CVC words with /ɪ/ in the middle.
- watch a video about school uniforms in other countries.
- identify the value of wearing clean clothes.

Language

Words

dress, jeans, pants, shirt, shoes, skirt, socks, T-shirt; boots, gloves, happy, hat, scarecrow

Grammar

- *Are these your shoes? Yes, they are.*
- *Are these your pants? No, they aren't.*
- *What color is his face? It's orange.*
- *What color are his eyes? They're black.*

Phonics

/ɪ/ big, bin, lip, sit, six

Twenty-First Century Skills

Collaboration
Complete questions and answers about clothes in pairs, Lesson 2

Communication
Talk about colors and clothes, Lesson 4

Creativity
Draw and speak about school uniforms, Lesson 7

Critical Thinking
Identify the value of wearing clean clothes, Lesson 5

In the Unit Opener, students will:

- respond to a photo of a girl in traditional Thai clothes.
- talk about clothes using colors.

Resources: Home School Connection Letter, Classroom Presentation Tool

Materials: a traditional costume from your country or photos of traditional costumes

Introduce the Theme

- Write the word *clothes* on the board. Point to your own clothes and say *These are my clothes.* Then point to a student's clothes and say *These are [Gia's] clothes.* Finally, give students an instruction. Say *Point to your clothes!* Have students listen and point. Say *In this unit, we're going to talk about clothes.*
- Call on a student to come to the front of the class. Point to each item of the student's clothing and to the class, ask *What color is this?*
- Bring a traditional costume into class to show students or display photos of traditional costumes. If students have traditional costumes of their own, have them bring the costumes or wear these costumes to class.
- Point to the costume and say *Look! These clothes are from [your country].* Show students each item of the costume and say *Look! This is for my [head].* Ask *What color is this?* and say *This is [blue].* Ask *Do you like these clothes?* Listen to several students' responses. Say *We wear these clothes in [name of your country]. People wear different clothes in other countries.*

Use the Photo

- Have students open their books to p. 89. Read aloud the instructions at the bottom of the page.
- Point to the child and ask *Is this a child?* (yes) Ask *How many children can you see?* (one) *Is this child a boy?* (no) *Is this child a girl?* (yes) Then say *Point to her face.* Repeat with *eyes, nose, mouth, arms, hands, legs.* Point to the child again and ask *Do you like these clothes?*
- Have students bring in a doll or a teddy bear and its own clothes for the Optional Activity in the next lesson. You may also wish to contact parents to let them know to send in a doll or a teddy bear with their child.

TEACHER TIP

Give students opportunities to bring in items for a *show-and-tell* session. Have students stand up and show something to the rest of the class and tell them a bit about it. For larger classes, keep a record of which students have had the chance to show and tell, so that other students can be given a chance next time. This activity encourages acceptance and helps to build confidence. You will need to scaffold the *tell* part of *show-and-tell.* This can be done by offering linguistic support with model sentences on the board. Alternatively, you can ask a series of questions about colors, numbers, what something can do, and so on, to keep students speaking English and using language they know.

My Clothes

A girl in Thailand

ABOUT THE PHOTO

This photo shows a girl in Thailand. She is wearing traditional Akha clothes. The Akha are indigenous people who live in small mountain villages. They are famous for their beautiful, handmade clothes. Girls wear a simple cap until the age of twelve. Then this is exchanged for a more elaborate headdress with colored decorations such as coins, feathers, beads, and fur. Each headdress is unique, as it's decorated by its owner.

Look at the photo. What can you see?

Words

1 Listen and point. 🎧 TR: 133

ABOUT THE PHOTO

This photo shows lots of colorful Indian shoes for sale. These shoes are called *jutti*. They are made from leather and are embroidered by hand. Hundreds of years ago, Indian royals wore jutti decorated with real gold and silver thread. The shoes start off with no left or right distinction. Then as they are worn, they mold to the shape of the feet and form a natural right and left pair. Both men and women wear jutti.

dress

jeans

pants

shirt

shoes

skirt

socks

T-shirt

2 Listen and repeat. 🎧 TR: 134

3 Point and say.

dress   jeans

Words

In this lesson, students will:

* talk about clothes.

Resources: Audio Tracks 133–134; Classroom Presentation Tool; Flashcards 108–109, 112–113, 121–128; Workbook p. 72; Workbook Audio Track 49; Online Practice

Materials: sticky tack, photos of different items of clothing or of people wearing different clothes, students' own dolls or teddy bears and their own clothes

Warm Up

* Display the *park* flashcard, the *playground* flashcard, the *swimming pool* flashcard and the *town center* flashcard from Unit 7 Lesson 1 on the board. Have students say the name of the place for each one. Then hold up photos of different items of clothing or of people wearing different clothes. Each time say *Look at these clothes. Where do you go with these clothes?* Mention other places and events, too, such as school or a birthday party. Have students share their ideas. Accept any reasonable answers at this stage. The important thing is for students to be thinking about different kinds of clothes.

* When you finish, say *Today we're going to learn words for clothes.*

* Point to your ear and say *Let's listen.* Play **TR: 133** and point to the photos one at a time as you hear the words.

* Use the flashcards to present and teach the clothes words. Hold up the *dress* flashcard and say *Look! A dress.* If anyone in the class is wearing a dress, point and say *Look! [Eva] has a dress. It's [blue].* Do the same with the other seven flashcards.

* Hold up each flashcard again and say *Raise your hand if you have [socks] on today!* Have students listen and raise their hands when you mention an item of clothing they are wearing. If everyone is wearing an item, say *Look! Today everyone has [shoes].*

* Read aloud the instructions. Then direct students' attention to the small photos. Play **TR: 133** again, and have students listen and point to the words and the photos.

* Say the colors of two or three items and have students point to the small photos. For example, say *Blue and green* and have them point to the photo of the socks; say *Blue, green, and white* and have them point to the photo of the shirt; say *Blue, white, and red* and have them point to the shoes.

* **Use the Photo** Point to the main photo and ask *What colors can you see?* Say *Point and say!* Have students work in pairs to point and say the colors.

* Read aloud the instructions. Play **TR: 134**. Pause after the first word to model repeating for students. Continue playing **TR: 134**, having students repeat the words as a class.

* Play **TR: 134** again and call on individual students around the class to repeat the words.

* **Extra Support** As you play **TR: 134**, hold up a flashcard or point to an item of clothing that one or more students is wearing as you hear it.

* Review the new words. Display the flashcards on the board and have students say the word for each item.

* Read aloud the instructions. Direct students' attention to the models. Point and say the words.

* Put students into pairs, A and B. Have Student A point to a photo and have Student B say a word. Have students take turns pointing and naming items in each of the photos.

* **Extra Challenge** Have students take turns pointing to an item of clothing their partner is wearing and saying the word. Have students repeat, this time pointing to items of clothing that other students in the class are wearing.

Optional Activity

* Have students bring in dolls and teddy bears and their clothes to have a fashion parade. Start by giving an example. Hold up a student's doll and talk about its clothes. If necessary, review different forms of *has* and *have* before you begin. For example, say *Look! This is [Rita]. Today she has blue jeans and a white shirt. She has shoes. Look! Her shoes are purple. [Rita] doesn't have socks today.* As you are talking about the doll's clothes, have the doll parade up and down the tabletop or up and down an aisle in the classroom. The most important thing is that everyone can see the doll's clothes.

* Allow time for students to take turns describing the clothes for their own toys. When they finish, have volunteers describe the clothes in front of the class.

Wrap Up

* Have students design an outfit for a party. To model, draw and color an outfit on the board. Add labels, such as, *A big blue hat* or *Brown shoes.*

* Have students draw and color their own clothes. Have them label each item with color and clothes words. When they finish, have them show their picture to a partner. If you'd like, make a classroom display with all the pictures, adding the heading *Our Party Clothes.*

Additional Practice: Workbook p. 72, Online Practice

Grammar

In this lesson, students will:

- ask and answer about clothes using *Are these your [shoes]? Yes, they are/No, they aren't.*
- say a chant.

Resources: Audio Tracks 135–136; Classroom Presentation Tool; Flashcards 144–151, 155; Workbook p. 73; Workbook Audio Track 50; Online Practice

Materials: a nice shirt; a funny or ugly hat; a pair of funny or ugly shoes; a pair of nice socks; paper cut-out dolls and their clothes (available for download on the Internet)

Warm Up

- Review the words from Lesson 1. Stand at the front of the class, point to your clothes, and describe them. Say *My [T-shirt] is [yellow]. My [shoes] are [black].* Have a student come to the front of the class and do the same. Then put students into groups to describe their clothes, one at a time. If the students wear a uniform, have them instead choose a photo of people in the book to describe.

- Have students open their books to p. 91. Direct students' attention to the chant. Use the *hat* flashcard (155) to teach the word *hat.* Ask students to find four clothes words in the chant. Have them work in pairs so that they can help each other. (shirt, hat, shoes, socks)
- Read aloud the instructions. Say *Listen to the chant.* Play **TR: 135.** Have students listen. Then play **TR: 135** again for students to chant. While they listen, hold up (in order) a nice shirt, a funny or ugly hat, a pair of funny or ugly shoes, and a pair of nice socks. Have students say the chant and when they give the negative responses, have them wrinkle their noses to show they really don't like the clothes.
- Play **TR: 135** again. Divide students into two groups, A and B. Point to the purple lines of the chant and say *Group A, say the purple lines.* Point to the green lines of the chant and say *Group B, say the green lines.*
- Play **TR: 135.** Have students say their lines of the chant.
- **Extra Support** Draw the four items of clothing on the board. Point to the shirt as you play **TR: 135** and draw a check next to it as the next line says *Yes, it is.* Repeat with the other three items of clothing on the board. Draw a check mark (yes) or an X (no) next to each item (hat—X, shoes—X, socks—check mark) as you listen to **TR: 135.**

- Read aloud the instructions. Direct students' attention to the grammar box. Say *Listen and read* and play **TR: 136.** Have students listen and read. Play **TR: 136** again and have students repeat the questions and answers as a class. Have them point to the items of clothing in the small photos in Lesson 1 as they speak.

- Call on a student to come to the front of the class and point to an item of clothing which is singular (dress, shirt, skirt, T-shirt). Ask *Is this your [dress]?* Emphasize *Is this.* Have the student answer *Yes it is,* emphasizing *it* and *is.* Then point to an item of clothing which is plural (shoes, socks). Ask *Are these your [shoes]?* Emphasize *Are these.* Have the student answer *Yes, they are,* emphasizing *they* and *are.* Then point to a pair of pants (one item but which takes the plural form). Ask *Are these your pants?* Emphasize *Are these.* Have the student answer *Yes, they are.* (NOTE: The question is *Are these your jeans?,* too.)
- If real clothes aren't available, use flashcards. Hold up the *T-shirt* flashcard and have students ask you *Is this your T-shirt?* Say *No, it isn't.* Then hold up the *shoes* flashcard and have students ask you *Are these your shoes?* Say *No, they aren't.*
- **Extra Support** Hold up the clothes flashcards one at a time. Ask *This or these?* each time. Have students respond.

- Point to the first picture and ask *Shoes?* (No, jeans.) Repeat for the other pictures, each time saying different items of clothing.
- Point to the questions and answers next to the pictures. Direct students' attention to the examples in item 1 and read aloud the question and answer.
- Have students complete the other questions and answers, while you monitor, encouraging and helping when necessary. Then check answers.
- **Extra Challenge** Have students add adjectives to the questions, such as *Are these your blue jeans, Xi?*

Optional Activity

- Make some paper dolls and cut-out clothes, or find and download templates of paper dolls from the Internet. Make one set for each group of four students. Allow time for students to dress their dolls. Then have them give their doll a name and describe its clothes. For example, a student may say *This is Bobby. He has brown pants and a red shirt.* Other students in the group study this doll's outfit. The remaining group members then describe their dolls' outfits.
- Have students take the clothes off the doll, mix them into a single pile, and take turns holding up random items asking, for example, *Are these your [pants], [Bobby]?* Students have to remember their dolls' clothes to respond.

Wrap Up

- Have each student draw two items of clothing on separate pieces of paper, one of which is singular and one of which is plural. Then, arrange students in groups of four to six. Have them put all their drawings together in a pile, shuffle them, and turn them facedown in the center of the table. Have students take turns choosing a drawing and asking a student *Is this your [dress]?* Have the student answer. If the questioner is correct, he/she gets to keep the picture. If not, it goes to the bottom of the pile. Have students continue until all the pictures are gone.

Additional Practice: Workbook p. 73, Online Practice

Grammar

1 Listen and chant. 🎧 TR: 135

Is this your shirt? Is this your shirt?
Yes, it is. This is my shirt.

Is this your hat? Is this your hat?
No, it isn't. This isn't my hat.

Are these your shoes? Are these your shoes?
No, they aren't. These aren't my shoes.

Are these your socks? Are these your socks?
Yes, they are. These are my socks.

2 Listen and read. 🎧 TR: 136

> Are these your shoes?
> Yes, they are.
>
> Are these your pants?
> No, they aren't.

3 Write.

 1. __Are__ these your jeans, Xi?

Xi: Yes, they __are__ .

 2. __Are__ __these__ your pants, Xi?

Xi: No, they __aren't__ .

 3. __Are__ __these__ __your__ shoes, Xi?

Xi: __Yes__ , __they__ are.

 4. __Are__ __these__ __your__ __socks__ , Xi?

Xi: No, __they__ __aren't__ .

3 Reading

1 Listen and repeat. 🎧 TR: 137

scarecrow   happy   boots   hat   gloves

2 Listen and read. 🎧 TR: 138

Look at this man. Is he real? No, he isn't! He's a **scarecrow**. A scarecrow is a big doll. You can see scarecrows on farms.

This scarecrow is **happy**. Look at his mouth! He has big eyes. What color is his face? It's orange.

What about his clothes? He has a blue and red shirt and jeans. He doesn't have shoes, but he has **boots**. They're black. He has a nice **hat** and two **gloves**.

Can you make a scarecrow?

3 Read again and match.

1. The scarecrow is   black.
2. His eyes are   blue and red.
3. His face is   happy.
4. His shirt is   orange.
5. His boots are   big.

ABOUT THE PHOTO

The photo shows a scarecrow with a jack-o'-lantern head—a head made from a pumpkin. Farmers around the world use scarecrows to scare off birds in order to stop them from eating their crops. In recent years, there has been a growing trend for scarecrow festivals in the UK, the United States, and the Philippines. Each festival is different, but you can expect to see scarecrow competitions and people dressed in scarecrow costumes as well as music, entertainment, food, and drink.

LESSON 3 Reading

In this lesson, students will:

- read about a scarecrow.
- describe a scarecrow.
- match sentence halves in a comprehension activity.

Resources: Audio Tracks 137–138, Classroom Presentation Tool, Flashcards 152–156, Workbook p. 74, Workbook Audio Track 51, Online Practice

Materials: glue, craft sticks, scissors, colored paper (including orange), yarn, sticky tack, foam blocks (optional)

Warm Up

- Review the names of clothes. Write *T-_ _ _ _* on the board. Point to the first letter and have students say the word. (T-shirt) Write *d _ _ _ _* on the board. Point to the first letter and have students say the word. (dress) Repeat with *jeans* and *pants*. Then repeat with all the other five-letter words, choosing one or more letters which belong to one word only each time. For example, write *_ h _ _ t* (shirt), *_ h _ _ s* (shoes), *_ k _ _ _* (skirt) and *_ _ _ k _* (socks).

- **Use the Photo** Have students open their books to pp. 92–93. Direct students' attention to the photo. Ask *Is this a real person?* (no) Give instructions. Say *Point to his [face].* Ask about the scarecrow's clothes. Point to the shirt and ask *What's this?* Point to the jeans and ask *What are these?*

- Read aloud the instructions. Play **TR: 137** and have students listen and repeat the words. Then use actions and descriptions to teach the new words.

- Point to the scarecrow in the photo again and say *Look! A scarecrow.* Then explain what a scarecrow does. Draw a simple scarecrow on the left of the board. Point and say *A scarecrow.* Then draw some simple birds on the right of the board and say *Look! Birds.* Then point to the scarecrow again and draw an arrow toward the right to indicate that the birds fly away when they see the scarecrow.

- Smile in an exaggerated manner and point to your mouth. Say *Look! I'm happy.* Call on a student and ask *Are you happy, [Marta]?* Do the same with a few other students, having them smile and look happy each time.

- Use the photo in the book to teach *boots, hat,* and *gloves.* Point to each item and say *Look! [A hat].* Then ask about colors and have students call out the answers.

- Point to the text and say *Find the words here.* Have students scan the text to find the five new words.

- Read aloud the instructions. Point to the text and play **TR: 138.** Have students listen to and read the whole text.

- Play **TR: 138** again, pausing after the first paragraph. Have students listen and read. Hold up the *scarecrow* flashcard and ask *What's this?* Then ask *Is a scarecrow big or small?* (big) *Where can you see scarecrows?* (on farms) Continue playing **TR: 138**, pausing after each paragraph and asking questions.

- Hold up a copy of the Student's Book open to p. 92 and point to the scarecrow's face. Say *He's happy.* Ask *Are you happy?* Say *His face is orange.* Ask *Is your face orange?* Personalize the other comprehension questions you asked about the scarecrow. For example ask *Do you have shoes?*

- **Reading Strategy: Making Personal Connections** One way to engage students while reading is to have them make personal connections with the text. As you check comprehension, pause and ask questions about the students themselves. Making personal connections helps students engage with the text more fully to better understand and retain.

- Read aloud the instructions. Hold up a copy of the Student's Book and point to the words on the right. Say *Black* and have students find this word in the text. Then say *Blue and red* and have students find these words in the text. Repeat with the other three words on the right. Then have students read aloud the sentences in the text which include these adjectives. Then point to the first words of item 1 (*The scarecrow is*). Point to the words on the right and have students call out *happy.* Use your finger to trace a line from *is* to *happy.* Have students draw the line in their books.

- Have students complete the matching activity on their own or in pairs. Check the activity by asking students to read aloud each of the complete sentences, one at a time.

- **Extra Challenge** Before students begin the matching, have them cover the sentence endings. In pairs, have them try to guess each ending. Then, have them reveal the endings and check their work.

- **Extra Support** Before students begin, have them look at the words on the right. Ask *What's black? What's blue and red? What's orange? What's big?* Have students point to things in the photo.

Optional Activity

- Have students make mini-scarecrows. Have them glue craft sticks in a T-shape so that the scarecrow's arms are extended. Cut out an orange head for each scarecrow. Then have students attach yarn for its hair and draw its face. Then have them use colored paper to cut out the scarecrow's clothes, and stick both the face and the clothes onto the scarecrow. Either display the scarecrows on a bulletin board or get some foam blocks (as used by florists) to stand them up. Have students describe their scarecrow's face and clothes, either in pairs or, for smaller classes, to the class.

Wrap Up

- Have students close their books and see how much they can remember from the reading text. Read the text aloud, one or two lines at a time, pausing before key words. Have students call out the words as a class.

Additional Practice: Workbook p. 74, Online Practice

Grammar

In this lesson, students will:

- talk about the color of things using *It's [black]*, *They're [green]*.

Resources: Audio Tracks 139–140, Classroom Presentation Tool, Workbook p. 75, Workbook Audio Track 52, Online Practice

Materials: photos of people wearing clothes students can name (optional), sticky tack

Warm Up

- Invite a male student to the front of the class. Point to the student's hair and say *Look at [Michael]! His hair is [brown]. His eyes are [green].* Then invite a female student to the front of the class. Point to the student's hair and say *Look at [Isla]! Her hair is [black]. Her eyes are [blue].* (If you have single-gendered classes, only teach either *his* or *her*.) Have the student point to you and say similar sentences.

- On the board, write *Look at the boy/girl! His/Her hair is [brown]. His/Her eyes are [green].* Have students take turns to point and say. Monitor students while they speak to make sure they are using *is* and *are* correctly.

- Have students open their books to p. 93. Direct students' attention to the grammar box. Say *Listen and read* and play **TR: 139** from beginning to end. Have students listen and read. Play **TR: 139** again and have students repeat the questions and answers as a class.

- Point to a student and ask *What color is [his] hair?* Answer yourself, and say *It's [brown].* Emphasize *it's.* Then ask *What color are [his] eyes?* Say *They're [blue].* Emphasize *They're.*

- Copy the two answers in the grammar box on the board. Circle *It's* and write *It is* under the first answer. Then circle *They're* and write *They are* under the second answer. Point and say *It's, It is* and *They're, They are.* Say *Use* it *for one; use* they *for two.*

- Point to things around the room and ask *What color are the pencils? What color is the board?* Elicit answers starting with *It's* and *They're.*

- Direct students' attention to the picture of the scarecrow, and have them name the clothes and their colors.

- Read aloud the instructions. Then point to item 1 and read aloud the question. Have students point to the scarecrow's hair and then say the answer. (It's black.) Direct their attention to the example in the book.

- Have students complete the activity in pairs. Have students take turns to ask and answer questions.

- Check answers by reading aloud each question and calling on a different student each time to give the answer.

- **Extra Challenge** Have students answer the same questions about the scarecrow's clothes in the photo on pp. 92–93.

- Read aloud the instructions. Make sure students are prepared with a pencil and paper or their notebooks and some colored crayons or markers. Play **TR: 140** from beginning to end. Then play **TR: 140** again, pausing after each instruction for students to listen, draw, and color.

- Have students compare their drawings in pairs to make sure they are the same.

- **Listening Strategy: Listening for Adjectives** Explain to students that it is very important to identify describing words, such as colors, in a listening text. Students can listen once for the describing words. Then, have them listen a second time to identify what is being described by each word.

- **Extra Support** Write the colors students will hear on the board: red, blue, black, and green.

Script for TR: 140

A: *Draw a girl. She's a scarecrow.*
B: *What clothes is she wearing?*
A: *She has a T-shirt, a skirt, socks, and shoes.*
B: *What color is her skirt?*
A: *It's red.*
B: *What color are her socks?*
A: *They're blue. Her T-shirt is blue, too.*
B: *What color is her hair?*
A: *It's black.*
B: *What color are her shoes?*
A: *They're green.*
B: *Done!*

- Read aloud the instructions. Model the conversation with a volunteer. Choose a girl in the class and have the volunteer begin the conversation by saying *Girl or boy?* Then choose a boy and model the conversation again.

- Have students work in pairs. Have them take turns to choose someone in the class, and to ask and answer questions. If the students are in uniform, this activity can be changed so that students are speaking about people in photos from a magazine or the Internet.

Optional Activity

- Have each student draw a picture of a child, dressed in pants, shoes, socks, a T-shirt, and a hat. Allow students to color the clothes any way they like. Display the pictures on the board. Ask students to say the name of the child and write the names under the children on the board.

- Have students, in pairs, take turns choosing a picture without telling their partner which one. Then have them ask and answer questions to guess the correct picture.

Wrap Up

- Have students ask and answer questions about people's clothes using photos and illustrations in the Student's Book. Put students into small groups. Have them take turns pointing to photos and asking *What color are [his jeans]?* Have students answer with complete sentences.

Additional Practice: Workbook p. 75, Online Practice

Grammar

1 Listen and read. 🎧 TR: 139

> What color is his face?
> It's orange.
>
> What color are his eyes?
> They're black.

2 Read and answer.

1. What color is his hair?
   It's black.
2. What color is his hat?
   It's blue.
3. What color are his pants?
   They're green.
4. What color is his shirt?
   It's white.
5. What color are his boots?
   They're brown.

3 Listen, draw, and color. 🎧 TR: 140

4 Say, ask, and answer.

Girl or boy?

Girl.

OK. What color are her shoes?

They're black.

5 Song

1 **Listen and read.** 🎧 TR: 141

2 **Listen and sing.** 🎧 TR: 142 and 143

3 **Sing and act.** 🎧 TR: 144

Chorus
***Are these your clothes
on the clothesline?
Are your clothes clean?
Yes, they are mine.
Yes, they're my clothes
on the clothesline.
Yes, my clothes are clean.
And they're all mine.***

**Dresses and T-shirts,
yellow and green.
Socks and pants,
dark blue jeans.**

**Gray and white jackets,
two pink skirts.
Lots and lots of
red and white shirts!**
Chorus

VALUE **Wear clean clothes.**
Workbook, Lesson 6

LESSON 5 Song

In this lesson, students will:
- listen to and sing a song about clothes on a clothesline.
- act out a song.
- identify the value of wearing clean clothes.

Resources: Audio Tracks 141–144, Classroom Presentation Tool, Workbook p. 77, Online Practice

Materials: two blue crayons (one dark and one light), two T-shirts (one clean and one dirty), a dirty shirt, coloured paper, string, clothespins or paper clips

Warm Up

- Review clothes words. Invite a colleague into the classroom. Have students note his/her clothes, and hair color. Then take a photo of the colleague. After this person has left the classroom, ask students questions about his/her clothes. For example, ask *What color are his/her shoes? What color is his/her shirt?* Have students answer all your questions. Then, hold up the photo so that they can check.
- **Use the Photo** Hold up a copy of the Student's Book open to p. 94. Say *Look! Lots of clothes.* Point to the clothesline, trace your finger along it, and say *This is a clothesline.*

- Review *dark* and *light*. Hold up two blue crayons, one dark blue and one light blue. Ask *What color are these?* Then point to one crayon and ask *Is this dark blue or light blue?*
- Draw a jacket on the board or point to a jacket in the class and say *This is a jacket.* Write *jacket* on the board. Teach the word *gray* by pointing to something gray in the classroom.
- Have students scan the words of the song quickly to find clothes words. Ask *How many words for clothes?* (eight)
- Read aloud the instructions. Play **TR: 141**.
- **Extra Support** Write the eight clothes words in a list on the board. Point to each word as you play **TR: 141**.

- Read aloud the instructions. Play **TR: 142**. Get a clapping or tapping rhythm going to accompany the song. Play **TR: 142** a second time and have students sing the whole song.
- Play **TR: 143**, the instrumental version of the song, for students to sing.

- Read aloud each line of the chorus and demonstrate an action. Have students make the action, too.
  Are these your clothes (Point to your own clothes.)
  on the clothesline? (Point upwards and move your finger along an imaginary clothesline.)
  Are your clothes clean? (Rub your hands together in a washing gesture and then hold them out.)
  Yes, they are mine. (Nod and point to your clothes.)
  Yes, they're my clothes (As above)
  on the clothesline. (As above)
  Yes, my clothes are clean. (As above)
  And they're all mine! (As above)

- Read aloud each line of the verses and demonstrate an action. Have students make the action, too.
  Dresses and T-shirts, (Point to yourself wearing an imaginary dress, then a T-shirt.)
  yellow and green. (Place left hand out to the left, right hand out to the right.)
  Socks and pants, (Point to your feet and then your legs.)
  dark blue jeans. (Point to your legs.)
  Gray and white jackets, (Touch the lapel of an imaginary jacket.)
  two pink skirts. (Hold up two fingers, then point to yourself wearing an imaginary skirt.)
  Lots and lots of (Point to lots of different things in a row in front of you.)
  red and white shirts! (Point to yourself wearing an imaginary shirt.)

- Play **TR: 144**, pausing after each line to make sure everyone remembers the actions. You can change or simplify the actions if necessary.
- Play **TR: 144** again. Have students sing the song again and do the actions.
- **Extra Challenge** Have students draw a clothesline with the items of clothing in the song (yellow and green dresses and T-shirts, socks and pants, dark blue jeans, gray and white jackets, two pink skirts, lots of red and white shirts).
- **Value: Wear clean clothes** At this point in the lesson, you can teach the value. Say *The value of this lesson is* Wear clean clothes. On the board write *Wear clean clothes.* Say *The clothes on the clothesline are clean.* Hold up a clean T-shirt. Ask *What's this?* (a T-shirt) Smile and say *This is a clean T-shirt.* Hold up a dirty T-shirt, frown, and say *This is a dirty T-shirt.* Hold up each T-shirt one at a time and have students react by smiling or frowning. Say *We wear clean clothes to school. We can wear dirty clothes at the playground.* Hold up a dirty shirt and ask *Is it OK at school?* (no) *Is it OK at the playground?* (yes) *Is it OK at the museum?* (no) *Is it OK at the park?* (yes) For additional practice, have students complete Lesson 6 of the Workbook in class or at home.

Optional Activity

- Have students draw and cut out clothes shapes from colored paper. Then have them use the clothes to play a game. Hang a clothesline, made from a piece of string, across the classroom between two chairs. Use clothespins or paper clips to attach all the clothes students made. Walk along the clothesline, point, and ask *What's this? What are these?* Have students answer in chorus. Then have students close their eyes. Remove an item of clothing from the clothesline. Have students look again and ask *What's missing from the clothesline?* Have students race to answer.

Wrap Up

- Put students into pairs or groups of three to invent two new verses for the song, changing clothes words and colors to describe their own clothes. Have students come to the front of the class to sing their verses, pointing to their clothes as they sing.

Additional Practice: Workbook p. 77, Online Practice

Phonics

In this lesson, students will:
- identify and pronounce CVC words with /ɪ/ in the middle.
- form three-letter words with the letter *i*.

Resources: Audio Tracks 145–147, Classroom Presentation Tool, Flashcards 157–161, Workbook p. 76, Workbook Audio Track 53, Online Practice

---

Warm Up

- Play a drawing game with students. Draw part of a number 6 on the board. Pause and ask *What number is it?* Then draw another part of the number 6 and repeat the question. Continue until a student is able to guess what number you have drawn. Do the same with a drawing of a bin. Then draw a big circle and a small circle, and point to the big one. Ask *Is it big or small?* (big) Then point and say *Six, bin, big.* Today we're learning words with the /ɪ/ sound in the middle.

- Have students open their books to p. 95. Direct students' attention to the photos and words. Read aloud the instructions. Play **TR: 145**, pointing to each photo and word as students hear it.
- Play **TR: 145** again. Have students repeat each word. Monitor students carefully, making sure they pronounce the target sound (/ɪ/) correctly. Ask *What sound are we learning today?* (/ɪ/) Remind students that they are practicing this sound in the middle of words. Remind them that *i* is a vowel and each of these words follows a consonant, vowel, consonant pattern with *i* in the middle.

- Read aloud the instructions. Point to the chant. Say *Listen. Can you hear the /ɪ/ sound?* Play **TR: 146**. Have students work in pairs and circle the letters. Check answers together as a class by saying each word, one at a time, and writing the word on the board.
- Play **TR: 146** again. This time have students read and chant.
- **Extra Challenge** Have students read the chant again and find any other words with the /ɪ/ sound (*It's, is, if*).

- Have students look at the picture. Say *Point to six, Point to bin,* and *Point to lip.* Then say *Point to something big* and *Point to the number six.* Have students listen, look, and point. Stand up and say *Stand!* Sit down and say *Sit!* Point to the girl sitting and ask *Stand or sit?* (sit) Then point to the photo illustrating *sit* in Activity 1. Do the same with the other four items so that students understand they can copy the words from Activity 1.
- Read aloud the instructions. Give students a minute to look at the picture again, read the words, and think about the sounds.
- Play **TR: 147**. Have students do the activity individually.
- Walk around the classroom, monitoring students as they do the activity and checking to see they have written the words correctly.
- **Extra Support** Before students do the activity, hold up a copy of the Student's Book open to p. 95 and point to parts of the picture. Ask *What's this? What are these? What color are [the books]? What's [next to] the [lamp]?*

Script for TR: 147 *sit, six, bin, lip, big*

Optional Activity

- Practice the new sound. Say a series of words, one after the other. Have students raise their hands if they hear the sound /ɪ/. Say *Six, pen, lip, big, man, jam, leg, bin, bed.*
- Have students make a list of nine words, using the phonics words from Units 7–9. Divide the class into pairs and have students read their words to their partner. Have students raise their hands if they hear the sound /ɪ/. Have them then repeat any words with the sound /ɪ/ that they heard.
- Have students change partners several times and repeat the activity, reading the list faster each time.

Wrap Up

- Hand out the five phonics flashcards to volunteers. Have them say the sentence in the chant that includes their word and have the rest of the class say the other sentences. For example, have the student with the *sit* flashcard say the first sentence, have the student with the *six* flashcard say the second sentence, have the student with the *lip* flashcard say the third sentence, and have all the students say the fourth sentence. When students have said the chant, collect the flashcards and then hand them out to five different students. Repeat the chant in this way several times.

Additional Practice: Workbook p. 76, Online Practice

---

1 Listen, point, and repeat. 🎧 TR: 145

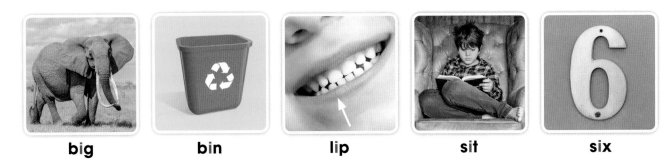

| big | bin | lip | sit | six |

2 Listen, chant, and circle. 🎧 TR: 146

Sit on the chair. Count to six.
Touch your lip. Touch your head.
Look at the bin. It's very big.
What color is it? It's red!

3 Listen and find. Write the word. 🎧 TR: 147

1. l i p
2. s i x
3. s i t
4. b i n
5. b i g

1 **Watch and match. Write the numbers.** ▶ Video 11

 1. Yurara   **2. Indiphile**   **3. Juan**

ABOUT THE VIDEO

In this video, the three children talk about school uniforms in their countries. Uniforms are common in elementary and secondary schools all over the world. They have been traced back to the sixteenth century in schools in the UK. In some schools in countries where there are extreme weather changes, students have two uniforms—one for the winter and another for the summer.

2 **Your turn! Ask and answer.**

Do you have a school uniform?

Yes, I have gray pants and a white shirt. I also have white socks and black shoes.

3 **Draw and say.**

At school

This is my _____ .

These are _____ .

At home

This _____ .

_____ .

Video

In this lesson, students will:

- watch a video about school uniforms in other countries.
- ask and answer about school uniforms.
- draw and speak about clothes for school and for home.

Resources: Video 11, Classroom Presentation Tool, Online Practice

End-of-Unit Resources: Worksheet 1.9, Unit 9 Test, ExamView Assessment Suite

Materials: a school uniform or a photo of a typical school uniform from the students' country (including a jacket, tie, and sweater)

Warm Up

- Show the class a school uniform. Have different students describe each item of clothing. Have them point and say *This is a [blue] shirt.* Review the word *jacket*, and teach *tie* and *sweater*.
- If students wear a school uniform, have them stand up, one at a time, and describe one part of it.
- Ask *Do you like your school uniform?* Or, if students don't have a school uniform, ask *Do you like school uniforms?* Listen to students' responses. Then say *Today we're going to learn about what children wear to school in other counties.*

- Have students open their books to p. 96. Direct students' attention to the three photos at the top of the page. Say the name of one of the children. For example, say *Juan* and have students say the corresponding number. Do the same with the other names.
- Point to the three photos of children wearing school uniforms. Give students instructions to point to different items of clothing. Use colors. Say *Point to [a white shirt].* Have students listen and point.
- Read aloud the instructions and play **Video 11** from beginning to end. Have students match the three numbers and names at the top with the photos at the bottom and write the numbers in the boxes.
- Play **Video 11** and pause after Yurara says *Yes, I do.* Ask *Does Yurara have a school uniform?* (yes) Continue and pause again when she says *For my books, I have a red bag.* Ask *What's her uniform?* Have students name as many items and colors as they can (gray skirt, white shirt, white socks, black shoes). Write the name *Yurara* and as many items and colors as students can name on the board. Continue playing **Video 11** and have students look at the photo on the right and point to the items of clothing as they listen.
- Repeat for Indiphile. Pause after she says *Yes, I do.* Ask *Does Indiphile have a school uniform?* (yes) Continue and pause again when she says *I have blue socks and brown shoes.* Ask *What's her uniform?* Have students name as many items and colors as they can (blue dress, blue shirt, blue socks, brown shoes). Write the name *Indiphile* and a list of items and colors on the board.

- Repeat for Juan. Continue playing **Video 11** and pause after he says *I can wear jeans and a T-shirt.* Ask *Does Juan have a school uniform?* (no) *What does he wear to school?* (jeans, T-shirt) Then continue playing **Video 11** to the end. Have students look at the middle photo and point to the items of clothing as they listen.
- Play **Video 11** again if necessary. Pause at the end of each segment for students to name more clothes the speakers wear to school. Write these words in the lists on the board.
- **Extra Support** Before playing **Video 11**, make sentences about the clothes the children in the three photos at the bottom are wearing. Say *The girls have [pink dresses]* or *The boy has [a yellow hat].* Encourage students to point to the child or children. Repeat with sentences about different colors and clothes.

The script for **Video 11** *is available on the Teacher's Resource Website.*

- Read aloud the instructions and model the conversation with a volunteer.
- Put students into pairs to ask and answer questions about what they wear to school.
- Monitor students while they speak and help when necessary.

Optional Activity

- Have students work in pairs to design a school uniform. Have them draw the uniform, then color it and add labels. When they finish, have students describe their uniform to their classmates. To extend the activity, have students draw separate uniforms for boys and girls.

- Read aloud the instructions. Use the board to demonstrate. Draw some clothes that you wear at home. Point to the picture and say *At home. This is my [T-shirt]. These are my [socks].*
- Have students draw two pictures—one for the clothes they wear at home and the other for the clothes they wear at school. Have students work individually to complete the activity. When they finish, have them walk around with their books and show their pictures to their classmates. Have them talk about their drawings.
- **Extra Challenge** When students show their pictures to classmates, encourage the students who are looking at the drawings to use *your.* For example, have them say *This is your shirt, These are your shoes.*

Wrap Up

- Divide the class into pairs and have students describe the children in the photos in Activity 1. Then have students tell each other what Yurara, Indiphile, and Juan wear to school. If necessary, write these colors and clothes on the board in random order (Yurara: gray skirt, white shirt, white socks, black shoes; Indiphile: blue dress, blue shirt, blue socks, brown shoes; Juan: jeans, T-shirt).

Additional Practice: Worksheet 1.9, Online Practice

In this unit, students will:

- talk about food and drink.
- talk about food preferences using *I like* and *I don't like.*
- read about a school lunch.
- use *Do you like…* and *Yes, I do/No, I don't; It's/They're OK* to ask and answer questions about food.
- listen to and sing a song about food.
- identify and pronounce CVC words with /a/ in the middle.
- watch a video about meals in other countries.
- identify the value of eating good food.

Language

Words

banana, bread, candy, lemon, milk, potato, rice, tomato, water; great, lunch, terrible, tray

Grammar

- *I like bananas. I don't like rice.*
- *Do you like apples? Yes, I do. They're great./They're OK.*
- *Do you like milk? No, I don't. It's terrible./It's OK.*

Phonics

/a/ dog, dot, fox, mop, nod

Twenty-First Century Skills

Collaboration
Work with a partner to practice words, Lesson 1

Communication
Take turns to talk about likes and dislikes, Lesson 2

Creativity
Draw and speak about a favorite food, Lesson 7

Critical Thinking
Identify the value of eating good food, Lesson 5

In the Unit Opener, students will:

- respond to a photo of an orange and lemon display.
- classify fruits and vegetables.

Resources: Home School Connection Letter, Classroom Presentation Tool

Materials: photos of fruits and vegetables

Introduce the Theme

- Bring to class photos of fruits and vegetables. Hold up a photo of a fruit and say *Fruit.* Write the word *fruit* on the board. Say the word aloud again. Hold up a photo of a vegetable and say *Vegetable.* Write the word *vegetable* on the board. Say it aloud again.
- Hold up a few more photos of fruit items and vegetable items, and have students respond by saying *Fruit* or *Vegetable.*
- Play a game. Have students stand up. Each time you hold up a fruit photo, have students clap their hands. Each time you show a vegetable photo, have them stomp their feet.
- Say *In this unit, we're going to talk about fruits and vegetables. We eat these things.* Hold up a copy of the Student's Book open to p. 97 and point to the unit title: *Eat and Drink.* Say *Eat,* and ask *What else do you eat?* Have students draw other foods they eat, and walk around as they work, reacting to their drawings.
- Then point to the word *Drink* in the unit title. Act out drinking a glass of water. Then ask *What do you drink?* Have students add drinks to their drawing.

Use the Photo

- Have students open their books to p. 97. Read aloud the instructions at the bottom of the page and point to the photo. Ask *Fruits or vegetables?* (fruits) Point to the oranges and ask *What color is this fruit?* (orange) Note that some of the oranges are in the foreground and some are on the wall of the house. Then point to the lemons on the wall and ask *What color is this fruit?* (yellow) Then give instructions. Say *Point to a house.* Then say *Point to a man* and *Point to a flower.* Each time, pause to make sure students are pointing to the correct item.
- Read aloud the caption. Point and ask *Is it fun? Yes or no?*

TEACHER TIP
Total Physical Response (TPR) activities are ideal for students of this age. Have students respond by doing different actions in reaction to something you say or do. Actions like clapping, turning around, jumping, touching their heads, and pointing are motivating and allow students to show their understanding without having to produce any language.

Eat and Drink

ABOUT THE PHOTO

This photo shows workers making an orange and lemon display for *La fête du citron*, The Lemon Festival, in Menton, France. The festival started in 1928, when a hotel manager had the idea of having an exhibition of citrus fruit and flowers in the Hôtel Riviera's gardens. The festival grew each year, spreading out into the surrounding streets and attracting many tourists. These days the festival continues with its exhibitions, but also has parades, entertainment, music, and light shows.

Orange and lemon festival in France

Look at the photo. What can you see?

Words

1 Listen and point. 🎧 TR: 148

banana   **bread**   **candy**   **lemon**   **milk**

potato   **rice**   **tomato**   **water**

2 Listen and repeat. 🎧 TR: 149

3 Point and say.

a banana

rice

ABOUT THE PHOTO

This photo shows a street vendor with a bicycle full of bananas in Vietnam. More than 1,000 varieties of bananas are grown in 150 countries around the world. They aren't always yellow. There is a blue variety (Blue Java), a black variety (the Macabu), and even a lemon-flavored variety (the Burro). Not all bananas are sweet. Some are savory. In some countries, people don't peel bananas. They eat the skin, too.

LESSON 1 Words

In this lesson, students will:

- talk about food and drink.

Resources: Audio Tracks 148–149; Classroom Presentation Tool; Flashcards 101, 162–169; Workbook p. 78; Workbook Audio Track 54; Online Practice

Materials: photos of food and drink (NOTE: Potatoes can be potato chips, rice can be cereal or rice cakes, etc.), colored paper, glue, poster paper

Warm Up

- Say *Today we're going to learn words for food.* On the board, draw a happy face and a sad face. If you use different-colored markers, use green for the happy face and red for the sad face. This will link to Lesson 4 of this unit. Point to the happy face and say *Yes! Yum! I like this.* Have students repeat *yes.* Then point to the sad face, shake your head, and say *No!* Have students repeat *no.* Write *yes* and *no* below the two faces on the board.

- Hold up a photo of a food item and point to the two faces on the board. Have students respond *yes* or *no* according to whether or not they like the food. Repeat with other food photos.

- **Use the Photo** Have students open their books to pp. 98–99. Point to the bananas in the main photo and say *Look! Fruit. They're bananas.* Say *Yes! I like bananas* and nod your head or say *No! I don't like bananas* and shake your head.

- Have students use the photo to listen, look, find, and point. Give instructions to find and point to different things in the main photo. Say *Point to something [yellow].* Repeat with other colors. Then say *Point to a woman.* Repeat with *her hat, a street, her shoes,* and *her pants.*

- Read aloud the instructions. Then direct students' attention to the small photos. Point and say *Look, food and drink.*

- Point to your ear and say *Let's listen.* Play **TR: 148** and point to the photos, one at a time, as you hear the words.

- Play **TR: 148** again, and model pointing to the photos under the instructions.

- Read aloud the instructions. Play **TR: 149.** Pause after the first word. Repeat the word to model the activity for students. Continue **TR: 149** and have students repeat the words as a class.

- Play **TR: 149** again and call on individual students around the class to repeat the words.

- **Extra Challenge** Have students hide the words under the photos with colored paper while they listen, repeat, and point.

- **Extra Support** Hold up the flashcard for each word you hear on the audio.

- Have students close their books. Use the flashcards to practice the words. Hold up the *tomato* flashcard and ask *Tomato or potato?* Repeat with the other flashcards, asking a question with *or* each time.

- Have students open their books again. Read aloud the instructions. Direct students' attention to the examples. Model pointing and saying the words.

- Put students into pairs. Have them take turns pointing to the food and drink photos and saying the words. Monitor students while they do the activity, making sure they are taking turns, and helping when necessary.

Optional Activity

- Have students make food and drink posters in small groups. Have them draw and color pictures. Then, have them glue the pictures to poster paper, add a heading, and label the words. Have them add happy and sad pictures to indicate which items they all like or dislike.

- Have groups of students take turns holding up their posters and saying the words.

Wrap Up

- Write the new words on the board with the letters scrambled.

a a a b n n
a b d e r
a c d n y
a e r t w
a m o o t t
a o o p t t
e l m n o
c e i r
i k l m

- Have students work in pairs to unscramble the letters and write the words in their notebooks. When they finish, have them look back at Activity 1 to check the spelling. (Answers: banana, bread, candy, water, tomato, potato, lemon, rice, milk)

Additional Practice: Workbook p. 78, Online Practice

LESSON 2 Grammar

In this lesson, students will:
- talk about food preferences using *I like* and *I don't like*.
- say a chant about likes and dislikes.

Resources: Audio Tracks 150–151; Classroom Presentation Tool; Flashcards 101, 162–169; Workbook p. 79; Workbook Audio Track 55, Online Practice

Materials: sticky tack, colored paper

Warm Up
- Review the words from Lesson 1. Display the flashcards on the board in a row in random order and number them 1–9. Call out two numbers. For example, say *Four* and *two*. Have students respond by calling out the corresponding words, for example, *water* and *rice*.
- Hold up a copy of the Student's Book open to p. 98. Point to the second photo and say *Bread!* Then point to one slice and say *One slice of bread.*

- Hold up a copy of the Student's Book open to p. 99. Point to and read aloud the instructions. Say *Listen to the chant.* Play **TR: 150.** Have students listen and clap to the rhythm.
- Play **TR: 150** again. This time have students chant, too.

- Read aloud the instructions. Direct students' attention to the grammar box. Say *Listen and read* and play **TR: 151.** Have students listen and read. Play **TR: 151** again and get students to repeat the sentences as a class.
- Hold up the *bread* flashcard. Say *Look! Bread. I like bread.* Emphasize the word *like.* Rub your stomach, and smile and lick your lips. Do the same with the *rice* flashcard and *rice.* Then hold up the *potato* flashcard. Say *Look! A potato. I don't like potatoes!* Emphasize the word *don't* and frown. Do the same with the *lemon* flashcard and *lemons.*
- On the board, write *I like milk. I like apples.* Say the two sentences aloud and underline the *s* in *apples.* Point and say *I like apples.* Ask *I like apple or I like apples?* (I like apples.) Say *That's right.* Write the two sentences *I like milk* and *I like apples* on the board. Direct students' attention to Activity 1 on p. 98. Point to each word, one at a time, and say *I like [bananas], I like [bread].* Write the words *bread, candy, rice,* and *water* under *milk* on the board, and write *bananas, lemons, potatoes,* and *tomatoes* under *apples* on the board. Say *I like bananas* and point to the final *s.* Repeat with the other plural words.
- Point to the chant and read aloud *I like bananas.* Then say a few more sentences with plural forms. For example, say *I like lemons. I like tomatoes. I like potatoes.* Emphasize the *s* each time.

- Hold up a copy of the Student's Book and point to the four pictures of food and drink items. Then point to each picture and ask *What is it?* (rice, a banana, a kiwi, milk)
- Read aloud the instructions. Point to the four items under the pictures. Point and read aloud item 1, and pause at the space. Point to the picture and ask *Like or don't like?* (like) Have students write *like* in the space.
- Have students work in pairs to look at the pictures, read the sentences, and write *like* or *don't like.*
- Monitor students as they work. Then call on students to read aloud each complete sentence for the rest of the class to check.
- **Extra Challenge** Before students write, have them cover the sentences with a piece of colored paper. Have them work in pairs to try to say the sentences themselves.
- **Extra Support** Before students write, have them point to each picture, and smile or frown to indicate whether the child likes the food or not.

- Read aloud the instructions. Model the sentences for the rest of the class to listen to. Rub your stomach and smile as you say the first sentence. Frown as you say the second.
- Put students into pairs. Have them take turns talking about food and drink they like and don't like. Monitor students while they do the activity, making sure they are taking turns to speak and helping when necessary.

Optional Activity
- Do a class survey about food and drink likes and dislikes. Put students into groups and give each group some food items to draw. Make sure each group has a similar number of food and drink items.
- Model the activity. Draw a lemon on the board, and draw a happy and a sad face next to the lemon. Then point to the picture and invite a student to say *I like lemons* or *I don't like lemons.* Write *1* under the happy or sad face depending on the answer. Ask more students and keep erasing the old number and writing the new one. When you have asked everyone, say *Look! [Eight] students like lemons and [six] students don't like lemons.* NOTE: If nobody likes the food, or if only one student likes the food, erase the drawing and move on to a different food, simply saying *Let's try again!* Avoid presenting *likes* at this stage.
- Have students conduct their surveys in groups. Then have them share the results with the rest of the class.

Wrap Up
- Practice using *like* and *don't like* in a memory game. Have each student say one sentence, such as *I don't like rice* or *I like water.* Have students then take turns pointing to one of their classmates and saying from memory what this person likes or dislikes. Show students how to use *You.* For example, say *[Gianni], you don't like rice. [Julian], you like water.*
- Have students play in groups of four or five. Monitor them as they play.

Additional Practice: Workbook p. 79, Online Practice

Grammar

1 **Listen and chant.** 🎧 TR: 150

I like bananas, and I like bread.
I don't like apples, green or red!

I like oranges, and I like rice.
I like bread. Can I have a slice?

2 **Listen and read.** 🎧 TR: 151

> I like **bananas**.
> I don't like **rice**.

3 **Write *like* or *don't like*.**

1. I ___like___ rice.

2. I ___don't like___ bananas.

3. I ___don't like___ kiwis.

4. I ___like___ water.

4 **Say.**

I like potatoes.

I don't like milk.

UNIT 10   Eat and Drink   **99**

3 Reading

1 Listen and repeat. 🎧 TR: 152

> lunch   tray   terrible   great

2 Listen and read. 🎧 TR: 153

Look at the photo. It's time for **lunch**! These boys and girls have **trays**. The trays are on the table. The lunch is a school lunch. How many trays can you see? What's on the trays? Can you see the food?

I like carrots, but I don't like potatoes. They're **terrible**! Look! Is that rice? Yes, it is. I like rice. It's **great**.

3 Read again. Complete the sentences.

> lunch   rice   table   trays   two

1. There are ___two___ boys in the photo.

2. The children eat ___lunch___ at school.

3. The lunches are on ___trays___ .

4. The trays are on the ___table___ .

5. The boys and girls eat ___rice___ for lunch.

 Reading

In this lesson, students will:

- read about a school lunch.
- use new words to talk about lunch.
- choose the correct words to complete sentences about a text.

Resources: Audio Tracks 152–153; Classroom Presentation Tool; Flashcards 101, 162–173; Workbook p. 80; Workbook Audio Track 56; Online Practice

Warm Up

- Play a guessing game about food and drink. Point to your head to show you are thinking. Then ask *Can you guess the food or drink?* Give clues, one at a time, and have students hold up their hands if they want to guess. Give clues using *big* or *small* and colors. Say *This is a fruit. It's small. It's green and brown.* (a kiwi)

- Call on a few students to describe a food or drink item for the rest of the class to guess. Use the Lesson 1 flashcards to select items. Show a flashcard to the student who is giving the clues. Make sure the other students don't see it.

- **Use the Photo** Have students open their books to pp. 100–101. Direct students' attention to the photo. Point and ask *What can you see?* (boys and girls) Ask *How many children can you see?* (four)

- Give students instructions. Say *Point to a boy.* Repeat the procedure with other words, such as *a girl, a table, rice, eyes, a nose, hair,* and so on. Have students listen, look, and point each time.

- Read aloud the instructions. Play **TR: 152** and have students listen and repeat the words.

- Use drawings, actions, and descriptions to teach the new words. For example, write some very simple math exercises on the board with correct answers: *1 + 2 = 3,* and so on. Check them all. Then point and say *That's good. It's very good. It's great!* Emphasize the word *great.* Write some very simple math exercises on the board, but write the wrong answers: *1 + 2 = 6,* and so on. Mark all of them wrong. Then point and say *Oh no! This is bad. It's very bad. It's terrible.* Emphasize the word *terrible.*

- Point to a tray in the main photo. Say *Look! This is a tray. Let's count the trays.* As you point, say *One tray, two trays, three trays, four trays.* Pretend to balance a tray of food. Say *Look! This is a tray.* Then point to the main photo again, this time pointing to the food in the different tray compartments. Say *Look! Lunch.* Say *This is the children's lunch.*

- Point to the text and say *Find the words here.* Have students scan the text to find the four words. Make sure they understand that they don't have to read the whole text—just find the words.

- Remind students of the word *carrot.* Draw a carrot on the board and point. Ask *What's this?* If nobody remembers, say *It's a carrot.*

- Read aloud the instructions. Then point to the text and say *Listen and read.* Play **TR: 153**. Have students listen to and read the whole text.

- Play **TR: 153** again, pausing after the first paragraph. Have students listen and read. Say *Now, read again.* Then, ask *Where are the trays?* (on the table) *Are the children at home?* (no) *Where are they?* (at school)

- Continue playing **TR: 153** to the end. Say *Now read again,* and ask *Is there rice for lunch?* (yes)

- Read aloud each sentence of the text. Have students point to things in the photo as you read, such as *photo, lunch, boys and girls,* and *trays.* Have them answer any questions in the text, such as *How many trays can you see?* (four) Also, have them make personal responses to statements in the text, such as *I like carrots.*

- **Reading Strategy: Pausing and Thinking** It can be helpful for students to pause every now and then and think about what they have just read in a text, either imagining a scene described or checking comprehension. Pausing and thinking helps students engage more with the text. If something isn't clear, they can go back and read that part again.

- **Extra Support** As students listen to the audio, help them understand the text by holding up flashcards of the new words as they appear.

- Read aloud the instructions. Point to the word box and the sentences. Point to item 1, read it aloud, and say *Mmm* to replace the word in the space. Point to the word box again and ask *Which word?* (two) Have students write *two* in the space.

- Have students complete the activity in pairs.

- Correct the activity by calling on students to read aloud each complete sentence.

- **Extra Challenge** Before students write, have them try to guess the missing words without looking at the word box.

Optional Activity

- Have students draw and label pictures of lunch on trays. Have them draw a tray like the ones in the photo and add different food to each compartment. Remind them to include at least one food item they don't like. Have them then hold up their pictures and talk about them. For example, they could say, *This is my lunch on a tray. I like [potatoes]. I don't like [bananas].*

Wrap Up

- Have students close their books. Write the new words on the board. Have students write a sentence with one of the words.

Additional Practice: Workbook p. 80, Online Practice

In this lesson, students will:

- use *Do you like…* and *Yes, I do/No, I don't; It's/They're OK* to ask and answer questions about food.

Resources: Audio Track 154; Classroom Presentation Tool; Flashcards 101, 162–169; Workbook p. 81; Workbook Audio Track 57; Online Practice

Materials: sticky tack, food cut into small pieces, toothpicks

Warm Up

- Use the Lesson 1 flashcards to review *I like* and *I don't like*. Display the nine cards across the board. Under each card, draw a happy face or a sad face. Point to the first flashcard and the face below it. Say *I [like bananas]*. Then call on students to say a sentence about each flashcard, using *I like* or *I don't like*, depending on the face below.

- Have students open their books to p. 101. Read aloud the instructions. Point to the grammar box and say *Listen.* Play **TR: 154.** Have students listen and read. Play **TR: 154** again and have students repeat the sentences.

- Display the *banana* flashcard on the board. Ask *Do you like bananas?* Have students answer *Yes, I do.* Have a student ask you the same question. Say *Yes, I do. They're great.* Emphasize the word *great.* Display the *tomato* flashcard on the board. Have a student ask *Do you like tomatoes?* Say *They're OK,* using your hands and shrugging to indicate you neither like nor dislike tomatoes.

- Display the *potato* flashcard on the board. Have a student ask *Do you like potatoes?* Say *No, I don't. They're terrible.* Emphasize the word *terrible* and frown. Repeat this with *apples, carrots, lemons,* and *oranges,* displaying these flashcards on the left side of the board. Then repeat with noncount food items: *bread, candy, milk, rice,* and *water.* Display these flashcards on the right side of the board. Have students ask you the questions and say *Yes, I do. It's great!* or *No, I don't. It's terrible!*

- **Extra Support** Copy the questions and answers from the green box onto the board. Draw two stick people next to the conversations. Then draw a happy face next to *Yes, I do. They're great,* a sad face next to *No, I don't. It's terrible,* and a neutral face next to *They're OK* and *It's OK.* If possible, use the same colors as the faces in Activity 2.

- Read aloud the instructions. Point to item 1 and read aloud the question. Direct students' attention to the face and then read aloud the example answer.

- Have students complete the questions and answers in pairs. Go through the missing words as a class. Have students take turns reading aloud each question and call on a different student to give the answer each time.

- **Extra Challenge** Have students ask and answer the questions in the activity again orally. Have them work in pairs and give their own answers.

Task Guidance Notes

Starters Speaking Part 4 Students have to answer personal questions about themselves, such as age, family, school, and friends. There is no visual prompt, but students only have to give short answers, such as *Yes/No* to show they understand (although they can give longer answers if they feel ready). This tests understanding and answering spoken questions.

Challenges Students can get nervous because there are no pictures to help them and they have to rely on listening. Explain that all the questions will be about them and things they know about themselves. Practice listening for key words in questions with the class, for example, *like* (in *Do you like*) or *old* (in *How old*).

Performance Descriptor

- Can respond to very simple questions with single words

- This activity practices *Do you like…?* personal questions. Do the example with the class. Make sure students understand they can say more than just *yes* or *no*—they should try to add an adjective.

- Have students around the class ask more *Do you like…?* questions using the words on the page. Encourage them to add an adjective.

- **Collaborate** Write two examples on the board of what you like and don't like, for example, *milk* ✔, *lemons* ✗. Have students ask you questions. Point to what you wrote on the board and answer. Have students in pairs each draw five things they like and three things they don't like. Have each pair exchange their drawings with another pair. Have students take turns asking *Do you like…?* questions from the drawings they are given. Monitor and help.

- **Second Chance** Teach *I don't understand.* Have students exchange their drawings with new classmates and repeat the activity. Encourage them to try and answer quickly or to say *I don't understand* if they need the question repeated. Monitor and help.

Optional Activity

- If there are no students with food allergies in your class, do a taste-testing activity. Bring to class some food cut into small pieces, such as a selection of fruit, a tomato, some potato chips, some bread, candy, and so on. Use toothpicks to serve the different food items and have students taste them while blindfolded. Ask *Do you like it? What is it?*

Wrap Up

- Have students choose three food or drink items and then write the words *great, OK,* and *terrible,* one with each. Have them also write one question, such as *Do you like milk?* Have them move around the class asking their question each time. Students can only answer if the food or drink item is on their list. Students then cross off the food or drink item and the adjective. The first student to give an opinion of all three items on his/her list is the winner.

Additional Practice: Workbook p. 81, Online Practice

Grammar

1 Listen and read. 🎧 TR: 154

> Do you like apples?
> Yes, I do. They're great.
>
> Do you like milk?
> No, I don't. It's terrible.
>
> Do you like apples? They're OK.
> Do you like milk? It's OK.

2 Write.

1. Do you like candy?

   You: _____Yes, I do._____ ☺

2. _____Do_____ you like apples?

   You: _____No, I don't._____ ☹

3. _____Do___you___ like rice?

   You: _____It's OK._____ 😐

4. _____Do___you___like_____ water?

   You: _____Yes, I do._____ ☺

3 Ask and answer.

Do you like candy?

Yes, I do! It's good.

Song

1 **Listen and read.** 🎧 TR: 155

2 **Listen and sing.**
🎧 TR: 156 and 157

3 **Sing and act.** 🎧 TR: 158

Chorus
Time for lunch!
I'm very hungry.
Time for lunch!
Yummy! Yummy!

Do you like carrots?
Yes, I do.
I like carrots and potatoes, too.
Do you like bread? Do you like rice?
Yes, I like bread, and I like rice.
Chorus

Do you like oranges?
Yes, I do.
I like oranges and bananas, too.
Do you like water? Do you like milk?
I like water, but I don't like milk!
Chorus

ABOUT THE PHOTO

The photo shows a child drinking a milkshake through a straw. People have been using straws for 5,000 years. However, in 1888, an inventor, Marvin Stone, patented the first mass-produced straws, which were made of paper. Straws are convenient, but these days there are lots of campaigns around the world to stop the use of disposable plastic straws, as the plastic often ends up in the oceans where it harms the environment. Estimates show that in the United States alone about 500 million straws are used each day. Scientists estimate that up to 8.3 billion plastic straws are lying on shores around the world.

VALUE **Eat good food.**
Workbook, Lesson 6

Song

In this lesson, students will:
- listen to and sing a song about food.
- act out a song.
- identify the value of eating good food.

Resources: Audio Tracks 155–158; Classroom Presentation Tool; Flashcards 24, 33, 73, 80, 95, 101, 162–163, 166–168; Workbook p. 83; Online Practice

Materials: photos of healthy and unhealthy food and drink items

Warm Up

- Review some of the words in the song with a drawing dictation. Have students listen and draw. Give instructions, pausing after each sentence to allow students time to think and draw. Say *Draw a lunch tray. Draw carrots. Now draw potatoes. Draw rice and bread. Draw an orange. Now draw some milk.*
- Have students compare their drawings in small groups or pairs. Then have them draw happy, sad, or neutral faces near each of the food and drink items.
- **Use the Photo** Have students open their books to p. 102. Point to the photo and say *Point to the boy.* Do the same with his hat, his hair, his nose, and so on. Point to the drink and say *Look! It's a drink. Is it milk? Is it water?* Accept any ideas. Then point to the straw and say *This is a straw.*

- Have students read through the song quickly and find all the food and drink words. Then, point to the photo and ask *What's the song about?* (lunch)
- Teach the word *hungry.* Rub your stomach and say *I'm hungry!*
- Read aloud the instructions. Play **TR: 155.** Have students listen to the song and follow in their books.

- Read aloud the instructions. Play **TR: 156.** Get a clapping or tapping rhythm going to accompany the song. Encourage students to sing along to the chorus.
- Hold up a copy of the Student's Book and point to the different-colored lines. Divide students into two groups, A and B. Explain that students in Group A sing the green lines and students in Group B sing the purple lines. Have all the students sing the black lines of the chorus together. Play **TR: 156** again for students to sing.
- Play **TR: 157,** the instrumental version of the song, for students to sing. Have students change roles this time.
- **Extra Challenge** Have students close their books and try to remember the words as they sing.
- **Extra Support** Play **TR: 157** again for students to sing. Hold up flashcards as food and drink items are mentioned.

- Read aloud each line of the song and demonstrate an action. Have students make the action, too.
  Time for lunch! (Point to your left wrist and then do an eating action, using a spoon.)
  I'm very hungry. (Make circular movements over your stomach with one hand.)
  Time for lunch! (As above)
  Yummy! Yummy! (Make a big smile.)
  Do you like carrots? (Point to someone next to you.)
  Yes, I do. (Nod your head.)
  I like carrots and potatoes, too. (Hold imaginary plates in your left then right hand.)
  Do you like bread? Do you like rice? (Point to someone next to you.)
  Yes, I like bread and I like rice. (Hold imaginary plates in your left then right hand.)
  Do you like oranges? (Point to someone next to you.)
  Yes, I do. (As above)
  I like oranges and bananas, too. (Hold imaginary plates in your left then right hand.)
  Do you like water? Do you like milk? (Point to someone next to you, then make a drinking action twice.)
  I like water, but I don't like milk! (Nod and make a drinking action, then shake your head and make a drinking action.)
- Play **TR: 158,** pausing after each line to make sure everyone remembers the actions. You can change or simplify the actions as necessary for your students.
- Play **TR: 158** again. Have students sing the song again and do the actions.
- **Value: Eat good food** At this point in the lesson, you can teach the value. Say *The value of this lesson is* Eat good food. Write *Eat good food* on the board. Say *The food in the song is good food.* Use photos of food and drink to help students understand the value. Hold up a photo and ask *Is it good food or bad food?* Have students respond together each time. Make sure some photos show junk food, such as candy, soda drinks, etc. Other photos should show healthy food, such as fruit, vegetables, fish, rice, etc. For additional practice, have students complete Lesson 6 of the Workbook in class or at home.

Optional Activity

- Read aloud the first question and answer in the first verse and draw two carrots on the board. Have students copy your drawing and then draw the other items in the song.
- As students are drawing, draw a glass of milk on the board. Draw a red line through the glass of milk. Again, have students copy your drawing.
- Have students hold up their drawings as they sing the song again.

Wrap Up

- Have students write a new verse for the song in groups, using other food and drink words and referring to the song as a model.

Additional Practice: Workbook p. 83, Online Practice

Phonics

In this lesson, students will:
- identify and pronounce CVC words with /ɑ/ in the middle.
- form three-letter words with the letter o.

Resources: Audio Tracks 159–161; Classroom Presentation Tool; Flashcards 20, 35, 51, 119–120, 125, 142–143, 157–161, 174–177; Workbook p. 82; Workbook Audio Track 58; Online Practice

Materials: sticky tack

Warm Up

- Use the phonics flashcards from Unit 9 to review the sound /ɪ/. Put all the flashcards together and mix them up. Hold up one flashcard at a time and have students say the word as a class. Listen to the pronunciation of /ɪ/ and say the word aloud yourself if you think students need to hear it correctly.

1

- Have students open their books to p. 103. Direct their attention to the photos and words. Read aloud the instructions. Play **TR: 159**, pointing to each photo and word as students hear it.
- Play **TR: 159** again. Have students repeat each word. Monitor students carefully, making sure they pronounce the target sound (/ɑ/) correctly. Ask *What sound are we learning today?* (/ɑ/) Remind students that they are practicing this sound in the middle of words.

Optional Activity

- Practice the new sound. Say a series of words, one after the other. Have students clap or raise their hands if they hear the sound /ɑ/. Say these words: *yes, bat, nod, pen, bag, mop, dog, big, leg, dot, jam, pet, map, fox,* and *bed*.

2

- Make sure students understand the word *floor*. Point to the floor and say *Look! This is the floor.*
- Read aloud the instructions. Point to the chant. Say *Listen. Can you hear the /ɑ/ sound?* Play **TR: 160**. Have students circle the letter o each time. Have students work in pairs. Check answers together as a class by holding up a copy of the Student's Book and circling each letter with your finger, so that students can see and check.
- Play **TR: 160** again. This time have students read and chant.

- **Extra Challenge** Have students work in pairs. Have one student with his/her book open do actions for each part of the chant. Have the other student with book closed remember the chant with his/her partner's help.
- **Extra Support** Before students read and chant, establish an action for each phrase. For example, say *Nod your head* and nod your head. Say *Mop the floor* and act out a mopping action. Create actions for the other words. As students read and chant, do the actions for each part of the chant. Then have students do the actions as they read and chant.

3

- Have students look at the picture. Give them instructions. Say *Point to the dot.* Repeat with *dog, fox, mop.* Have students listen, look, and point. Point to the image of the head nodding and ask *What's this word?* (nod) Then point to the photo of the nodding head in Activity 1.
- Read aloud the instructions. Give students a minute to look at the picture again, read the words, and think about the sounds.
- Play **TR: 161**. Have students do the activity individually.
- Walk around the classroom, monitoring students as they do the activity and checking to see they have written the words correctly.

Script for TR: 161 *mop, fox, dog, nod, dot*

Wrap Up

- Use the four walls of the classroom to play a game. Display four phonics flashcards representing the sounds /æ/, /ɛ/, /ɪ/, /ɑ/, one on each of the four walls. Point to each wall and say the sound (/æ/, /ɛ/, /ɪ/, or /ɑ/).
- Hold up phonics flashcards from Units 7–10 in random order. Use the *bag, bat, jam, man, map, bed, leg, pen, pet, yes, big, bin, lip, sit, six, dog, dot, fox, mop,* and *nod* flashcards. Have students say each word in chorus and turn to face and point to the corresponding wall each time.

Additional Practice: Workbook p. 82, Online Practice

1 **Listen, point, and repeat.** 🎧 TR: 159

dog   dot   fox   mop   nod

2 **Listen, chant, and circle.** 🎧 TR: 160

Nod your head and mop the floor.
Draw a dot and count to four.
I like the dog, I like the fox.
Draw a dot inside a box!

3 **Listen and find. Write the word.** 🎧 TR: 161

1. d o t
4. n o d
2. d o g
5. m o p
3. f o x

1 **Watch and match. Write the numbers.** ▶ Video 12

  1. Tracy and Jessica

 2. Marcel

 3. Lara

 4. Pablo

 2

 1

 4

 3

ABOUT THE VIDEO

In this video, Pablo talks about Spanish *tortilla*. This is a traditional omelet dish made from eggs and potatoes. Sometimes, onion and other ingredients are added. Tortilla can be eaten hot or cold and is often eaten as an appetizer or snack. The word *tortilla* is the diminutive of *torta*, meaning cake.

2 **Your turn! Ask and answer.**

What's your favorite food?

I like oranges and apples.

3 **Draw and say.**

This is one of my favorite foods.

It's _____ .

_____ .

_____ .

LESSON 7 Video

In this lesson, students will:
- watch a video about meals in other countries.
- ask and answer questions about favorite foods.
- draw and speak about favorite foods.

Resources: Video 12, Classroom Presentation Tool, Online Practice

End-of-Unit Resources: Anthology Story 5, Anthology Teaching Notes p.140, Worksheet 1.10, Unit 10 Test, ExamView Assessment Suite

Materials: photos of familiar dishes, dictionaries, paper plates (one per student), crayons

Warm Up

- Hold up a photo of a dish such as moussaka, chow mein, or vegetable soup. Say *This is [moussaka].* If the dish doesn't have an English translation, say the name in your language. Point and name any ingredients that are visible. For example, say *This is [meat] and these are [potatoes].* When you finish, say whether you like the dish. Then to several students, ask *Do you like [moussaka]?*

- Ask *What's your favorite food?* Help students find out how to say the name of the dish in English or the name of some ingredients. Use online dictionaries, picture dictionaries, or an online translator. Then go around the class calling on each student to say what his/her favorite food is.

- Read aloud the instructions and play **Video 12** from beginning to end. Have students match the four numbers and names on the left with the photos on the right and write the numbers in the boxes.

- Play **Video 12** a second time, pausing after Jessica says *We can't have it every day* and ask *What color are the cakes?* (green) Continue playing **Video 12** and pause after Marcel says *I love cake.* Ask *What vegetables does he like? Potatoes or carrots?* (carrots) Play and then pause again after Lara says *We eat it with tomatoes* and ask *Which fruit can you see?* (a lemon) Play and pause after Pablo says *I like rice and fish.* Ask *Does Pablo like fish?* (yes) Play and pause again after the narrator asks *Wait, are those insects?* and the candy insects appear on the screen again. Point to the insects and ask *What are these?* (candy) Then continue playing **Video 12** to the end.

- Play segment 1 from **Video 12** with the sound off. Say *The girls talk about bahn tet cakes and bananas.* Ask *Do they like this food?* (yes) Ask *What can you do to show you like something?* Have students demonstrate that you can smile, nod your head, or rub your stomach.

- **Listening Strategy: Noticing Body Language** Explain that when students watch someone talking in a video, they can find clues about what is being said from the speakers' facial expressions and gestures. Try showing a video with no sound to see how much students understand about how the speakers are feeling. Or have students copy the facial expressions, shrugs, nods, etc. that the speakers make.

- **Extra Challenge** Divide the class into pairs. Have students prepare short conversations in which they use both words and gestures to show what they like.

- **Extra Support** Before students watch the video, have them look at the four food photos and name the items they can see. If necessary, point to and teach *cake, omelet, fried banana,* and *fish.* Write these words on the board.

The script for **Video 12** *is available on the Teacher's Resource Website.*

- Ask *What do Tracy and Jessica like?* If necessary, play the first segment of **Video 12** again. Have students name the basic foods the girls mention and start a list on the board. (rice, meat, bananas) Then ask *Marcel?* and play the second segment of **Video 12.** Add *fish* and *cake* to the list on the board. Then ask *Lara?* and add *lamb, yogurt, tomatoes,* and *bread* to the list. Do the same for Pablo. (eggs, potatoes, candy)

- Read aloud the instructions and model the conversation with a volunteer. Have other students ask you the question and answer with some of the food items from the video.

- Put students into pairs to ask and answer questions about their favorite food. Encourage them to use gestures and facial expressions as they speak.

- Read aloud the instructions. Use the board to demonstrate. Draw a picture of your favorite food. Point to the food and say *This is one of my favorite foods. It's [rice].*

- Have students work individually to complete the activity. When they finish, have them show their pictures to their classmates. Have them ask and answer questions about their drawings. Encourage students to show their drawings to at least three other students.

Optional Activity

- Give each student a paper plate and crayons. Have them draw and color their favorite meal on the plate. Then have them label the ingredients. If necessary, help students with any unknown words.

- Make a display of the meals. Have each student point to his/her plate and describe the meal he/she has drawn.

Wrap Up

- Ask questions to find out how much students remember about the video. If necessary, play **Video 12** again.

- Suggested questions:
  Bahn tet cakes are in a leaf from a plant. Banana or tomato? (banana)
  Marcel likes a cake from Brazil. What fruit is in the cake? (bananas)
  Which vegetable is inside gözleme bread? (potato)
  Pablo talks about Spanish omelet. He eats it on bread with what? (tomatoes)

> **Additional Practice:** Anthology Story 5, Worksheet 1.10, Online Practice

Function 3: Classroom language 3

In this lesson, students will:

- use functional language for communicating in the classroom.
- look at the language in a classroom conversation.

Resources: Audio Tracks 162–163, Classroom Presentation Tool, Workbook p. 84, Workbook Audio Track 59, Online Practice

Materials: index cards

Warm Up

- Review the alphabet. Have students say the letters of the alphabet. Then do a spelling dictation. Dictate some new words from Units 9–10, letter by letter. Have students listen and write the words. Write a list yourself so that you can check answers. Call on one student to say a word, and another to write it. Repeat with different pairs.
- Have students make a list of words from Units 9–10. Then, put them in pairs and have them take turns dictating words to each other.
- Direct students' attention to the green box. Say *Today we're going to learn words for speaking in the classroom.* Read aloud the expressions, pausing to have students repeat each one.

- Read aloud the instructions. Point to the conversation. Ask *Who's speaking?* (Sandra and her teacher) Play **TR: 162** from beginning to end. Have students listen and follow in their books.
- Play **TR: 162** again, pausing after Sandra's first line. Point to the space in the line and ask *What's the question?* (What page?) Point to the expression in the green box as a reminder.
- Continue playing and pausing **TR: 162**. Have students listen to the conversation and write the words in the spaces as they hear them. Play **TR: 162** again, if necessary.

- Read aloud the instructions. Play **TR: 163** for students to check their answers.
- Play **TR: 163** again, pausing after each of Sandra's sentences so that students can read them aloud.

- Read aloud the instructions. Hold up a copy of the Student's Book open to p. 105 and point to the four questions. Have students find similar questions (or the same questions) in the conversation, such as *How do you spell duck?*
- Have students complete the activity in pairs. Check answers. Read each question aloud, one at a time, and have students call out the answer.

- **Extra Challenge** Write *What does owl mean?* on the board and call on students to read aloud the answer. Erase the word *owl* and replace it with *huge*. Ask *What does huge mean?* and call on students to read aloud the answer from the conversation. Now, erase the word *huge* from the question on the board and replace it with *tiny*. Again, read aloud the question. Call on students to answer it.
- **Extra Support** Before students begin the activity, review the alphabet. Then, direct their attention to the first question *How do you spell your name?* Start spelling the name of a student in the class and have everyone else point to the student when they know who it is. Repeat with the spelling of other students' names. Then, to the remaining students, ask *How do you spell your name?*

Optional Activity

- Write a word in English on one side of each index card and then the translation into students' own language on the other side. Use words from Units 1–10. Make enough cards for each student, with some extras.
- Direct students to the three sentences in the top right of the green box. Give them time to think of ways to complete the three sentences and then have three students read aloud their sentences. For example, *How do you say [great] in [Spanish]? How do you spell [great]? What does [great] mean?*
- Demonstrate the activity with a volunteer as your partner. Hold up one of the cards and ask a question about the English word. For example, show the student the word in English and then ask *How do you say [terrible] in [Spanish]?* Have the student say *It's* and give the translation in their own language. Show him/her the word in his/her language on the card. Or ask *How do you spell [terrible]?* Have the student say *It's* and spell the word. Show him/her the word in English on the card. Alternatively, ask *What does [terrible] mean?* Have the student say *It means* and give the translation in your language. Show him/her the word in your language on the card.
- Divide the class into pairs and give each student a card, putting any extras in a pile on your desk. Have students take turns asking and answering questions. When they finish, have students put their card on your desk and choose another card from the pile. Have them repeat the activity with a different partner. Continue this until each student has asked about three words.

Wrap Up

- Have students write and act out new conversations using at least four of the expressions from the green box. Have a few pairs act out their conversations for the rest of the class, using classroom objects as props.

Additional Practice: Workbook p. 84, Online Practice

Function 3: Classroom language 3 (student to teacher)

> Can I go to the bathroom?　　How do you say...?
>
> What page?　　How do you spell...?
>
> I don't know/understand.　　What does...mean?
>
> Can you repeat that, please?

1 Listen and complete. 🎧 TR: 162

Teacher: Now look at the picture of the farm.

Sandra: What ___page___ ?

Teacher: Page fifteen, Sandra.

Sandra: Thank you.

Sandra: How do you ___say___ "pato" in English?

Teacher: It's *duck*, Sandra. *Duck.*

Sandra: How do you ___spell___ *duck*?

Teacher: It's d-u-c-k.

Sandra: I ___don't___ understand. What does *huge* ___mean___ ?

Teacher: It means "very big," Sandra. Anything else?

Sandra: Yes! Can I go to the ___bathroom___ ?

2 Listen again and check. 🎧 TR: 163

3 Read and match.

1. How do you spell your name?　　Page nineteen.
2. What page?　　Yes, OK.
3. What does *owl* mean?　　It's M-a-x.
4. Can I go to the bathroom?　　It's a bird with big, round eyes.

Otavalo Market, Ecuador

In this lesson, students will:

- watch a video about Otavalo Market, Ecuador.
- use new words to talk about a market.
- make an animal mask.
- present a project to the class.

Resources: Video 13, Classroom Presentation Tool, Project Guide, Workbook p. 85, Online Practice

Materials: sticky tack; paper plates (one per student); rubber bands (two per student); construction paper; glue; scissors; crayons or markers; photos of an elephant, a monkey, a lion, a zebra, and a meerkat

ABOUT THE VIDEO

Otavalo is a town in the Andes. It is famous for its beautiful natural surroundings and friendly people. The Otavalo Market is one of the most famous and culturally significant markets in Latin America. The Otavaleños are indigenous people who have lived in this area for many hundreds of years. They are known for their brightly-colored clothes, embroidered blouses, and beaded necklaces. People from all over the world buy their arts and crafts when they visit the market and take them back home as gifts and souvenirs.

At the market, you can buy lots of other things, too, from live cattle, goats, and chickens to plants, food, drinks, and sweets.

Warm Up

- Write the word *market* on the board. Say *Today, we're going on a school trip. We're going to Otavalo Market in Ecuador.* To teach the meaning of *market*, ask *What's a market?* Have students share their ideas. Say *A market is a place for shopping.* Then use the students' local environment. Say *Do you know a market in [name of town]?*

- Say *Otavalo Market is outside.* Make sure students understand the meaning of *inside* and *outside.* Point to the area inside the classroom and say *We're inside the classroom.* Then point out of the window or to the general area outside and say *That's outside the classroom.* Point and repeat and say *inside* and *outside.*

- Ask *What things can we find in a market?* Have students make suggestions and write each word on the board. Accept any reasonable ideas.

- Leave the list on the board. Say *Today we're watching a video of Otavalo Market in Ecuador. Let's see the things in the market in the video.*

Introduce the Theme

- Have students open their books to pp. 106–107. Read aloud the title. Hold up a copy of the Student's Book and point to the bags in the market stall. Say *Look! This is at the market.* Point to the bags and ask *What are these?* (bags) Say *Yes. They're bags.* Ask *What colors can you see? Which is your favorite bag?* Have students point or say *I like the [red and white] bag.*

- Hold up a copy of the Student's Book open to pp. 106–107. Read aloud the instructions and point to the three questions. Then read aloud the first question. Ask *What can you see?* (bags) Say *That's right. Bags.* Then read aloud the second question. Ask *What's the answer? Outside or inside?* (outside) Say *That's right. This is outside.* Then read aloud the third question. Ask *What is this place?* (a market)

- Read aloud the instructions. Then hold up a copy of the Student's Book and point to the six photos with words. Point to each of the photos, one at a time, and read aloud the words. Then play **Video 13** from beginning to end.

- Play **Video 13** again. Pause after the narrator says *Is it a blue bag?* and ask *What do you think? Is it a bag?* (no) Continue playing the video and pause after the narrator says *Look at this woman!* Ask *Is she happy?* (yes)

- Continue playing **Video 13** and pause again after the narrator says *What's your favorite color?* Repeat the question to students and listen to their favorite colors. Continue playing **Video 13** and pause again after the narrator says *Can you see the masks?* Call on a volunteer to come to the screen and say *Point to a blue mask.* Repeat the question with other students and other colors. (orange, green, and yellow) Guide students back to the photo of the masks on the page and have them check the box. Continue playing **Video 13** and pause again after the narrator says *There are boy and girl dolls. And animals, too.* Say *Point to a girl.* Repeat the instruction with boy, animal, and doll.

- Continue playing **Video 13**. Then play it a second time and have students check their answers. To review answers, read aloud each word, one at a time, and have students say *yes* or *no.*

Script for Video 13

Let's go on a trip. Let's go to a market.

Look at this woman. What does she have on her back? Is it a blue bag? No! She has a small child on her back. Otavalo Market is very big. You can see a lot of things.

Look at this woman. She has a happy face. Look at her hands. She's making something. What is it? A hat? A bag? Let's look closer.

Look! Can you see the bags? What's your favorite color? I like the orange and gray bag.

Look! Can you see the masks? A mask is a face, but it isn't a real face. Look! A funny face. It's a man. And a blue bird face. And an orange monkey face!

There are a lot of colors in Otavalo Market. Look! Can you see a girl? Yes! I can see her head, but I can't see her arms or legs.

There are toys in the market, too. Look at these dolls. There are boy and girl dolls. And animals, too. They're cool!

3

- Ask *Is Otavalo Market cool? What do you think?* Listen to several students' responses before beginning the activity.
- Read aloud the instructions and the first sentence, saying both words in bold. Say *Remember the video. What word is it? Is it man or woman?* (woman) *That's right. We circle the word woman.* Then allow time for students to complete the activity on their own.
- Have students compare their answers with a partner. To review their work, read each sentence aloud with the correct word.
- **Extra Challenge** Have students write two true and one false sentence about the video. Divide the class into pairs. Have students take turns saying or reading their sentences about the video. Have them say which of their partner's sentences is false.
- **Extra Support** Read aloud each sentence twice as students choose the correct word. The first time, read aloud the first word in bold. The second time, read aloud the second word in bold.

Optional Activity

- Make sure students have a pencil, colored crayons or markers, and paper. Say *Draw a market stall in Otavalo Market.* Use the main photo to help students understand the word *stall.* Point and say *This is a stall with bags. What about your stall?*
- Have students draw and color a market stall selling one product. NOTE: You may want to ask each student, one at a time, what they are going to draw before they start, to make sure they draw a variety of products in the stalls. Make sure they know the English word for their product. Alternatively, assign students different stalls to ensure variety.
- Call on individual students to come to the front and hold up their drawings. Have them talk about their market stall and their product, for example, *These are hats. There are lots of hats in my stall. This hat is green. This hat is blue and red.*
- When students finish, have them make one large display so that the stalls are all in a row, resembling a real market.

4 Project

- Direct students' attention to the blue project box at the bottom of p. 107. Read aloud the instructions and make sure that students have the necessary materials to make an animal mask: a paper plate, pencil, two thin rubber bands, construction paper, glue, scissors, and crayons or markers.
- Give each student a copy of the project guide or display the instructions. Say *Let's make animal masks.* Read aloud Step 1 and point to the picture. Say *Think about animals. What animal mask do you want to make?* Allow students time to think and choose an animal. If necessary, show some animal photos. Have students tell you which animals they have chosen. Monitor students while they draw and color their animal faces.

- Read aloud Step 2 and point to the picture. Ask *Does you animal have whiskers?* Hold your fingers up by the sides of your face and wiggle them to teach the meaning of whiskers. *Does it have ears? Let's add these things. Cut and paste.* Hold up scissors and glue as you say each word so students understand what to do.
- Walk around as students work on Step 2, offering help as needed. As you do, cut out the eyes on each student's mask. Punch holes on either side, and thread the rubber bands through for students to wear their masks. Point to Step 3 and 4 on the project guide so that students understand that you're completing that step.
- When their masks are finished, have students put them on by pulling each rubber band behind their ear. Then, have students describe their masks, one at a time. For example, a student may say *This is my [cat] mask. It has [blue] ears and a [red] nose.*
- To assess the project, check that students followed directions and worked neatly and efficiently. You may also want to offer points for creativity. Be certain to explain feedback orally so that students understand why they are receiving the grade they're getting.

Wrap Up

- Write the words *mask* and *market* on the board. Point to the word *mask,* and call on a student to use that word in a sentence about the video, such as *A mask is a face.* Then call on a different student to give another sentence using the same word, such as *There's a bird mask.*
- Continue until students make at least two sentences using each word. Challenge the class to go beyond two sentences if possible.

> **Additional Practice:** Workbook p. 85, Online Practice

1 BEFORE YOU WATCH Look at the photo. Answer.

1. What can you see?
   bags
2. Is this outside or inside?
   outside
3. What is this place?
   a market

2 WHILE YOU WATCH What things are in the video? Check (✔). ▶ Video 13

bag

car

chicken

doll

kite

mask

3 AFTER YOU WATCH Read and circle.

1. A **man** / **woman** at the market is happy.

2. The **bird** / **monkey** has a blue face.

3. You can see the girl's **head** / **legs**.

4. There are **toys** / **TVs** at the market.

4 PROJECT Make an animal mask.

This is my cat mask. It has blue ears and a red nose.

1 Look and write.

1. n s a e j

   j e a n s

2. h r i t s

   s h i r t

3. k c s o s

   s o c k s

4. s r e d s

   d r e s s

2 Look and read. Write (✔) or (✘).

1. There's milk on the table. ✔

2. There are two bananas, too. ✔

3. There's an orange. ✘

4. There are three candies. ✘

3 Listen and color. 🎧 TR: 164

4 Write *like* or *don't like*.

1. I _____ like _____ oranges.

2. I _____ don't like _____ milk.

3. I _____ like _____ water.

4. I _____ don't like _____ kiwis.

In this lesson, students will:

- review words and grammar from Units 9–10.

Resources: Audio Track 164, Classroom Presentation Tool, Workbook pp. 86–87, Workbook Audio Track 60, Online Practice

Warm Up

- Have students work in pairs to review the language they learned in Units 9–10. Have each pair take turns pointing and saying one thing about each page.

- Direct students' attention to the example. Have them work individually to complete the activity. Then check answers.

Optional Activity

- Have students work in pairs to write two lists—one of ten words from Units 9–10 and the other of scrambled versions of these words. Then, have pairs exchange scrambled words, unscramble them and then compare their words.

- Have students complete the activity. Then check answers.
- **Extra Support** Before students do the activity, have them name the items in the picture and make sentences with *There is* and *There are*.

Task Guidance Notes

Starters Listening Part 4 Students have to look at a big picture which has seven identical objects. They have to listen to a conversation with instructions to locate five of the objects and color correctly. There is a pause in the conversation after each instruction. This tests words for objects including clothing, colors, and prepositions.

Challenges Students need to listen very carefully to identify which object is the one to be colored. They also have to choose the correct color crayon, so sometimes they get flustered because there are several things to do. Young students worry about coloring nicely, but they only have to color roughly to show understanding. Make sure they can do this quickly.

Performance Descriptors

- Can understand very simple spoken descriptions of people and everyday objects
- Can understand simple spoken instructions given in short, simple phrases

- **Predict** Have students look at the drawing and think about what they can see. Give them one minute, then ask them to say words for the clothes. Write the words on the board.
- **Build Confidence** Check students can find the colors quickly. Have them put all their crayons on their desk. Say a color and have students show the correct crayon.
- Play **TR: 164**. Have students complete the activity. Play **TR: 164** again for students to check their answers.

Script for TR: 164

N: Narrator, **G**: girl, **M**: man

N: *1*
M: *Look at the girl and color her dress.*
G: *OK. What color is her dress?*
M: *It's green.*
G: *OK. I have a green crayon.*
M: *Great! Color the dress with your green crayon.*

N: *2*
M: *And can you see her socks?*
G: *Yes, I can see her socks and shoes. What color are her socks?*
M: *They're red. She has red socks.*
G: *Good! I have a red crayon, too.*

N: *3*
M: *Now look at her shoes.*
G: *Yes, I can see her shoes.*
M: *They're brown.*
G: *OK. Where's my brown crayon? Oh, good. I have it.*
M: *The boy has shoes, too.*
G: *Are they brown, too?*
M: *Yes, they are.*

N: *4*
M: *The boy has pants.*
G: *And what color are his pants? Are they brown, too?*
M: *No, they aren't. They're black.*
G: *OK. I can use my pencil for his pants. I can color them black with my pencil.*
M: *Good.*

N: *5*
M: *The boy has a T-shirt, too.*
G: *What color's his T-shirt? Is it black, too?*
M: *No, his T-shirt isn't black. It's blue.*
G: *OK. I have a blue crayon. I can color it blue.*
M: *Thank you.*

- Direct students' attention to the example. Read aloud the first sentence and have students point to the oranges in the first picture.
- Have students work in pairs to complete the sentences. Then, check answers.
- **Extra Challenge** Hold up a copy of the Student's Book and point to each item on the trays, one at a time. Say your likes and dislikes. Then have students describe their likes and dislikes.

Wrap Up

- Give each of the following instructions one at a time. Elicit the answers from the class.
  1. *Name six clothing items.*
  2. *Name six food and drink items.*
  3. *Describe a classmate's hair and eyes.*
  4. *Ask and answer a question using* What color is/are...?
  5. *Say two foods or drinks you like and two you don't like.*

Additional Practice: Workbook pp. 86–87, Online Practice

UNIT 11 Beach Vacations

In this unit, students will:

- talk about beach vacations.
- talk about objects using *There isn't* and *There aren't*.
- read about children snorkeling.
- ask and answer questions about things using *Is there…?/Are there…?* and *Yes, there is/are, No there isn't/aren't*.
- listen to and sing a song about the beach.
- identify and pronounce CVC words with /ʌ/ in the middle.
- watch a video about beaches in other countries.
- identify the value of playing outside in the sun.

Language

Words

beach, beach ball, boat, ice cream, ocean, sand, sandcastle, shell, sun hat; breathe, flippers, mask, snorkel

Grammar

- *There isn't a sun hat on my head. There aren't boats on the ocean.*
- *Is there a boat in the water? No, there isn't.*
- *Are there fish in the water? Yes, there are.*

Phonics

/ʌ/ *bus, cup, jug, jump, run*

Twenty-First Century Skills

Collaboration
Work with a partner to practice new words, Lesson 1

Communication
Talk about what's in your bag, Lesson 4

Creativity
Draw and speak about what you can do at the beach, Lesson 7

Critical Thinking
Identify the value of playing outside in the sun, Lesson 5

In the Unit Opener, students will:

- respond to a photo of camels on a beach.
- describe beaches.

Resources: Home School Connection Letter, Classroom Presentation Tool

Materials: a bucket and shovel, a sun hat, sunglasses, a towel, drawing paper (one sheet per student), crayons

Introduce the Theme

- Bring a bucket and shovel, a sun hat, sunglasses, and a towel into class to show students. Point to the items and say *Look! I'm going somewhere.* Ask *Am I going to the town center?* Shake your head *no.* Ask *Am I going to a farm?* Wait for students to say *no.* Repeat with *a park, a library, a playground,* and *a swimming pool.* Then say *I'm going to the beach.* Ask *Do you like the beach?* Listen to several students' responses.
- Write *vacation* on the board and say it aloud. Then ask *Are we on vacation or are we at school?* (at school) Then say *I go on vacation to [typical vacation destination].* To a few students, ask *Where do you go on vacation?* Accept any reasonable answers.
- Give students a sheet of drawing paper and make sure they have crayons. Have students draw themselves on a beach vacation and write their names on the back of the paper. Collect their drawings, and hold them up one at a time. Each time, say *Look! [Raina] is at the beach! Look. Toys! Water! How fun!*

Use the Photo

- Have students open their books to p. 109. Read aloud the instructions at the bottom of the page. Then read aloud the caption. Point to the camels and say *Look! These are camels. How many camels are on the beach?* Have students count the camels. (12) Point and ask *How many people can you see? How many are on a camel?* Point to each person, one at a time, and start counting. Say each number and have students say the numbers with you. Have students continue past 20 if they can. Continue to 27. Ask *What colors can you see?* (blue, pink) Hold up a copy of the Student's Book and point to the reflection in the photo just above the instructions and next to the caption. Say *Look! What's this?* Have a student respond, and then say *That's right. It's water.*

TEACHER TIP

When students play a team game or take a quiz, select a captain each time. The role of the captain is to liaise between the team players and the teacher. This will prevent lots of students talking at the same time or students calling out the answers too soon. Make sure to select a different captain each time.

Beach Vacations

ABOUT THE PHOTO

This photo shows people riding camels on the beach in Broome, Australia. Though camels are mostly found in North Africa, the Middle East, and Central Asia, they were imported to Australia in the nineteenth century. There are two types of camels: dromedary camels (one hump) and Bactrian camels (two humps). Camels usually live in desert climates. They can survive for days without food and water because they store fat in their humps. Camels' eyes are unique. They have two sets of eyelashes and extra eyelids that serve as protection from the sand. They can also close their nostrils when it gets windy.

Camels on the beach in Australia

Look at the photo. What can you see?

Words

1 Listen and point. 🎧 TR: 165

beach

beach ball

boat

ice cream

ocean

sand

sandcastle

shell

sun hat

2 Listen and repeat. 🎧 TR: 166

3 Point and say.

beach

beach ball

Words

In this lesson, students will:
- talk about beach vacations.

Resources: Audio Tracks 165–166, Classroom Presentation Tool, Flashcards 178–186, Workbook p. 88, Workbook Audio Track 61, Online Practice

Materials: sticky tack

Warm Up

- Write *summer vacation* on the board. Say *During summer vacation, I go to the beach.* Say *Raise your hands if you like the beach!* Ask a few questions about going to the beach. Ask *Is there a beach near our town?* If not, ask *Where is there a beach in our country? Who goes to the beach with you? What can you see at the beach?* Accept any reasonable answers.
- Have students open their books to pp. 110–111. Point to the photo and ask *Is this a park or a beach?* (a beach) Point to the sandcastle and say *This is a sandcastle.*
- Say *Today we're going to learn words for a beach vacation.*

- Read aloud the instructions. Then direct students' attention to the small photos.
- Point to your ear and say *Let's listen.* Play **TR: 165** and point to the photos, one at a time, as you hear the words.
- Play **TR: 165** again, and model pointing to the photos under the instructions.
- Use the flashcards to teach the new words. Hold up the *beach* flashcard and say *Look! A beach.* If there is a beach in the students' town, say *[Name of your town] has a beach.* Hold up the *beach ball* flashcard and ask *What's this?* (a ball) Say *Yes, it's a ball. It's a beach ball.* Hold up the *boat* flashcard and say *Look! A boat.* Ask *Is there a boat on a street?* (no) *Where do you see a boat?* (in water/on the ocean) Hold up the *ice cream* flashcard and say *Look! Ice cream.* Ask *Do you like ice cream?* Hold up the *ocean* flashcard and say *Look! The ocean.* Hold up the *sand* flashcard and say *Look! Sand.* Ask *Where can we see sand?* (on the beach) Hold up the *sandcastle* flashcard and say *Look! A sandcastle.* Point to the main photo and say *This is a big sandcastle.* Hold up the *shell* flashcard and say *Look! A shell.* Ask *Where can we see a shell?* (on the beach) Finally hold up the *sun hat* flashcard. Say *Look! A sun hat.* Ask. *Is this for your feet or your head?* (head)

- Read aloud the instructions. Play **TR: 166**. Pause after the first word. Repeat the word to model the activity for students. Continue with **TR: 166** and have students repeat the words as a class.
- Play **TR: 166** again and call on individual students around the class to repeat the words.
- **Extra Support** Point to each compound word, one at a time, and say the individual words: *Beach ball, ice cream, sun hat* and *Sandcastle.* Review or teach the meaning of each individual word to help students understand the meanings of the compound words.

- Review the words. Display the flashcards on the board. Say a clue about each item and have students call out the word. For example, say *You can eat it.* (ice cream)
- Read aloud the instructions. Direct students' attention to the examples. Model pointing and saying the words.
- Put students in pairs. Have them take turns pointing to a photo for their partner to say the word.
- **Extra Challenge** Say *Beach* and call on students to say the next word in the sequence. Encourage them to say *beach ball.* Then say *Beach, beach ball* and encourage students to say the third word in the sequence. Repeat until students say all the words. Help when necessary.

Optional Activity

- Have students act out being at the beach. Give instructions. Have students listen and do the actions. For example, say *You're at the beach. Put on a sun hat. Nice! Oh, look. An ice cream. Eat the ice cream now. Can you see the beach ball? Pick up the beach ball! Throw it to your friend. Look, a shell. Pick it up. Look at it. Now put it in your bag. Look at the ocean. Put your feet in the water. The water's great!* Pause after each item. Any student who does the wrong action sits down, and the last few students standing are the winners.

Wrap Up

- Draw a simple beach scene on the board with sand, the ocean, a boat on the ocean, and a big sandcastle. Draw a beach ball and some shells. As you draw each item, say *Look! This is a boat,* etc. Draw a stick person in the ocean. Point and say *Look! This is me. I'm in the ocean.*
- Have students come up to the board to draw themselves in the scene, write their name, and say where they are. For larger classes, have students do this in groups. Have them copy the scene on a piece of paper and follow the same steps.

Additional Practice: Workbook p. 88, Online Practice

Grammar

LESSON 2

In this lesson, students will:

- talk about objects using *There isn't* and *There aren't*.
- say a chant about what's on and what isn't on the beach.

Resources: Audio Tracks 167–168, Classroom Presentation Tool, Workbook p. 89, Workbook Audio Track 62, Online Practice

Warm Up

- Review the words from Lesson 1. Dictate the words in order and have students write them. Start with *One word* or *Two words* each time. Then, have one student spell a word and another write it on the board. Encourage them to start with *one word* or *two words*. Repeat with all the words. Alternatively, students can turn back to p. 110 and check their spelling.

- Have students open their books to p. 111. Direct students' attention to the chant. Ask students to find two objects in the chant. Have students scan the chant to find the objects (*beach ball, sun hat*).
- Read aloud the instructions. Play **TR: 167**. Have students listen to the chant and clap to the rhythm.
- Play **TR: 167** again for students to say the chant.
- **Extra Support** Draw a large square on the board and divide it into four equal squares. In the top square on the left, draw one beach ball. In the bottom square on the left, draw three beach balls. In the top square on the right, draw one sun hat. In the bottom square on the right, draw three sun hats. Draw a big X over each picture on the right. Point to the pictures on the board, one at a time, as students say the chant.

- Read aloud the instructions. Direct students' attention to the grammar box. Play **TR: 168**. Have students listen and read. Play **TR: 168** again and get students to repeat the sentences as a class.
- Place some classroom objects on your table, some single objects (for example, one eraser) and more than one of other objects (for example, two crayons). Point to the eraser and say *Look! There's an eraser on my table*. Remove the eraser. Point and say *There isn't an eraser on my table*. Emphasize the word *isn't*. Point to the crayons and say *Look! There are crayons on my table*. Remove the crayons. Point and say *There aren't crayons on my table*. Emphasize the word *aren't*. Repeat with more objects, using *isn't* and *aren't*.

- Hold up a copy of the Student's Book open to p. 111. Read aloud the instructions. Point to each picture, one at a time, and have students say what they can see.
- Point to and say *Sandcastles* in item 1. Direct students' attention to the first picture again and to item 1. Ask *Is there a sandcastle in this picture?* (no) *That's right. I see sand, I see water, I see an umbrella, but no sandcastles. There's an s on sandcastles in the sentence, so There aren't is the answer.* Read aloud the complete sentence.
- Have students complete the activity individually. Then check answers by calling on a different student each time to read aloud each complete sentence.
- **Extra Challenge** Have students work in pairs. Have them write another negative (but true) sentence for each picture, such as *There isn't a boat* for picture 1.

- Read aloud the instructions. Model the sentences for the rest of the class to listen to. If one or more of the sentences is true about your classroom, then use *is* or *are* instead. Say other sentences about your classroom with *isn't* and *aren't*.
- Put students into pairs. Have them take turns talking about things that aren't in the classroom. Monitor students while they do the activity, making sure they are taking turns and helping when necessary.
- **Extra Support** Provide students with a list of items to discuss, such as a TV, a shower, a baby, potatoes, and kites.

Optional Activity

- On the board, write *…on the beach* and draw a simple picture of a beach (sand by the ocean). Then point to the beach on the board and make a negative sentence ending with *on the beach*. For example, say *There aren't shells on the beach.* Call on each student in the class to make a negative sentence about the beach on the board. Have students use the new words from Lesson 1 as well as other words, such as *boys, girls, store, trees,* to make logical sentences.

Wrap Up

- On the board write *…in our school.* Say true sentences using *isn't* or *aren't.* For example, say *There isn't a sandcastle in our school. There aren't beds in our school.*
- Write a list of nouns, including logical and illogical items, and have students respond. Nouns could include *car, pencil case, elephant, bananas, students, chickens, scarecrows.* Use a mix of singular and plural words and say some things that are in the school and some things that aren't.
- Call on a student to come to the board and give him/her a word, for example, *elephant.* Have the student write a sentence using *is, isn't, are,* or *aren't* and *in our school,* such as *There isn't an elephant in our school.* Continue, calling on a different student each time, until all the words on your list are used.

Additional Practice: Workbook p. 89, Online Practice

Grammar

1 **Listen and chant.** 🎧 TR: 167

There's a beach ball next to me.
There are beach balls, one, two, three!

There isn't a sun hat on my head.
There aren't sun hats, blue or red.

2 **Listen and read.** 🎧 TR: 168

> There isn't a sun hat on my head.
> There aren't boats in the ocean.

3 **Write *There isn't* or *There aren't*.**

1. ___There aren't___ sandcastles.

2. ___There isn't___ a sun hat.

3. ___There aren't___ shells.

4. ___There isn't___ ice cream.

4 **Say.**

There isn't a poster in this classroom.

And there aren't lamps.

3 Reading

1 **Listen and repeat.** 🎧 TR: 169

> mask   breathe   snorkel   flippers

2 **Listen and read.** 🎧 TR: 170

It's vacation time. The sun is in the sky. It's a nice day.

These two children aren't at school. They're at the beach. Look! They're in the ocean. But they aren't in a boat. They're in the water.

The children can see—they have **masks** on their faces. They can **breathe** under the water, too—they have **snorkels**. And they have special shoes called **flippers**.

Are there fish in the water? Yes, there are! Look! How many fish can you see?

ABOUT THE PHOTO

The photo shows children snorkeling at Goat Island Marine Reserve in Leigh, New Zealand. This was New Zealand's first marine reserve and it covers just over five square kilometers of coast. The reserve has more than 100 species of fish and other marine animals, including dolphins, whales, crabs, crayfish, and sea stars. Fur seals, orca, and a species of birds called *pied shags* also live on the reserve.

3 **Read again. Answer the questions.**

1. How many children are there?   two
2. Where are the children?   in the water
3. What do they have on their faces?   masks
4. Can they breathe under the water?   yes
5. What animals can the children see?   fish

Reading

In this lesson, students will:

• read about children snorkeling.

• use new words to talk about snorkeling.

• answer questions about a text.

Resources: Audio Tracks 169–170, Classroom Presentation Tool, Flashcards 187–190, Workbook p. 90, Workbook Audio Track 63, Online Practice

Materials: a mask, a snorkel, flippers, a video of someone diving (optional)

Warm Up

• **Use the Photo** Have students open their books to pp. 112–113 and direct their attention to the photo. Ask *Where are these children?* (in the water/ocean) *What animals can you see?* (fish) *Are the fish big or small?* (big) Give instructions to practice other vocabulary, such as *Look at the children. Point to an arm,* etc.

1

• Read aloud the instructions. Play **TR: 169** and have students listen and repeat the words.

• Use the flashcards to introduce the words or try to bring the real items into class. Let students see and touch them. Alternatively, find a video of a diver wearing the items. As you play it, pause, point, and say *Look! This is a [mask].* Point to the word *breathe* and say it aloud. Then say *Watch me breathe.* Breathe deeply, in and out a few times. Then say *Breathe with me.* Have students copy you as you breathe deeply in and out.

• Point to the text and say *Find the words here.*

• **Extra Support** Have students work in pairs, taking turns pointing and saying the four words. Have them act out the meaning of the four words as they say them.

2

• Read aloud the instructions. Then point to the text and say *Listen and read.* Play **TR: 170.** Have students listen to and read the whole text.

• Play **TR: 170** again, pausing after the first paragraph. Ask *Is the weather good or bad?* (good) Continue playing the audio, pausing after the second paragraph. Ask *How many children are there?* (two) *Where are they?* (at the beach/in the water/in the ocean) Continue playing **TR: 170,** pausing after the third paragraph. Ask *What do the children need to see?* (masks) *What do they need to breathe?* (snorkels) *Where are their flippers?* (on their feet)

• Continue playing **TR: 170** to the end. Have students listen and read. Ask *How many fish can you see?*

• Divide the class into pairs. Give students time to read the questions in Activity 3. Then have them read the text aloud. Have students take turns after every two or three sentences.

• **Reading Strategy: Setting a Purpose for Reading** Have students look closely at any task connected with the text before reading so that they know what information to look for as they read.

Task Guidance Notes

Starters Speaking Parts 1 & 2 Students have to point to objects in a big picture, then place two small picture cards in the big picture according to the examiner's instructions. Then students have to answer questions about the big picture, such as number, color, size, location. This includes a *Tell me about* (an object/a person in the picture) question. The focus is on familiar words as well as prepositions. This tests understanding and following spoken instructions.

Challenges Students can be very nervous at the beginning of the exam, so remind them the picture will show familiar objects. Explain that the examiner will give them thinking time and repeat the question if necessary. They can say *Sorry, I don't understand,* so practice this in class.

Performance Descriptors

• Can understand some simple spoken instructions given in short, simple phrases

• Can name some familiar people or things

• Can give very basic descriptions of objects and animals

• Ask students to look at the photo and give them one minute to think about what they can see. Then say *Point to the water, fish, boys,* etc. Remind students to point to all the objects if plural.

• Go around the class and ask *Where is…?/How many...?/Is it...?* questions.

• **Collaborate** Have students look at the photo and, in pairs, think about what they can say about the children and the fish, such as their size, age, color, and so on. Get ideas from the class and write the words on the board. Then say *Tell me about the child. Tell me about the fish. Tell me about the water.* Give everyone a turn and make mental notes on any pronunciation points.

• **Second Chance** Have students in pairs take turns asking and answering the questions in Activity 3. (NOTE: Students can also find the answers to these questions in the text.) Monitor and help.

• **Extra Challenge** Have students write three more questions about the text and photo. Have them exchange questions with a partner and answer them.

Optional Activity

• Have students write one sentence each about the main photo. Encourage them to use *There is/isn't* or *There are/aren't* in their sentence. Have students share their sentence with the class.

Wrap Up

• Have students look at the text and the main photo again. Say *You're one of the children in the photo.* Call on students to make one sentence each with *I,* for example, *I have a mask on my face* or *I can breathe.*

Additional Practice: Workbook p. 90, Online Practice

Grammar

In this lesson, students will:

- ask and answer questions about things using *Is there…?/Are there…?* and *Yes, there is/are; No, there isn't/aren't.*

Resources: Audio Track 171, Classroom Presentation Tool, Workbook p. 91, Workbook Audio Track 64, Online Practice

Warm Up

- Say *There's a board in this classroom* and have students nod their heads to indicate *yes*. Say *There are four walls in this classroom* and have students nod their heads. Then say *There isn't a [sandcastle] in this classroom* and have students shake their heads to indicate *no*. Finally, say *There aren't [toys] in this classroom* and have students shake their heads. Then call on individual students to make one sentence each about the classroom and other students to either nod or shake their heads.

- Have students open their books to p. 113. Read aloud the instructions. Point to the grammar box and say *Listen and read*. Play **TR: 171**. Have students listen and read. Play **TR: 171** again and have students repeat the questions and answers, first as a class and then individually.
- Ask *Is there a board in the classroom?* Answer yourself. Point to the board and say *Yes, there* is. Emphasize *is*. Then ask *Is there a sandcastle in the classroom?* Answer yourself. Shake your head and say *No, there* isn't. Emphasize *isn't*. Repeat with plural items. Emphasize *are* and *aren't*.
- Call on students to ask questions to the rest of the class. If necessary, give them help by providing singular and plural nouns (clock, beach balls, etc.).
- **Extra Support** Copy the two questions and two answers on the board. Circle *Is* and *isn't* and draw a line to connect the two words. Then do the same with *Are* and *are*. This shows the link between the verb used in the question and the verb used in the answer. Remind students that *Yes, there is* and *No, there aren't* are also possible answers to the questions.

- Hold up a copy of the Student's Book open to pp. 112–113. Write *One* and *Two* on the board as headings. Say *Boat*, point to the word in the reading text (line 6), and write it under *One*. Then point to *Two* on the board and have students say *boats*. Say another word, such as *Face*, and have students say *one face* and *two faces*. Write these words under the headings on the board. Say *One boat is singular. Two boats is plural*. Underline the final *s* in *boats* and *faces*.
- Have students scan the text and find words that end with *s*. Have them call out *masks, faces, snorkels, shoes, flippers* and then read the sentences again with these words slowly. Point out the irregular plurals *children* and *fish*. Say *These two words are plural, too. We ask* Is there [a] *with singular words and* Are there *with plural words. For example, Are there many children in class?*

- Read aloud the instructions. Point to the conversation and say *Look! Three questions and three answers*. Ask *Who asks the questions, A or B?* (A) *Who answers, A or B?* (B)
- Point to the first question and read it aloud. Direct students' attention to the example. Read the question again. Emphasize *Is* and *a beach*.
- Have students complete the activity in pairs. Remind them to complete the questions and answers. Go through the missing words as a class. Have students read aloud each question, one at a time, and call on a different student to give the answer each time.
- **Extra Challenge** Have students work in pairs. Have them ask and answer the questions in the activity again orally, replacing the original word in each question with place words from Unit 7 (zoo, library, swimming pool, etc.).
- **Extra Support** Before students begin the activity, write the six missing words on the board: *is, is, is, isn't, are,* and *aren't*.

- Read aloud the instructions. Then put your bag on the table and put various classroom objects in it, including a pencil case. Have a volunteer model the question. As you take the pencil case out of your bag, model the answer.
- Have other students ask you questions with *Is there*, for example, *Is there a clock in your bag?* If there is a clock in your bag, take it out and show the class as you respond. If there isn't a clock, frown and shake your head as you say *No, there isn't*.
- Repeat with plural objects and *Are there* questions. Put two pencils, two crayons, two rulers, etc. in your bag. Have individual students ask you questions.
- Put students into pairs. Have them take turns asking and answering questions about each other's schoolbags. Remind them to use *Is there* and *Are there*.
- Monitor students while they do the activity, checking on their use of the new grammar and helping when necessary.

Optional Activity

- Have students work in pairs. Have them take turns asking and answering questions like those in Activity 3 about their homes. Write these words on the board for students to ask about: *a beach ball, a board, a lamp, a swimming pool, a TV, animals, beds, cabinets, chairs,* and *walls*.

Wrap Up

- Play a memory game using the picture of the house on pp. 58–59. Give students one minute to look at the picture and then say *Close your books!*
- Ask *Is there* and *Are there* questions about the picture. For example, ask *Is there a lamp in the bedroom?* Ask about: *a bed, a cat, a game, a kitchen, a shower, children, pictures,* and *toys*. Have different students answer each time.

Additional Practice: Workbook p. 91, Online Practice

Grammar LESSON 4

1 **Listen and read.** 🎧 TR: 171

> Is there a boat in the water?
> No, there isn't.
>
> Are there fish in the water?
> Yes, there are.

2 **Write *is*, *isn't*, *are*, or *aren't*.**

A: _____Is_____ there a beach in your town?

B: Yes, there ___is___ .

A: Great! And ___is___ there an ice cream shop?

B: No, there ___isn't___ .

A: ___Are___ there candy shops?

B: No, there ___aren't___ !

3 **Ask and answer.**

Is there a pencil case in your bag?

Yes, there is!

Song

1 **Listen and read.**

🎧 TR: 172

2 **Listen and sing.**

🎧 TR: 173 and 174

3 **Sing and act.**

🎧 TR: 175

Chorus
Let's go to the beach.
Let's play in the sun.
Let's look for shells.
Vacations are fun!

Is there sand on the beach?
Are there fish? Can you see?
Are there shells on the beach?
Yes, there are! Come with me!
Chorus

Are there trees on the beach?
Are there boats? Can you see?
Is there sun every day?
Yes, there is! Come with me!
Chorus

VALUE Play outside in the sun.
Workbook, Lesson 6

ABOUT THE PHOTO

The photo shows a child holding shells in Jutland, Denmark. Seashells are the external skeletons of mollusks, and there are over 50,000 types of mollusk shells in oceans around the world. In tourist areas, shells are big business. Large ones are sold as bowls and other household items. Smaller ones are used to decorate clothes or made into jewelry and other souvenirs.

Song

In this lesson, students will:
- listen to and sing a song about the beach.
- act out a song.
- identify the value of playing outside in the sun.

Resources: Audio Tracks 172–175, Classroom Presentation Tool, Flashcards 178–186, Workbook p. 93, Online Practice

Materials: nine large index cards, sticky tack, photos of children playing inside and outside in the sun

Warm Up

- Play a game to review beach vacation words. Draw four lines across the board. Write the nine new words from Lesson 1 on index cards. Display them facedown on the second line, in a row on the board. Give each one a letter (*A* to *I*) and write the letters above the index cards, in a row on the top line. Then display the nine flashcards facedown on the third line, in a row below the index cards. Give each flashcard a number (1 to 9) and write the numbers below the flashcards in a row on the fourth line. Put students into teams, A and B. Have Team A call out a number and a letter. Turn the two cards over. If they match, have Team A keep the cards. If they don't match, turn the cards over again. Have Team B do the same. Continue playing until there are no cards left on the board. The team with the most cards at the end of the game wins.
- **Use the Photo** Have students open their books to p. 114. Point to the photo. Ask *Where is this child?* (at the beach) Say *Look! What does the child have?* (shells) Point and ask *Where are the shells?* (in the child's hands) *How many shells are there?* (ten) *What's on the shells?* (sand) Ask *Do you like shells?* Listen to students' responses, then say *We're going to learn a song about the beach and about shells.*

- Have students read through the song quickly. Ask *Which words can you find for beach vacations?* (beach, sun, shells, vacations, sand, fish, boats)
- Read aloud the instructions. Play **TR: 172**. Have students listen to the song and follow in their books.
- **Extra Support** Play **TR: 172** again and hold up flashcards of the beach vacation words as they are sung.

- Read aloud the instructions. Play **TR: 173**. Get a clapping or tapping rhythm going to accompany the song. Encourage students to sing along to the chorus.
- Hold up a copy of the Student's Book and point to the different-colored lines. Divide students into two groups, A and B. Explain that Group A has to sing the green lines and Group B has to sing the purple lines. Have all the students sing the black lines of the chorus together. Play **TR: 173** again for students to sing. Then play **TR: 173** again for Groups A and B to change roles.
- Play **TR: 174**, the instrumental version of the song, for students to sing.

- Read aloud each line of the song and demonstrate an action. Have students make the action, too.
  Let's go to the beach. (Spread out your arms and hands to indicate a beach.)
  Let's play in the sun. (Point up to the sun in the sky.)
  Let's look for shells. (Place your downturned hand above your eyes, look from left to right.)
  Vacations are fun! (Wave your hands in the air in joy.)
  Is there sand on the beach? (Shrug and spread out your arms and hands to indicate a beach.)
  Are there fish? Can you see? (Do a fish swimming action with your hands, then point to yourself and then to your eyes.)
  Are there shells on the beach? (Shrug and spread out your arms and hands to indicate a beach.)
  Yes, there are! Come with me! (Nod and smile, then beckon with one hand.)
  Are there trees on the beach? (As above)
  Are there boats? Can you see? (Do a boat rowing action with your hands, then point to yourself and then to your eyes.)
  Is there sun every day? (Point up to the sun in the sky.)
  Yes, there is! Come with me! (As above)
- Play **TR: 175**, pausing after each line to practice doing the actions. You can change or simplify the actions as necessary for your students.
- Play **TR: 175** again. Have students sing the song again and do the actions.
- **Extra Challenge** Have students read aloud the song, replacing one word in each line of the verses.
- **Value: Play outside in the sun** At this point in the lesson, you can teach the value. Say *The value of this lesson is* Play outside in the sun. Write this on the board. Review the words *inside* and *outside*. Take some photos into the classroom of children playing inside and outside in the sun. Hold up one of the photos, point to the children, and have students call out *They're [inside]*. Repeat with the other photos. If possible, take students outside to play in the sun. When they come back inside, ask them how they feel. For additional practice, have students complete Lesson 6 of the Workbook in class or at home.

Optional Activity

- Divide the class into pairs, A and B. Have Student A dictate the first verse of the song to Student B. Then have Student B dictate the second verse to Student A. When students finish, have them read the verses of the song in their books again and check their work.

Wrap Up

- In pairs or small groups, have students think of a title for the song. Write their ideas on the board. Then, have them vote for their favorite.
- Have students bring in photos of their favorite vacation places for the Optional Activity in Lesson 7. You may also wish to contact parents to ask them to send in photos with their child.

Additional Practice: Workbook p. 93, Online Practice

Phoncis

 In this lesson, students will:
- identify and pronounce CVC words with /ʌ/ in the middle.
- form three-letter words with the letter *u*.

Resources: Audio Tracks 176–178; Classroom Presentation Tool; Flashcards 125, 157–161, 174–177; Workbook p. 92; Workbook Audio Track 65; Online Practice

Materials: sticky tack

Warm Up

- Use the flashcards to review the phonics from Units 9–10 (/ɪ/ and /ɑ/). Draw a line down the board to divide it into two. Write *i* on one side and *o* on the other side as headings. Shuffle the *big, bin, lip, sit, six, dog, dot, fox, mop,* and *nod* flashcards. Then hold up the flashcards one at a time.
- Have students say the word for each flashcard, and call on a volunteer to display the flashcard under the correct heading on the board. Continue until all the flashcards are on the board, five on each side.
- Then run in place for a few moments. Say *Run.* Have students stand up and run in place, too. Ask *Does* run *have an* /ɪ/ *sound?* (no) *Does* run *have an* /ɑ/ *sound?* (no) *Does* run *have an* /ʌ/ *sound?* (yes) Say *Run! Today we're learning words with the* /ʌ/ *sound in the middle.*

1

- Have students open their books to p.115. Direct students' attention to the photos and words. Read aloud the instructions. Play **TR: 176**, pointing to each photo and word as students hear it.
- Play **TR: 176** again. Have students repeat each word. Monitor students carefully, making sure they pronounce the target sound /ʌ/ correctly.
- **Extra Challenge** Before students listen, have them try to say the words aloud. Then have them listen and check.

Optional Activity

- Say a series of words, one at a time. Have students write the word in their notebooks if they hear the sound /ʌ/. Say these words: *bed, boy, bug, bus, cup, map, jam, jug, leg, man, pen, run,* and *six.* Write the answers on the board for students to check.

 2

- Read aloud the instructions. Point to the chant. Say *Listen. Can you hear the* /ʌ/ *sound?* Play **TR: 177**. Have students circle the letter *u* each time. Have students work in pairs. Check answers together as a class by saying each sound one at a time and writing the word on the board.
- Play **TR: 177** again. This time say the first sentence on the top line, the first sentence on the second line, the third sentence as far as and including *table,* and the fourth sentence as far as and including *jug.* Have students complete the lines. Then change roles and have students start each line for you to complete.
- **Extra Challenge** Have students work in small groups to see if they can think of one more word with the /ʌ/ sound, such as *fun, sun, up, us.*

 3

- Read aloud the instructions. Give students a minute to look at the picture again and to think about the words.
- Play **TR: 178**. Have students do the activity individually.
- Walk around the classroom, monitoring students as they do the activity and checking to see they have written the words correctly.
- **Extra Support** Before students do the activity, call on them to point and make sentences about the picture. For example, *Look! There's a boy. There's a table, too. There's a jug on the table.*

  Script for TR: 178 *jug, bus, bug, cup, run*

Wrap Up

- Write each sentence on the board, one at a time, and read it aloud at the same time. Have students draw a picture to illustrate each sentence as you say and write it. When they finish, erase the sentences on the board. Have them say aloud the sentences from memory in pairs, referring to their pictures.
  There's a bus in the street.
  The boy can run.
  There's a bug on the table.
  The jug's on the table, too.
  It's next to a cup.
- Have students bring in photos of their favorite vacation places for the Optional Activity in the next lesson. You may also wish to contact parents to ask them to send in photos with their child.

Additional Practice: Workbook p. 92, Online Practice

1 Listen, point, and repeat. 🎧 TR: 176

bug   bus   cup   jug   run

2 Listen, chant, and circle. 🎧 TR: 177

There's a bus on the street! Run! Run!
There's a bug on the table. Bug! Bug!
There's a jug on the table and two cups, too.
There's milk in the jug for me and you.

3 Listen and find. Write the word. 🎧 TR: 178

1. b u s
4. c u p
5. j u g
3. r u n
2. b u g

Video

1 **Watch and match. Write the numbers.** ▶ Video 14

 1. Mati

 2. Safia

 3. Juan

 4. Indiphile

 4

 1

 2

 3

ABOUT THE VIDEO

In this video, Juan talks about Playa del Carmen, in the southeast of Mexico. This is a popular vacation destination for thousands of tourists every year. They are attracted to the beautiful white sand and blue-green ocean. Visitors enjoy water sports and activities such as windsurfing, kayaking, and especially snorkeling and diving. Besides seeing fish, visitors can see the spectacular Maya coral reef.

2 **Your turn! Ask and answer.**

 What can you do at the beach?

 I can run and I can swim.

3 **Draw and say.**

What can you do at the beach?

I can _____ .

_____ ?

_____ .

Video

> **In this lesson, students will:**
> - watch a video about beaches in other countries.
> - ask and answer questions about what you can do at the beach.
> - draw and speak about what you can do today.
>
> **Resources:** Video 14, Classroom Presentation Tool, Online Practice
>
> **End-of-Unit Resources:** Worksheet 1.11, Unit 11 Test, ExamView Assessment Suite
>
> **Materials:** students' own photos of vacation places

Warm Up

- Talk about what you can do in different places. Ask *What can you do in the park?* Have students share their ideas. Then ask about other places, such as, *in the town center, at home, at school,* and *on the playground.* Finish and ask *What can you do at the beach?* Accept any reasonable ideas.

- Have students open their books to p. 116. Direct students' attention to the four photos on the left. Say the name of one of the children and have students say the corresponding number. Do the same with the other names.
- Point to the four photos of places. Point to each photo and ask *What can you see?* Have students share their ideas.
- Read aloud the instructions and play **Video 14** from beginning to end. Have students match the four numbers and names on the left with the photos on the right and write the numbers in the boxes.
- Play **Video 14** with the sound off. During the first segment, pause while *Do you like the beach?* is on the screen. Say *You're Mati. What's the answer?* Accept all reasonable answers. Repeat and pause while *Are there good beaches in Poland?* is on the screen. Again, have students answer. Repeat with the two other questions in segment 1 and then with all the other segments. Then, play **Video 14** again.
- **Listening Strategy: Using Text Clues** Have students use text clues to help them understand what is being said. Questions are the most common type of text clue and these can feature either on the page or in a video. Have students look at questions before they listen or before they watch a video with the sound on. Have them think about the words they are most likely going to hear in response. Then when they listen to the audio or watch the video with the sound on, they will hear words they are expecting and will find the activity easier.
- **Extra Challenge** Write some of the questions from the video on the board, such as *Do you like the beach? Are there good beaches in [your town]? Is [your town] near the ocean? Where do you go to the beach?* Divide students into pairs and have them think about their answers to the questions. Then call on students to ask and answer the questions.

*The script for **Video 14** is available on the Teacher's Resource Website.*

- Read aloud the instructions and model the conversation with a volunteer.
- Put students into pairs to ask and answer questions about what they can do at the beach.
- Monitor students while they speak and help when necessary.
- **Extra Support** Give students a list of verbs they can use, such as *eat, drink, play, eat, jump,* and *make.*

Optional Activity

- If students have brought in photos of their favorite vacation places, have them write a few sentences about the place and what you can do there. (NOTE: If more than one student has chosen the same place, students can work in small groups.) Give students an example first. For example, hold up a photo or photos of your favorite vacation place and say *This is [Punta Arenas]. It has a [museum]. There are [boats in the museum].*
- Give students time to prepare their sentences. Then, call on individual students to hold up their photo or photos and tell the class about the place they have chosen.

- Read aloud the instructions. Use the board to demonstrate. Draw a beach activity. Point to the beach activity and say *I can [eat an ice cream].*
- Have students ask other questions, such as *What can you do in the park/at school/at the swimming pool?* Write the places on the board.
- Have students work individually to complete the activity. Remind them to choose a different activity and a different place for their second question and answer.
- When students finish, have them show their pictures to their classmates. Have them ask and answer questions about their drawings. Encourage students to show their drawings to at least three other students.

Wrap Up

- Ask questions to find out how much students remember about the video. If necessary, play **Video 14** again.
- Suggested questions:
  Where is the playground in Poland—in the town center or at the beach? (at the beach)
  What color are the houses in Essaouira? (white)
  Who goes snorkeling? (Juan)
  What does Juan have on his feet in the water? (flippers)
  Where is Playa del Carmen? (Mexico)
  Remember the sandcastle in Indiphile's video? What can you see on it, people or animals? (people)

> **Additional Practice:** Worksheet 1.11, Online Practice

12 Free Time

In this unit, students will:

- talk about free-time activities.
- make and respond to suggestions using *Let's*.
- read about being in the park.
- use *We're* and *We aren't* to talk about their current location.
- listen to and sing a song about free time.
- review, identify, and pronounce CVC words with /æ/, /ɛ/, /ɪ/, /ɑ/, and /ʌ/ in the middle.
- watch a video about free-time activities in other countries.
- identify the value of using your time well.

Language

Words

fly a kite, make a cake, paint a picture, play a game, play soccer, read a book, sing a song, write a story; hot, paper, swing

Grammar

- *Let's fly a kite! Great idea!*
- *Let's play soccer! No!*
- *We're in the park. We're on the beach. We aren't at school.*

Phonics

/æ/ hat, /ɛ/ red, /ɪ/ kid, /ɑ/ hot, /ʌ/ sun

Twenty-First Century Skills

Collaboration

Work with a partner to practice words, Lesson 1

Communication

Make suggestions and respond, Lesson 4

Creativity

Draw and speak about what you can do today, Lesson 7

Critical Thinking

Identify the value of using your time well, Lesson 3

In the Unit Opener, students will:

- respond to a photo of children playing in the rain.

Resources: Home School Connection Letter, Classroom Presentation Tool

Materials: ten photos of children doing different activities, sticky tack

Introduce the Theme

- Bring to class ten photos of children doing different free-time activities. Make sure there are a mix of outdoor and indoor activities, sports, games, and quiet activities like reading or drawing. Hold up a photo and say *Look! Children.* Ask *Is this fun?* Have students call out *Yes, it is!* or *No, it isn't!* Repeat with the other photos.
- On the board, write the numbers 1–10 in a column, leaving space to display a photo next to each number. Draw a smiling face next to 1 and say *This is fun!* Draw a sad face next to 10 and say *This isn't fun.* Hold up the photos again and have students rank the activities from the most fun (1) to the least fun (10).
- Hold up each photo again, one at a time. Say each number as you hold up a photo. Have students raise their hands as you say each number.
- Say *These photos are free-time activities. This unit is about free time. When you're at school, it isn't free time. Your free time is at home, at the park, or at the beach.*

Use the Photo

- Have students open their books to p. 117. Read aloud the caption and the instructions at the bottom of the page, and point to the photo. Ask *Are the children inside or outside?* (outside) Then give instructions. Say *Look at the girl. Point to her hair.* Repeat with *arms, mouth, eyes, skirt,* and *shirt.* Then say *Look at the boy in the middle. Point to his mouth.* Repeat with body parts and clothes. Then ask *Can you see a tree or a train?* (a tree) *Are the children happy or sad?* (happy) *Is this fun?* Listen to students' responses.

TEACHER TIP

Give parents guidance on how to help students practice English at home. Direct them to audio tracks with vocabulary and language models. Have them encourage their children to listen to the tracks and repeat them at home. Encourage parents to set a few moments aside, two or three times a week, to review English with their children. Remind parents to continue this even after the course ends so that students can maintain their level of English when they are not in school.

Free Time

ABOUT THE PHOTO

This photo shows schoolchildren enjoying themselves as they play outside in the rain. They don't mind getting wet. The largest amount of rain on record fell during Cyclone Denise in Foc-Foc, La Reúnion, in 1966. In a 24-hour period, 182.5 centimeters of rain fell. The largest amount of rain to fall in a single year was 25.4 meters, in Cherrapunji, India.

Playing in the rain

Look at the photo. What can you see?

117

1 Words

1 Listen and point. 🎧 TR: 179

fly a kite

make a cake

paint a picture

play a game

play soccer

read a book

sing a song

write a story

2 Listen and repeat. 🎧 TR: 180

3 Point and say.

Fly a kite!

Make a cake!

ABOUT THE PHOTO

This photo shows children painting a *mandala* on the ground in a village in India. Traditionally, mandalas act as a support for meditation. They are circular in form, representing wholeness and the cycle of life. Most mandalas are decorated with ancient symbols that represent different beliefs or elements of nature. Mandalas can be found as paintings and tapestries, stained-glass windows, and rugs, and as decorations on plates and bowls.

Words

In this lesson, students will:
- talk about free-time activities.

Resources: Audio Tracks 179–180, Classroom Presentation Tool, Flashcards 196–203, Workbook p. 94, Workbook Audio Track 66, Online Practice

Materials: colored chalk, crayons or markers, a large piece of paper

Warm Up

- **Use the Photo** Have students open their books to pp. 118–119. Point to the children and ask *Are they boys or girls?* (girls) *How many girls?* (two) *Is this a picture or a game?* (a picture) *Is the picture on the wall or on the floor?* (on the floor)
- Have students listen, look, find, and point. Give instructions to find and point to different things in the photo. Say *Point to something [white], Point to a [head]*, etc. Point to the photo again and ask *Is this fun?* Listen to students' responses.

Task Guidance Notes

Starters Speaking Part 3 Students have to answer questions about four small picture cards. The examiner asks what each object is and then asks personalized questions, for example, *Do you have a [x]?, Do you like [x]?* This tests understanding and answering spoken questions.

Challenges Students can get nervous because the examiner can ask a variety of personalized questions, for example, *Do you...? What...? Have you...?*, etc. Make sure students can quickly identify question types. Have a fast round of questions at the beginning of class.

Performance Descriptors
- Can name some familiar people or things
- Can respond to very simple questions with single words

- This activity practices identifying objects and answering simple questions. Have students cover the words and look at the photos under the instructions. Ask *Can you see a...?, Is it a...?*, and *What is it?* questions around the class about people and objects in the photos.
- Read aloud the instructions. Then direct students' attention to the photos. Point and say *Look. Activities. These are things we can do in our free time.* Ask *Do we have free time after school?* (yes) Say *That's right. We have free time after school, and during vacations.*
- Point to your ear and say *Let's listen.* Play **TR: 179** and point to the photos, one at a time, as you hear the words.
- Play **TR: 179**, and model pointing to the photos under the instructions.

- Read aloud the instructions. Play **TR: 180**. Pause after the first word. Repeat the word to model the activity. Continue with **TR: 180** and have students repeat the words as a class.
- Play **TR: 180** again and call on individual students to repeat the words.
- **Extra Challenge** Have students close their books when they listen and repeat.

- Have students close their books. Use actions to practice the words. Point to the first photo and say *Look! Fly a kite. I can fly a kite.* Pretend to fly a kite by looking up and holding the handle and kite string in your hands. Then say *Fly a kite with me.* Have students copy the action. Repeat with the other photos, doing an action each time and having students join in, too.
- Hold up the *fly a kite* flashcard and ask *Fly a kite or play soccer?* (fly a kite) Repeat with the other flashcards, asking a question with *or* each time.
- Have students open their books again. Read aloud the instructions. Direct students' attention to the examples. Model pointing and saying the words.
- Put students in pairs. Have them take turns pointing to a photo for their partner to say the words. Monitor students while they do the activity, making sure they are taking turns to point and say.
- **Extra Support** Say *Fly a kite* and write this on the board. Then say *Fly* and look through the Student's Book to find the word. Hold up a copy of the Student's Book open to p. 79 and point to the word in the third line of the chant in Activity 1. Underline the word on the board. Repeat with *kite.* Hold up your book open to p. 18 and point to the word in Activity 1. Again, underline the word on the board. Then say *Make a cake* and write this on the board. Have students look for the words in their books. Have them underline only the words that they have already seen. (fly p. 79 / kite p. 18, make p. 27 / cake p. 40, paint p. 9 / picture p. 87, play p. 8 / game p. 18, read p. 5 / book p. 10, sing p. 14 / song p. 14, write p. 15)

Optional Activity

- If possible, take students to an area outside of school, such as the playground, and have them draw and color a picture using colored chalk. Have them design a picture in class on paper first and then transfer the design to the ground or to a wall. If you don't have a space to do this, put a large piece of paper on the classroom floor instead, and give students crayons or markers. Have students describe the completed drawings to the class.

Wrap Up

- Pretend to do one of the actions in Activity 1. Have students raise their hands and guess what you are doing. Then have students act out the activities in small groups. Have them take turns acting out and guessing.

Additional Practice: Workbook p. 94, Online Practice

LESSON 2 Grammar

In this lesson, students will:
- make and respond to suggestions using *Let's*.
- say a chant about what to do.

Resources: Audio Tracks 181–182, Classroom Presentation Tool, Flashcards 196–203, Workbook p. 95, Workbook Audio Track 67, Online Practice

Warm Up
- Review the words from Lesson 1. Organize students into small groups of four or five. Have students take turns acting out an activity from Lesson 1. Have the rest of the group call out the activity.

- Read aloud the instructions. At the same time, point to Activity 1. Say *Listen to the chant.* Play **TR: 181**. Have students listen to the chant and clap to the rhythm.
- Put students into two groups, A and B. Have students in Group A say the purple words and students in Group B say the green words. Play **TR: 181** again for students to say the chant.
- Have the groups change roles and say the chant again.

- Read aloud the instructions. Direct students' attention to the grammar box. Play **TR: 182**. Have students listen and read. Play **TR: 182** again and get students to repeat the sentences as a class.
- Hold up the *make a cake* flashcard. Say *Let's make a cake!* Emphasize the word *Let's* and act enthusiastically as if you've just had the idea and are excited to make a cake. Have students respond with *Yes!* Then say *Great idea!* Have students repeat it after you. Show them how to say this enthusiastically. Say *I like to make cakes. It's fun. Yes, let's do this!* On the board write *Let's = Let us* and then put an X through *Let us* and say Let's *means* Let us. *But we don't say* Let us. *We say* Let's.
- Hold up the *write a story* flashcard. Say *Let's write a story!* Emphasize the word *Let's* and act enthusiastically as if you've just had the idea and are excited to write a story. Have students respond with *No!* Show them how to say this as if they really don't feel like writing a story. Have them shake their heads and use body language to express that they don't want to do this.

Optional Activity
- Divide the class into two groups, A and B. Hold up a Lesson 1 flashcard and have Group A make a suggestion, enthusiastically, using *Let's*. Smile and nod at Group B and have them respond using *Great idea!* Hold up another flashcard for Group A to make a suggestion. This time shake your head and frown at Group B so that they respond with *No!* Repeat the procedure with two more flashcards. Then play again. Use the remaining flashcards, and have the two groups change roles and play again.

- Point to the picture and ask *How many children?* (two) *Are they girls or boys?* (girls) Then say *Look at A. What's in her hand?* (paper)
- Read aloud the instructions. Direct students' attention to the example. Point and read aloud the suggestion in the first conversation. Say *Let's sing a song!* Point to the picture again and to the two pieces of paper the girls are holding. Say *Look at A! There's* sing a song *on her paper. So, A says* Let's sing a song. *Now look at B! There isn't* sing a song *on her paper. So, B says* No! Have students write the missing word, *No.*
- Have students work in pairs to look at the picture again, read the two papers, and complete the second conversation.
- Monitor students as they work. Call on two students to read aloud the second conversation for the rest of the class to check. If necessary, explain that students should write *Great idea* because both girls have *fly a kite* on their lists.
- **Extra Challenge** Have students write two activities on their own pieces of paper. Then have them have conversations with their classmates. When the activities don't match, have them respond with *No!* When they find a classmate with the same activity, have them respond with *Great idea!*
- **Extra Support** Write the missing words from the conversation on the board in a random order (fly, great, idea, let's, let's, no, sing). Have students use this list as they work.

Wrap Up
- Have students suggest how to spend the last five minutes of class time. Say *What can we do in the last five minutes today? What's your suggestion?* Remind students to use *Let's* and give an example yourself. For example, say *Let's listen and chant again.* Have students respond *Great idea!* or *No!* Then have students raise their hands to make suggestions and the rest of the class respond each time with *Great idea!* or *No!* If necessary, provide some prompts on the board: *book, game, picture, song*, etc.
- Have students agree on an activity. Then end the class by doing that activity, showing how you've taken their choice into consideration.

Additional Practice: Workbook p. 95, Online Practice

Grammar

1 **Listen and chant.** 🎧 TR: 181

Let's make a cake! Great idea!
Let's fly a kite! Great idea!
Let's paint a picture of a house!
No! No! A picture of a mouse!

Let's read a book! Great idea!
Let's play a game! Great idea!
Let's write a story about a dog!
No! No! A story about a frog!

2 **Listen and read.** 🎧 TR: 182

> Let's fly **a kite!**
> Great idea!
>
> Let's play **soccer!**
> No!

3 **Write.**

1. **A:** ___Let's sing___ a song!

   B: ___No___ !

2. **A:** ___Let's___ ___fly___ a kite!

   B: ___Great___ ___idea___ !

LESSON 3 Reading

1 Listen and repeat. 🎧 TR: 183

> hot   paper   swing

2 Listen and read. 🎧 TR: 184

It's a nice day. The sun is in the sky, and it's **hot**. We aren't at school today. We're in the park. I don't have a soccer ball, but I have a pencil and **paper**. What can we do? Let's write a story. And let's paint a picture, too. I like stories. Let's think of a story. What can we see in the park?

Look at that boy in the sky! Can he fly? No, he can't! Birds can fly, but children can't fly. The boy is on a **swing**. He's high in the sky, but he can't fly!

I have an idea! Let's write a story about a flying boy and his friend, a bird!

3 Read again. Write _T_ for True or _F_ for False.

1. The writer is in the park.   `T`

2. The writer has a soccer ball.   `F`

3. The boy can fly.   `F`

4. The boy is on a swing.   `T`

5. The story is about two birds.   `F`

> **VALUE** Use your time well.
> _Workbook, Lesson 6_

LESSON 3 Reading

> **In this lesson, students will:**
> - read about being in a park.
> - use new words to talk about free time.
> - decide whether sentences about a text are true or false.
> - identify the value of using your time well.
>
> **Resources:** Audio Tracks 183–184; Classroom Presentation Tool; Flashcards 204–206; Workbook pp. 96, 99; Workbook Audio Track 68; Online Practice

Warm Up

- **Use the Photo** Have students open their books to pp. 120–121. Direct students' attention to the photo. Point and ask *Is this a boy or a man?* (a boy) Ask *Is he inside or outside?* (outside) Point to the swing and ask *Is this fun?* Have students answer *yes* or *no*.

- Read aloud the instructions. Play **TR: 183** and have students listen and repeat the words.
- Use visuals, objects, and actions to teach the new words. For example, hold up the *hot* flashcard and say *Look! Hot.* Act as though you feel hot, brushing the perspiration from your brow and panting. Say *I'm hot. It's a hot day.* Have students act hot, too. Pick up a piece of paper and say *Look! Paper.* Have students hold up a piece of paper, too. Hold up the *swing* flashcard and say *Look! A swing.* Have students point to the swing in the main photo. Then ask *Do you like swings?* Listen to several students' responses.
- Point to the text and say *Find the words here.* Make sure students understand that they don't have to read the whole text—just find the words.
- **Extra Support** Help students understand the text and **TR: 183** by holding up flashcards of the new words as they appear (hot, paper, swing).

- Teach the meaning of *we.* Gesture to yourself and say *I'm at school.* Then gesture to indicate yourself and the class and say *We're at school.*
- Read aloud the instructions. Then say *Listen and read.* Play **TR: 184.** Have students listen to and read the whole text.
- Play **TR: 184** again, pausing after the first paragraph. Have students listen and read. Say *The reading text is about a group of children.* Then ask *Where are the children today?* (in the park) *What two things can they do?* (write a story and paint a picture) Continue playing **TR: 184** to the end. Remind students that they saw the word *idea* in the previous lesson. Ask *Where is the boy?* (in the sky/on a swing) *What's the story about?* (a flying boy and a bird) *Is this a good idea for a story?*
- Draw a question mark (?) on the board and say *This shows a question.* Then draw an exclamation mark (!) and say *Oh, Wow!* with a lot of emotion. Direct students' attention to the exclamation marks on p. 119. Point to the first line of the chant and say *Look!*

- Point to the punctuation marks on the board and have students read aloud the sentences in the text that end in these punctuation marks.
- **Reading Strategy: Looking at Punctuation** Periods (.), exclamation marks (!), and question marks (?) can help students understand a reading text. For example, a text with lots of exclamation marks shows excitement and energy. Direct students' attention to the punctuation as they listen to the text being read aloud. Have them notice the different intonation for the three punctuation marks. Then have them notice how a question is followed by an answer.

- Read aloud the instructions. Then point to and read aloud item 1. Ask *Is this sentence true or false?* Have students look back at the reading text to find the answer. Have one of the students read aloud the sentence *We're in the park.* Then ask *Is sentence 1 true or false?* (true) Ask *What do we write in the box?* (T)
- Have students complete the activity individually and then check their answers in pairs.
- Correct the activity by reading aloud each sentence and having students call out *True* or *False.*
- **Extra Challenge** Have students work in pairs, A and B. Have A students look at the first half of the text and B students look at the second half of the text. Have them write two more true or false sentences on paper. Then have them exchange papers and decide whether their partner's sentences are true or false.
- **Value: Use your time well** At this point in the lesson, you can teach the value. Say *The value of this lesson is* Use your time well. Write this on the board. Pretend to read a book. Then ask *Do I use my time well?* (yes) Then gaze out of the window, daydreaming. Ask *Do I use my time well?* (no) Have students draw pictures in which they are using their time well. Have each student draw three pictures. Then call on students to hold up their pictures and say how they use their time well. For additional practice, have students complete Lesson 6 of the Workbook in class or at home.

Optional Activity

- Read aloud the last two lines of the reading text again. Say *Think about this story. It's about a flying boy and his friend, a bird. Now imagine the story is a book. Is it a good book?* Have students design the cover of the book. Have them think of a title and draw a picture. Make a display with their book covers. Then have students describe their cover using simple sentences. For example: *This is a bird and this is a boy. They can fly.*

Wrap Up

- Have students close their books. Play the audio for the text one more time, pausing midsentence now and then for students to complete the sentences. Then continue to play the audio for students to check. Call on a different student each time.
- If you plan to do the next lesson's Optional Activity, have students bring in a self-addressed, stamped envelope.

> **Additional Practice:** Workbook pp. 96, 99; Online Practice

LESSON 4 Grammar

In this lesson, students will:

- use *We're* and *We aren't* to talk about their current location.

Resources: Audio Track 185, Classroom Presentation Tool, Flashcards 196–203, Workbook p. 97, Workbook Audio Track 69, Online Practice

Materials: two index cards; self-addressed, stamped envelopes from parents/caregivers

Warm Up

- Play a game to review the grammar from Lesson 2. Take two index cards. Draw a smiling face on one and a frowning face on the other. Divide students into two groups, A and B, on opposite sides of the class.
- Hold up one of the Lesson 1 flashcards and show it to Group A. At the same time, hold up one of the index cards and show it to Group B. Have students in Group A say *Let's [fly a kite]!* Have them act enthusiastically. Have students in Group B respond according to the face you have shown them, saying either *Yes! Great idea!* or *No!*
- Repeat five or six times. Then have the groups change roles and repeat, using different card combinations each time.

- Have students open their books to p. 121. Point to the grammar box and say *Listen and read.* Play **TR: 185**. Have students listen and read. Play **TR: 185** again and have students repeat the sentences, first as a class and then individually.
- Say *OK. Let's act! We* aren't *in the classroom. We're at the library.* Emphasize the word *aren't*. Have students pretend to be at a library. Demonstrate choosing a book from a shelf, taking it down, opening it, reading a bit, and then putting it back. Say *Now, we* aren't *at the library. Now, we're on the beach.* Emphasize the word *aren't* again. Have students pretend to be on the beach. Demonstrate putting on a sun hat and making a sandcastle with a bucket and shovel.
- **Extra Support** Draw illustrations on the board for each of the sentences to help students understand their meaning.

- Read aloud the instructions. Point to the first photo and ask *Where's this?* (the park) Then point to *at school* at the end of the first sentence and read it aloud. Point to the first photo again and have students say *We aren't at school.*
- Have students complete the activity in pairs. Review answers as a class. Call on a different student to read each of the complete sentences.

- Read aloud the instructions and model the conversation with a volunteer. Then put students into pairs to read the conversation.
- Have students look at the free-time activities on p. 118 again. Remind them to use these activities as their suggestions.
- Have students complete the activity in pairs. Have them take turns saying *We aren't in…* and *That's right. We're in…* and to make a suggestion of what to do there.
- Monitor students while they speak and help when necessary.
- **Extra Challenge** Have students make at least two suggestions for each place they name, adding information as possible. For example, a student might say *Let's make a cake for Grandma.* and *Let's sing the birthday song.*

Optional Activity

- Have students write a note or a postcard from school to a parent or relative.
- Copy these sentences on the board for students to use as a model.

```
Hi _____ ,
We're _____ today.
We aren't _____ .
Bye,
_____
```

- Have students put the note into the self-addressed, stamped envelope they brought into class. Then, mail the notes or postcards to parents' homes. Make a note to follow up with parents after several days to see if they received their notes.

Wrap Up

- Write *We're at home* on the board. Divide students into pairs and have them make a list of all the activities they can do at home. For example, they can paint a picture, read a book, jump on the bed, sit on the sofa, etc. Then have someone from each pair make a suggestion one at a time. For example, they could say *Let's paint a picture.* Other pairs cross off the expression *paint a picture* if it is on their list. Continue so that students make more suggestions until all the expressions on their list are used.

Additional Practice: Workbook p. 97, Online Practice

Grammar

1 **Listen and read.** 🎧 TR: 185

> We're in the park.
> We're on the beach.
> We aren't at school.

2 **Write *We're* or *We aren't*.**

1. ___We aren't___ at school.

2. ___We're___ on the beach.

3. ___We aren't___ at the zoo.

4. ___We aren't___ on the playground.

3 **Say.**

> We aren't in the living room.

> That's right. We're in the kitchen.

> OK. Let's make a cake!

> Great idea!

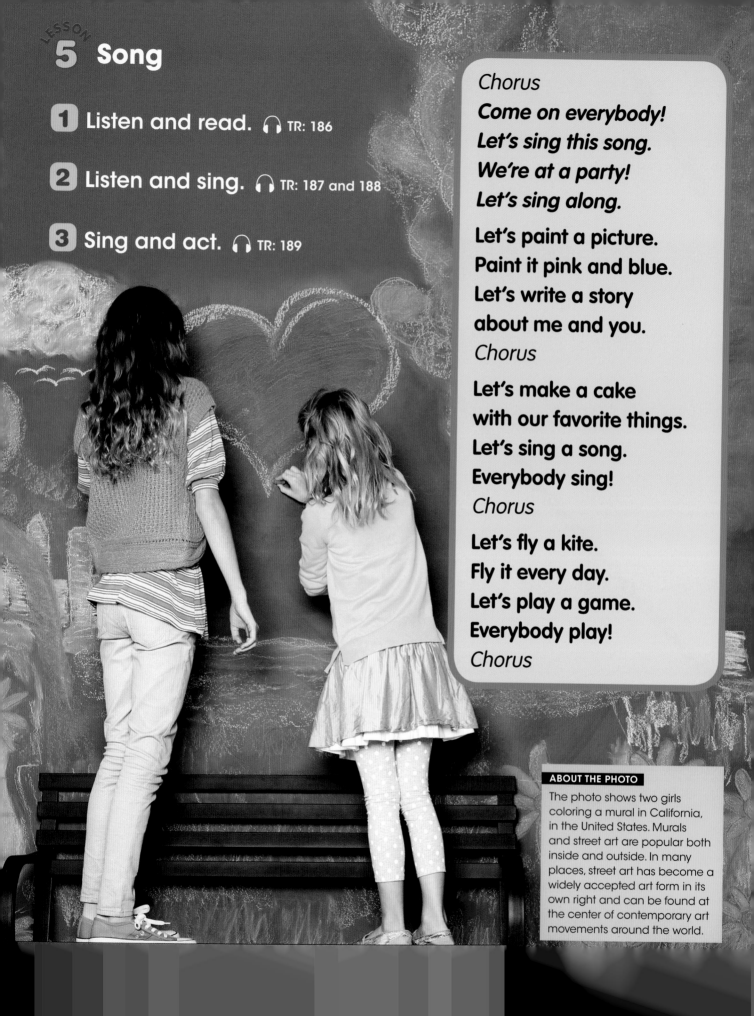

5 Song

1 Listen and read. 🎧 TR: 186

2 Listen and sing. 🎧 TR: 187 and 188

3 Sing and act. 🎧 TR: 189

Chorus
Come on everybody!
Let's sing this song.
We're at a party!
Let's sing along.

Let's paint a picture.
Paint it pink and blue.
Let's write a story
about me and you.
Chorus

Let's make a cake
with our favorite things.
Let's sing a song.
Everybody sing!
Chorus

Let's fly a kite.
Fly it every day.
Let's play a game.
Everybody play!
Chorus

ABOUT THE PHOTO

The photo shows two girls coloring a mural in California, in the United States. Murals and street art are popular both inside and outside. In many places, street art has become a widely accepted art form in its own right and can be found at the center of contemporary art movements around the world.

Song

In this lesson, students will:
- listen to and sing a song about free time.
- act out a song.

Resources: Audio Tracks 186–189; Classroom Presentation Tool; Flashcards 196–199, 202–203; Online Practice

Warm Up

- On the board write *We're at a party!* Say *We're at a party. What can we do?* Have students share their ideas for activities you can do at a party. Have them use *Let's* to make suggestions. Have students raise their hands to make a suggestion. They might say, for example, *Let's eat ice cream. Let's make a cake. Let's play a game. Let's sing.*
- **Use the Photo** Have students open their books to p. 122. Point to the photo. Ask *How many children can you see?* (two) *Are they boys or girls?* (girls) Give instructions to point. Say *Point to her [hair].* Ask *Can you name something [orange]?* Ask *Do you like this picture?* Listen to several students' responses.

- Have students read through the song quickly and find all the words for free-time activities. Then, point to the photo and ask *What's the song about?* (a party)
- Read aloud the instructions. Play **TR: 186**. Have students listen to the song and follow in their books.

- Read aloud the instructions. Play **TR: 187**. Get a clapping or tapping rhythm going to accompany the song. Encourage students to sing along to the chorus.
- Play **TR: 187** again for students to sing.
- Play **TR: 188**, the instrumental version of the song, for students to sing.
- **Extra Challenge** Have students close their books. Onto the board, copy the lines from the verses which begin with *Let's* and end with a noun. (NOTE: These are the first and third lines of each verse.) Do not copy the noun at the end of the line. Have students guess the missing words and write them in their notebooks. Then have them open their books and check their answers.
- **Extra Support** Hold up the flashcard for each activity as it appears in the song (sing a song [chorus], paint a picture, write a story, make a cake, fly a kite, play a game).

- Read aloud each line of the song and demonstrate an action. Have students do the action, too.
  Come on everybody! (Beckon people to come to you.)
  Let's sing this song. (Hold a microphone like a pop singer.)
  We're at a party! (Use both hands to show the area around you.)
  Let's sing along. (Hold a microphone again.)
  Let's paint a picture. (Make a painting action.)
  Paint it pink and blue. (Continue painting action.)
  Let's write a story (Make a writing action.)
  about me and you. (Point to yourself and a student.)
  Let's make a cake (Make a mixing in a bowl action.)
  with our favorite things. (Continue mixing in a bowl action.)
  Let's sing a song. (Hold a microphone again.)
  Everybody sing! (Gesture to the whole class.)
  Let's fly a kite. (Make a kite flying action, looking up.)
  Fly it every day. (Continue making a kite flying action, looking up.)
  Let's play a game. (Jump as in hopscotch.)
  Everybody play! (Contine jumping as in hopscotch and point to lots of people one at a time.)
- Play **TR: 189**, pausing after each line to make sure everyone remembers the actions. You can change or simplify the actions as necessary for your students.
- Play **TR: 189**. Have students sing the song again and do the actions.
- **Extra Challenge** Play **TR: 189** again. Have students sing along to the instrumental version of the song, doing the actions, without their books.

Optional Activity

- Divide the class into six groups. Have everyone sing the chorus and each group sing two other lines only. For example, have one group sing the first two lines of verse 1 and everyone else act out the activity of painting a picture, have another group sing the last two lines of verse 1 and everyone else act out the activity of writing a story. Repeat with other groups and other lines of the song. Then have students change lines and sing the song again.

Wrap Up

- Review the actions for the *Let's* sentences. Then put students into two groups. Have one group sing the song while the other group does the actions. Then have students change roles and do it again.

Additional Practice: Online Practice

Phonics

In this lesson, students will:

- review, identify, and pronounce CVC words with /æ/, /ɛ/, /ɪ/, /ɑ/, and /ʌ/ in the middle.
- form three-letter words with the letters *a, e, i, o,* and *u.*

Resources: Audio Tracks 190–192; Classroom Presentation Tool; Flashcards 17, 20, 35, 51, 119–120, 125, 142–143, 155, 157–161, 174–177, 204, 207–208; Workbook p. 98; Workbook Audio Track 70; Online Practice

Materials: sticky tack, a bag

Warm Up

- Use the phonics flashcards to review the vowel sounds from Units 7–11: /æ/, /ɛ/, /ɪ/, /ɑ/, and /ʌ/. Draw five columns on the board and write the headings *a, e, i, o,* and *u.* Then put all the phonics flashcards from Units 7–11 together and mix them up. Hold up one flashcard at a time and have students say the word as a class. Listen to the pronunciation of the vowel sound and point to the columns on the board. Have students indicate where the flashcard belongs. Display the flashcard in the correct column. Continue with the other flashcards.

- Have students open their books to p. 123. Direct students' attention to the photos and words. Read aloud the instructions. Play **TR: 190**, pointing to each photo and word as students hear it.
- Play **TR: 190** again. Have students repeat each word. Monitor students carefully, making sure they pronounce the target sounds correctly. Say *Today we're practicing five sounds, /æ/, /ɛ/, /ɪ/, /ɑ/, and /ʌ/, in the middle of words.*

Optional Activity

- Practice the phonics sounds. Have students listen to a word and then say the vowel sound three times. For example, say *Dog* and then have them say /ɑ/, /ɑ/, /ɑ/. Say *Lip* and then have them say /ɪ/, /ɪ/, /ɪ/. Repeat with other words from Units 7–11 and their sounds.

- Read the instructions aloud. Point to the chant. Say *Listen. Can you hear the five sounds? Can you hear /ɪ/, /ʌ/, /ɑ/, /æ/, and /ɛ/?* Play **TR: 191**. Have students work in pairs to circle the letters.
- Check answers together as a class by saying each sound, one at a time, and writing the word on the board.
- Play **TR: 191** again. This time have students read and chant.
- **Extra Challenge** Dictate the chant for students to write down, but only dictate the words with the vowel in the middle one time each. For example, say *This is a kid, He's in the sun, It's very hot,* etc. Have students work in pairs to check that they have spelled the last word in each line correctly.
- **Extra Support** Before chanting, say a series of rhyming words for each of the target sounds from Unit 12. Have students listen carefully and repeat. Start and finish with the target words each time. For example: *hat, cat, fat, mat, hat; red, bed, Ted, red; kid, did, lid, kid; hot, dot, lot, pot, hot; sun, bun, fun, run, sun.* Note that it doesn't matter whether students know all these words. They are focusing on sound, not meaning.

- Have students look at the picture. Give them instructions. Say *Point to the sun.* Have students listen, look, and point. Point to the hat and ask *What's this?* (hat) Then point to the photo of the hat in Activity 1. Do the same with *kid* and *sun* so that students understand they can copy the words from Activity 1. Then say *Point to something red in the big picture.* Then do the same with something *hot.*
- Read aloud the instructions. Give students a minute to look at the picture again, read the words, and think about the sounds.
- Play **TR: 192**. Have students do the activity individually.
- Walk around the classroom, monitoring students as they do the activity and checking to see they have written the words correctly.

Script for TR: 192 *hat, red, sun, kid, hot*

Wrap Up

- Play a game to review the five sounds. Place all the phonics flashcards from Units 7–11 in a bag and arrange students in a circle. Have students take turns picking out a flashcard from the bag without showing anyone. Have them look at the flashcard and say the sound (not the word). Then have the rest of the students try to guess the word. When a student guesses the word correctly, it is his/her turn to take a flashcard from the bag. Continue until all the flashcards are out of the bag.

Additional Practice: Workbook p. 98, Online Practice

1 Listen, point, and repeat. 🎧 TR: 190

hat   red   kid   hot   sun

2 Listen, chant, and circle. 🎧 TR: 191

This is a kid, kid, kid, kid.
He's in the sun, sun, sun, sun.
It's very hot, hot, hot, hot.
He has a hat, hat, hat, hat.
It's big and red, red, red, red.

3 Listen and find. Write the word. 🎧 TR: 192

1. r e d
2. h o t
3. h a t
4. k i d
5. s u n

1 **Watch and match. Write the numbers.** ▶ Video 15

 1. Tracy and Jessica   **2. Shiven**   **3. Lara**

ABOUT THE VIDEO

In this video, Lara talks about ebru painting. This art form has been popular in Turkey and Central Asia for thousands of years. Artists use a water-based solution with dyes and paints and a special tool called an *awl* to create patterns and motifs which are then transferred to paper or fabric. Ebru painting is also known as *marbling* because of the marble effect that paint has when it mixes with water.

2 **Your turn! Ask and answer.**

What can we do today?

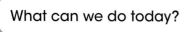

Let's play a game in the yard!

3 **Draw and say.**

Let's _____ in the park!

Great _____ !

Let's _____ !

_____ !

Video

In this lesson, students will:

- watch a video about free-time activities in other countries.
- make and respond to suggestions.
- draw and talk about free-time activities.

Resources: Video 15, Classroom Presentation Tool, Online Practice

End-of-Unit Resources: Anthology Story 6; Anthology Teaching Notes p. 141; Worksheet 1.12; Unit 12 Test; Units 7–12 Tests; Units 1–12 Tests, Workbook: Cambridge English Qualifications Pre-A1 Starters Practice Test; ExamView Assessment Suite

Warm Up

- Ask *What places are in our town?* Allow students a couple of minutes to think. Then go around the class asking for their ideas and list them on the board. Then point to the list of places and give an example sentence. Say *There's a park in our town. Let's fly a kite in the park!* Call on students around the class to make similar suggestions using the places on the board and following your example.

- Have students open their books to p. 124. Direct students' attention to the photos at the top. Say the name of one of the children. For example, say *Jessica*, and have students say the corresponding number. Do the same with the other names.
- Point to the three photos at the bottom. Say *Look! What can you see?* Ask *What activity is this?* Accept any reasonable ideas. For example, students could say *paint a picture, go to the town center, play a game.*
- Read aloud the instructions and play **Video 15** all the way through. Have students do the matching activity. Then play **Video 15** again for students to check their answers.
- Write the word *Let's* on the board. Play **Video 15**, pausing after the first segment, and ask students to suggest ways of finishing this phrase, such as *Let's do something fun; Let's go to the town center; Let's go to the market; Let's get clothes, toys…and some candy, too; Let's go to the beach; Let's sit in the sand and make sandcastles; Let's fly kites.*
- If students can't identify the phrases, write these words on the board: *Let's do, Let's go, Let's get, Let's sit, Let's make,* and *Let's fly.* Play the first segment of **Video 15** and have students suggest ways of finishing the phrases. Repeat for the other video segments. If necessary, write these words on the board: *Let's play* (segment 2) and *Let's paint* (segment 3).
- Make sure these expressions are on the board: *Let's go, Let's get, Let's sit, Let's make, Let's fly, Let's play,* and *Let's paint.* Divide students into pairs and have them decide another idea they could finish the phrase with, such as *Let's go to the zoo, Let's get pens at the store, Let's sit in the garden.* To finish the activity, have students make suggestions to the class.

- **Listening Strategy: Extending** Listening doesn't finish when the audio stops playing and the task has been completed. Having students personalize the language that they heard in the audio or video encourages them to really think about the topic and remember it better later.

The script for **Video 15** *is available on the Teacher's Resource Website.*

Optional Activity

- Write five known words from each video segment in random order on the board. Divide students into pairs or small groups and have them put the 15 words into three groups and match the words with the names of the speakers. If necessary, play **Video 15** again.
  Suggested words:
  Segment 1: candy, clothes, kite, sand, toys
  Segment 2: family, house, park, soccer, swim
  Segment 3: bread, flower, food, kitchen, water

- Read aloud the instructions and model the conversation with a volunteer. Then put students into pairs to have similar conversations. Have them take turns to start by asking *What can we do today?* Have them make suggestions and respond with *Great idea!* or *No!*
- Monitor students while they speak and help when necessary. Encourage them to use some of the free-time activities from the video.
- **Extra Support** Write a list of verbs on the board to guide students' suggestions. Make sure you include these verbs from the video: *go, get, sit, make, fly, play,* and *paint.*

- Read aloud the instructions. Use the board to demonstrate. Draw a picture of a kite flying. Point to the kite and say *Let's fly a kite in the park.* Have students say *Great idea!*
- Have students work individually to complete the activity. Remind them to choose a different activity and a different place for their second suggestion and response.
- When they finish, have students show their pictures to their classmates. Have the student who did the drawing make a suggestion and the other student respond. Encourage students to show their drawings to at least three other students.

Wrap Up

- Ask questions to find out how much students remember about the video. If necessary, play **Video 15** again.
- Suggested questions:
  Remember the market at night? Can you name one thing we can buy there? (clothes, toys, candies)
  Remember Shiven's game, carom? What three colors are the game pieces? (red, black, and white)
  Who does he play with? His family or his friends? (his family)
  Remember the ebru painting? What color were the flowers? (pink)

Additional Practice: Anthology Story 6, Worksheet 1.12, Online Practice

Game 3

In this lesson, students will:
- review words and grammar from Units 9–12.
- ask and answer questions about photos.
- play a game.

Resources: Classroom Presentation Tool; Flashcards 101, 145–156, 162–173, 178–190, 196–206; Workbook p. 100

Materials: one coin per pair of students, one game piece per student, nine sticky notes per pair of students

Warm Up

- Use flashcards to review words from Units 9–12. Shuffle all the flashcards and place them facedown on the table. Put students into two or four teams, depending on the size of the class.
- Turn over and hold up one flashcard at a time. Have teams take turns saying three true sentences about the item. For example, hold up the *socks* flashcard. Say *They're socks. Today I have gray socks. My socks are on my feet.*
- Make sure each team is given the same number of turns to make sentences about the flashcards. Award one point for each correct response. Add up the points at the end. The team with the most points is the winner.

- Draw two circles on the board to represent coins. Hold up a real coin for students to see and say *Look! A coin.* Show students the side with the head and say *Look! Heads.* Draw a picture of a head on one coin on the board. Write *Heads* next to it. Write *Heads = 1* on the board. Repeat the procedure with the other side of the coin and say *Look! Tails.* Write *Tails = 2* on the board.
- Hold up a few game pieces for students to see. Say *Look! Game pieces!* Draw a few squares on the board. Write *Game pieces* next to them. Leave the drawings on the board.
- Give each pair of students a coin and two different-colored game pieces to play the game. Have students practice flipping, or tossing, the coin.
- Put students into pairs, A and B. Have each pair share a book. Have them open their books to p. 125. Read aloud the instructions and direct students' attention to the game.
- Say *Look! This is a game. It's called* Snakes and Ladders. Point to a snake and say *Look! This is a snake.* Point to a ladder and say *Look! This is a ladder.* Then point to START and say *You start here. Put your game pieces here.* Then point to END and say *Look! You end here.* Trace the direction students have to move in, from START to END, with your finger.

- Give students simple instructions to play the game, pointing and modeling as you explain. Say *Take turns, Student A and Student B. Student A, you toss the coin.* If the coin lands heads-up, say *Heads! That's one! Move the game piece one square.* Point to the question in square 1. Say *This is a question. For a question, we read and answer.* Then read aloud the question and answer it. Say *Yes, I like milk. It's great.* If the coin lands tails-up, say *Tails! That's two! Move the game piece two squares.* Point to the photo in square 2 and say *This is a photo. For a photo, we point and say.* Say *Look! These are jeans. They're blue.* (NOTE: The odd numbers are questions and the even numbers are photos.)
- Point to a ladder. Say *Look! A ladder. When you see a ladder, you answer the question or say something about the photo. If your sentence is correct, you go up the ladder.* Emphasize *up.* Say *If your sentence isn't correct, you don't go up the ladder. You wait your turn, throw the coin, and move your game piece one or two squares.* Trace your finger up the ladder to the square at the top. Point to a snake. Say *Look! A snake. When you see a snake's head, you answer the question or say something about the photo. If your sentence isn't correct, you go down the snake.* Emphasize *down.* Trace your finger down the snake to the square at the bottom. Then say *If your sentence is correct, you don't go down the snake.*
- Have students play the game in pairs. Walk around the classroom, monitoring them while they play the game and helping when necessary. The first student to reach END is the winner. (NOTE: Students may know another way of playing the game—as soon as they land on a square with a snake or a ladder, they go down the snake and up the ladder. Have students play with these rules if time is limited.)
- **Extra Challenge** Have students say an extra sentence in the negative for each photo. For square 2, for example, *These aren't socks!*
- **Extra Support** Before students play the game, have them work in pairs and take turns saying words for the things they see in the photos.

Optional Activity

- Divide the class into pairs. Give each pair nine sticky notes. Have students replace part of each question with words which they write on the sticky note. For example, for square 1 they could write *like water?* and attach the note under *Do you,* for square 3 they could write *color is his/her hair?* and attach the note under *teacher.* Then have students play the game again in their pairs.

Wrap Up

- Use the photos in the game to review the words in a personalized way. Point to the first photo and then point to yourself. Say a sentence that is true for you. For example, say *My pants are blue.*
- Have students work in groups of three or four, working their way through the photos, one at a time, and saying something true about themselves. If necessary, write words such as *can, have, my,* and *like* to guide students.

> **Additional Practice:** Workbook p. 100

1 Work in pairs. Read, say, and answer.

16

17 Is there a beach in your town?

18

END

15 Look at the board. Are there numbers on the board?

14

13 Look at your friend. What color are his/her shoes?

12

8

9 Look at your bag. What color is it?

10

11 Look outside. Are there trees?

7 Is there a ball in the classroom?

6

5 Is there a picture of a beach in this book?

4

START

1 Do you like milk?

2

3 Look at your teacher. What color are his/her eyes?

Colors

The Color Wheel

A color wheel shows us how we can mix different colors to make new colors.

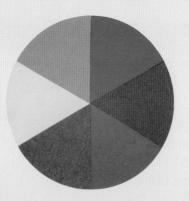

Primary Colors

There are three primary colors. They're red, blue, and yellow. We can't make a primary color by mixing other colors. We can make all the colors of the rainbow when we mix primary colors together.

Secondary Colors

There are three secondary colors. They're green, orange, and purple. Look at the color wheel. We can make a secondary color by mixing the two primary colors next to it! We can make orange when we mix yellow and red.

Haystacks in Brittany
by Paul Gauguin

Black and White

We can add white to a color to make it lighter. We can make gray when we mix black and white, and pink when we mix red and white. And what happens when we add black to a color? That's right—it makes it darker!

In this lesson, students will:
- respond to a famous painting.
- read about the color wheel.
- find out how to mix colors to make new ones.

Resources: Audio Track 193, Classroom Presentation Tool, Workbook p. 101, Workbook Audio Track 71, Online Practice

Materials: finger paints or watercolor paints (various colors), water, paper, and paintbrushes (enough for students working in groups of three or four)

ABOUT THE PICTURE

This picture is *Haystacks in Brittany* by Paul Gauguin (1848–1903). It was painted in 1890, using oil on canvas, and it hangs in the National Gallery of Art, in Washington, D.C., in the United States. Gauguin started his artistic career in France with the Impressionist painters. He later moved to Brittany, in France, where he painted lots of landscapes like this one. At the end of his career, Gauguin moved to French Polynesia.

Warm Up
- Bring watercolor paints, water, paper, and paintbrushes into class. Display everything on your table at the front of the class and make sure students can see. Point to the different-colored paints and ask *What color is this?* Have students name the colors.
- Take a piece of paper that you will draw on. Display it at the front of the class so students can see your work. Paint a yellow ball on the piece of paper. Say *Look! It's a ball. It's yellow.* Then paint a red ball overlapping with the first ball. Point and say *Look! It's a ball.* Ask *What color is it?* (red) Point to the overlapping, orange area and ask *What color is this?* (orange) Shrug your shoulders and look puzzled. Point to the two paints you used and then to the three colors on the paper. Say *Two paints, red and yellow. But three colors, red, yellow, and orange.* Leave students with this thought. Say *Later, you can paint, too.*
- **Use the Picture** Have students open their books to pp. 126–127. Point to the painting. Say *Look! This is a painting.* Ask *Do you like it?* Read aloud the title and the painter's name Paul Gauguin (/pɔːl goʊˈɡæn/). Then point to a haystack and say *This is a haystack. Brittany is a place.* Ask students to point to different parts of the painting. Say *Point to a woman.* Repeat with *the sky, cows, trees,* and *a haystack.* Each time, have students point to the word you say.

- Read aloud the instructions. Direct students' attention to the scene around them (the classroom). Ask students to raise their hands to share their ideas about how many colors they need to paint the scene. Have them point to items in the classroom and say the color while keeping count of the number of colors. Write the colors on the board as students mention them. If necessary, point out items in the classroom that have colors that students haven't mentioned.
- Direct students' attention to the glossary on p. 127. Point to the first photo of the wheel. Say *Look! This is a wheel.* Then ask *Where can we see wheels?* Accept any reasonable ideas (for example, a car). Point to the second photo and say *Look!* Do a mixing action and ask *What things can we mix?* Accept any reasonable ideas, such as food, paint colors, or sand and water. Point to the third picture and use your finger to indicate as you say *Look! Lighter, darker. Lighter gray, darker gray.* Point to two other items of clothing of the same color, one of which is lighter than the other. Say *This one is lighter [blue]. This one is darker [blue].*

- **Listen and Read** Read aloud the instructions. Point to the text. Play **TR: 193** from beginning to end.
- Play **TR: 193** again, pausing at the end of the first paragraph. Have students listen to and read the first paragraph. Ask some questions to check students understand. Point to the color wheel and ask *What's this?* (a color wheel) *How many colors can you see in the wheel?* (six)
- Continue playing **TR: 193**, pausing after *mix primary colors together.* Have students listen to and read the second paragraph. Ask some questions to check they understand. Ask *How many primary colors are there?* (three) *What are they?* (red, blue, and yellow) *Can we make a primary color from other colors?* (no)
- Continue playing **TR: 193**, pausing at the end of the third paragraph. Have students listen to and read the third paragraph. Ask some questions to check they understand. Ask *How many secondary colors are there?* (three) *What are they?* (green, orange, and purple) *Can we make a secondary color from other colors?* (yes)
- Explain that *add white to red* is the same as *mix white and red.* Then play the last part of **TR: 193**. Have students listen to and read to the end of the text. Ask some questions to check understanding. Ask *How can I make a color lighter?* (add white) *How can I make a color darker?* (add black) *How can I make gray?* (mix black and white)
- Have students read the text again and find the four new words from the glossary. Have students work in pairs, helping each other.
- Review the reading strategy *looking at visual clues.* Say *Look at the different pictures. Point and say.* Have students point to different diagrams (the color wheel, the primary colors, the secondary colors), and say what they can see. Encourage them to say, for example, *These are three primary colors.*

Reading Extra 3

- **Listen Only** If you choose to do this as a listening-only activity, have students close their books. Play **TR: 193** and follow the instructions above, pausing after each section of the text and asking the comprehension questions. Play **TR: 193** again and have students raise their hands when they hear each of the four new words from the glossary. Allow students to work in pairs, helping each other.

- Read aloud the instructions and point to the questions. Model the activity to show how students can look back at the text to find the answers. Read aloud the first question. Say *Hmm, what is a color wheel?* Tap the side of your head to show students you are thinking. Then point back to the text and the first paragraph and say *I think the answer is here. Let's read.* Read aloud the sentence. Then say *That's it. That's the answer. Let's write* A color wheel shows us how to make new colors. Trace the words as you pretend to write.
- Have students work in pairs to answer the remaining questions. Then check answers by asking aloud each question and calling on different students to provide the answers.
- **Listen Only** Play **TR: 193** again. Make a sign when an answer is coming (the first sentence of the four paragraphs and the last two sentences of the fourth), and pause after each section for students to write their answers.

- Read aloud the instructions. Hold up a copy of the Student's Book and point to the five items. If necessary, explain what the symbols mean (+ and =). Ask *Red and yellow make… ?* (orange) Look at item 5, too. Ask *Blue and white make… ?* Accept both *lighter blue* and *light blue.* Then ask *Blue and black make… ?* Accept both *darker blue* and *dark blue.*
- Have students work individually to complete the activity. Then have them compare their answers in pairs.
- Use the watercolor paints to confirm the answers. Have students read aloud the first two colors (red and yellow). Display a paper for painting where students can see it. Paint two overlapping balls, using red for one and yellow for the other, and show students the color of the overlapping section (orange). Call on four other students to come to the front, one at a time, and paint balls using the other four pairs of colors.

- Put students into groups of three or four, and give each group a set of finger paints or watercolors. Have them read the questions and underline the colors they need to mix. Then, have students mix the colors and say what the result is.

Optional Activity

- Put students into pairs or groups of three or four to share paints and water. Give each student some paper and a paintbrush.
- On the board write *three primary colors, three secondary colors, one lighter color, one darker color, gray.* Have students paint anything they want to paint but with all the colors on the board. When they finish, have a show-and-tell session. Have each student stand up and show his/her picture to the class, explain what the picture shows, and point out a few colors. For larger classes, have students share their pictures in small groups.

Wrap Up

- Write the four words from the glossary on the board. Have students work in pairs to make four sentences, each one containing one of the new words.

> **Additional Practice:** Workbook p. 101, Online Practice

Glossary

wheel

mix

lighter   darker

1 Imagine you want to paint the scene around you. How many different color paints do you need?

2 Listen and read. How many colors are in the text? 🎧 TR: 193   eight

3 Answer the questions.

1. What is a color wheel?
A color wheel shows us how to make new colors.
2. How many primary colors are there?
Three
3. How many secondary colors are there?
Three
4. How can we make a color lighter?
We can add white.
5. How can we make a color darker?
We can add black.

4 Think and write a color.

1. red + yellow = ___orange___

2. yellow + blue = ___green___

3. blue + red = ___purple___

4. red + white = ___pink___

5. blue + black = ___dark blue___

5 Work in groups. Answer these questions.

1. What color can we make when we mix red and green?   brown

2. What color can we make when we mix black and white?   gray

1 Read and match.

1. I have a sun hat — on my head.
2. I can see a boat — in the ocean.
3. Look at that big, yellow — beach ball!
4. This ice cream is — very good!

2 Read and complete. Use four words.

book
cake
game
~~kite~~
picture
soccer

A: Let's go outside. Let's fly a ___kite___ !

B: No. Let's play a ___game___ in the living room! That's fun.

A: No. Let's go in the kitchen. Let's make a ___cake___ !

B: Mom is in the kitchen, and there aren't eggs.

A: You're right! Let's paint a ___picture___ !

B: No. Let's go in the yard. Let's read a ___book___ !

A: Great idea! We can sit under a tree. Come on!

3 Write is, isn't, are, or aren't.

1. ___Is___ there a beach ball in the store? Yes, there ___is___ .

2. ___Are___ there shells in the ocean? No, there ___aren't___ .

3. ___Is___ there an apple in the bag? No, there ___isn't___ .

4. ___Are___ there boys in the park? Yes, there ___are___ .

4 Write.

1. ___We're___ in the living room. Let's ___sing___ a song!

2. ___We're___ in the classroom. Let's ___write___ a story!

3. ___We're___ ___in___ the yard. Let's ___play___ a game!

4. ___We're___ ___on___ ___the___ beach. Let's ___fly___ a kite!

In this lesson, students will:
- review language from Units 11–12.

Resources: Classroom Presentation Tool, Flashcards 178–186, Workbook pp. 102–103, Workbook Audio Track 72, Online Practice

Materials: a photo of an egg

Warm Up
- Have students work in pairs to review the language they learned in Units 11–12. Have each pair share a book and take turns pointing and saying something about each page.

- Use the Lesson 1 flashcards from Unit 11 to review the words. Hold up the *sandcastle* flashcard. Say *Look! Is this a sun hat?* Have students say *No, it isn't. It's a sandcastle!* Repeat with the other eight flashcards, saying an incorrect word each time.
- Read aloud the instructions. Direct students' attention to the example. Read aloud the first part, and trace the blue line with your finger as you read the second part.
- Have students work individually to complete the activity.
- When everyone finishes, check answers.
- **Extra Challenge** Before doing the activity have students work in pairs to invent endings for each sentence beginning. Have them cover the endings before they start.

Task Guidance Notes
Starters Reading & Writing Part 4 Students have to read a semi-factual text which has five spaces. Below the text, they are given a box of nouns and must choose the correct word to write in each space. Each noun has a picture to support the meaning. There are also two extra words that they do not need. This tests understanding of a longer text and writing missing words.

Challenges Students tend to try and fill each space immediately from the list. Encourage students to read the whole text first and think about what they know about the subject before starting to choose words. They may be able to use information they know from lessons in other subjects, but the word must fit the sentence.

Performance Descriptors
- Can follow some very short stories written in very simple language
- Can copy words

- **Collaborate** Have students close their books. Write five verbs from the conversation on the board: *fly, make, paint, play,* and *read.* Have students in pairs write any words they know that go with these verbs. Check ideas with the class and write the words next to the verbs on the board. At this point, show the photo of an egg and teach the word *egg.*

- This activity practices identifying words that go together and articles with nouns. Have students read the whole conversation and underline the verbs you have just focused on. Then have them circle *fun, eggs, under a tree* and match with the words in the box, for example, *fun = game, soccer; eggs = cake; under a tree = book, picture.* This will help students understand that there are several clues to help them, so they need to read everything.
- Have students complete the activity individually, then check in pairs. Check answers with the class. Point out that *soccer* is not possible because there is an article before each space in the conversation.

- Read aloud the instructions. Direct students' attention to the examples in the first line.
- Have students work individually to complete the activity. Then, check the answers.
- **Extra Support** Write two options for each space, the correct option and one distractor, on the board.

Optional Activity
- Play a game to practice *there is, there isn't, there are,* and *there aren't.* Divide students into two pairs within a group of four, A and B. Have Pair A choose a word from p. 128 and have Pair B make a question with this word. For example, if Pair A chooses *kitchen,* then the question could be *Are there lemons in the kitchen? Is there a kitchen in the house?* Have students in Pair A answer the question. Have pairs take turns to choose a word.

- Say *We're in the living room!* Have students suggest something to do using *Let's.* For example, *Let's play a game.* Repeat using other places. Have students raise their hands to make a suggestion. Suggested places: bedroom, kitchen, library, park, store, town center, and yard.
- Read aloud the instructions. Direct students' attention to the examples in the first line.
- Have students work in pairs to complete the sentences. Then, check the answers.
- NOTE: You might like to mention that item 4 is *on* or *at (the beach)* but every other place in the activity is preceded by *in.*

Wrap Up
- Give each of the following instructions one at a time. Elicit the answers from the class.
  1. *Name five things you see on the beach.*
  2. *Name five activities you can do.*
  3. *Make three suggestions using* Let's.
  4. *Point and say where three things are in the classroom.*
  5. *Make a suggestion and respond with a partner using* We're [in the classroom]. Let's….

Additional Practice: Workbook pp. 102–103, Online Practice

One More Look

> **In this lesson, students will:**
> - name their favorite parts of the book.
> - name their favorite words from the book.
> - choose an activity for vacation.
>
> **Resources:** Classroom Presentation Tool

Warm Up

- Hold up a copy of the Student's Book and say *This is the end of this book. Let's look at the book again.* Open some pages of the Student's Book at random and show the class. Make comments and ask a few questions, depending on the page you open to. For example, say *Look! I like this unit. This lesson is fun. Look! These are words to talk about [a town]. This [game] is good.*
- Write *This game is good* on the board and underline the word *good*. Read the sentence again, but replace the word *good*. Say *This game is great.* Write *great* on the board under *good*. Call on students to read the sentence and replace the word *good*. Encourage them to use *fun, terrible,* and *OK*. Circle *game* in the sentence on the board. Then say *This is my favorite game* and write this sentence on the board. You can also say *I like this game* and *I don't like this game* and write these sentences on the board.
- Have students work in pairs to look back at the different parts of each unit: games, readings, songs, and so on. Guide them to use the sentences on the board to comment. Have them share one book to make sure they are both looking at the same pages. Give them two minutes to do this.

- Hold up a copy of the Student's Book open to p. 129 and point to the photo. Ask *Do you remember this unit? What was the unit about?* (places in a town) Say *That's right!*
- Point to the first sentence and the example. Read aloud the example. Then point to the photo again and say *This is Unit 7. Unit 7 is about places in a town.* Point to the character and say *This is his favorite unit.* Then ask *What's your favorite unit?*
- Hold up a copy of the Student's Book open to p. 117 and show the class. Say *Unit 12.* Then flip back through the book to p. 109 and show the class. Say *Unit 11.* Have them flip back to p. 97 and say *Unit 10.* Then ask *What's your favorite unit?* Give students time to think about the question and then write their favorite unit number. Ask a few students around the class to say their favorite unit.
- Read aloud the second sentence. If necessary, remind students that the songs are in Lesson 5. Give students time to look back at the songs and then write the unit number of their favorite. Call on a few students to share.
- Read aloud the third sentence. Give students time to look back at the games (Games 1, 2, and 3) and then write their favorite. Call on a few students to share.

Optional Activity

- Have a vote to find out the class's favorite song. Then, have students open to the page with that song. Play that song's audio track for students to sing the song.

- Read aloud the instructions. Then point to the box and say *Look at the book again and find your favorite six words. Write the words here.* (NOTE: If students have the Workbook, it will be much easier for them to work with the Word List which starts on p. 133.)
- Give students a limited time to find and write their words. Then have them compare their words with a partner to see if they have any words that are the same. Then ask a few students around the class to tell you some of their favorite words.
- Say *One of my favorite words is* yellow. *I like* yellow *because it's my favorite color.* Then choose another word and make another sentence about it. For example, say *I like the word* bread. Bread *is good.* Then have students say sentences to the rest of the class about some of their favorite words.
- **Extra Challenge** Have students write six sentences using their favorite words.
- **Extra Support** Before students do the activity, have them find the new words in the Lesson 1 and Lesson 3 pages. Then have them work in pairs, looking at each Lesson 1 and finding one word they like in each unit. When they finish, have them choose their six favorite words.

- Read aloud the instructions. Say *You can practice English during vacation. It's fun.* Point to the three activities and read them aloud. Then divide the board into three parts and model one of the options in each section of the board.
- Read aloud item 1 again. Then draw yourself with some friends. Don't try and draw with accuracy—stick people will be fine. Write three sentences. For example: *I'm with Tom and Jo. We're good friends. We go to the park.*
- Read aloud item 2 again. Then draw the beach, the park, or the playground. Write a few sentences. For example: *I like the beach. There are shells on the beach. There is a sandcastle, too.* Read the sentences aloud.
- Read aloud item 3 again. Hold up a copy of the Student's Book open to p. 129 and point to the question. Say *What do you like doing* means *What are your favorite activities or things.* Then draw three simple pictures and write three sentences. For example, draw pictures of a kite, a museum, and an ice cream cone. Write: *This is my kite in the park. I like the museum in the town center. I like ice cream.*
- Have students discuss their choice with a partner, thinking about what is involved in each activity and choosing the option they find most appealing.
- Ask students around the class which activity they have chosen to do during vacation. Have them copy the activity into their notebooks so that they don't forget.

Wrap Up

- Remind students of the game they chose in Activity 1. Group students according to the game they have chosen and then give them five minutes to play the game again in their groups.

1 Look and say.

- My favorite unit is Unit ___ .
- My favorite song is in Unit ___ .
- My favorite game is ___ .

My favorite unit is Unit 7.

2 Write.

My six favorite words are:

_____ _____ _____

_____ _____ _____

3 Choose one activity for vacation.

- Draw you and your friends. Write sentences.
- Draw the beach, the park, or the playground. Write sentences.
- What do you like doing during the school vacation? Draw three pictures and write sentences.

International kite festivals

International kite festival, Cha-Am beach, Thailand

In this lesson, students will:

- watch a video about the International Kite Festival in Leba, Poland.
- use new words to talk about a kite festival.
- make a kite.
- present a project to the class.

Resources: Video 16, Classroom Presentation Tool, Project Guide, Flashcard 196, Workbook p. 104, Online Practice

Materials: a globe or map of the world, sticky tack, black construction paper (one sheet per student), clear contact paper (one sheet per student), colored tissue paper, glue, a ruler, poster paper, crayons or markers

---

ABOUT THE VIDEO

The International Kite Festival featured in the video is in Leba, Poland. Leba is a beautiful town in Poland where the river Leba meets the Baltic Sea. There are lakes, forests, beaches, sand dunes, and even a dinosaur park. Not surprisingly, Leba is a popular location for tourists. Every summer, an international kite festival is held on the beach there. Kite enthusiasts come from many different countries to take part—either to fly kites or to enjoy the spectacle. Other highlights include a parade through the town (in which people wear funny costumes) and evenings of light and music. Workshops are organized to teach visitors how to make and fly kites.

Warm Up

- Hold up the *fly a kite* flashcard and have students identify the activity. Write the word *kite* on the board. Say *Today, we're going on a school trip. We're going to the International Kite Festival in Leba, Poland.* To teach the meaning of *international*, say International *means* from all around the world. Hold up a globe or a map and say the sentence again as you move your finger around the world.
- Say *Let's think about international kite festivals. What things can we see at a kite festival?* Have students make suggestions and write each word on the board. Accept any reasonable ideas.
- Leave the list on the board. Say *Today we're watching a video of the International Kite Festival in Leba, Poland. Let's see what things we can see.*

Introduce the Theme

- Have students open their books to pp. 130–131. Read aloud the title. Hold up a copy of the Student's Book and point to the kites. Say *Look! This is a kite festival.* Point to the caption and read it aloud. Say *Another international kite festival is in this photo. It isn't in Poland. It's in Thailand.*

- Read aloud the instructions. Then ask *What can you see?* (kites) *That's right. A lot of kites.* Say *Look at the kites in the photo. Can you see the animal kites?* Say *Point to the* cat *kite.* Ask *How many* bird *kites can you see?* (five) Ask *Which kite do you like?* Have students point or say *I like the [red, yellow, and green] kite.*

- Say *Let's go to the International Kite Festival in Leba, Poland.* Read aloud the instructions. Then hold up a copy of the Student's Book and point to the six animal photos with words. Point to each of the photos, one at a time, and read aloud the words. Then play **Video 16** from beginning to end.
- Play **Video 16** again and pause after the narrator says *up and down.* Ask *What colors can you see on this kite?* (blue, green, orange, red, and yellow) Continue playing the video and pause after the narrator says *The kite festival is at the beach.* Ask *Can you see a red and white kite? Can you see a black, white, and orange kite?* Continue playing **Video 16** and pause after the narrator says *Some kites are animals.* Direct students' attention to the crocodile kite and say *Look! What animal is this?* (a crocodile) Have students look back to the photos on the page and check the box.
- Continue playing **Video 16**, pausing to allow students to check each animal.
- Play **Video 16** a third time and have students check their answers. To review answers, read aloud each animal word one at a time and have students say *yes* or *no*.

Script for Video 16

Let's go on a trip. Let's go to a festival.
Look! What can you see in the sky? What is it? Up and down. Up and down. It's red, orange, yellow, blue, and green. It's a kite!
The kite festival is at the beach. Can you see the sand? Can you see the ocean? There are a lot of boys and girls at the kite festival. There are a lot of kites, too! Some kites are animals. Can you see the fish? Let's look closer at some kites. Wow! Look at this kite. It's fantastic. It has big eyes and a lot of legs. How many legs can you see? One, two, three, four, five, six, seven, eight. Eight legs! Do you know this animal? It's an octopus.
Oh, look! This is my favorite kite. It's a boy. He has a big blue hat on his head. It's a helmet. And he has brown boots. He's happy! A happy boy kite! What a great kite festival!

- Ask *Is the kite festival cool? What do you think?* Listen to several students' responses before beginning the activity.
- Read aloud the instructions and the first sentence, saying all the words in bold. Say *Remember the video. What words are they? Are they at the beach or in the park?* (at the beach) *That's right. We circle* at the beach. Then give students time to complete the activity on their own.
- Have students compare their answers with a partner. To review their work, read each sentence aloud with the correct words.

- **Extra Challenge** Describe a kite from the video in detail. Have students listen carefully. Then play the video again and have students call out *I can see the kite!* and point when they see the kite you described.
- **Extra Support** Before students do the activity, play the video again. Make a sign that the answer is about to be given before the narrator says: *The kite festival is at the beach, Some kites are animals, My favorite color is purple,* and *And he has brown boots.*

Optional Activity

- Have students work in pairs to list all the animals they know. Allow them to look back through the Student's Book to remind themselves of animals. Give students a limited time (two or three minutes). Then say *Stop!* Have students count the animals. Invite the pair with the most animals to read aloud their list while you write the words on the board. Then invite students to add any other animals the pair might have missed.

4 Project

- Before starting the project, make sure students understand the actions *measure* and *stick*. Demonstrate measuring something with a ruler and say *Measure.* Demonstrate sticking two pieces of paper together with glue and say *Stick.* Write the words on the board, then say aloud each word and have students pretend to do each action.
- Direct students' attention to the blue project box at the bottom of p. 131. Read aloud the instructions and make sure that students have the necessary materials to complete the poster: black construction paper (one sheet), clear contact paper (one sheet), colored tissue paper, glue, a ruler, and a pencil.
- Give each student a copy of the project guide or display the instructions. Say *Let's make kites.* Read aloud Step 1 and point to the picture. Say *First, you need the black paper, a ruler, and a pencil. I will come and measure your strips. You cut.* To save time, you might prefer to cut the necessary strips out for students before class, using a paper cutter. Then, simply give the six strips of paper to each student at the start of the project.
- Read aloud Step 2 and demonstrate how to assemble the kite. Take the 20-cm strip and the 14-cm strip, and arrange them to look like a lowercase *t*. Then, place the two 16-cm strips in a diagonal, from the bottom of the *t* to either end of the 14-cm strip. Place the two 10-cm strips in a diagonal from the top of the *t* to either end of the 14-cm strip. Pause after you arrange each piece to make sure that students are arranging their papers on their desks in the same way.
- Read aloud Step 3 and point to the picture. Hold up a piece of clear contact paper and say *This is very sticky! Be careful.* Help students to remove the backing of the contact paper and stick their kite pieces into place. Remind students to wait for you if they think they need help, so that they don't get sides of the contact paper stuck together, ruining the sheet. To ensure students get this right, you may wish to call students to your desk for this, so that you can help them one at a time.

- Read aloud Step 4 and point to the picture. Say *Look! Now it's time to decorate the kite.* Demonstrate how to stick small pieces of tissue paper into place. (NOTE: It is a good idea for students to prepare the tissue paper before they begin this stage. Have them tear up the paper into small pieces and put them into separate piles, organized by color.)
- Give time for students to cover the clear areas of the kite with colored tissue paper.
- Read aloud Step 5 and point to the picture. Hold up a pair of scissors and say *Use the scissors. Be careful!* Demonstrate how to cut off the extra contact paper. Have students throw the extra paper in the garbage can immediately, so that it does not get stuck to the classroom furniture or the floor.
- Point to the picture of the completed kite in the window and say *Hold up your kites.* Have students hold up their kites to show the rest of the class. Point to the model in the blue project box, and call on individual students to describe their kites in the same way.
- Collect all of the kites and display them on the window so that the sun shines through the colored paper, giving a stained-glass effect. If you don't have enough window space, hang them on a bulletin board or from the ceiling.
- To assess the project, check that students followed directions and worked neatly and efficiently. You may also want to offer points for creativity. Be certain to explain feedback orally so that students understand why they are receiving the grade they're getting.
- When all the kites are finished, make a kite festival poster as a class. Alternatively, with larger classes, have students make posters in smaller groups. Have students draw small pictures of their kites. Use the pictures to make a montage. Then use the montage as the basis for a kite festival poster. Have students think of a title and location for the festival. Have them add this information to the poster. You might want to make a digital version and take photos of the students' kites to form the montage.
- **Extra Support** Prepare several kites on contact paper before class and give them to students who may not be able to create the kite themselves.

Wrap Up

- Play **Video 16** again, pausing when there are animal kites (crocodile, penguin, octopus, fish, etc.). Give clues about the animal kites in the video. Say *I see a kite of an animal that lives near water. It has a big mouth. It goes CHOMP* (make chomp gesture with arms). If students don't guess the word, say *It's a crocodile.* Then have them point to the crocodile kite in the video. Repeat this with the other animals, and similar clues.

> **Additional Practice:** Workbook p. 104, Online Practice

1 **BEFORE YOU WATCH** Look at the photo. What can you see?

2 **WHILE YOU WATCH** What animal kites are in the video? Check (✔). ▶ Video 16

cat

crocodile

fish

monkey

octopus

penguin

3 **AFTER YOU WATCH** Read and circle.

1. The kite festival is (at the beach) / in the park.

2. Some kites are (animals) / planes and trains.

3. The octopus kite is **blue** / (**purple**)

4. The boy kite has **black** / (**brown**) boots.

4 **PROJECT** Make a kite. Then make a kite festival poster.

Look! My kite is green and orange.

What's an Elephant?

Mom Mouse has six baby mice. The baby mice can't see very well. They're small.

"I can see an elephant," Mom Mouse says. "It's under the trees." "What's an elephant?" Baby Mouse One asks. "Go and ask the elephant," Mom Mouse says.

The six baby mice go under the trees. They touch the elephant. They touch its body. "What's this?" Baby Mouse One asks. "Is it a wall?" "I don't know," Baby Mouse Two says.

They touch its leg. "What's this?" Baby Mouse Three asks. "Is it a tree?" "I don't know," Baby Mouse Four says.

They touch its tail. "What's this?" Baby Mouse Five asks. "Is it a rope?" "I don't know," Baby Mouse Six says. "Let's ask the elephant."

In this lesson, students will:

- respond to a picture of a country scene.
- read a story about an elephant and mice.
- draw and talk about an animal.

Resources: Audio Track 194, Classroom Presentation Tool, Workbook p. 105, Workbook Audio Track 73, Online Practice

Materials: a rope (such as a jump rope), a large piece of paper (one per group of students)

ABOUT THE STORY

What's an Elephant? is based on an Indian fable that tells the story of six blind men who come across different parts of an elephant on their journeys through life. The men each create their own version of reality from that limited experience. There is even a poem called "Blind Men and the Elephant" written by John Godfrey Saxe in the nineteenth century.

Warm Up

- Review words for body parts. Write *Person* and *Animal* on the board as headings. Say *Head. Person? Animal? Both?* (both) Write *head* under each heading. Go around the room, calling on students to say a body part word for either category. If students don't say *tail* (from School Trip 2), you can say it. Then have students point to each part of the body as you read the words in the list. When it comes to *tail*, have them pretend to be an animal.

- Explain the meaning of *rope*. Take a rope (such as a jump rope) into the classroom. Hold it up and say *This is a rope.*

- **Use the Picture** Have students open their books to pp. 132–133. Point to the elephant in the picture and ask *What's this animal?* (an elephant) *Is it big or small?* (big) Then point to a mouse and ask *What's this animal?* If students don't know the word, say *Mouse* and have students repeat. Then point to the three mice on p. 132 or all six mice and tell students that the plural of *mouse* is *mice*. Do this by pointing and counting. Say *One mouse, two mice.* Emphasize the word *mice* each time. Then ask *How many mice are in the picture?* (six) *What other things can you see?* (trees, flowers) Point to the elephant again and say *Today we're going to read a story about an elephant.*

- Read aloud the instructions. Have students look at the example and at the first word in the lower box (*big*). Ask *What is big? An elephant or a mouse?* (an elephant) *That's right. An elephant is big. We draw a line to match the word* big *with the word* elephant.

- Have students look at the picture again if necessary and work individually to match the other words. (NOTE: Mice can be gray and elephants can be brown, so students must look at the picture for their answers.) Then, have them compare their answers in pairs. Check their answers by calling out each word in the lower box, one at a time, and having the class call out *elephant* or *mouse*.

- **Listen and Read** Read aloud the instructions. Point to the story. Read aloud the title and call on a few students to share their ideas. Accept any reasonable answers.

- Play **TR: 194** all the way through.

- Play **TR: 194** again, pausing at the end of the second paragraph. Have students listen to and read the first two paragraphs of the story. Ask some questions to check understanding. Ask *How many baby mice are there?* (six) *Who can see an elephant?* (Mom Mouse) *Where is the elephant?* (under the trees)

- Continue playing **TR: 194**, pausing at the end of the third paragraph. Have students listen to and read the next paragraph of the story. Ask a question to check they understand. Say *The baby mice touch the elephant's body. One mouse thinks it's something else. What?* (a wall)

- Continue playing **TR: 194**, pausing at the end of the fourth paragraph. Have students listen to and read the next paragraph of the story. Ask a question to check they understand. Say *The baby mice touch the elephant's leg. One mouse thinks it's something else. What?* (a tree)

- Continue playing **TR: 194**, pausing at the end of the fifth paragraph. Have students listen to and read the next paragraph of the story. Ask a question to check they understand. Say *The baby mice touch the elephant's tail. One mouse thinks it's something else. What?* (a rope)

- Continue playing **TR: 194**, pausing at the end of the sixth paragraph. Have students listen to and read the next paragraph of the story. Ask some questions to check they understand. Ask *What do the baby mice touch?* (their body, their legs, and their tail) *Do an elephant and a mouse have the same number of legs?* (yes) *Do an elephant and a mouse have a tail?* (yes)

- Play the last part of **TR: 194**. Have students listen to and read the last two paragraphs of the story. Ask some questions to check they understand. Ask *What color are the mice?* (brown) *What color is the elephant?* (gray)

- Read aloud the question again and ask *What's an elephant? Is it a, b, c, or d?* (c) Have students circle the answer.

- **Listen Only** Have students close their books. If you choose to do this as a listening-only activity, write the question and the four options on the board. Then say *Listen carefully.*

- Play **TR: 194** all the way through. Then point to the board and ask the question again. Ask *What's an elephant? Is it a, b, c, or d?* Have students choose from the options on the board and call out the answer (c).

BONUS Reading Extra

- Prepare an activity on the board for students to copy into their notebooks and do while they listen a second time. Write the following animals in the left column. Then write these sentences and questions in the right column, but change the order so that the sentences and questions do not match the speakers. These are the answers.

Mom Mouse	I can see an elephant.
Baby Mouse One	Is it a wall?
Baby Mouse Two	I don't know!
Baby Mouse Three	Is it a tree?
Baby Mouse Five	Is it a rope?
Baby Mouse Six	Let's ask the elephant.
Elephant	This is my body!

- Have students listen again to **TR: 194** and match the animals in the story with their sentences and questions. To check answers, say each sentence or question and have students call out the animal. For example, say *I can see an elephant* and have students call out *Mom Mouse*.

 3

- Read aloud the instructions. Ask *How many things do we have to do?* (two) *What are they?* (write, match) Say *Good. Let's look at the first activity—write.* Hold up a copy of the Student's Book and point to the word box. Say *Here are the words.* Point to the three pictures of body parts with the lines underneath and say *Write the words here.*
- Point to the first picture and then back to the word box. Ask *Is this a picture of a body, a leg, or a tail?* (a leg) Say *That's right. It's* a leg. *So we can write* leg *here.* Point to the line. Have students write the word and then repeat with the other two words.
- Hold up a copy of the Student's Book again to check answers. Point to the pictures, one at a time, and have students call out the word as a class.
- Point to the three pictures on the right and then to the instructions again. Read aloud *Match.* Say *Remember the story.* Point to the picture of the wall and say *This is a wall. The mice call the elephant's…what?…a wall.* (body) Say *That's right. The mice call the elephant's body a wall.* Then make sure that students draw a line matching *body* to *wall.*
- Have students match the other pictures. Walk around and monitor students as they do the matching activity to check their answers.
- **Extra Challenge** Write these sentences on the board.

This is my hair. It isn't a ____ .
These are my eyes. They aren't ____ .
This is my ____ . It isn't ____ .

Have students copy and complete the sentences in their notebooks in pairs. Have students read aloud their sentences. For example, *This is my hair. It isn't a flower. These are my eyes. They aren't marbles. This is my hand. It isn't a glove.*

- **Extra Support** Before students do the activity, copy these sentences from the story onto the board.

This is my body. It isn't a wall.
This is my leg. It isn't a tree.
This is my tail. It isn't a rope.

Draw the first two items on the board (an elephant's body and a wall). Read aloud the first sentence and point to the pictures. Say *Look! A body and a wall. They are the same.* Point to each picture one at a time again, and make sure students notice they are similar. Then do the same with the other two sentences and four pictures.

 4

- Read aloud the instructions. Give students some time to think before they start drawing. Ideally students will draw different animals but all with a body, a tail, and legs. Go around the class, and to each student ask *What's your animal?* Have students name their animal each time. Make sure there are a variety of animals.
- Have students work individually to draw their animals. When they finish, have them hold up their pictures and describe the animals in simple sentences. Remind them to point to different parts of the body as they speak. For example, have them point to the body and say *This isn't a wall. It's a body.* Have them point to the tail and say *This isn't a rope. It's a tail.* Have them point to the legs and say *These aren't trees. They're legs.*

Optional Activity

- Have students work in groups of three or four to make a storyboard for the story. First have them decide how many pictures they need to draw. Model the first frame of the storyboard on the board. Draw a square. Have students suggest what the first picture should be. Draw the picture.
- Give each group a large piece of paper to make their storyboards. Give them ten minutes to draw and color their pictures. Walk around and help as necessary. When they finish, make a display and have students read each other's storyboards. Call on several groups to use their storyboards to retell the story.

Wrap Up

- Call on eight students to come to the front of the class. Assign each student a role. As you read the story aloud (or play **TR: 194** again), have each student act out his/her assigned role. (NOTE: Avoid having students touch one another.)

Additional Practice: Workbook p. 105, Online Practice

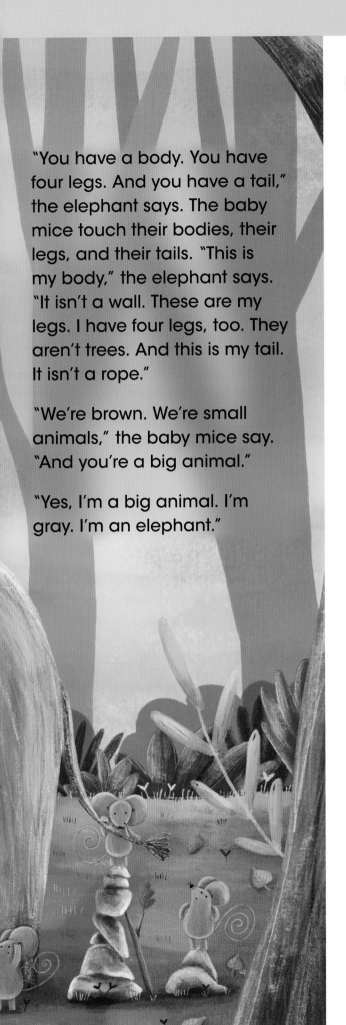

"You have a body. You have four legs. And you have a tail," the elephant says. The baby mice touch their bodies, their legs, and their tails. "This is my body," the elephant says. "It isn't a wall. These are my legs. I have four legs, too. They aren't trees. And this is my tail. It isn't a rope."

"We're brown. We're small animals," the baby mice say. "And you're a big animal."

"Yes, I'm a big animal. I'm gray. I'm an elephant."

1 **Look at the picture. Match.**

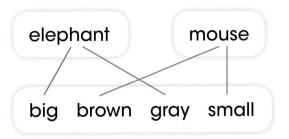

elephant   mouse

big   brown   gray   small

2 **Listen and read. What's an elephant?** 🎧 TR: 194

a. a wall   **c.** a big animal

b. a tree   **d.** a small animal

3 **Write. Then match.**

body   leg   tail

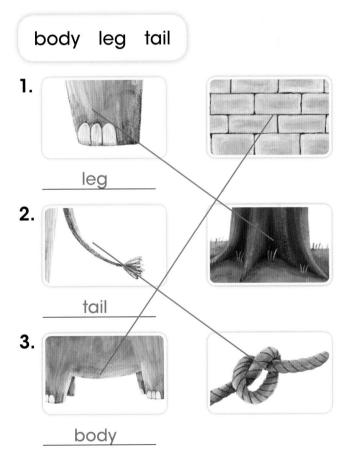

1. leg

2. tail

3. body

4 **Draw a different animal.**

1 **What can you remember about the texts in this book?**

1
Unit 1

A _____ is in the classroom.
- a. bag
- b. pencil case
- c. poster

2
Unit 2

A marble is a _____ .
- a. ball
- b. color
- c. game

3
Unit 3

The dinosaur is in a _____ .
- a. classroom
- b. museum
- c. school

4
Unit 4

Atdhetare is _____ today! Happy birthday!
- a. five
- b. six
- c. seven

5
Reading Extra 1

The _____ is black at night.
- a. moon
- b. sky
- c. sun

6
Unit 5

The boy has _____ and white paint on his face.
- a. black
- b. brown
- c. green

7
Unit 6

In the bedroom, the game is on the _____ .
- a. bed
- b. cabinet
- c. table

8
Unit 7

There's a _____ in the photo.
- a. playground
- b. swimming pool
- c. town

In this lesson, students will:

- review the reading texts in this book.
- answer questions about reading texts.
- play a game.

Resources: Classroom Presentation Tool; Flashcards 28–31, 41–43, 53–55, 69–71, 82–85, 99–101, 115–118, 129–131, 152–156, 170–173, 187–190, 204–206

Materials: one coin per pair of students, one game piece for each student, sticky notes, masking tape, a beanbag

Warm Up

- Use the Lesson 3 flashcards to review the new words that are in the reading texts. Shuffle all the flashcards and place them facedown on the table. Put students into two or four teams, depending on the size of the class.
- Turn over and hold up one flashcard at a time. Have teams take turns responding to three *true* or *false* sentences that you make about the flashcard. For example, hold up the *scarecrow* flashcard and say three sentences. For example, say *It's a scarecrow.* (true) *We can see a scarecrow in a museum.* (false) *Scarecrows aren't real people.* (true)
- Make sure each team is given the same number of turns. Award one point for each correct response. The team with the most points at the end is the winner.

- Hold up a coin for students to see and say *Look! A coin.* Show students the side with the head and say *Look! Heads.* Repeat with the other side of the coin and say *Look! Tails.*
- Hold up a few game pieces for students to see. Say *Look! Game pieces.* Draw two squares on the board and color them in two different colors. Write *game pieces* next to the squares. Leave the drawings on the board. Put students into pairs, and give each pair of students a coin and a pair of different-colored game pieces to play the game. Write *Heads = 1* and *Tails = 2* on the board. Say *Heads* and have students show you the side of the coin with the head. Then say *Tails* and have students show you the other side of the coin.
- Have each pair share a book. Have them open their books to pp. 134–135. Read aloud the instructions and direct students' attention to the game. Have one student from each pair count the questions (1–16) and have the other student say the number of the unit or the Reading Extra.
- Say *Look! This is a game with questions.* Ask *How many questions are there?* (16) Point to the instructions and say *You start here. Put your game pieces here.* Then point to the heading BONUS Game on page 135 and say *You finish here.* Trace the direction.

- Give students simple instructions to play the game, pointing and modeling as you explain. Say *Take turns, Student A and Student B. Student A, you toss the coin.* If the coin lands heads up, say *Heads! That's one! Move your game piece one square.* Point to sentence 1. Read aloud the sentence. Say the three options and have students say *a*, *b*, or *c* if they know the answer. If not, have them look back at the reading text in Unit 1 to find it. If the coin lands tails up, say *Tails! That's two! Move your game piece two squares.* Point to sentence 2. Read aloud the sentence. Say the three options and have students say *a*, *b*, or *c* if they know the answer. If not, have them look back at the reading text in Unit 2 to find it.
- Say *One student completes the sentence and the other student checks the answer in the reading text in the unit.* Have students play in pairs. Walk around the classroom, monitoring while pairs play the game and helping when necessary. The first student to complete sentence 16 or jump two squares from sentence 15 is the winner.
- Check answers. Have individual students read one sentence each.
- **Extra Challenge** Have students create another board game of their own, writing sentences and options on small sticky notes, and placing them on top of the current sentences and options. Then have students play the game for additional practice. Alternatively, they can exchange games to play.
- **Extra Support** Before students play the game, give them time to read through the sentences and the options.

BONUS Game

Optional Activity

- Have students play a beanbag toss game. Make a circular shape with masking tape on the floor. Make a small middle ring, a larger inner ring, and an even larger outer ring. Mark the number of points: ten points in the middle, five points in the inner ring, and two points in the outer ring.
- Have students take turns tossing the beanbag from a distance. When the beanbag lands, have them get an instruction. The higher the point value, the more difficult the instruction. Prepare instructions in advance.
- Suggested instructions:

Ten points

Use three sentences to describe your teacher.
Use three sentences to describe your house.
Use three sentences to describe your town or city.
Use three sentences to describe your family.
Count from 11 to 20.
Say the alphabet.
Name three things in a park.
Make three suggestions for free-time activities.

Five points

Name three things in the ocean.
Name three things on a beach.
Name three things in the classroom.
Name three people at school.
Name three toys.
Name three colors.
Name three rooms in a house.
Count from one to ten.

Two points

Say one word. Ears, hair, nose, and…? (eyes, mouth, etc.)
Say one word. Arms, head, feet, and…? (hands, legs, etc.)
Say one word. Jeans, T-shirt, socks, and…? (hat, shoes, etc.)
Say one word. Chicken, elephant, horse, and…? (dog, sheep, etc.)
Say one word. Jam, tomato, yogurt, and…? (carrot, rice, etc.)
Say one word. Lamp, shower, TV, and…? (bed, cabinet, etc.)
Say one word. Aunt, dad, sister, and…? (cousin, grandpa, etc.)
Say one word. Crayon, pen, ruler, and…? (eraser, pencil, etc.)

Wrap Up

- Hold up a copy of the Student's Book open to pp. 134–135 and point to the first photo on the left. Ask *What's this animal?* (a dinosaur) *Are there dinosaurs now?* (no) *Is the dinosaur big or small?* (big) *What color is it?* (gray) *What color are its eyes?* (black and yellow)
- Have students describe the photos that illustrate the game. Have them work in pairs to point and say what they can about each photo.

Student Feedback

- It's clear that your students are in class to learn from you. But what you might not realize is how much *you* can learn from your students. By asking students for their opinion on the class you're teaching, you are:
  - demonstrating that you value students' ideas and opinions
  - opening lines of communication between yourself and your students
  - modeling the process of giving and responding to feedback
  - giving yourself an opportunity to adjust your teaching to meet students' needs
  - finding about your students' activity preferences
- An end-of-year survey is one way to get students' reaction to the class. Alternatively, you could request instant feedback at the end of a specific lesson or unit. This is useful if you've tried out a new method or technique and want to gauge students' response to it.
- To help you collect feedback on the class as a whole, a survey template has been created and can be accessed on the *Look* Teacher's Resource Website. Print a copy for each student, distribute it on the last day of class, and guide students through the survey questions, using their first language whenever necessary.
- Emphasize that students are not to put their names on the surveys, and as such, will not be penalized in any way for their answers.

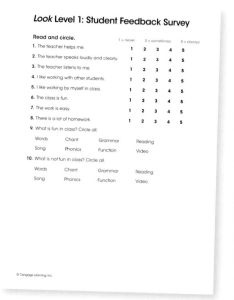

Look **Level 1: Student Feedback Survey**

Read and circle.

1 = never   3 = sometimes   5 = always

1. The teacher helps me.   1   2   3   4   5
2. The teacher speaks loudly and clearly.   1   2   3   4   5
3. The teacher listens to me.   1   2   3   4   5
4. I like working with other students.   1   2   3   4   5
5. I like working by myself in class.   1   2   3   4   5
6. The class is fun.   1   2   3   4   5
7. The work is easy.   1   2   3   4   5
8. There is a lot of homework.   1   2   3   4   5
9. What is fun in class? Circle all.

Words   Chant   Grammar   Reading
Song   Phonics   Function   Video

10. What is not fun in class? Circle all.

Words   Chant   Grammar   Reading
Song   Phonics   Function   Video

© Cengage Learning, Inc.

16
BONUS Reading Extra

The elephant is _____ the trees.
a. in
b. next to
c. under ⓒ

9
Unit 8

The farmer has food for the _____ .
a. chickens
b. ducks
c. sheep ⓒ

15
Reading Extra 3

The three primary colors are red, _____ , and yellow.
a. blue ⓐ
b. green
c. orange

10
Reading Extra 2

The frog has strong _____ .
a. feet ⓐ
b. hands
c. legs

14
Unit 12

The writer has a _____ and some paper.
a. crayon
b. pen
c. pencil ⓒ

11
Unit 9

The scarecrow has _____ .
a. boots ⓐ
b. shoes
c. socks

13
Unit 11

There are _____ in the water.
a. balls
b. fish ⓑ
c. shells

12
Unit 10

There's _____ on the lunch trays.
a. bread
b. rice ⓑ
c. water

Click! Click!

> **Resources:** Anthology 1, Story 1; Story 1 Audio
>
> **Materials:** a camera or smartphone; large sheet of paper with a hole cut in the middle; a bag with some toys and classroom objects (for example, a doll, a teddy bear, a car, toy animals, a book, a pencil, a bag, a crayon, etc.)

About the Story

This story is about what happens when a little girl finds a camera lying around the house. She starts taking photos of things she sees from different angles and gets her younger brother to guess what each item is. Suddenly the owner of the camera turns up!

Warm Up

- Show students your camera or smartphone, or a photo of a camera. Say *Look! It's a camera. Let's take a class photo!* Hold up the camera, or pretend to hold one up to take a photo. Say *Look at me! Smile. Look happy!* Smile at students and encourage them to smile back. As you pretend to take the photo, say *Click! Click!*

- Continue taking photos and giving different, simple instructions, acting out the actions or expressions as you do so, for example, *Look sad! Look cold! Say Hello! Look big! Look small!* Wait for students to show the correct expression or action before you pretend to take the photo and say *Click! Click!* If there are any concerns about taking photos, make sure students understand it is only pretend.

 1

- Have students open their books to Story 1, p. 3. Hold up a book and direct students' attention to the picture. Ask *What can you see?* (a girl, a boy, a camera, a photo) Ask *Do you like looking at photos?* (Yes, I do./No, I don't.) *Do you take photos?*

- Read aloud the title of the story and act out taking a photo. Say *This story is about a girl with a camera. She takes photos. The camera goes Click! Click!* Say *Let's read the story and find out what photos the girl takes.*

 2

- Play **Story 1** and ask students to listen and follow along in their books.

- Ask students to read the story again. Then point to p. 3. Ask *Is it a toy?* (No. It's a camera.) *The girl takes a photo. Click! Click! What is it? Is it a rabbit?* (No, it isn't.)

- Point to p. 4. Ask *What is it?* (It's a cat, it's Lola.)

- Point to p. 5. Say *Click! Click! Juan says "Can I see?" What is it? Is it a car?* (No, it isn't.)

- Point to p. 6. Ask *What is it?* (Juan's robot) *That's right, it's a robot. The girl says "Good ...?"* (Good job, Juan!)

- Point to p. 7. Say *Click! Click! What's this?* (a shoe) *That's right, it's a shoe. It's a man's shoe.*

- Point to p. 8. Ask *Who is this?* (Dad) *Yes, it's Dad. The girl says "Uh-oh!" And Juan says ...?* (Sorry, Dad!)

- Ask *How do the children feel?* (They're sorry)

- **Extra Challenge** Ask students to try and remember all the photos the girl takes in the story in the order she takes them. (cat, robot, shoe)

- **Extra Support** Listen to the story again. Ask students to join in with the 'Click Click' sound every time the girl takes a photo.

 3

- Help students open their books to p. 42. Read aloud the instructions: *Match and write.* Say *Look at the photos.* Hold up a copy of the book and point to the close-up of the pencil. Say *What's this?* (It's a pencil) *Yes, it's a pencil. Now match.* Point to the teddy bear at the top and ask *Is this photo a pencil?* (No, it isn't.) Point to the pencil on the second line and ask *Is this photo a pencil?* (Yes, it is.) *Yes it is. Match the pencil and the pencil.* Trace the line with your finger to show students how to match the photos. Then ask students to write the words to complete the sentences.

- Have students compare their answers in pairs.
  Answers: 1. It's a teddy.; 2. It's a pencil.; 3. It's a tennis racket.; 4. It's a chair.

Optional Activity

- Put students into pairs and ask them to think of three things in the classroom or around school that they could take interesting photos of. Encourage students to imagine they're taking photos. Have them draw pictures of their ideas.

- Ask students to share their ideas with the class.

Wrap Up

- Hold the sheet of paper in front of you with the bag of objects hidden behind. Take an object out of the bag and hold it behind the hole, so students can only see part of it. Say *Look! What is it?* Call on students to try to name the object.

- Continue with different objects. Then call on a student to come to the front of the class, choose an object and hold it up behind the hole, asking the question *What is it?* Have the class make guesses, and encourage the student to answer *Yes, it is.* or *No, it isn't.* Have several students take a turn.

The Granny Cloud

Resources: Anthology 1, Story 2; Story 2 Audio

Materials: a soft ball (optional)

About the Story

This story takes place in India. It is about The Granny Cloud, an organization which was created by an Indian professor, Sugata Mitra from the University of Newcastle, in the UK. At The School in the Cloud, volunteer grannies use Skype to help some of the world's poorest children learn English. This cultural exchange encourages students to be autonomous with computer technology and learn a different language.

Warm Up

- Pretend to go out of the classroom door and come back in again. Wave to the class. Ask *What do you say?* (Hello. How are you? I'm fine, thank you.) Write the expressions on the board. Read them aloud together as a class.
- Have students walk around the room. When you clap your hands, get them to greet someone using the expressions on the board. Repeat as necessary.

- Have students open their books to Story 2, p. 9. Hold up a book and direct students' attention to the photo.
- Ask *Look at the photo. What can you see?* (A school, children, teachers) *Where is it?* (India) Read aloud the title of the story. Pretend to look puzzled and ask *What is a Granny Cloud? A granny is another word for* grandma. Draw a cloud on the board and say *This is a cloud. So what is a granny cloud?* Say *Let's read the story and find out.*

- Play **Story 2** and ask students to listen and follow along in their books.
- Ask students to read the story again. Then point to p. 9. Ask *What do the children want to learn?* (English).
- Point to p. 10. Ask *What can you see?* (girls, a computer) Point to the woman on the computer screen and say *Who is it?* (a granny) *That's right. It's a granny. She speaks English. She can help the girls. Where are the students?* (India.) *Where's the granny?* (the UK or maybe in the US)
- Point to p. 11. Ask *What can the boys and girls learn?* (English) *Who can they talk to?* (a granny) *What is it called?* (the Granny Cloud)
- Point to p. 12. Ask *Do the students want to learn English?* (Yes, they do.) *What does the lady say?* (Hello! How are you? I can help you.)
- Point to p. 13. Ask *When do they speak English with the lady?* (every week) *Is the lady happy to help them?* (Yes, she is.)

- Point to p. 14. Ask *Is it one school?* (No, it's a lot of schools.)
- **Extra Challenge** Ask students to make a list of English-speaking countries where they would like to talk to a granny on the Granny Cloud (for example, the US, the UK, Australia, Canada, etc.)
- **Extra Support** Have students practice the first exchanges they would have with a granny on the Granny Cloud (Hello. How are you? We're fine, thank you.)

- Help students open their books to p. 43 *Look at the pictures. What can you see in the pictures?* (A granny and students.)
- Read aloud the instructions: Say *Look and write.* Explain that students need to write the correct sentence or question from the box to complete each conversation.
- Have students compare their answers in pairs.
  Answers: 1. How are you?; 2. It's a book.; 3. How many dogs?; 4. It's orange and blue.

Optional Activity

- Have a class discussion about learning English from other people. Ask students to think about things we can learn from each other.
- Say *Imagine you can talk to a granny on the Granny Cloud.* Ask *What questions do you want to ask? What can you show the granny from your country?* (for example, songs, poems, photos, or pictures)
- Put students into pairs and ask them to think of three things they want to show or tell a granny about themselves, their school, etc. They can draw their ideas or write simple sentences.
- Ask students to get into groups of four to share their ideas. Write their ideas on the board for the class to see.

Wrap Up

- Throw a soft ball to a student and ask him or her to say one thing that he or she would tell a granny (for example, My name's [Pedro]. I have a dog, I like chicken, my [shirt] is [blue].) then throw the ball back to you. If the sentence is incorrect, throw the ball back to the student until he or she gets it right. If the sentence is correct, throw the ball to another student, and so on. Encourage and support students as you go around the classroom.

We're All Superheroes!

> **Resources:** Anthology 1, Story 3; Story 3 Audio

About the Story

This is a rhyme about superheroes. Children love dressing up and inventing. In this rhyme children talk about their superpowers and describe their bodies and their costumes. The rhyme shows that anyone can be a superhero!

Warm Up

- Ask *Do you like superheroes? What's your favorite superhero?* Listen to students' answers.
- Say *I'm a superhero. Watch me! I can run!* Pretend to run very fast on the spot. Have the students stand up and pretend to run. Say *I can run!* and have students repeat. Then act out and say a series of superhero actions and have students copy you and repeat. *I'm a superhero. I have strong legs and strong arms! I'm a superhero. I can fly! I'm a superhero. I can help people!*

- Have students open their books to Story 3, p. 15. Hold up a book and direct students' attention to the photo. Ask *What can you see?* (a superhero) *What can he do?* Listen to students ideas, for example, *He can fly; He can run; He can help people.*
- Read aloud the title of the story. Ask *Is it true?* Listen to students' ideas. Then say *We are all superheroes because we are all special. Let's read the story and find out about these superheroes.*

- Play **Story 3** and ask students to listen and follow along in their books.
- Ask students to read the story again. Point to p. 15. Ask *What does this superhero have?* (a special red cape)
- Point to p. 16. Ask *What does this superhero have?* (strong arms and legs) Ask *What can he do?* (He can run.)
- Point to p. 17. Ask *What color are this superhero's eyes?* (blue) *What can she do?* (She can fly.)
- Point to p. 18. Ask *How many stars does this superhero have?* (one) *Can she help you?* (Yes, she can.)
- **Extra Challenge** Have students look at the story again and find all the pairs of words that have the same sound at the end. Ask them to write the words down. (fun/run, eyes/fly, star/are, ears/near, see/be)
- **Extra Support** Listen to the story again and have students raise their hands every time they hear a part of the body. (arms, legs, hair, eyes, body, ears)

- Help students open their books to p. 44. Say *Look at the superhero family.*
- Read aloud the instructions: *Look and write.* Explain that students need to complete each sentence the superheroes say using the words in the box.
- Have students compare their answers in pairs.
  Answers: 1. These are my strong arms.; 2. These are my blue eyes.; 3. These are my strong legs.; 4. This is my super body.

Optional Activity

- Ask students to look at the photos in the story again. Ask them to choose the one they like the most and say why they like him or her. (For example, *I like this superhero. He has a special red cape. I like this superhero. She can fly.*)
- Ask students to get into pairs. Say *Imagine you're a superhero.* Ask *What superhero do you want to be? What is your superpower?*
- When everyone has finished, encourage each pair to talk about their superhero with the rest of the class.

Wrap Up

- Write these single words on the board in a mixed-up order and get students to match the words in pairs from the rhyme.

red	cape
strong	arms
strong	legs
long	hair
blue	eyes
super	smile

- Tell students to look carefully and, when they find a pair (for example *strong arms*), to raise their hand. Go around the class encouraging students to say the answers.

Where's Rosie?

> **Resources:** Anthology 1, Story 4; Story 4 Audio
>
> **Materials:** large sheets of paper, crayons (optional)

About the Story

This story is about a little boy called Ben who lives on a farm. Ben has a pet sheep that follows him everywhere, but one day he can't find her anywhere. He looks around the farm mistaking some of the other farm animals for his sheep. Eventually he finds her in the vegetable patch eating cauliflowers!

Warm Up

- Write the word *Farm* on the board and ask students to tell you all the farm animals they know. Write students' ideas on the board (for example, *cow, sheep, duck, dog,* etc.). Make the noise for a duck and ask *What animal am I?* (a duck) Do the same for all the animals on the board.
- Call on individual students to make an animal noise for other students to guess.

- With books closed, write the title of the story (*Where's Rosie?*) on the board. Ask students to guess who Rosie might be.
- If they don't have any ideas, say *It's an animal.* Have students guess which animal they think the story is about. Say *Let's read the story and find out.*

- Have students open their books to Story 4, p. 21. Direct students' attention to the picture. Ask *What animal is Rosie?* (a pet sheep)
- Play **Story 4** and ask students to listen and follow along in their books.
- Ask students to read the story again. Then point to p. 21. Ask *Does Ben love Rosie?* (Yes, he does.) *Does Rosie love Ben?* (Yes, she does) Say *She follows him everywhere. Look! I'm Ben.* Walk around the classroom as if you are out for a walk. Then stop and look behind you and wave at an imaginary Rosie and say *Hello, Rosie! Rosie follows me.*
- Point to pp. 22–23. Ask *Ben can't find Rosie. Where is she?* Point to the tree. *Is she under the tree?* (No, she isn't.) *What animal is this, under the tree?* (a goat)
- Point to p. 24. Ask *What animal is this, in the flowers?* (a cat) *What color is the cat?* (white) *That's right, the cat's white, and the flowers are white.*
- Point to p. 25. Say *Ben says "Maybe she's ...?"* (in the pond) *Oh no! Is that good?* (No!) *Why not?* (She can't swim!) *What animals are these, in the pond?* (ducks) *How many ducks?* (four) *What color are the ducks?* (white)

- Point to p. 26. Ask *What animal is this, in the vegetable patch?* (A sheep. It's Rosie.) *How does Ben feel?* (He's happy.)
- **Extra Challenge** Have students close their books and try to remember the order of the animals Ben sees and where he sees them. (a goat under a tree, a cat in some flowers, some ducks in the pond)
- **Extra Support** Listen to the story again. Have students make the correct animal sound each time they hear an animal word (sheep, goat, cat, duck). Pause the audio appropriately.

- Help students open their books to p. 45. Say *Look at the photos. What animals can you see?* (ducks, goats, a cat, and a donkey)
- Read aloud the instructions: *Look, read, and circle.* Point to the first photo and say *Three white ducks.* Hold up three fingers. *There's or There are three white ducks?* (there are) *That's right, there are three ducks.* Have students circle the correct words for each sentence.
- Have students compare their answers in pairs.
  Answers: 1. There are three white ducks in the pond.; 2. There are two goats under a tree.; 3. There's a cat in the flowers.; 4. There's a donkey in a field.

Optional Activity

- Ask students to look back at the pictures in the story. Ask *What color is Rosie? Why can't Ben see Rosie?* (She's in the white cauliflowers.)
- Put students into pairs and ask them to draw a map of a farm with a farmhouse, different fields, a pond, and some enclosures. Ask them to draw small farm animals in each place and one hidden sheep (Rosie) somewhere in the picture. Hand out large pieces of paper and crayons for them to draw their farms on.
- Ask students to get into groups of four. Have each pair say what they can see in the other pair's map until they find Rosie the sheep. (There's a cow, but I can't find Rosie, etc.)

Wrap Up

- Read out the following sentences about what some animals can or can't do. Then get students to say together *Yes, it can* or *No, it can't.* If you want, do actions for the verbs to help students understand them.

  A cat can jump. (Yes, it can.)

  A fish can fly. (No, it can't.)

  A duck can swim. (Yes, it can.)

  A monkey can climb. (Yes, it can.)

  A rabbit can read. (No, it can't.)

  A sheep can walk. (Yes, it can.)

  A goat can eat. (Yes, it can.)

The Farmer and the Rock

> **Resources:** Anthology 1, Story 5; Story 5 Audio
>
> **Materials:** Level 2 flashcards 66–70, large pieces of paper, crayons (optional)

About the Story

This story is a folktale from Myanmar in Asia. It tells the story of a caring and honest farmer who is always considerate toward other people. He is the only person that moves the rock that is blocking the road in order to help travelers continue on their journey. Because of his honesty and good nature, he receives a precious reward.

Warm Up

- Bring a small rock to class or make a pretend rock out of scrunched up paper. Hide the rock somewhere in the classroom before the class starts or when the students aren't looking.
- Ask two students to look for the rock while you give instructions as to how close they are: *Cold* (far away), *Warm* (getting closer) or *Hot* (very close).
- When they find it, they can choose the next two students to look. Have these two students face the wall while they hide the rock in a new place. Repeat the game as you wish.

- Have students open their books to Story 5, p. 27. Hold up a book and direct students' attention to the picture. Ask *What can you see?* (There's a big rock in the road.)
- Read aloud the title of the story. Ask *What's a farmer?* Hold up one of the other flashcards for jobs from Level 2, for example, *doctor*, and ask *Is this a farmer?* (No, it isn't.) *No, it isn't. A farmer works on a farm, with cows and sheep.* Continue holding up flashcards and asking the question, then finally show the *farmer* flashcard. *Is this a farmer?* (Yes, it is.) Say *Let's read the story.*

- Play **Story 5** and ask students to listen and follow along in their books.
- Ask students to read the story again. Then point to p. 27. Ask *Where's the big rock?* (in the road)
- Point to p. 28. Say *Look! The man has a hole in his pants! What does he say?* (Oh no! I don't like this rock.)
- Point to p. 29. Ask *What can you see?* (two women) Say *One woman says "My dress is dirty."* Point to the dirty marks on the women's clothes. *Look! Her dress is dirty. Her skirt is dirty. Do they like the rock?* (No, they don't.)
- Point to pp. 30–31. Ask *What does the old farmer say?* (This rock is in the way. I can move the rock.) Put a chair in a bad place in front of the teacher's desk or in front of the door and pretend to try to get past it. Say *This chair is in the way. I can't go past! I can move the chair.* Pick the chair up and put it back in the correct place.
- Point to p. 32 Say *The farmer moves the rock. What does he find?* (a bag of jewels) *Who do the jewels belong to?* (the king)
- Point to p. 33. Ask *Does the king keep the jewels?* (No, he doesn't.) *No, he doesn't. He says "You can have them." You're ... ?* (kind and honest)
- Point to p. 34. Say *Everyone says "Thank you." Why? Because the farmer is ...?* (kind) *That's right. He helps them.*
- **Extra Challenge** Write these sentences on the board and have students write the sentences in the correct order. *A. An old farmer moves the rock. B. He takes the jewels to the king. C. A man can't go past the rock. D. Everyone thanks the farmer. E. Two women can't go past the rock. F. The king gives the jewels to the farmer. G. The farmer finds some jewels under the rock. H. There's a big rock in the road.* (Answers: 1H, 2C, 3E, 4A, 5G, 6B, 7F, 8D)
- **Extra Support** Ask students to try to remember the correct sequence of what happened in the story and draw pictures to show the eight stages.

- Help students open their books to p. 46. Say *Look at the pictures.*
- Read aloud the instructions: *Look and answer Yes, it is* or *Yes, they are.* Explain that students need to write the appropriate phrase to complete each conversation.
- Have students compare their answers in pairs.
  Answers: 1. Yes, they are.; 2. Yes, it is.; 3. Yes, it is.; 4. Yes, they are.

Optional Activity

- Ask *What can we learn from the farmer in the story?* (It's important to help other people.)
- Put students into small groups and give each group a large piece of paper and crayons.
- Tell them to draw a road down the middle and then draw something large blocking the way. (If you need to, suggest ideas like a large pile of sand, a truck, a herd of cows, etc.).
- Have them add a place where the road goes to (for example, a palace, the seaside, a beautiful garden, etc.).
- Now have them discuss and draw a solution about how they can all help to unblock the road.
- When they finish, get each group to present their ideas to the rest of the class.

Wrap Up

- Have students work in small groups to write down all the things you can do to help each other at school. Give them some examples on the board.
- When all the groups are finished, get them to read out their ideas using the structure, *You can...*, etc.

STORY

6 A Sandy Surprise

Resources: Anthology 1, Story 6; Story 6 Audio

Materials: colored chalk or crayons, roll of paper (optional)

About the Story

This story is about four friends who go exploring on a beach and find some art drawn in the sand. They start to draw some of their own designs but get a surprise when they see a large jellyfish sculpture! They're so inspired by the jellyfish sand sculpture that they decide to build one, too.

Warm Up

- Ask students to tell you all the words they know about going to the beach and write them on the board (for example, *beach, sand, ice cream, ocean,* etc.).

- Ask students to sit in pairs, A and B. Ask Student A to think of a simple object that you can find at the beach and draw it on Student B's back with their finger. Student B then has to guess what the object is. The pairs then swap roles.

 1

- Have students open their books to Story 6, p. 35. Hold up a book and direct students' attention to the picture. Ask *Where are the children?* (at the beach) Ask *Do you like going to the beach?* (Yes, I do./No, I don't.) *What can you do at the beach?* (for example, I can swim; I can look for shells; I can draw in the sand.) Write students' ideas on the board.

- Read aloud the title of the story. Act out being surprised and say *The children in the story find a* sandy surprise. Ask students to guess what they think the sandy surprise could be. Write students' ideas on the board. Say *Let's read the story and find out.*

 2

- Play **Story 6** and ask students to listen and follow along in their books.

- Ask students to read the story again. Then point to p. 35 and ask *How many children are in the story?* (four)

- Point to p. 36. Ask *What do they do?* (go for a walk, climb)

- Point to p. 37. Ask *What can Silvia see?* (a boat) *Is the boat in the ocean?* (No, it isn't. It's on the beach. It's a drawing in the sand.)

- Point to p. 38. Ask *What do they do?* (draw pictures in the sand) *What does Edu find for Silvia?* (pretty shells)

- Point to pp. 40–41. Ask *What's the sandy surprise?* (There's a big sand jellyfish.) *What does Silvia say?* (Let's build a sand jellyfish, too!)

- **Extra Challenge** Have students tell you what happens at the end of the story. (The children find a jellyfish sand sculpture. Then they build a sand jellyfish.) Now have them change the ending of the story. Ask them to use their imagination and write or draw their ideas about what happens, then present them to the rest of the class.

- **Extra Support** Listen to the story again and have students write a list of all the things the children do at the beach (go for a walk, climb, draw pictures in the sand, find a sand jellyfish).

 3

- Help students open their books to p. 47. Say *Look at the picture of the beach.* Read aloud the instructions: *Look and answer.* Explain that students need to choose the correct answer from the box for each question.

- Have students compare their answers in pairs.
  Answers: 1. Yes, there is.; 2. No, there aren't.; 3. Yes, there are.; 4. No, there isn't.

Optional Activity

- Ask *Are the children happy on the beach?* (Yes, they are.) *Do they like drawing in the sand?* (Yes, they do.) *Do you like drawing in the sand at the beach? What do you draw?* Listen to students' answers.

- Get students into pairs and ask them to think about a beach picture that they would like to draw. Give them a piece of paper and some colored chalk or crayons and ask them to roughly sketch their ideas.

- Ask students to get into groups of four to share their ideas. Then write all the different things in their pictures on the board.

- Lay out a large roll of paper on the classroom floor and get students to draw their ideas and organize them into one large piece of art. Ask them to invent a title for their picture, for example, *A day at the beach!* Display their picture in the classroom.

Wrap Up

- Choose a student to come to the board. Ask him or her to draw something that you can find at the beach.

- Get the rest of the class to guess what it is. Encourage them to use the question *Is it a …?*

- Call on different students to come to the board and repeat the activity.

Formative Assessment Framework

How to use the framework

The framework below gives a list of performance descriptors for the level based on the Common European Framework of Reference (CEFR). The assessment activities suggest how activities in the Student's Book could be used to assess how well students are doing in attaining each performance descriptor. Make sure the activities focus on the specific skill being assessed. In order to assess progression, it is a good idea to plan two formative assessment activities. The table also includes suggestions for remedial activities, which you may need to implement if the first assessment indicates students need extra help.

Activity References	Performance Descriptors	Assessment Activity 1	Remedial Activity	Assessment Activity 2
READING				
Units 1–6, Lesson 6	CAN recognize the letters of the English alphabet	Ask students individually to match lowercase and uppercase letters.	**Visual:** Put lowercase letters around the class, students find and match uppercase. Do five per lesson, not in order.	After Unit 8, repeat Assessment Activity 1.
Units 1–4, Lesson 7	CAN understand simple written instructions	On the board, draw eyes, a pen, a crayon, ears, and a mouth with a question mark. Write a mix of instructions from Lesson 7 on a worksheet or the board; students match to your drawing.	**Visual:** Ask students to draw eyes, etc. (as Assessment Activity 1) and cut them out. Put instructions from Lesson 7 around the class walls. Students match drawings to instructions.	After Unit 6, repeat Assessment Activity 1.
LISTENING				
Units 1–5, Lesson 2, Activity 1	CAN understand simple sentences about things around them	Choose ten statements from the units. Say to the class using pictures, realia, or actions. Students individually write *true* or *false* in their notebooks.	**Competition:** Practice three statements per lesson (from mixed units). Students in pairs compete to be first to say *true* or *false*.	After Unit 6 or 7, repeat Assessment Activity 1 with similar statements.
Functions pages after Units 2 and 6	CAN understand and follow simple classroom instructions	After Unit 6, say instructions, students act or respond individually.	**Random Practice:** In every lesson, include one instruction when the class is not expecting it; note how quickly they respond.	After Unit 9, repeat Assessment Activity 1.
SPEAKING				
Units 2–6, Lessons 2 and 4	CAN respond to personal questions on topics such as age, family, home	Choose ten questions from the units. Students all stand. Ask individual students a question. If correct, they sit until whole class is sitting. Note that you can repeat questions to help students if necessary.	**Speed Game:** Repeat Assessment Activity 1 weekly at speed, getting faster and faster.	After Unit 9, repeat Assessment Activity 1.
Functions pages after Units 2, 6, and 10	CAN respond to simple expressions of communication	Choose ten examples of communicative expressions across the units that require a verbal response. Ask students in pairs to respond.	**Competition:** Repeat Assessment Activity 1 with groups competing. Focus on correct pronunciation.	After Unit 11, repeat Assessment Activity 1.
Units 1–6, Lesson 1, Activity 1	CAN listen to and repeat words and phrases appropriate to the level	Select ten words from the units. Draw pictures on the board. Say each word, and students point to the correct drawing.	**Visual:** In each lesson, say one word from Assessment Activity 1 and students draw the word. Observe speed of response.	After Unit 7, repeat Assessment Activity 1.
WRITING				
Units 1–5, Lesson 6, Activity 3	CAN write letters of the English alphabet and spell their name and simple words	After Unit 6, choose eight letters and eight words. Say and ask students to write. Observe speed and accuracy.	**Competition:** Repeat Assessment Activity 1 with groups competing. Focus on handwriting.	After Unit 8, repeat Assessment Activity 1.
Units 1–6, Lesson 6, Activity 3	CAN recognize and copy words from a text, a book, or the board	After Unit 6, choose ten words. Write on the board, students copy. Observe speed and accuracy.	**Competition:** Repeat Assessment Activity 1 with pairs competing. Focus on handwriting.	After Unit 9, repeat Assessment Activity 1.
LINGUISTIC				
Units 2, 6, and 7, Lessons 2 and 4	CAN use very simple principles of word order	Choose eight sentences from the units. Write on the board with words scrambled. In groups, students put the words in order.	**Physical:** Each student is a word; ask them to stand in a line to make a correct sentence.	After Unit 10, repeat Assessment Activity 1.

How to assess in the classroom

Repeating activities or tasks is a safe way to assess young learners. For very young students, regular repetition of activities is an important part of learning. You know learning has taken place if they can repeat the activity more quickly than the first time. Observe your students—watch learners as they are reading to see how much attention they pay and how quickly they respond. Watch and listen as they are listening or speaking and make notes for feedback and as part of your progress log. If you have permission, you may wish to record students so both they and you can listen back and check.

Giving feedback

It's important for young learners to have some form of feedback on how they perform, especially in an assessment situation. It is a good idea to let them know that they are being assessed before you start the activity. Use a range of ways to give feedback across the term or year. If students need to improve, give them feedback that includes one small tip for how to improve so they can remember and focus.

To the class: say what students generally did well and give one specific tip about how to improve or remember.

To a group: say what students did well and give one tip about how they can help each other improve.

To an individual student: students need individual praise, but keep "how to improve" feedback to group or class situations.

Self-reflection: Ask students to put their hand up, for example, if they are confident they know something.

- -

Student Progress Log

A = excellent   B = satisfactory   C = needs to improve

Student's Name: _____

Student can	Progress 1 Assessment	Feedback Notes	Progress 2 Assessment
READING			
recognize the letters of the English alphabet	Date _____ Grade A B C		Date _____ Grade A B C
understand simple written instructions	Date _____ Grade A B C		Date _____ Grade A B C
LISTENING			
understand simple sentences about things around them	Date _____ Grade A B C		Date _____ Grade A B C
understand and follow simple classroom instructions	Date _____ Grade A B C		Date _____ Grade A B C
SPEAKING			
respond to personal questions on topics such as age, family, home	Date _____ Grade A B C		Date _____ Grade A B C
respond to simple expressions of communication	Date _____ Grade A B C		Date _____ Grade A B C
listen to and repeat words and phrases appropriate to the level	Date _____ Grade A B C		Date _____ Grade A B C
WRITING			
write letters of the English alphabet and spell their name and simple words	Date _____ Grade A B C		Date _____ Grade A B C
recognize and copy words from a text, a book, or the board	Date _____ Grade A B C		Date _____ Grade A B C
LINGUISTIC			
use very simple principles of word order	Date _____ Grade A B C		Date _____ Grade A B C

Workbook

1 **Match.**

four three one five two

1 2 3 4 5 6 7 8 9 10

nine eight six ten seven

2 **Count and circle.**

1. one / (two)
2. four / (five)
3. (seven) / eight

3 **Read and draw.**

1. three
2. six
3. nine

1 **Listen, read, and circle.** 🎧 TR: 1

Hello! Hello!
What's your (name) / old?
My name's Xi.
Me / (My) name's Wayne.

Hello! Hello!
How **fine** / (old) are you?
Hello, I'm six.
(I'm) / **My** six, too!

Hello, Xi.
How are you?
I'm fine, thanks.
And I'm fine, (too) / **you**.

2 **Match.**

1. What's your name? — I'm fine, thanks.
2. How old are you? — My name's Han.
3. How are you? — I'm seven.

3 **Write about you.**

1. What's your name? _____
2. How old are you? _____
3. How are you? _____

1 **Color.**

1. purple
2. black
3. red
4. white
5. yellow
6. green
7. brown
8. orange
9. blue

2 **Listen and color.** 🎧 TR: 2

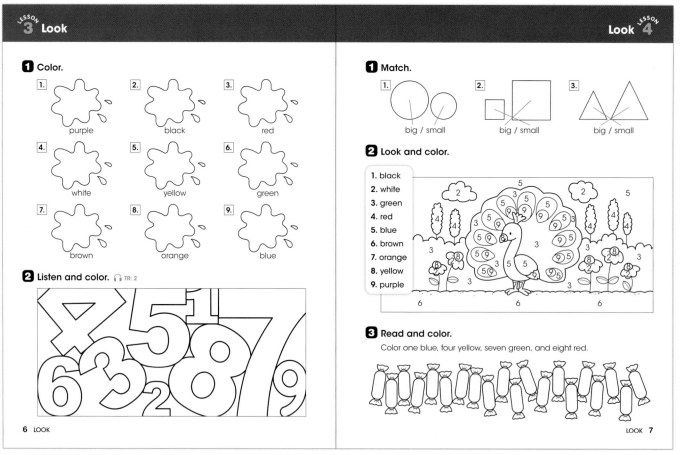

1 **Match.**

1. big / small
2. big / small
3. big / small

2 **Look and color.**

1. black
2. white
3. green
4. red
5. blue
6. brown
7. orange
8. yellow
9. purple

3 **Read and color.**

Color one blue, four yellow, seven green, and eight red.

144

1 Things for School

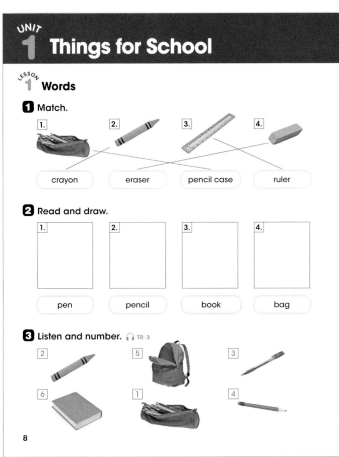

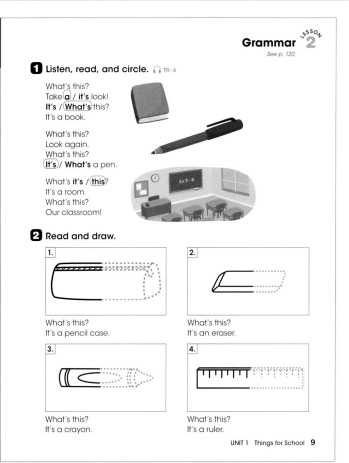

LESSON 1 Words

1 Match.

1. 2. 3. 4.

crayon | eraser | pencil case | ruler

2 Read and draw.

1. 2. 3. 4.

pen | pencil | book | bag

3 Listen and number. TR: 3

2 5 3
6 1 4

1 Listen, read, and circle. TR: 4

What's this?
Take **a** / **it's** look!
It's / **What's** this?
It's a book.

What's this?
Look again.
What's this?
It's / **What's** a pen.

What's **it's** / **this**?
It's a room.
What's this?
Our classroom!

2 Read and draw.

1. 2.

What's this? | What's this?
It's a pencil case. | It's an eraser.

3. 4.

What's this? | What's this?
It's a crayon. | It's a ruler.

8

UNIT 1 Things for School **9**

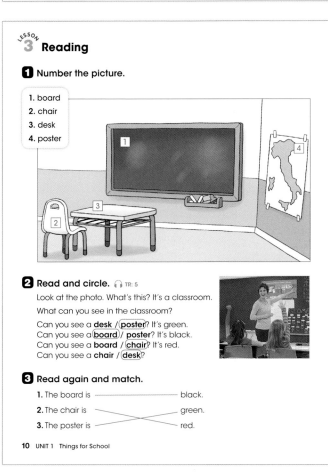

LESSON 3 Reading

1 Number the picture.

1. board
2. chair
3. desk
4. poster

2 Read and circle. TR: 5

Look at the photo. What's this? It's a classroom.

What can you see in the classroom?

Can you see a **desk** / **poster**? It's green.
Can you see a **board** / **poster**? It's black.
Can you see a **board** / **chair**? It's red.
Can you see a **chair** / **desk**?

3 Read again and match.

1. The board is ———— black.
2. The chair is ———— green.
3. The poster is ———— red.

1 Read and check (✓).

1. What's this?
Is it a pencil?
✓ Yes, it is.
☐ No, it isn't.

2. What's this?
Is it a crayon?
☐ Yes, it is.
✓ No, it isn't.

3. What's this?
Is it a ruler?
✓ Yes, it is.
☐ No, it isn't.

4. What's this?
Is it a book?
☐ Yes, it is.
✓ No, it isn't.

2 Listen and check (✓). TR: 6

1. ☐ Yes, it is.
✓ No, it isn't.

2. ✓ Yes, it is.
☐ No, it isn't.

3. ☐ Yes, it is.
✓ No, it isn't.

4. ☐ Yes, it is.
✓ No, it isn't.

145

Workbook

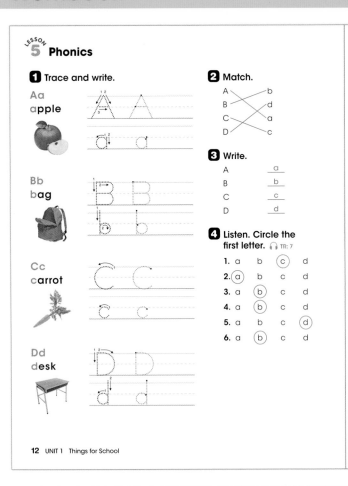

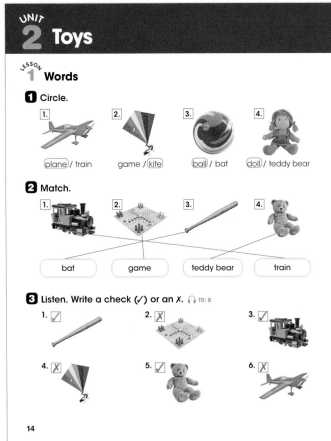

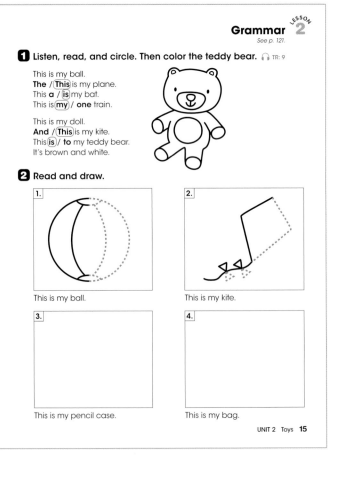

146

Reading

1 Circle the word for a toy.

favorite   fun   (marble)

2 Read and circle. 🎧 TR: 10

Look at the photo. This is a game of marbles. Marbles is my favorite (game) / **play**. It's fun!

A marble is small. It's a small (ball) / **color**.

Find a blue marble. Find a red and white **game** / (marble). Find a yellow marble. Yellow is my favorite (color) / **marble**. Is this your (favorite) / **fun** color, too?

3 Read again. Color the marbles.

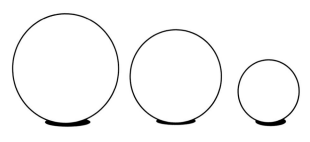

Grammar
See p. 121.

1 Read and check (✓).

1. Is this your bat, Tom?
☑ Tom: Yes, it is.
☐ Tom: No, it isn't.

2. Is this your teddy bear, Tom?
☐ Tom: Yes, it is.
☑ Tom: No, it isn't.

3. Is this your ball, Tom?
☑ Tom: Yes, it is.
☐ Tom: No, it isn't.

4. Is this your plane, Tom?
☐ Tom: Yes, it is.
☑ Tom: No, it isn't.

2 Listen and number. Then check (✓). 🎧 TR: 11

3 ☑ Yes, it is.
☐ No, it isn't.

4 ☐ Yes, it is.
☑ No, it isn't.

2 ☑ Yes, it is.
☐ No, it isn't.

1 ☐ Yes, it is.
☑ No, it isn't.

Phonics

1 Trace and write.

Ee
elephant

Ff
fish

Gg
goat

Hh
horse

2 Match.

E ⟍⟋ g
F ⟋⟍ e
G ⟋⟍ h
H ⟋⟍ f

3 Write.

E   e
F   f
G   g
H   h

4 Listen. Circle the first letter. 🎧 TR: 12

1. e (f) g h
2. (e) f g h
3. e f (g) h
4. e f g (h)
5. e f (g) h
6. e f g (h)

VALUE Share your toys.   **Value**

1 Who shares their toys? Look and check (✓).

1. ☑
2. ☐
3. ☐
4. ☑

2 Read and draw.

I share my toys.

147

Workbook

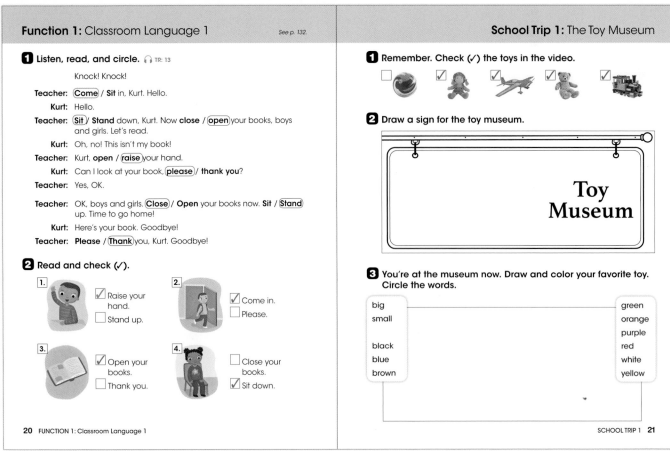

Function 1: Classroom Language 1

See p. 132.

1 Listen, read, and circle. TR: 13

Knock! Knock!

Teacher: (Come) / **Sit** in, Kurt. Hello.

Kurt: Hello.

Teacher: (Sit) / **Stand** down, Kurt. Now **close** / (open) your books, boys and girls. Let's read.

Kurt: Oh, no! This isn't my book!

Teacher: Kurt, **open** / (raise) your hand.

Kurt: Can I look at your book, (please) / thank you?

Teacher: Yes, OK.

Teacher: OK, boys and girls. (Close) / **Open** your books now. **Sit** / (Stand) up. Time to go home!

Kurt: Here's your book. Goodbye!

Teacher: **Please** / (Thank) you, Kurt. Goodbye!

2 Read and check (✓).

1. ✓ Raise your hand.
   ☐ Stand up.

2. ✓ Come in.
   ☐ Please.

3. ✓ Open your books.
   ☐ Thank you.

4. ☐ Close your books.
   ✓ Sit down.

School Trip 1: The Toy Museum

1 Remember. Check (✓) the toys in the video.

☐ ✓ ✓ ✓ ✓

2 Draw a sign for the toy museum.

Toy Museum

3 You're at the museum now. Draw and color your favorite toy. Circle the words.

big
small

black
blue
brown

green
orange
purple
red
white
yellow

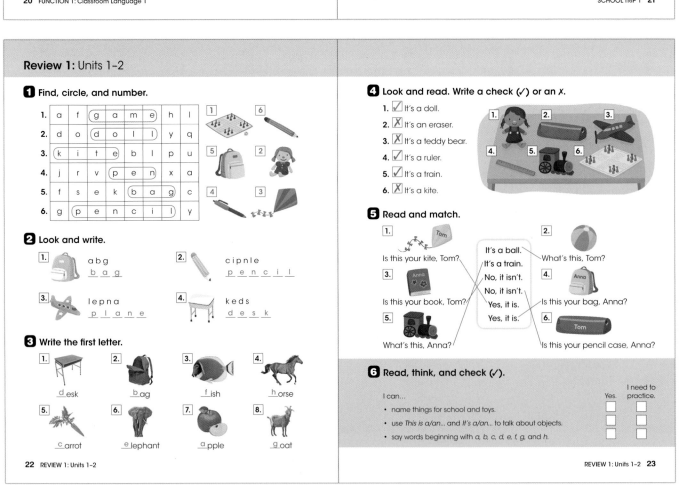

Review 1: Units 1–2

1 Find, circle, and number.

1. a f (g a m e) h l
2. d o (d o l l) y q
3. (k i t e) b l p u
4. j r v (p e n) x a
5. f s e k (b a g) c
6. g (p e n c i l) y

2 Look and write.

1. a b g
   b a g

2. c i p n l e
   p e n c i l

3. l e p n a
   p l a n e

4. k e d s
   d e s k

3 Write the first letter.

1. d esk
2. b ag
3. f ish
4. h orse
5. c arrot
6. e lephant
7. a pple
8. g oat

4 Look and read. Write a check (✓) or an X.

1. ✓ It's a doll.
2. X It's an eraser.
3. X It's a teddy bear.
4. ✓ It's a ruler.
5. ✓ It's a train.
6. X It's a kite.

5 Read and match.

1. Is this your kite, Tom?
2. What's this, Tom?
3. Is this your book, Tom?
4. Is this your bag, Anna?
5. What's this, Anna?
6. Is this your pencil case, Anna?

It's a ball.
It's a train.
No, it isn't.
No, it isn't.
Yes, it is.
Yes, it is.

6 Read, think, and check (✓).

I can…	Yes.	I need to practice.
• name things for school and toys.	☐	☐
• use *This is a/an…* and *It's a/an…* to talk about objects.	☐	☐
• say words beginning with *a, b, c, d, e, f, g,* and *h.*	☐	☐

UNIT 3 People

LESSON 1 Words

1 Number.

1. boy
2. girl
3. man
4. woman

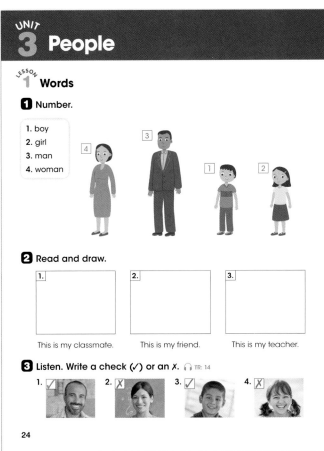

2 Read and draw.

1.	2.	3.
This is my classmate.	This is my friend.	This is my teacher.

3 Listen. Write a check (✓) or an ✗. TR: 14

1. ✓ 2. ✗ 3. ✓ 4. ✗

24

Grammar LESSON 2
See p. 122.

1 Listen, read, and circle. TR: 15

Who's this?
This is Dan.
He's / She's a boy.
He's / She's a student.
He's / She's my classmate.
He's / She's my friend, too.

Who's this?
This is Kim.
He's / **She's** a girl.
He's / **She's** a student.
He's / **She's** my classmate.
He's / **She's** my friend, too.

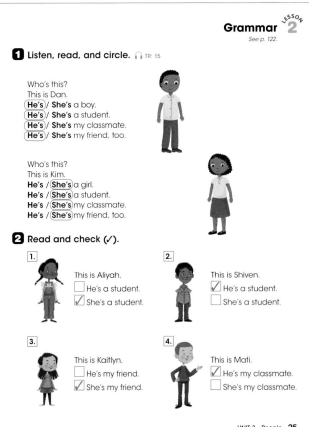

2 Read and check (✓).

1. This is Aliyah.
☐ He's a student.
✓ She's a student.

2. This is Shiven.
✓ He's a student.
☐ She's a student.

3. This is Kaitlyn.
☐ He's my friend.
✓ She's my friend.

4. This is Mati.
✓ He's my classmate.
☐ She's my classmate.

UNIT 3 People 25

LESSON 3 Reading

1 Match.

1. 2. 3.

dinosaur   museum   trip

2 Read and circle. TR: 16

Look at the photo. Is it a classroom?
Point to the girl. She's a
student / teacher.

This isn't a classroom. It's a
board / **museum**. Look! A
dinosaur / classroom! It's big!
The girl is on a school class / **trip**.
This museum is good / **fun**!

3 Read again and match.

1. The girl in the photo is — big.
2. The museum is — small.
3. The dinosaur in the museum is — fun.

26 UNIT 3 People

Grammar LESSON 4
See p. 122.

1 Read and match.

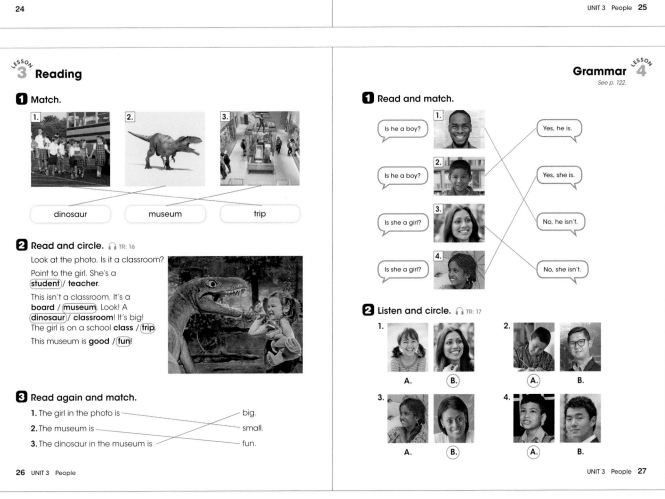

Is he a boy?   1.   Yes, he is.
Is he a boy?   2.   Yes, she is.
Is she a girl?   3.   No, he isn't.
Is she a girl?   4.   No, she isn't.

2 Listen and circle. TR: 17

1. A. **B.** 2. **A.** B.
3. A. **B.** 4. **A.** B.

UNIT 3 People 27

149

Workbook

Phonics

1 Trace and write.

Ii
insect

Jj
jellyfish

Kk
kiwi

Ll
lamp

2 Match.

I — j
J — i
K — l
L — k

3 Write.

I   i
J   j
K   k
L   l

4 Listen. Circle the first letter. 🎧 TR: 18

1. i   j   k   (l)
2. i   j   (k)   l
3. i   (j)   k   l
4. (i)   j   k   l
5. i   j   (k)   l
6. (i)   j   k   l

VALUE Make friends at school.

Value LESSON 6

1 Who makes friends at school? Look and circle.

2 Read and draw.

I make friends at school.

UNIT 4 My Family

Words

1 Match.

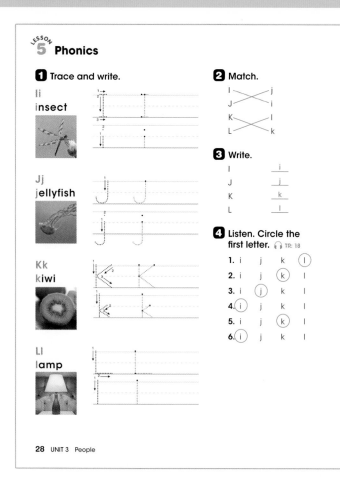

dad   mom   grandma   grandpa

2 Listen and number. 🎧 TR: 19

3 Read and draw.

This is my family.

Grammar LESSON 2

See p. 123.

1 Listen, read, and circle. 🎧 TR: 20

(I have) / I don't have two brothers and a sister, too.
I have / (I don't have) a cousin. What about you?

(I have) / I don't have two grandmas and a grandpa, too.
I have / (I don't have) an uncle. What about you?

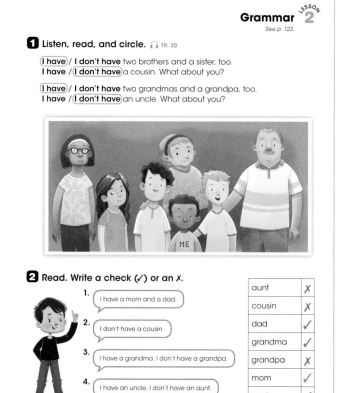

2 Read. Write a check (✓) or an ✗.

1. I have a mom and a dad.
2. I don't have a cousin.
3. I have a grandma. I don't have a grandpa.
4. I have an uncle. I don't have an aunt.

aunt	✗
cousin	✗
dad	✓
grandma	✓
grandpa	✗
mom	✓
uncle	✓

1 Read and number the picture.

1. This is a birthday cake.
2. This is a birthday party.
3. This is in the middle.

2 Read and circle. 🎧 TR: 21

Look at the photo. It's a **class** / **family**. Can you see Mom?

Count the **boys** / **girls**. One, two, three. Look at the girl in the middle. Her name's Atdhetare. She's **four** / **five** today! Her sister Arneta is five today, too. And her sister Agnesa…she's five, too!

This is a birthday party. Look! A birthday **bag** / **cake**. Happy birthday, Atdhetare, Arneta, and Agnesa!

3 Read again and match.

1. This is a ————————— in the middle.
2. Atdhetare is ————————— birthday party.
3. Agnesa and Arneta ————————— five today.
4. The girls are ————————— are sisters.

Grammar LESSON 4
See p. 123.

1 Read and check (✓).

1. ☐ Her name is Chris.
   ✓ His name is Chris.

2. ✓ Her name is Nicky.
   ☐ His name is Nicky.

3. ☐ Her name is Lee.
   ✓ His name is Lee.

4. ✓ Her name is Pat.
   ☐ His name is Pat.

2 Listen and match. 🎧 TR: 22

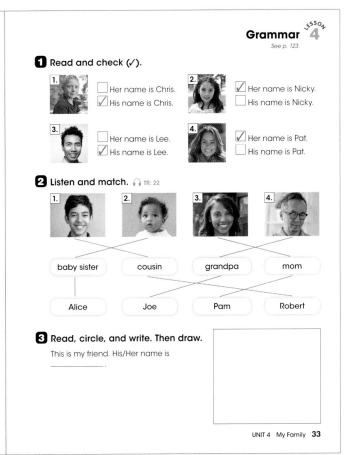

| 1. | 2. | 3. | 4. |

baby sister   cousin   grandpa   mom

Alice   Joe   Pam   Robert

3 Read, circle, and write. Then draw.

This is my friend. His/Her name is
—————————— .

---

1 Trace and write.

Mm
mom

Nn
nose

Oo
orange

Pp
pencil

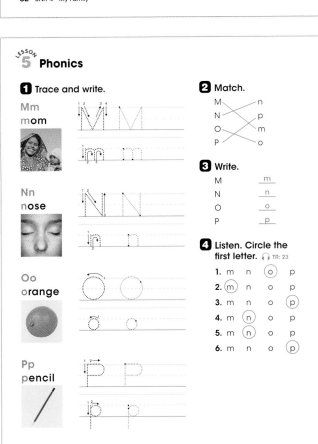

2 Match.

M ——— n
N ——— p
O ——— m
P ——— o

3 Write.

M   m
N   n
O   o
P   p

4 Listen. Circle the first letter. 🎧 TR: 23

1. m   n   (o)   p
2. (m) n   o   p
3. m   n   o   (p)
4. m   (n) o   p
5. m   (n) o   p
6. m   n   o   (p)

VALUE Give things to your friends.

Value LESSON 6

1 Who gives things to their friends? Look and check (✓).

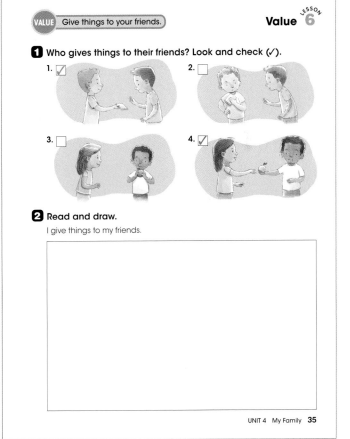

1. ✓
2. ☐
3. ☐
4. ✓

2 Read and draw.

I give things to my friends.

151

Workbook

Game 1

1 Look, find, and color. Then point and say.

bag
ball
bat
classmate
dad
friend
grandpa
mom
pencil case
ruler
teacher
teddy bear

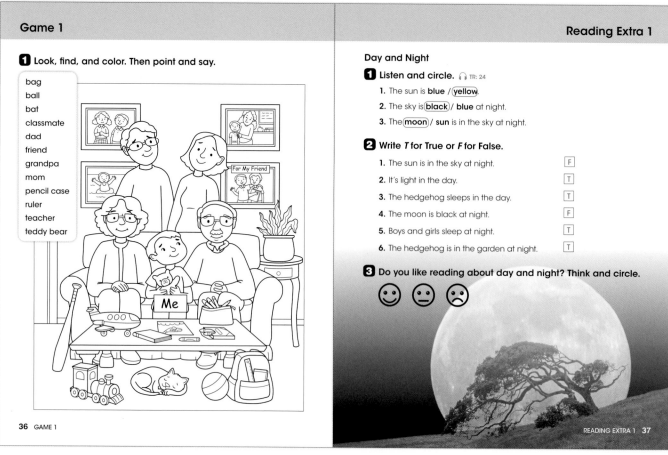

For My Friend

Me

Reading Extra 1

Day and Night

1 Listen and circle. 🎧 TR: 24

1. The sun is **blue** /(yellow).
2. The sky is(black)/ blue at night.
3. The(moon)/ sun is in the sky at night.

2 Write *T* for True or *F* for False.

1. The sun is in the sky at night.   F
2. It's light in the day.   T
3. The hedgehog sleeps in the day.   T
4. The moon is black at night.   F
5. Boys and girls sleep at night.   T
6. The hedgehog is in the garden at night.   T

3 Do you like reading about day and night? Think and circle.

☺ 😐 ☹

Review 2: Units 3–4

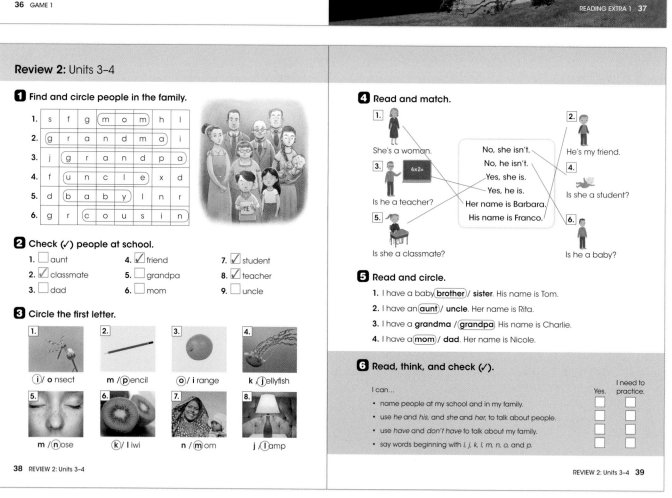

1 Find and circle people in the family.

1.	s	f	g |(m	o	m)| h	l
2. |(g	r	a	n	d	m	a)| i
3.	j |(g	r	a	n	d	p	a)
4.	f |(u	n	c	l	e)| x	d
5.	d |(b	a	b	y)| l	n	r
6.	g	r |(c	o	u	s	i	n)

2 Check (✓) people at school.

1. ☐ aunt
2. ✓ classmate
3. ☐ dad
4. ✓ friend
5. ☐ grandpa
6. ☐ mom
7. ✓ student
8. ✓ teacher
9. ☐ uncle

3 Circle the first letter.

1. (i)/ o nsect
2. m /(p)encil
3. (o)/ i range
4. k /(j)ellyfish
5. m /(n)ose
6. (k)/ l iwi
7. n /(m)om
8. j /(l)amp

4 Read and match.

1. She's a woman.
3. Is he a teacher? 6x2=
5. Is she a classmate?

No, she isn't.
No, he isn't.
Yes, she is.
Yes, he is.
Her name is Barbara.
His name is Franco.

2. He's my friend.
4. Is she a student?
6. Is he a baby?

5 Read and circle.

1. I have a baby(brother)/ sister. His name is Tom.
2. I have an(aunt)/ uncle. Her name is Rita.
3. I have a grandma /(grandpa)His name is Charlie.
4. I have a(mom)/ dad. Her name is Nicole.

6 Read, think, and check (✓).

I can…	Yes.	I need to practice.
• name people at my school and in my family.	☐	☐
• use *he* and *his*, and *she* and *her*, to talk about people.	☐	☐
• use *have* and *don't have* to talk about my family.	☐	☐
• say words beginning with *i, j, k, l, m, n, o,* and *p*.	☐	☐

UNIT
5 My Body

LESSON 1 Words

1 Circle.

1. (arm) / ear
2. eye / (leg)
3. (hand) / mouth
4. (foot) / head

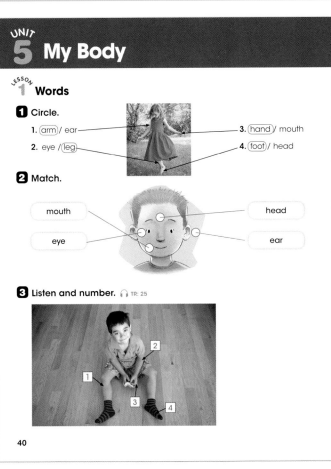

2 Match.

mouth

eye

head

ear

3 Listen and number. 🎧 TR: 25

40

Grammar LESSON 2
See p. 124.

1 Listen, read, and circle. 🎧 TR: 26

(This is) / **These are** my mouth.
My mouth is red.
This is / (These are) my ears.
(This is) / **These are** my head!

This is / (These are) my eyes.
My eyes are blue.
This is / (These are) my hands.
One and two!

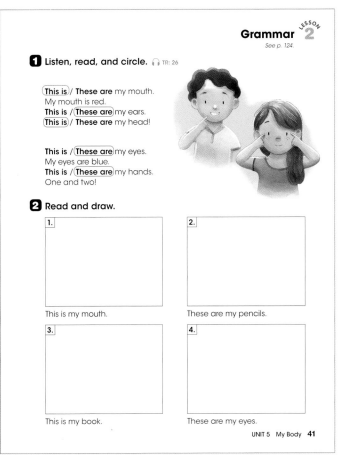

2 Read and draw.

1.	2.
This is my mouth.	These are my pencils.

3.	4.
This is my book.	These are my eyes.

UNIT 5 My Body **41**

LESSON 3 Reading

1 Number the picture.

1. body
2. face
3. hair
4. skeleton

2 Read and circle. 🎧 TR: 27

Look at the photo. Is it a skeleton? No! Look again. This is a (boy) / girl.

He has black hair and brown arms / (eyes). He isn't a skeleton! He doesn't have a skeleton body.

Look at his (face) / hair. He has white paint on his face and black paint on his eyes and **hands** / (mouth).

Face **color** / (paint) is fun!

3 Read again. Write *T* for True or *F* for False.

1. This is a photo of a boy. T
2. His hair is brown. F
3. Paint is on his face. T
4. Paint is on his hair. F
5. Face paint is fun. T

42 UNIT 5 My Body

Grammar LESSON 4
See p. 124.

1 Read and color.

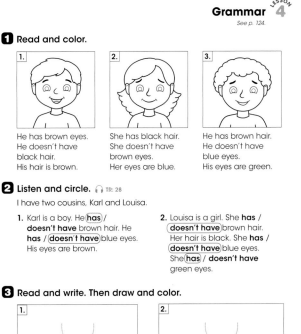

1.	2.	3.
He has brown eyes. He doesn't have black hair. His hair is brown.	She has black hair. She doesn't have brown eyes. Her eyes are blue.	He has brown hair. He doesn't have blue eyes. His eyes are green.

2 Listen and circle. 🎧 TR: 28

I have two cousins, Karl and Louisa.

1. Karl is a boy. He (has) / doesn't have brown hair. He **has** / (doesn't have) blue eyes. His eyes are brown.

2. Louisa is a girl. She **has** / (doesn't have) brown hair. Her hair is black. She **has** / (doesn't have) blue eyes. She (has) / **doesn't have** green eyes.

3 Read and write. Then draw and color.

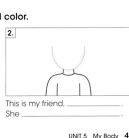

1.	2.
This is my friend, _____. He _____.	This is my friend, _____. She _____.

UNIT 5 My Body **43**

153

Workbook

Phonics

1 Trace and write.

Qq
queen

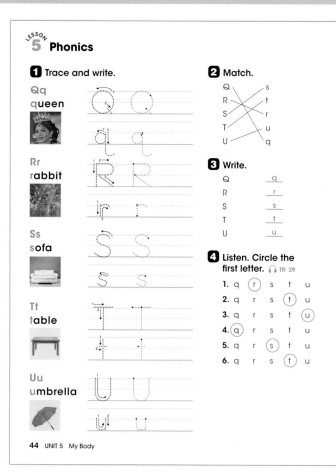

Rr
rabbit

Ss
sofa

Tt
table

Uu
umbrella

2 Match.

Q — s
R — t
S — r
T — u
U — q

3 Write.

Q	q
R	r
S	s
T	t
U	u

4 Listen. Circle the first letter. 🎧 TR: 29

1. q (r) s t u
2. q r s (t) u
3. q r s t (u)
4. (q) r s t u
5. q r (s) t u
6. q r s (t) u

VALUE | Be active.

Value

1 Who's active? Look and check (✓).

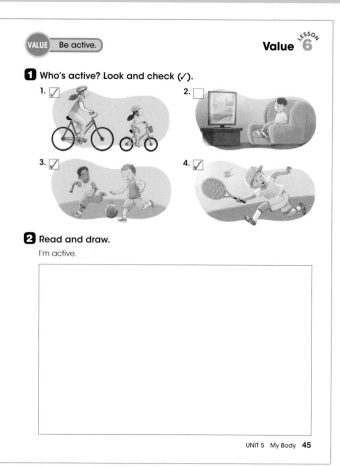

1. ✓   2. ☐
3. ✓   4. ✓

2 Read and draw.

I'm active.

UNIT 6 Homes

Words

1 Circle.

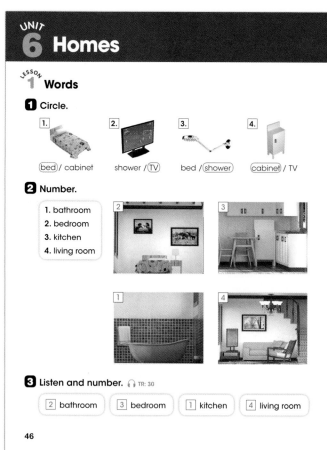

1. (bed) / cabinet
2. shower / (TV)
3. bed / (shower)
4. (cabinet) / TV

2 Number.

1. bathroom
2. bedroom
3. kitchen
4. living room

3 Listen and number. 🎧 TR: 30

[2] bathroom   [3] bedroom   [1] kitchen   [4] living room

Grammar

See p. 125.

1 Listen, read, and circle. 🎧 TR: 31

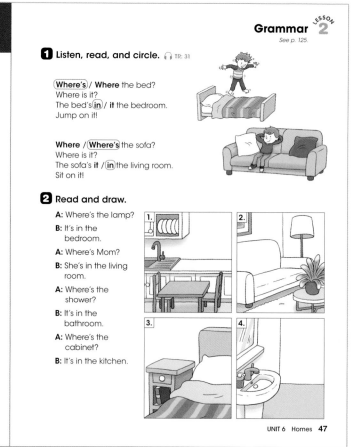

(Where's) / Where the bed?
Where is it?
The bed's (in) / it the bedroom.
Jump on it!

Where / (Where's) the sofa?
Where is it?
The sofa's it / (in) the living room.
Sit on it!

2 Read and draw.

A: Where's the lamp?
B: It's in the bedroom.
A: Where's Mom?
B: She's in the living room.
A: Where's the shower?
B: It's in the bathroom.
A: Where's the cabinet?
B: It's in the kitchen.

1.   2.
3.   4.

1 Match.

1. water
2. house
3. clock

clock | house | water

2 Read and circle. 🎧 TR: 32

Look at the photo. This is a **bathroom** / **bedroom**. It isn't in a house. It's in an aquarium. Can you see the table? The table is next to the **bed** / **chair**. It's white. The clock is on the table. It's **big** / **small**. The **game** / **train** is on the bed. It's yellow, red, and blue. The toy fish are on the **bed** / **table**, too.

Look at the fish in the water. This bedroom is under the water!

3 Read again and match.

1. The bedroom isn't — the table.
2. The bed is next to — in a house.
3. The game is red, — blue, and yellow.
4. The toy fish — are on the bed.

---

1 Read and circle.

1. The boy is **next to** / **on** / **under** the sofa.
2. The clock is **next to** / **on** / **under** the photo.
3. The train is **next to** / **on** / **under** the sofa.
4. The photo is **next to** / **on** / **under** the table.
5. The lamp is **next to** / **on** / **under** the TV.

2 Listen and circle. 🎧 TR: 33

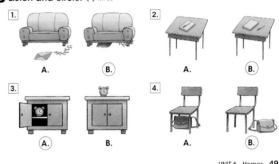

1. A. B.
2. A. B.
3. A. B.
4. A. B.

---

1 Trace and write.

Vv violin

Ww wall

Xx box

Yy yogurt

Zz zebra

2 Match.

V — z
W — w
X — v
Y — x
Z — y

3 Write.

V — v
W — w
X — x
Y — y
Z — z

4 Listen. Circle the first letter. 🎧 TR: 34

1. v (w) x y z
2. v w (y) z
3. v w x y (z)
4. (v) w x y z
5. v (w) x y z
6. v w x (y) z

---

1 Who plays with their friends? Look and check (✓).

1. ✓
2. ☐

3. ✓
4. ✓

2 Read and draw.

I play with my friends.

155

Workbook

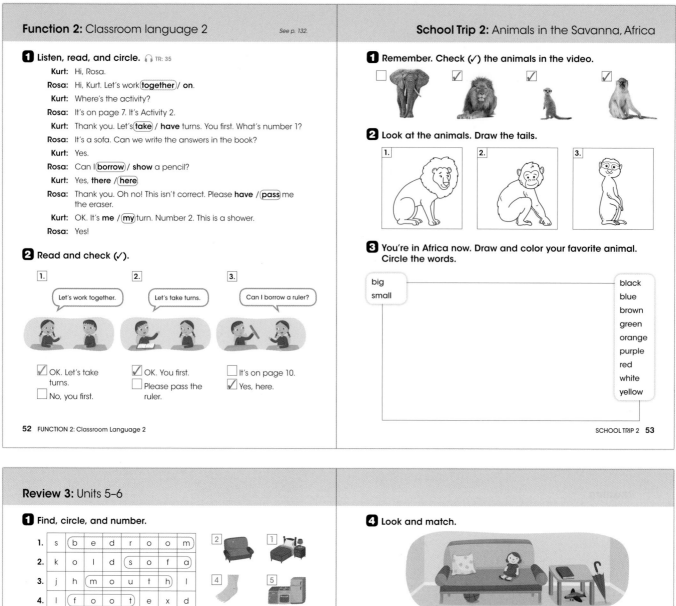

Function 2: Classroom language 2 See p. 132.

1 Listen, read, and circle. 🎧 TR: 35

Kurt: Hi, Rosa.

Rosa: Hi, Kurt. Let's work (together) / on.

Kurt: Where's the activity?

Rosa: It's on page 7. It's Activity 2.

Kurt: Thank you. Let's (take) / have turns. You first. What's number 1?

Rosa: It's a sofa. Can we write the answers in the book?

Kurt: Yes.

Rosa: Can I (borrow) / show a pencil?

Kurt: Yes, there / (here)

Rosa: Thank you. Oh no! This isn't correct. Please have / (pass) me the eraser.

Kurt: OK. It's me / (my) turn. Number 2. This is a shower.

Rosa: Yes!

2 Read and check (✓).

1.
> Let's work together.

2.
> Let's take turns.

3.
> Can I borrow a ruler?

☑ OK. Let's take turns.
☐ No, you first.

☑ OK. You first.
☐ Please pass the ruler.

☐ It's on page 10.
☑ Yes, here.

School Trip 2: Animals in the Savanna, Africa

1 Remember. Check (✓) the animals in the video.

☐ ☑ ☑ ☑

2 Look at the animals. Draw the tails.

1. 2. 3.

3 You're in Africa now. Draw and color your favorite animal. Circle the words.

big
small

black
blue
brown
green
orange
purple
red
white
yellow

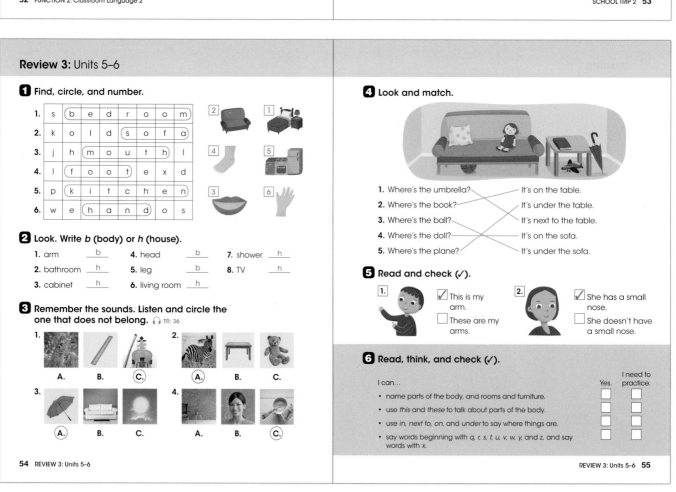

Review 3: Units 5–6

1 Find, circle, and number.

1.	s	(b	e	d	r	o	o	m)
2.	k	o	l	d	(s | o | f | a)
3.	j	h	(m	o	u	t	h)	l
4.	l	(f | o | o | t)	e	x	d
5.	p	(k	i	t	c	h	e	n)
6.	w	e	(h | a | n | d)	o	s

2 Look. Write b (body) or h (house).

1. arm _b_
2. bathroom _h_
3. cabinet _h_
4. head _b_
5. leg _b_
6. living room _h_
7. shower _h_
8. TV _h_

3 Remember the sounds. Listen and circle the one that does not belong. 🎧 TR: 36

1. A. B. (C.)
2. (A.) B. C.
3. (A.) B. C.
4. A. B. (C.)

4 Look and match.

1. Where's the umbrella? — It's on the table.
2. Where's the book? — It's under the table.
3. Where's the ball? — It's next to the table.
4. Where's the doll? — It's on the sofa.
5. Where's the plane? — It's under the sofa.

5 Read and check (✓).

1.
☑ This is my arm.
☐ These are my arms.

2.
☑ She has a small nose.
☐ She doesn't have a small nose.

6 Read, think, and check (✓).

I can…	Yes.	I need to practice.
• name parts of the body, and rooms and furniture.	☐	☐
• use *this* and *these* to talk about parts of the body.	☐	☐
• use *in*, *next to*, *on*, and *under* to say where things are.	☐	☐
• say words beginning with q, r, s, t, u, v, w, y, and z, and say words with x.	☐	☐

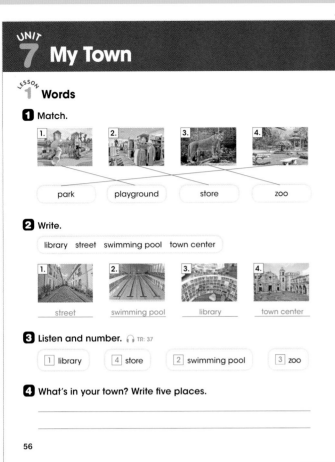

UNIT 7 My Town

See p. 126.

LESSON 1 Words

1 Match.

1. 2. 3. 4.

park | playground | store | zoo

2 Write.

library street swimming pool town center

1. street
2. swimming pool
3. library
4. town center

3 Listen and number. TR: 37

1 library   4 store   2 swimming pool   3 zoo

4 What's in your town? Write five places.

56

Grammar LESSON 2

See p. 126.

1 Listen, read, and write. TR: 38

There's a street, a street, a street in the town.
There's __a__ store, a store, a store on the street.
There's __a__ girl, a girl, a girl __in__ the store.
There's __a__ store, a store, a store __on__ the __street__.
There's __a__ street, a street, a street __in__ the __town__.

2 Write.

1. the park / in / a playground / there's
There's a playground in the park.

2. there's / the store / in / a man
There's a man in the store.

3. the car / a woman / in / there's
There's a woman in the car.

4. a library / on / there's / the street
There's a library on the street.

UNIT 7 My Town **57**

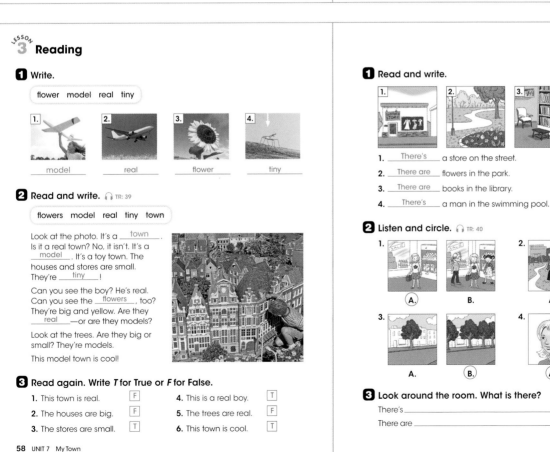

LESSON 3 Reading

1 Write.

flower model real tiny

1. model
2. real
3. flower
4. tiny

2 Read and write. TR: 39

flowers model real tiny town

Look at the photo. It's a __town__. Is it a real town? No, it isn't. It's a __model__. It's a toy town. The houses and stores are small. They're __tiny__!

Can you see the boy? He's real. Can you see the __flowers__, too? They're big and yellow. Are they __real__—or are they models?

Look at the trees. Are they big or small? They're models.

This model town is cool!

3 Read again. Write *T* for True or *F* for False.

1. This town is real.   F
2. The houses are big.   F
3. The stores are small.   T
4. This is a real boy.   T
5. The trees are real.   F
6. This town is cool.   T

58 UNIT 7 My Town

Grammar LESSON 4

See p. 126.

1 Read and write.

1. 2. 3. 4.

1. ____There's____ a store on the street.
2. ____There are____ flowers in the park.
3. ____There are____ books in the library.
4. ____There's____ a man in the swimming pool.

2 Listen and circle. TR: 40

1. A. B.   2. A. B.
3. A. B.   4. A. B.

3 Look around the room. What is there?

There's _____

There are _____

UNIT 7 My Town **59**

157

Workbook

Phonics

1 Check (✓) the words with *a*.

☑ ☑ ☑ ☑

2 Write.

1. j <u>a</u> m
2. m <u>a</u> n
3. m <u>a</u> p
4. b <u>a</u> t

3 Listen and write the words with *a*. 🎧 TR: 41

1. <u>b</u> <u>a</u> <u>t</u>
2. <u>m</u> <u>a</u> <u>n</u>
3. <u>j</u> <u>a</u> <u>m</u>
4. <u>m</u> <u>a</u> <u>p</u>
5. <u>c</u> <u>a</u> <u>t</u>
6. <u>d</u> <u>a</u> <u>d</u>

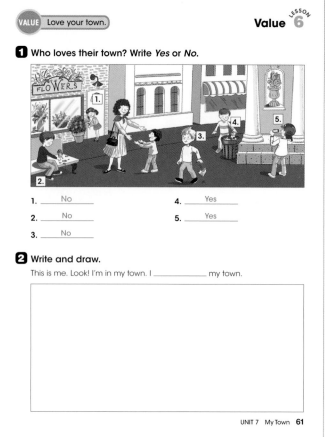

VALUE Love your town.

Value LESSON 6

1 Who loves their town? Write *Yes* or *No*.

1. No
2. No
3. No
4. Yes
5. Yes

2 Write and draw.

This is me. Look! I'm in my town. I _____ my town.

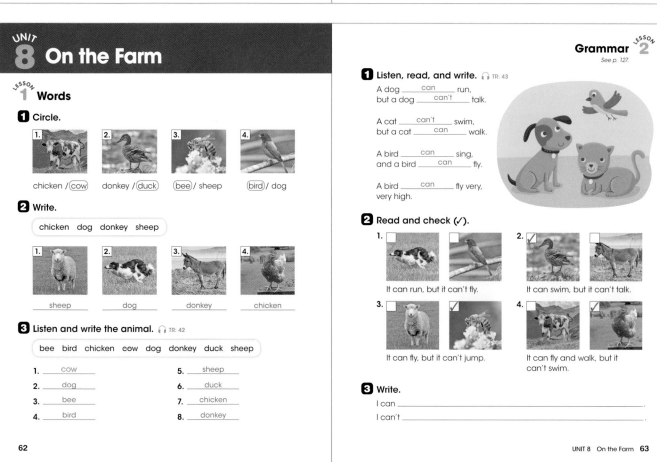

UNIT 8 On the Farm

Words

1 Circle.

1. chicken / (cow)
2. donkey / (duck)
3. (bee) / sheep
4. (bird) / dog

2 Write.

| chicken   dog   donkey   sheep |

1. sheep
2. dog
3. donkey
4. chicken

3 Listen and write the animal. 🎧 TR: 42

| bee   bird   chicken   cow   dog   donkey   duck   sheep |

1. cow
2. dog
3. bee
4. bird
5. sheep
6. duck
7. chicken
8. donkey

62

Grammar LESSON 2
See p. 127.

1 Listen, read, and write. 🎧 TR: 43

A dog ___can___ run,
but a dog ___can't___ talk.

A cat ___can't___ swim,
but a cat ___can___ walk.

A bird ___can___ sing,
and a bird ___can___ fly.

A bird ___can___ fly very,
very high.

2 Read and check (✓).

1. ☐ ✓ It can run, but it can't fly.
2. ✓ ☐ It can swim, but it can't talk.
3. ☐ ✓ It can fly, but it can't jump.
4. ☐ ✓ It can fly and walk, but it can't swim.

3 Write.

I can _____.
I can't _____.

158

Reading

1 Write.

farmer food pen

1. food   2. pen   3. farmer

2 Read and write. 🎧 TR: 44

boy farmer food school sheep

Can you play with animals at school?
No! You can play with your friends at
school . Can you play with animals
on a farm? Yes! Look at this farm.

This is a pen. But it isn't a pen for writing. It's a ____sheep____ pen. A pen
is a sheep's "house." Look! Can you see the ____farmer____? She has
____food____ for the sheep.

Look at the ____boy____! He has food for the sheep, too. Do you like
this farm?

3 Read again and circle.

1. You **can** / **(can't)** play with animals at school.

2. You **(can)** / **can't** play with your friends at school.

3. A sheep's house is a **(pen)** / **pencil**.

4. The farmer has food for the **boy** / **(sheep)**.

Grammar
See p. 127.

1 Read and circle.

1. Can a bird fly?   **(Yes, it can.)** / No, it can't.

2. Can a dog jump?   **(Yes, it can.)** / No, it can't.

3. Can a donkey fly?   Yes, it can. / **(No, it can't.)**

4. Can a chicken draw a picture?   Yes, it can. / **(No, it can't.)**

5. Can a cat run?   **(Yes, it can.)** / No, it can't.

2 Write. Then listen and check. 🎧 TR: 45

 (read)

Can a duck read?
No, it can't.

 (fly)

Can a cow fly?
No, it can't.

 (jump)

Can a cat jump?
Yes, it can.

 (swim)

Can a fish swim?
Yes, it can.

 (sing)

Can a sheep sing?
No, it can't.

 (run)

Can a horse run?
Yes, it can.

Phonics

1 Check (✓) the words with *e*.

 ✓   ✓   ☐   ✓

 ✓   ☐   ✓   ☐

2 Write.

1. l e g   2. p e n   3. b e d   4. t e n

3 Listen and write the words with *e*. 🎧 TR: 46

1. r e d

2. l e g

3. b e d

4. t e n

5. y e s

6. m e n

VALUE Be kind to animals.

Value

1 Who's kind to animals? Write *Yes* or *No*.

1. Yes   4. No

2. Yes   5. Yes

3. Yes   6. Yes

2 Write and draw.

This is me. Look! I'm kind to animals.

159

Workbook

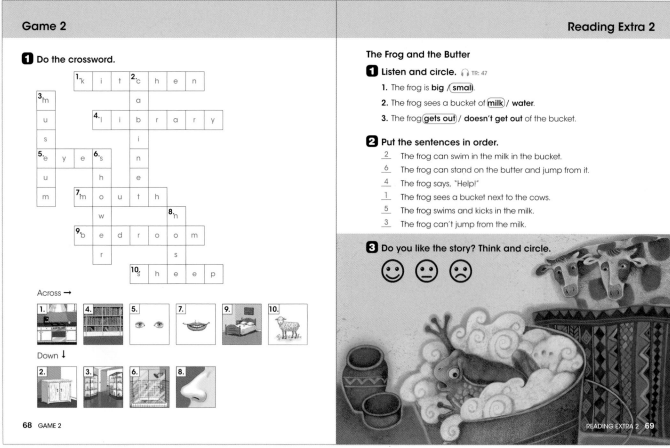

1 Do the crossword.

Across →

1. 4. 5. 7. 9. 10.

Down ↓

2. 3. 6. 8.

The Frog and the Butter

1 Listen and circle. TR: 47

1. The frog is **big** / **small**.
2. The frog sees a bucket of **milk** / **water**.
3. The frog **gets out** / **doesn't get out** of the bucket.

2 Put the sentences in order.

2 The frog can swim in the milk in the bucket.

6 The frog can stand on the butter and jump from it.

4 The frog says, "Help!"

1 The frog sees a bucket next to the cows.

5 The frog swims and kicks in the milk.

3 The frog can't jump from the milk.

3 Do you like the story? Think and circle.

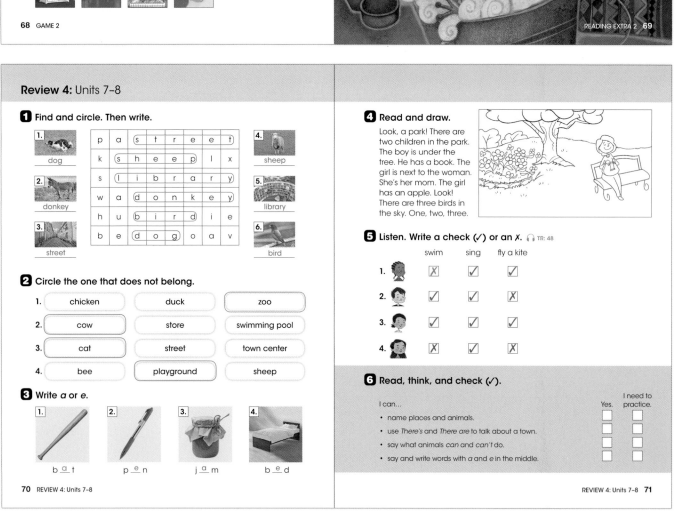

Review 4: Units 7–8

1 Find and circle. Then write.

1. dog
2. donkey
3. street
4. sheep
5. library
6. bird

2 Circle the one that does not belong.

1.	chicken	duck	zoo
2.	cow	store	swimming pool
3.	cat	street	town center
4.	bee	playground	sheep

3 Write *a* or *e*.

1. b_a_t
2. p_e_n
3. j_a_m
4. b_e_d

4 Read and draw.

Look, a park! There are two children in the park. The boy is under the tree. He has a book. The girl is next to the woman. She's her mom. The girl has an apple. Look! There are three birds in the sky. One, two, three.

5 Listen. Write a check (✓) or an *X*. TR: 48

	swim	sing	fly a kite
1.	X	✓	✓
2.	✓	✓	X
3.	✓	✓	✓
4.	X	✓	X

6 Read, think, and check (✓).

I can...	Yes.	I need to practice.
• name places and animals.	☐	☐
• use *There's* and *There are* to talk about a town.	☐	☐
• say what animals *can* and *can't* do.	☐	☐
• say and write words with *a* and *e* in the middle.	☐	☐

160

UNIT 9 My Clothes

See p. 128.

LESSON 1 Words

1 What is it? Circle.

1. shoes / (T-shirt)
2. (dress) / pants
3. (jeans) / socks
4. shirt / (skirt)

2 Look and write. Use words from Activity 1.

1. shirt
2. pants
3. shoes
4. socks

3 Listen and color. TR: 49

72

Grammar LESSON 2

See p. 128.

1 Listen, read, and write. TR: 50

Is this your shirt? Is this your shirt?
Yes, it __is__. This is my shirt.
__Is__ this your hat? Is __this__ your hat?
No, it __isn't__. This isn't my hat.

Are these your shoes? Are these your shoes?
No, they __aren't__. These aren't my shoes.
Are __these__ your socks? Are these your socks?
Yes, they __are__. These are my socks.

2 Read and circle.

Ben

1.
A: Is this your T-shirt, Ben?
B: (Yes, it is.) / No, it isn't.

2.
A: Are these your socks, Ben?
B: Yes, they are. / (No, they aren't.)

3.
A: Are these your shoes, Ben?
B: Yes, they are. / (No, they aren't.)

4.
A: Are these your pants, Ben?
B: (Yes, they are.) / No, they aren't.

UNIT 9 My Clothes **73**

LESSON 3 Reading

1 Match.

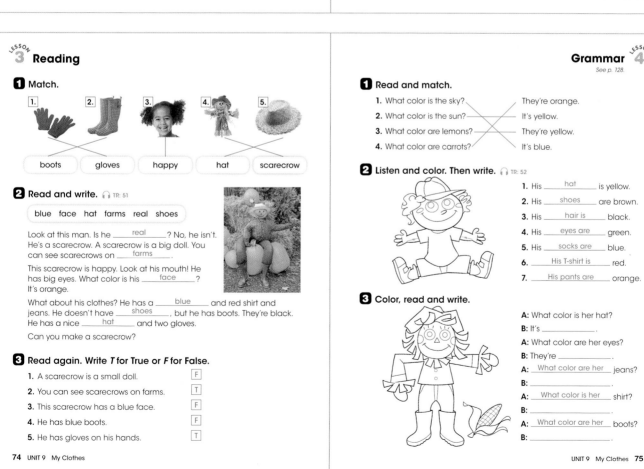

boots   gloves   happy   hat   scarecrow

2 Read and write. TR: 51

blue face hat farms real shoes

Look at this man. Is he __real__? No, he isn't.
He's a scarecrow. A scarecrow is a big doll. You
can see scarecrows on __farms__.

This scarecrow is happy. Look at his mouth! He
has big eyes. What color is his __face__?
It's orange.

What about his clothes? He has a __blue__ and red shirt and
jeans. He doesn't have __shoes__, but he has boots. They're black.
He has a nice __hat__ and two gloves.

Can you make a scarecrow?

3 Read again. Write T for True or F for False.

1. A scarecrow is a small doll.   F
2. You can see scarecrows on farms.   T
3. This scarecrow has a blue face.   F
4. He has blue boots.   F
5. He has gloves on his hands.   T

74 UNIT 9 My Clothes

Grammar LESSON 4

See p. 128.

1 Read and match.

1. What color is the sky?   They're orange.
2. What color is the sun?   It's yellow.
3. What color are lemons?   They're yellow.
4. What color are carrots?   It's blue.

2 Listen and color. Then write. TR: 52

1. His __hat__ is yellow.
2. His __shoes__ are brown.
3. His __hair is__ black.
4. His __eyes are__ green.
5. His __socks are__ blue.
6. __His T-shirt is__ red.
7. __His pants are__ orange.

3 Color, read and write.

A: What color is her hat?
B: It's _____.
A: What color are her eyes?
B: They're _____.
A: __What color are her__ jeans?
B: _____.
A: __What color is her__ shirt?
B: _____.
A: __What color are her__ boots?
B: _____.

UNIT 9 My Clothes **75**

161

Workbook

Phonics

1 Check (✓) the words with *i*.

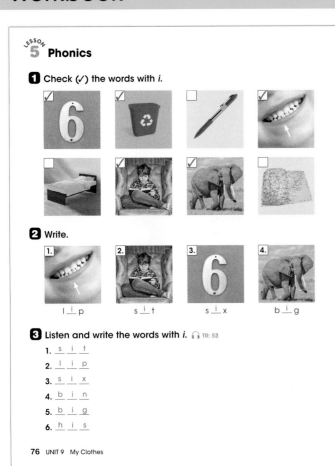

2 Write.

1.	2.	3.	4.
l <u>i</u> p	s <u>i</u> t	s <u>i</u> x	b <u>i</u> g

3 Listen and write the words with *i*. 🎧 TR: 53

1. <u>s</u> <u>i</u> <u>t</u>
2. <u>l</u> <u>i</u> <u>p</u>
3. <u>s</u> <u>i</u> <u>x</u>
4. <u>b</u> <u>i</u> <u>n</u>
5. <u>b</u> <u>i</u> <u>g</u>
6. <u>h</u> <u>i</u> <u>s</u>

VALUE Wear clean clothes.

Value LESSON 6

1 Who wears clean clothes? Look and check (✓).

2 Read and draw.

This is me. Look! I wear clean clothes.

UNIT 10 Eat and Drink

Words

1 Circle.

1.	2.	3.	4.
(lemon) / tomato	(bread) / rice	banana / (water)	(candy) / milk

2 Write.

banana   milk   potato   rice

1.	2.	3.	4.
potato	rice	milk	banana

3 Listen, number, and write. 🎧 TR: 54

3	1	2	4
milk	tomato	banana	bread

Grammar LESSON 2

See p. 129.

1 Listen, read, and write. 🎧 TR: 55

I <u>like</u> bananas and
I <u>like</u> bread.
I <u>don't like</u> apples, green or red!
I <u>like</u> oranges and
I <u>like</u> rice.
I <u>like</u> bread. Can I have a slice?

2 Read and number.

1. I like apples and oranges. I like water, too. I don't like milk.

2. I like apples and bananas. I like milk, too. I don't like oranges.

3. I like bananas and oranges. I like water, too. I don't like milk.

2

3

1

3 Draw and write.

1.

2.

I like _____ and _____. I _____, too.

I don't like _____ and I don't _____.

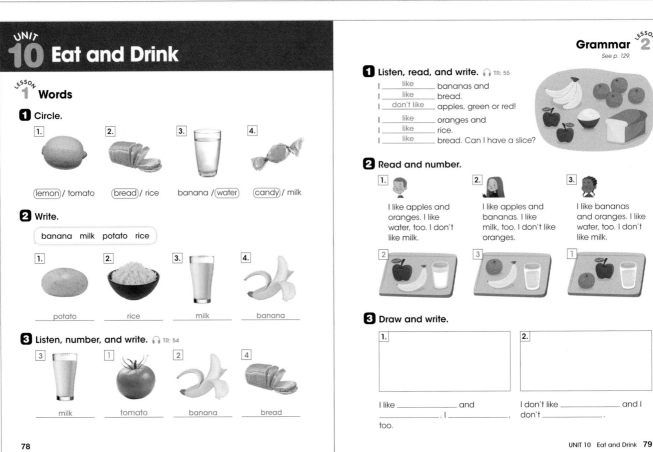

LESSON 3 Reading

1 Read and number the pictures.

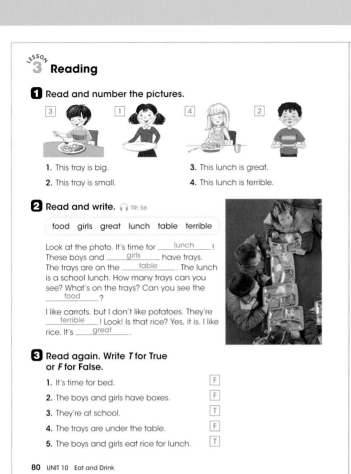

`3` `1` `4` `2`

1. This tray is big.
2. This tray is small.
3. This lunch is great.
4. This lunch is terrible.

2 Read and write. 🎧 TR: 56

| food girls great lunch table terrible |

Look at the photo. It's time for ___lunch___ !
These boys and ___girls___ have trays.
The trays are on the ___table___ . The lunch
is a school lunch. How many trays can you
see? What's on the trays? Can you see the
___food___ ?

I like carrots, but I don't like potatoes. They're
___terrible___ ! Look! Is that rice? Yes, it is. I like
rice. It's ___great___ .

3 Read again. Write *T* for True or *F* for False.

1. It's time for bed. `F`
2. The boys and girls have boxes. `F`
3. They're at school. `T`
4. The trays are under the table. `F`
5. The boys and girls eat rice for lunch. `T`

Grammar LESSON 4

See p. 129.

1 Read and write.

| It's OK. They're OK. Yes, I do. No, I don't. |

1. Do you like bananas? ☺
___Yes, I do.___
2. Do you like potatoes? ☺
___They're OK.___
3. Do you like milk? ☺
___It's OK.___
4. Do you like bread? ☹
___No, I don't.___

2 What about you? Write.

1. Do you like water?
_____
2. Do you like tomatoes?
_____
3. Do you like rice?
_____
4. Do you like apples?
_____

3 Listen and draw. 🎧 TR: 57

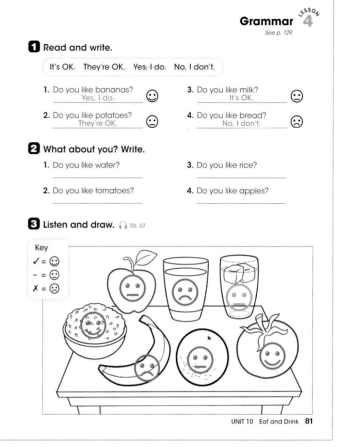

Key
✓ = ☺
– = ☺
✗ = ☹

LESSON 5 Phonics

1 Check (✓) the words with *o*.

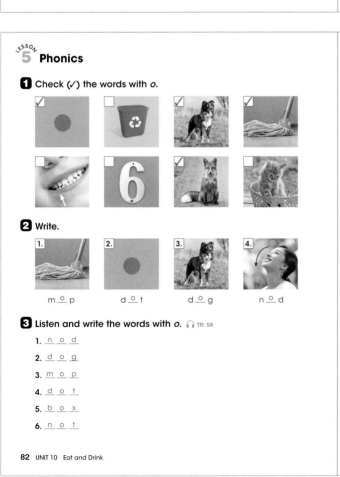

2 Write.

1. m _o_ p
2. d _o_ t
3. d _o_ g
4. n _o_ d

3 Listen and write the words with *o*. 🎧 TR: 58

1. _n_ _o_ _d_
2. _d_ _o_ _g_
3. _m_ _o_ _p_
4. _d_ _o_ _t_
5. _b_ _o_ _x_
6. _n_ _o_ _t_

VALUE: Eat good food.

Value LESSON 6

1 What's good food? Look and check (✓).

1. ✓
2. ☐
3. ✓
4. ✓
5. ☐
6. ✓

2 Read and draw.

Look! I eat good food.

163

Workbook

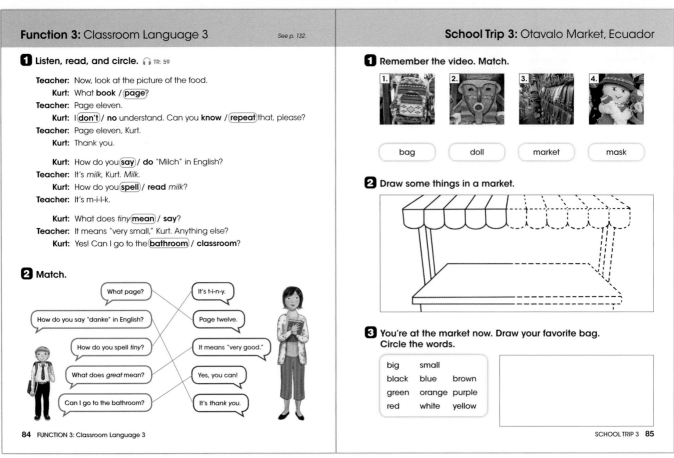

Function 3: Classroom Language 3

See p. 132.

1 Listen, read, and circle. 🎧 TR: 59

Teacher: Now, look at the picture of the food.
Kurt: What **book** / **page**?
Teacher: Page eleven.
Kurt: I **don't** / **no** understand. Can you **know** / **repeat** that, please?
Teacher: Page eleven, Kurt.
Kurt: Thank you.

Kurt: How do you **say** / **do** "Milch" in English?
Teacher: It's *milk*, Kurt. *Milk.*
Kurt: How do you **spell** / **read** *milk*?
Teacher: It's m-i-l-k.

Kurt: What does *tiny* **mean** / **say**?
Teacher: It means "very small," Kurt. Anything else?
Kurt: Yes! Can I go to the **bathroom** / **classroom**?

2 Match.

- What page?
- How do you say "danke" in English?
- How do you spell *tiny*?
- What does *great* mean?
- Can I go to the bathroom?

- It's t-i-n-y.
- Page twelve.
- It means "very good."
- Yes, you can!
- It's *thank you.*

84 FUNCTION 3: Classroom Language 3

School Trip 3: Otavalo Market, Ecuador

1 Remember the video. Match.

1.   2.   3.   4.

- bag
- doll
- market
- mask

2 Draw some things in a market.

3 You're at the market now. Draw your favorite bag. Circle the words.

big	small	
black	blue	brown
green	orange	purple
red	white	yellow

SCHOOL TRIP 3 85

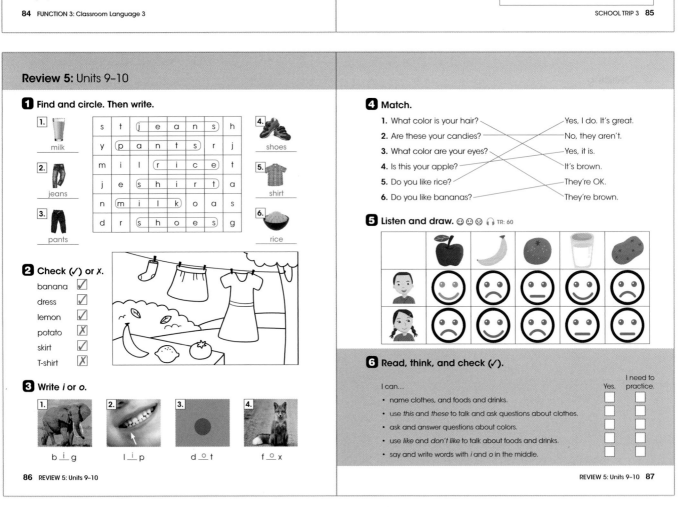

Review 5: Units 9–10

1 Find and circle. Then write.

1. milk
2. jeans
3. pants
4. shoes
5. shirt
6. rice

s	t	j	e	a	n	s	h
y	p	a	n	t	s	r	j
m	i	l	r	i	c	e	t
j	e	s	h	i	r	t	a
n	m	i	l	k	o	a	s
d	r	s	h	o	e	s	g

2 Check (✓) or ✗.

- banana ✓
- dress ✓
- lemon ✓
- potato ✗
- skirt ✓
- T-shirt ✗

3 Write *i* or *o*.

1. b i g
2. l i p
3. d o t
4. f o x

4 Match.

1. What color is your hair?
2. Are these your candies?
3. What color are your eyes?
4. Is this your apple?
5. Do you like rice?
6. Do you like bananas?

- Yes, I do. It's great.
- No, they aren't.
- Yes, it is.
- It's brown.
- They're OK.
- They're brown.

5 Listen and draw. 😊 😐 😞 🎧 TR: 60

6 Read, think, and check (✓).

I can...	Yes.	I need to practice.
• name clothes, and foods and drinks.	☐	☐
• use *this* and *these* to talk and ask questions about clothes.	☐	☐
• ask and answer questions about colors.	☐	☐
• use *like* and *don't like* to talk about foods and drinks.	☐	☐
• say and write words with *i* and *o* in the middle.	☐	☐

86 REVIEW 5: Units 9–10

REVIEW 5: Units 9–10 87

UNIT 11 Beach Vacations

LESSON 1 Words

1 Match.

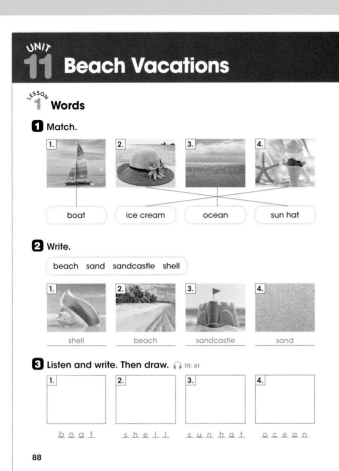

1. | 2. | 3. | 4.

boat | ice cream | ocean | sun hat

2 Write.

beach sand sandcastle shell

1. | 2. | 3. | 4.

shell | beach | sandcastle | sand

3 Listen and write. Then draw. 🎧 TR: 61

1. | 2. | 3. | 4.

b o a t | s h e l l | s u n h a t | o c e a n

88

Grammar LESSON 2

See p. 130.

1 Listen, read, and write. 🎧 TR: 62

_____There's_____ a beach ball next to me.
_____There are_____ beach balls, one, two, three!

_____There isn't_____ a sun hat on my head.
_____There aren't_____ sun hats, blue or red.

2 Read and number.

1. There aren't shells.
2. There isn't a sandcastle.
3. There aren't sun hats.
4. There isn't a teddy bear.

UNIT 11 Beach Vacations **89**

LESSON 3 Reading

1 Match.

breathe | flippers
mask | snorkel

2 Read and write. 🎧 TR: 63

beach fish flippers masks vacation water

It's _____vacation_____ time. The sun is in the sky. It's a nice day.

These two children aren't at school. They're at the _____beach_____. Look! They're in the ocean. But they aren't in a boat. They're in the _____water_____.

The children can see—they have _____masks_____ on their faces. They can breathe under the water, too—they have snorkels. And they have special shoes called _____flippers_____.

Are there _____fish_____ in the water? Yes, there are! Look! How many fish can you see?

3 Read again. Write *Yes* or *No*.

1. Are the children at school? _____No_____
2. Are they in the ocean? _____Yes_____
3. Are they in a boat? _____No_____
4. Can they see in the water? _____Yes_____
5. Can they breathe in the water? _____Yes_____

90 UNIT 11 Beach Vacations

Grammar LESSON 4

See p. 130.

1 Read and write.

Shiven: _____Is_____ there a beach in your town?

Aliyah: No, there _____isn't_____.

Shiven: I see. _____Is_____ there an ice cream shop?

Aliyah: Yes, there _____is_____!

Shiven: Great! And _____are_____ there candy shops?

Aliyah: No, there _____aren't_____.

2 Listen and draw. 🎧 TR: 64

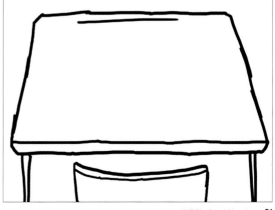

UNIT 11 Beach Vacations **91**

165

Workbook

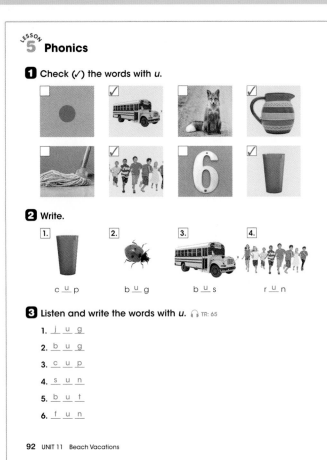

1 Check (✓) the words with *u*.

2 Write.

1. c_u_p
2. b_u_g
3. b_u_s
4. r_u_n

3 Listen and write the words with *u*. 🎧 TR: 65

1. j_u_g
2. b_u_g
3. c_u_p
4. s_u_n
5. b_u_t
6. f_u_n

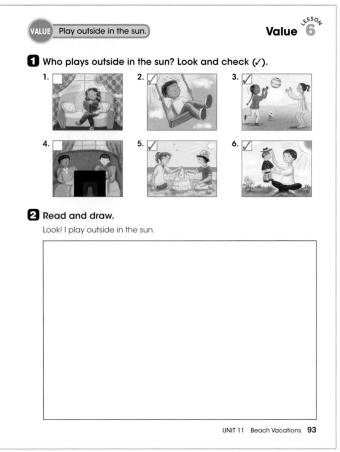

VALUE Play outside in the sun.

Value LESSON 6

1 Who plays outside in the sun? Look and check (✓).

1. 2. 3. ✓
4. 5. ✓ 6. ✓

2 Read and draw.

Look! I play outside in the sun.

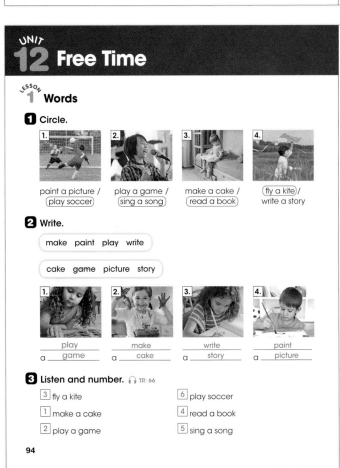

UNIT 12 Free Time

1 Circle.

1. paint a picture / (play soccer)
2. play a game / (sing a song)
3. make a cake / (read a book)
4. (fly a kite) / write a story

2 Write.

make paint play write

cake game picture story

1. play a game
2. make a cake
3. write a story
4. paint a picture

3 Listen and number. 🎧 TR: 66

3 fly a kite
1 make a cake
2 play a game

6 play soccer
4 read a book
5 sing a song

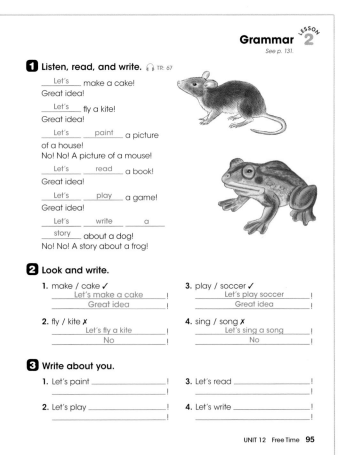

Grammar LESSON 2

See p. 131.

1 Listen, read, and write. 🎧 TR: 67

___Let's___ make a cake!
Great idea!
___Let's___ fly a kite!
Great idea!
___Let's___ ___paint___ a picture
of a house!
No! No! A picture of a mouse!
___Let's___ ___read___ a book!
Great idea!
___Let's___ ___play___ a game!
Great idea!
___Let's___ ___write___ ___a___
___story___ about a dog!
No! No! A story about a frog!

2 Look and write.

1. make / cake ✓
   Let's make a cake!
   Great idea!

2. fly / kite ✗
   Let's fly a kite!
   No!

3. play / soccer ✓
   Let's play soccer!
   Great idea!

4. sing / song ✗
   Let's sing a song!
   No!

3 Write about you.

1. Let's paint _____!
   _____
2. Let's play _____!
   _____
3. Let's read _____!
   _____
4. Let's write _____!
   _____

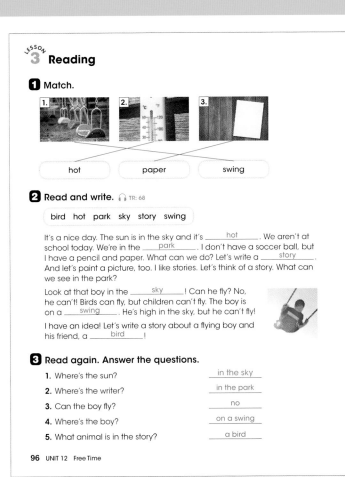

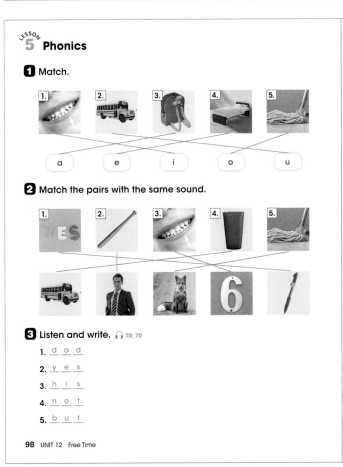

LESSON 3 Reading

1 Match.

1. 2. 3.

hot   paper   swing

2 Read and write. 🎧 TR: 68

bird hot park sky story swing

It's a nice day. The sun is in the sky and it's ___hot___. We aren't at school today. We're in the ___park___. I don't have a soccer ball, but I have a pencil and paper. What can we do? Let's write a ___story___. And let's paint a picture, too. I like stories. Let's think of a story. What can we see in the park?

Look at that boy in the ___sky___! Can he fly? No, he can't! Birds can fly, but children can't fly. The boy is on a ___swing___. He's high in the sky, but he can't fly!

I have an idea! Let's write a story about a flying boy and his friend, a ___bird___!

3 Read again. Answer the questions.

1. Where's the sun? — in the sky
2. Where's the writer? — in the park
3. Can the boy fly? — no
4. Where's the boy? — on a swing
5. What animal is in the story? — a bird

96 UNIT 12 Free Time

Grammar LESSON 4
See p. 131.

1 Write.

1. 2. 3. 4.

1. ___We aren't___ at the store.
2. ___We're___ in the park.
3. ___We're___ in the library.
4. ___We aren't___ at the swimming pool.

2 Listen and circle. 🎧 TR: 69

1. A. B.
2. (A.) B.
3. A. (B.)
4. (A.) B.

UNIT 12 Free Time 97

LESSON 5 Phonics

1 Match.

1. 2. 3. 4. 5.

a   e   i   o   u

2 Match the pairs with the same sound.

1. 2. 3. 4. 5.

3 Listen and write. 🎧 TR: 70

1. d a d
2. y e s
3. h i s
4. n o t
5. b u t

98 UNIT 12 Free Time

VALUE Use your time well.

Value LESSON 6

1 Who uses their time well? Look and check (✓).

1. 2.
3. 4.

2 Read and draw.

This is me. Look! I use my time well.

UNIT 12 Free Time 99

167

Workbook

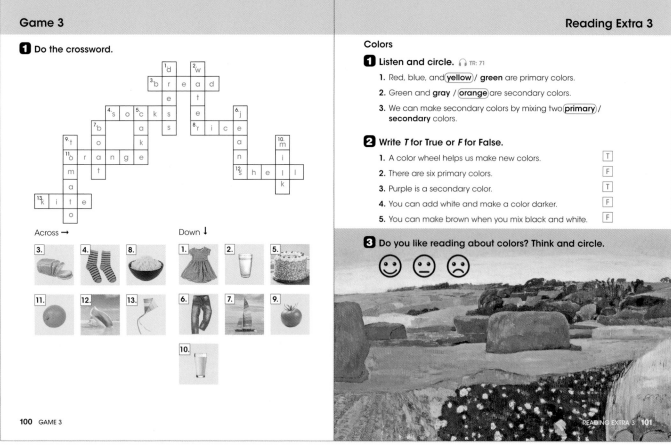

1 Do the crossword.

Across →
Down ↓

3. 4. 8. | 1. 2. 5.
11. 12. 13. | 6. 7. 9.
| 10.

Colors

1 Listen and circle. TR: 71

1. Red, blue, and **yellow** / **green** are primary colors.
2. Green and **gray** / **orange** are secondary colors.
3. We can make secondary colors by mixing two **primary** / **secondary** colors.

2 Write *T* for True or *F* for False.

1. A color wheel helps us make new colors. [T]
2. There are six primary colors. [F]
3. Purple is a secondary color. [T]
4. You can add white and make a color darker. [F]
5. You can make brown when you mix black and white. [F]

3 Do you like reading about colors? Think and circle.

☺ ☺ ☹

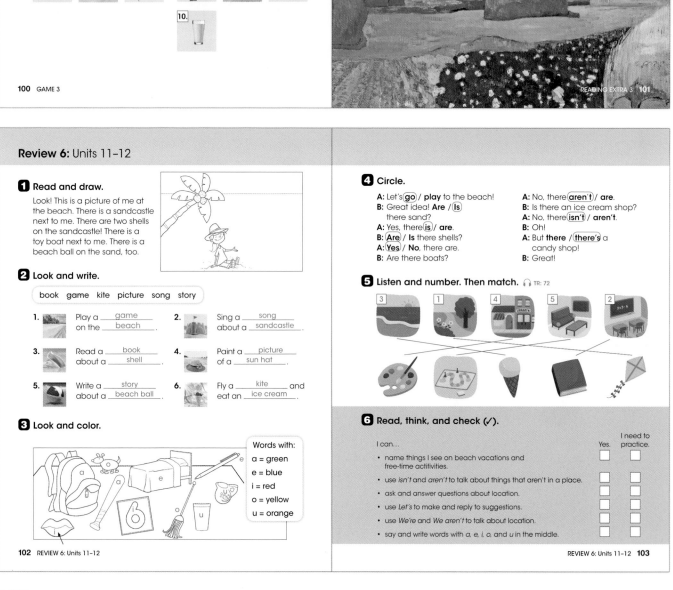

Review 6: Units 11–12

1 Read and draw.

Look! This is a picture of me at the beach. There is a sandcastle next to me. There are two shells on the sandcastle! There is a toy boat next to me. There is a beach ball on the sand, too.

2 Look and write.

book game kite picture song story

1. Play a ___game___ on the ___beach___
2. Sing a ___song___ about a ___sandcastle___
3. Read a ___book___ about a ___shell___
4. Paint a ___picture___ of a ___sun hat___
5. Write a ___story___ about a ___beach ball___
6. Fly a ___kite___ and eat an ___ice cream___

3 Look and color.

Words with:
a = green
e = blue
i = red
o = yellow
u = orange

4 Circle.

A: Let's **go** / **play** to the beach!
B: Great idea! Are / **Is** there sand?
A: Yes, there **is** / **are**.
B: **Are** / Is there shells?
A: **Yes** / **No**, there are.
B: Are there boats?

A: No, there **aren't** / **are**.
B: Is there an ice cream shop?
A: No, there **isn't** / **aren't**.
B: Oh!
A: But **there** / **there's** a candy shop!
B: Great!

5 Listen and number. Then match. TR: 72

3 1 4 5 2

6 Read, think, and check (✓).

I can...	Yes.	I need to practice.
• name things I see on beach vacations and free-time acitivities.	☐	☐
• use *isn't* and *aren't* to talk about things that aren't in a place.	☐	☐
• ask and answer questions about location.	☐	☐
• use *Let's* to make and reply to suggestions.	☐	☐
• use *We're* and *We aren't* to talk about location.	☐	☐
• say and write words with *a, e, i, o,* and *u* in the middle.	☐	☐

1 Remember the video. Match.

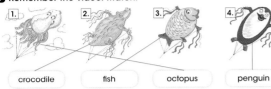

1. 2. 3. 4.

(crocodile) (fish) (octopus) (penguin)

2 Draw an animal kite.

3 You're at the kite festival now. Draw and write about your favorite kite. Use the words in the box.

big	small	
black	blue	brown
green	orange	purple
red	white	yellow

My favorite kite is a/an _____.

It's _____. (size)

It's colorful. I can see _____ and _____.

What's an Elephant?

1 Listen and circle. 🎧 TR: 73

1. Baby mice can't (see) / hear very well.
2. The elephant is **in a tree** / (under the trees).
3. The elephant **asks** / (answers) a lot of questions.

2 Put the sentences in order.

5 The baby mice speak to the elephant.

2 The baby mice think the elephant's body is a wall.

4 The baby mice think the elephant's tail is a rope.

1 Mom Mouse sees an elephant.

6 The elephant talks to the baby mice.

3 The baby mice think the elephant's leg is a tree.

3 Do you like the story? Think and circle.

☺ 😐 ☹

Starters Listening **Part 1** 5 questions

Listen and draw lines. There is one example. 🎧 TR: 74

Tom Lucy Hugo Alice

Mark Ben Kim

Starters Listening **Part 2** 5 questions

Read the questions. Listen and write a name or a number. There are two examples. 🎧 TR: 75

Examples

What is the new girl's name? _____Sue_____

What is her last name? _____Ball_____

Questions

1. How old is the girl? _____7_____
2. Where is her home? on _____Park_____ Street
3. What number is her house? _____13_____
4. What's the name of her friend? _____May_____
5. What number is the Music Room? _____10_____

Workbook

Listen and check (✓) the box. There is one example. 🎧 TR: 76

What animal does the teacher have?

A. ☐   B. ☐   C. ✓

1. Which is Matt's kite?

A. ☐   B. ✓   C. ☐

2. What are Eva's clothes for the party?

A. ✓   B. ☐   C. ☐

108

3. What's Nick's favorite fruit?

A. ☐   B. ☐   C. ✓

4. What's the children's activity after school?

A. ✓   B. ☐   C. ☐

5. Which is Anna's bag?

A. ☐   B. ✓   C. ☐

109

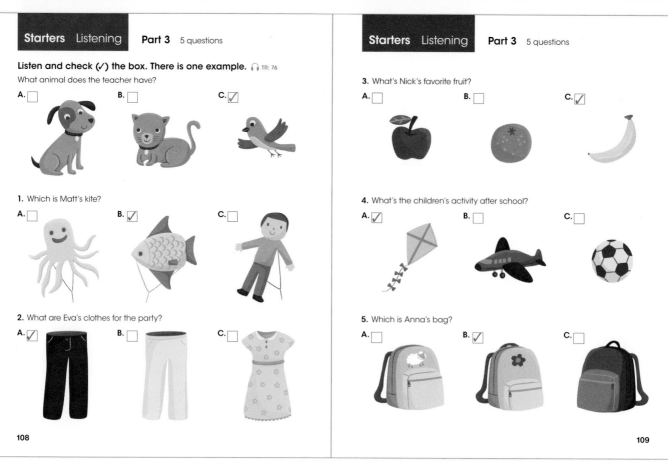

Listen and color. There is one example. 🎧 TR: 77

110

**Look and read. Put a check (✓) or an X in the box.
There are two examples.**

Examples

This is a tomato. ☒

These are balls. ✓

Questions

1. This is a skirt. ✓

2. These are socks. ☒

3. This is a train. ☒

4. These are dolls. ✓

5. This is a sandcastle. ✓

111

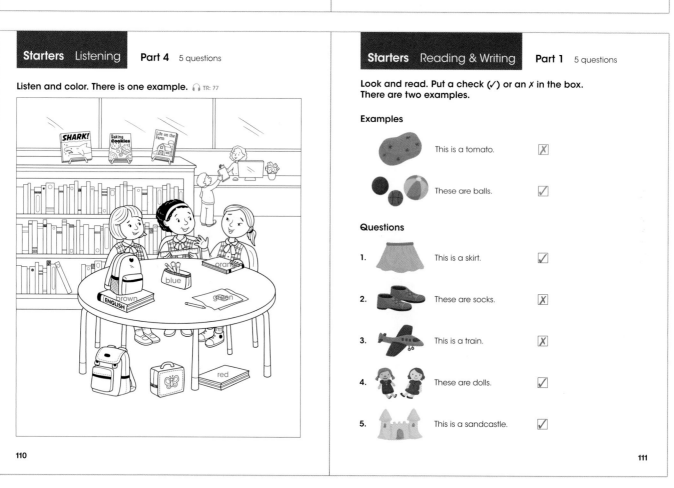

170

Look and read. Write *Yes* or *No*.

Examples

There are two trees in the picture.	yes
There are flowers in the park.	no

Questions

1. The man has a kite.	yes
2. There is a teddy bear next to the baby.	no
3. The woman has a sun hat.	no
4. There is a bird in one of the trees.	yes
5. The girl has a banana.	yes

112

Look at the pictures. Look at the letters. Write the words.

Example

 h o r s e

Questions

1. d o g

2. b i r d

3. d o n k e y

4. s h e e p

5. c h i c k e n

113

Read. Choose a word from the box. Write the correct word next to numbers 1–5. There is one example.

A Puppet

This isn't a real ___boy___ . It's a puppet. A puppet is a (1.) ___doll___ , but you can move parts of its body. You can make a puppet walk and dance. There are a lot of different puppets. This puppet has a big, round (2.) ___head___ . It moves from side to side. And look at the puppet's (3.) ___eyes___ . Now they are open, but they can close, too. His arms and (4.) ___legs___ can move up and down. Look at his (5.) ___shoes___ ! They are big and funny.

Example

boy　head　shoes　girl

eyes　gloves　legs　doll

114

Look at the pictures and read the questions. Write one-word answers.

Examples

Where are the people?	on a ___boat___
How many children are there?	___two___

Questions

1. What's the children's toy?	a ___game___

115

171

Workbook

2. What does Grandpa have?   a big _____fish_____

3. Where is his sun hat?   on the girl's _____head_____

4. Where are the children and Grandpa?   on the _____beach_____

5. What's in the sky?   the _____moon_____

116

Look at the picture. Read the questions and point.

Where is the woman?

Where is the picture?

Where is the bag?

Read and draw.

Where is the clock? Put the clock on the cupboard.

Where is the ball? Put the ball under the table.

Where are the bananas? Put the bananas next to the bread.

Where is the chair? Put the chair in the living room.

117

Look at the picture. Answer the questions.

1. How many girls are there?   There are three girls.

2. Where is the boy?   He's on the sofa.

3. Can you see a duck?   Yes, I can. (It's in the picture.)

4. Where is the kite?   It's next to the cupboard.

5. What's on the sofa?   The violin is on the sofa.

6. Can you see an umbrella?   Yes, I can. (It's under the sofa.)

118

Look at the pictures. Answer the questions.

1.   2.   3.   4.

Questions

1. What's this?   It's a cow.
Can a cow sing?   No, it can't.
What's your favorite animal?   Sample answer: My favorite farm animal is a horse.

2. What's this?   It's a park.
Is there a park in your town?   Sample answer: Yes, there is.
What can you do at the park?   Sample answer: I can fly my kite and play soccer.

3. What's this?   It's a T-shirt.
Is it your T-shirt?   No, it isn't.
What color is your favorite T-shirt?   Sample answer: It's red and yellow.

4. What's this?   It's a pencil case.
Is there a pencil case in your bag?   Sample answer: Yes, there is.
What's in your pencil case?   Sample answer: There's a pen, a pencil, an eraser and crayons in my pencil case.

Answer the questions.

How old are you?   Sample answer: I'm six.

What color are your eyes?   Sample answer: My eyes are brown.

Can you run?   Sample answer: Yes, I can. I can run.

119

172

Unit 1

LESSON 2
1. What's, a bag
2. What's, It's

LESSON 4
1. B
2. A
3. B
4. A

Unit 2

LESSON 2
Students' own drawings of: a plane, a bag

LESSON 4
1. A
2. B
3. A
4. B

Unit 3

LESSON 2
1. A
2. B
3. A

LESSON 4
4, 2, 1, 3

Unit 4

LESSON 2
1. ✓
2. ✓
3. ✗
4. ✓
5. ✓
6. ✗

LESSON 4
1. Her
2. Her
3. His
4. His

Unit 5

LESSON 2
4, 3, 2, 1

LESSON 4
Students' own coloring of: girl with black hair and any color eyes except brown; boy with any color hair except brown and blue eyes

Unit 6

LESSON 2
1. Where's, in
2. Where

LESSON 4
3, 2, 4, 1

Unit 7

LESSON 2
1. zoo in the park.
2. a table in the kitchen.
3. 's a library in the town center.
4. in the store.

LESSON 4
1. There's, There are
2. There are, There's

Unit 8

LESSON 2
1. can't
2. can
3. can
4. can't
5. can
6. can

LESSON 4
1. Yes, it can.
2. Yes, I can.
3. No, it can't.
4. No, I can't.

Unit 9

LESSON 2
1. Are, are
2. these, No

LESSON 4
1. They're blue.
2. It's yellow.
3. They're yellow.
4. It's blue.

Unit 10

LESSON 2
1. I like
2. I like
3. I don't like

LESSON 4
1. student's drawing of a smiling face
2. student's drawing of a smiling face
3. student's drawing of a frowning face
4. student's drawing of a neutral face

Unit 11

LESSON 2
2, 3, 4, 1

LESSON 4
1. No, there isn't.
2. Yes, there is.
3. Yes, there are.
4. No, there aren't.

Unit 12

LESSON 2
1. Let / Great
2. 's / No / idea

LESSON 4
1. A
2. B
3. A
4. B

STUDENT'S BOOK CREDITS

WORKBOOK CREDITS

Thank you to the educators who provided invaluable feedback during the development of *Look*:

CONSULTANTS

Gabriela Klečková, Teacher Trainer, University of West Bohemia, Czech Republic
Luciana Fernández, Teacher Trainer/Academic Consultant, ESSARP, Argentina
Mari Nakamura, Owner/Teacher Trainer/Teacher, English Square, Kanazawa
Nguyen Quoc Hung, MA, Teacher, Hanoi University, Hanoi
Dr Sagrario Salaberri, Professor, University of Almería, Spain

ADVISORS

Aisha Khawaja, Early Childhood and EAL Specialist, GEMS Dubai American Academy, United Arab Emirates
Alis Valenzuela, Junior Manager, Children & Teenagers Program, Instituto Guatemalteco Americano (IGA), Guatemala
Amanda Fonseca, Academic Advisor, Brasil
Andy Changan Li, Teaching Director, Keyword Education, Shenzhen
Carmen Virginia Pérez Cervantes, Academic Director, La Salle México-Sur, México
Emma Heyderman, Director of Education, Lacunza - International House San Sebastian, Spain
Jennifer Wu, Vice President, American Eagle Institute, Taipei
Julie Hwang, Educational Consultant, Seoul
Kevin McDonal, M.A.Ed., Curriculum Developer, Centro Cultural Costarricense-Norteamericano (CCCN), Costa Rica
Maria-Araxi Sachpazian, Managing Director, Input on Education, Greece
Mayumi Tabuchi, English Department Supervisor, Notre Dame Elementary School, Kyoto
Paulo Rogerio Rodrigues, Escola Mobile, Brasil
Dr Stephen Louw, Principle Trainer, Chichester College, Bangkok
Streamline Language School, Belarus
Teresa Haeok Park, Professor, International Graduate School of English (IGSE), Seoul

REVIEWERS

LATIN AMERICA

André Hedlund, Centro Cultural Brasil - Estados Unidos (CCBEU) - Goiânia, Brasil
Dulce Stoll, Colégio Miguel de Cervantes, Brasil
Itana Lins, Colégio Anchieta, Brasil
Isabella Oliveira Campos Titoneli Alvim, Instituto Brasil-Estados Unidos (IBEU) - Rio de Janeiro, Brasil
Lorena Stern, Colegio Madrid, México
María Consuelo Velasco, Colegio Santa Francisca Romana, Colombia
Maria Eugenia Rodriguez, Centro Cultural Salvadoreño Americano (CCSA), El Salvador
Thays Ladosky, Associação Brasil América (ABA) - Recife, Brasil
Viviana María Valenti, Universidad Nacional de Rosario, Argentina

EUROPE

Ainhoa Estella, Simon Says, Spain
Jennifer Chang, A++ School, Spain
Liana Boogaars, Bilingual Kids, the Netherlands
Sandy Millin, IH Bydgoszcz, Poland
Shay Coyne, Spain

ASIA

Fu Nuocheng, 51 Talk, Beijing
LV Yang, 51 Talk, Beijing
Wei Wang, Beijing Haidian Teachers Training College, Beijing
Su Jing, Chencent Education, Beijing
Rivers He, Houhai Education, Beijing
Junjun Guo, Improve Education, Beijing
Xu Huan, New Oriental School, Beijing
Wang Jing, Rise Education, Beijing

Song Haoyue, TAL Education, Beijing
Irene Chen, Owen English, Chongqing
Lily Ren, Dalian Maple Leaf, Dalian
Yuki Zheng, Guangzhou Panyuzhixin Middle School, Guangzhou
Rebecca Liu, Hui Da Hai Wen Education, Guangzhou
Nymark Wilkie, Panyu Zhixin Zhongxue, Guangzhou
Pingyuan Liu, PTE Testing Center Guangzhou Office, Guangzhou
Andrew W. Shewbart, ALO7 Education, Shanghai
Xiaofeng Shen, DaDa, Shanghai
Xiaobo Wang, Only Education Group, Shanghai
Liu Jun, 3rd Stage, Shenzhen
Katrina Li, Acadsoc Limited, Shenzhen
Fangfang Yan, Keyword Education, Shenzhen
Jinbo Shen, Little Oxford Education, Shenzhen
Natasa Natalie Radovanic, Nankai Primary Shenzhen School, Shenzhen
Keke Xu, Xue Er Si, Shenzhen
Monica, Xue Er Si, Shenzhen
Tanyuan Wang, Freelance, Shenzhen
Will Fu, Aston English, Xian
Wai Ling Nancy Chan, Baptist Sha Tin Wai Lui Ming Choi Primary School, Hong Kong
Dr Micaela de Senna Fernandes, Centre for International Cooperation in Education, Macau
Chloe Yu, Chuan Kids, Taipei
Steve Lambert, Shane English School, Taipei
Leonardo Tjen, Teach Indonesia School, Jakarta
Dr Tomohisa Machida, Akita International University, Akita

Ryan Hagglund, MY English School, Higashine
Marybeth Kamibeppu, Hiroshima International School, Hiroshima
Toshiyuki Niimura, Kyoshin, Kawasaki
Cynthia Akazawa, Interact English School, Kurashiki
Daniel Stoffers, No Borders International School, Nagoya
David Gonzales, No Borders International School, Nagoya
Kenn Gale, No Borders International School, Nagoya
Kori Herlein, No Borders International School, Nagoya
Michael Pettovello, No Borders International School, Nagoya
Chika Miyashita, Joy World English Academy, Obihiro
Eric Kane, ELF Learning, Omihachiman
Ai Murphy, Murphy School of English, Onga
Corazon Kato, Chubu Gakuin University, Seki
Dr Curtis Kelly, Kansai University, Suita
Nick Weston, British Council Japan, Tokyo
Leah Arai, Kyoshin, Tokyo
Reiko Hitomi, Showa Elementary School, Tokyo
Rie Hatai, Showa Elementary School, Tokyo
Chiyuki Yanase, Sunny Field English, Tokyo
Akiko Nagashima, Tact Kodomomirai, Tokyo
Rie Kobayashi, Tact Kodomomirai, Tokyo
Juwon Noh, BCN Kids, Seoul
Jinhee Lee, YBM ECC, Seoul
Tantiwa Neawjantuek, Ban Kru Am, Ban Khoi
Nguyen Thi Thu Phuong, American English School (AMES), Hanoi

Kathleen Steenkamp, Apollo, Hanoi
Zach Pinson, Atlantic Education & Training, Hanoi
Vu Thi Phuong Hien, BINH MINH Group, Hanoi
Do Thuy Duong, IEG Global, Hanoi
Tran Thanh Huyen, Language Link, Hanoi
Ann Brown, Le Quy Don+VAS Hanoi, Hanoi
Mitchell Baker, Ocean Edu, Hanoi
Nguyen Thi Huong, Star Hanoi Primary School, Hanoi
Tran Thi Thanh Phuc, Vinschool, Hanoi
Danh Nguyen, AMA, Ho Chi Minh City
Peter Waters, Apollo, Ho Chi Minh City
Giang Nguyen, CEFALT, Ho Chi Minh City
Malamatenia Gatsou, ILA, Ho Chi Minh City
Nguyen Thi Thanh Hien, IPS, Ho Chi Minh City
Nguyen Tri Nhu Quynh, Pathway School, Ho Chi Minh City
Trinh Thi Hoa My, SEAMEO, Ho Chi Minh City
Nguyen Thi Bao Khuyen, Vietnam USA Society English Centers (VUS), Ho Chi Minh City
Tran Thi Minh Nguyet, Vietnam USA Society English Centers (VUS), Ho Chi Minh City
Tran Ngoc Thuy Nhien, Vinschool, Ho Chi Minh City
Pham Huu Loc, Vstar, Ho Chi Minh City
Chris Nicholson, Wellspring Saigon Int'l, Ho Chi Minh City
Gia Linh Lam, Yola, Ho Chi Minh City